Life & Health

PATHFINDER

COMMEMORATIVE EDITION

William H. Cummings M.B.A.

D1289791

PATHFINDER   PUBLISHERS

3500 DePauw Blvd. Suite 1111   Indianapolis, IN 46268   (317) 872-1100

email: info@PathFinderEdu.com   visit our website: www.PathFinderEdu.com

SPECIAL THANKS TO SPECIAL PEOPLE

A text as comprehensive and detailed as the PATHFINDER Life and Health text could not be written without the help of many talented and caring individuals.

For their technical help and insurance expertise we thank the late H. P. "Pete" Hudson, Gregg Huey, Randy Montgomery, and John Stanley.

Thanks to Jen and Will Doss for their graphic arts, page layout, and attention to detail; and to Phil Apsey for his humor and creative style. And a special thanks to Mary Ellen Cummings, whose inspiration drove the process of developing a new look for PATHFINDER'S special Commemorative Edition.

TABLE OF CONTENTS

FOREWORD

The dictionary defines a *Pathfinder* as, "One who discovers a way, especially one who explores untraveled regions to mark out a new route." We chose the name PATHFINDER for this text for you, the student. The PATHFINDER will chart a course for your journey into a challenging and exciting new frontier – a career as a Life and Health insurance professional.

The PATHFINDER has been carefully constructed to make your first steps into this new frontier the right ones! It is designed to eliminate the most annoying problem in basic insurance training – frustration . . . frustration for new Agents, managers, and trainers. The source of this frustration is easy to identify. During the next few months you will be expected to learn a tremendous amount of information that is often technical, occasionally confusing and, in the beginning, totally foreign to you. This task in itself is a challenge. It can become unbearable if your study material is written at a level that only experienced Agents can comprehend. Students can become disheartened, and managers can resent the amount of time required to "translate" illogically constructed manuals filled with ill-defined jargon.

Relax! The PATHFINDER eliminates all of these frustrations. It employs hundreds of illustrations and examples that you can relate to your everyday life. It is written with the assumption that you know nothing about insurance, and insurance terms are defined before they are used. The PATHFINDER reduces complex insurance concepts to a level that is easy to grasp, and then builds upon your growing knowledge and confidence. If you do not have a doctorate in business administration, finance or economics – relax. If insurance is new to you, the PATHFINDER was written with you in mind! The authors of the PATHFINDER are professional insurance trainers who have prepared tens of thousands of new Agents like you to take state licensing examinations.

As you thumb through the PATHFINDER, you will discover many unique features, such as a section devoted to improving your test taking skills, and a unique combination Glossary-Index which provides a quick, easy-to-use tool for finding specific information . . . eliminating an endless safari through the pages. And the PATHFINDER offers something else you will appreciate – a sense of humor. It is written in a crisp conversational manner that will take the weariness out of your journey. The PATHFINDER actually makes studying fun.

The PATHFINDER's usefulness will not end when you earn your license. As your career develops, the PATHFINDER will remain an invaluable reference, and the cornerstone of your future insurance training and development. The clear, precise examples that will help you pass your exam will be just as helpful in communicating complex insurance concepts to your clients – and that will put dollars in your pockets.

Sit back. Relax, and allow the PATHFINDER to show you the way. Welcome to the world of Life and Health insurance.

The PATHFINDER

Trails to Your Success

Illustrations aren't just window dressing. They provide hooks where you can "hang" facts. Does something affect the customer or the company? Is there coverage or not? The illustrations provide a quick visual reference and make organization easier.

Glossary not only defines important terms, but gives a quick reference to where they are used in the text.

Notes columns line every page. These columns are for two kinds of notes — first, those we've written you — key points outlined for easy reference. Second, space for those you write yourself.

Sample test is found in Part 5. To be licensed, you must not only know the material but be able to transfer that knowledge to a testing situation. Towards that end, you'll find a part of the text that is **NEVER** passed over by successful students . . .

Tips on test-taking, and taking this test in particular. Pathfinder has been in the business for over three decades, and we pass on to you what we've learned about taking tests. Remember, not only do you need to **know** — you must **show** what you know.

Pathfinder Gives You The Keys

 KEY ideas are contained in the NOTES and ILLUSTRATIONS
They can give a framework for your thoughts.

 ENRICH your understanding of technical terms with the plain
language GLOSSARY & easy to use INDEX.

 SKILLS — Develop your test-taking skills with the SAMPLE TEST
and TEST-TAKING TIPS.

INTRODUCTION TO CHARACTERS

Two of the most powerful teaching devices that can be used in a text are pictures and examples. An illustration is a particularly succinct method, as an artist can often express very complex ideas with a few strokes of the pen. Examples, on the other hand, are often counterproductive if a completely new example is used to portray each important point. For this reason, we have created some imaginary characters that we use repeatedly in our examples and our illustrations. After you have worked with these characters for a time, they will become a type of symbolic shorthand for you as they always represent the same viewpoints. This process allows us to use many more examples to aid your learning process than space might otherwise permit.

This text uses two primary symbols. Joe Insured, on the left, represents the insuring public. The role of the insurance company is played by Mr. Policy.

A third important symbol is "the Other Guy" whom Joe has injured.

Both Joe and Mr. Policy are journeymen actors and can play many characters, and assume various personalities as represented by their numerous costumes.

Like the average client, Joe has a job (he is a restaurant owner) and a family – a typical family. Meet his wife, Jolene, and their three children: Joe College, Betty Jo, and Little Joe.

A less human symbol that often appears is the umbrella. When it is shown to be up and open, coverage exists. If it is folded, spindled or mutilated, Joe is out of luck as there is no coverage.

Another inanimate, but important, symbol is the red flag. This is used to emphasize a point that is either critical to your understanding, or frequently misunderstood, or both.

As used, these symbols provide a mental "hook" upon which your mind can hang the new ideas and concepts which will be introduced.

How Insurance Was Invented
or Is Lloyd's of London Stealing Zeus' Thunder?

There was a time very, very long ago when the gods often left their homes on Mt. Olympus to walk among men, learn their ways, and help them solve their problems.

It was after one of these forays that Zeus returned to Olympus, his brow etched with worry. For days the heavens were wrapped in the gloom of dark clouds, for nothing could rouse the king of the gods from his black mood. All of Olympus was abuzz with worry. What could be done? Surely something must be done to wrest their master from this state. It fell to Apollo, Zeus' favorite, to approach the king . . .

"Sire, what is troubling you, for surely none of us has caused you such displeasure?"

"Ah, no, my son, not you – it's man."

"Man," the godly chorus affirmed. "Ever since he was spawned, there has been nothing but trouble . . ."

"No," Zeus muttered, shaking his head, **"not this time. This time it is not man's fault, for the world I have created for him is full of risk and peril. A man can work and prosper all his life, only to lose all with a single stroke of misfortune."**

"Ah . . ." the gods now understood. Zeus was angry with himself, for it was he who created the world that man now called his own, and it was he who created the risks and perils which robbed man of the fruits of his labors.

"But what can be done?" they asked among themselves, for surely no one would dare suggest that Zeus undo his own handiwork.

Finally Athena, wisest of the goddesses, stepped forward. "Father, may I suggest a contest?"

"A contest?"

"Yes, Sire, for surely one of us on Olympus should be able to invent a tool that will make man equal to the world's perils."

"Bully," shouted Zeus in his best Teddy Roosevelt imitation. **"Grand idea! But we must be careful, for to give man too much would destroy his will to work. Mercury! Heralds! Spread the word to all on Olympus . . . a contest, honors and glory for he who gives man a fighting chance."**

Quickly, word of the quest spread through the heavens. All were eager to participate, for all knew the value of Zeus' friendship and respect.

Soon the day for judging the entries was at hand. All of the gods and goddesses, the important and the unimportant, gathered near the throne of Zeus to see who would win . . . who would give man his chance.

First to show his entry was Vulcan, armorer of the gods. His answer was a sword . . . keen of blade, massive in size, yet so perfectly balanced that a child could wield it without strain.

All were impressed. Zeus, however, was not.

"Fine as your blade is, oh Vulcan, can it stop fire? – for I have seen man lose all by fire."

The bearded god grew silent and hung his head. "No, Sire, it cannot fight the blast of fire."

"Then you have failed, my friend."

And so it was . . . one after another . . . the gods failed. If their tool could conquer the wind, it was of no use against the hail. If it was able to offer protection from the lightning, it could not stop the wind, and so on and so on. Finally, all of the major gods had displayed their answers to man's dilemma, only to have Zeus point out the weakness in each.

"Is there no one with an answer?" lamented the heavenly king.

All looked around for an answer. None was sounded. Finally, a small voice piped out from the very rear of the throne. "Sire, I have the tool which will give man a chance."

"Who said that? Come forward!"

Like the waves on the shore, the crowd parted, and before Zeus stood a minor god . . . one so minor that in fact none knew his name.

"And what is your answer, small one?"

"This," the stranger replied, producing a scroll of paper.

Laughingly, the divine audience jeered at the newcomer – but Zeus did not laugh. **"You do not amuse us,"** thundered the master of Olympus as he prepared to hurl a lightning bolt.

"Wait!", cried Athena, "hear him out. Perhaps he can succeed where strength and magic have failed."

"Yes, Sire, my magic comes only from logic, and my strength only from numbers."

"Very well, explain."

"First, Sire, man loses all to the perils of the world because he faces them alone. Sire, do all men suffer the fate that has so disturbed you?"

"No, only a very few lose all, but there are many that lose a great deal."

"And some that lose nothing, Sire?"

"Yes, there are those who lose nothing, but . . ."

"Suppose, Sire, that groups of men would join together and that each member of these groups would pay a little of what they own to a pool, and that out of this pool would come the wealth to make whole the losses of any one member . . ."

"Hmmm, wise, small one, but what if one man faced greater risk of loss than another? – say a farmer as opposed to a teacher. A farmer has property to measure his wealth, while the teacher has ideas, which are difficult to destroy."

"Well, Sire, we would group only like risks together. Thus, all would be equal among the members of each group."

"Don't some men lead riskier lives than others?"

"Yes, Sire, but with experience we could predict which type of man is more likely to suffer a loss, and have him pay more into the pool."

"But how would we know what a man's risks truly are?"

"Sire, we would have many men to deal with. Although some would surely surprise us with greater losses, there would be others who would be just as surprising with fewer losses. We could accurately predict the picture among all men in a group by using this Law of Large Numbers."

"But how do we assign man to the proper group?"

"Sire, we have men make statements to us on something called an application – and these statements, which I humbly have named Representations, would give us an accurate picture of each man's risk.

"But what if man did something purposely to cause his own loss? Surely then your plan would fail."

"Ah, your majesty. I, too, have considered this. We would announce to each man that there would be certain risks, like the one that concerns you, for which we could not offer protection – these, Sire, I call Exclusions."

"Interesting, stranger. Pray continue."

"With variations, Sire, my plan could protect all that man owns – his animals, his crops, his house – even, Sire, his health – and, may I be so bold, his life." The stranger noticed a dark look form on the imperial brow. "No, Sire, man would not become immortal, but he could guarantee that his family would not suffer financially if he were to travel across the River Styx before his time."

Zeus pulled himself to his feet, **"Stranger,"** he trumpeted. **"Come forward. You have done well. What do you call this plan of yours?"**

"Sire, I call it Insurance – and this piece of paper I hold in my hand is the most important part of the plan – for it contains the promises the group makes to each man."

"The most important part, you say. Then from now on, all shall know this paper by your name. What is your name, young god?"

"Policius, Sire."

"Good, then I proclaim that all shall call these papers, 'Insurance Policies' for all time."

So you see that long before those crusty British sea captains met in the dark of the London coffeehouse named Lloyd's, Zeus, with a little help, gave man the gift of insurance on those lofty slopes of Mt. Olympus

Part I
INSURANCE BASICS

INTRODUCTION TO INSURANCE

THE PURPOSE OF LIFE AND HEALTH INSURANCE

1   In the earliest days of insurance, policies were written to insure property — tangible assets. Merchants wanted to insure goods being transported on the high seas — raw materials coming in and finished goods being shipped out. Somewhat later, property that did not move — buildings, inventory, equipment and the like — became the subject of insurance. Even in the early 20th century, very little life insurance was being issued. The small amounts which were sold were designed to do little more than pay for a funeral. Health insurance took even longer to evolve. It was not until the 1950's that health insurance became rather commonplace.

Your Greatest Asset

2   By the 1950's, owning life insurance and health insurance had become almost a necessity for most Americans. Today, it is an absolute necessity, ranking right in there with food, shelter, heat and day-care. The question is, "What happened?" Why did we begin to buy life and health insurance as readily as we purchase property insurance?

Actually, we can best answer that question by asking another question.

What is your greatest asset?

1. Without a lot of thought, many of you might say, "my house, my car, my boat or my bank account". But for most of us, that answer would be wrong. For most of you, your *earning ability* is your greatest asset. Your ability to go into the workplace and bring home a paycheck is your greatest asset. Any disruption could be viewed as a **financial loss**.

2. For example, if Joe Insured works for 40 years and has an average income of a rather modest $25,000 a year, he will earn $1,000,000 over his lifetime. If his wife, Jolene, has the same earning capacity and also works for 40 years, they have a combined lifetime earning ability of $2,000,000. With adequate planning, they should be able to enjoy a relatively good life together.

3. However, there are any number of events which could shatter this blissful picture. Like all of us, Joe and Jolene have a degree of risk in their lives. In insurance, we **define risk as the uncertainty of financial loss**. And certainly, Joe and Jolene have to live with the risk or **exposure** that either of them could lose their ability to bring home a paycheck. We can characterize this potential financial loss as **economic death**.

Pure Risk - insurance (only a chance for loss; inherent)

Responding To Risk

4. Unless you are independently wealthy, you must deal with the risk of economic death. The many ways you can respond to such risk are of great importance to insurance companies. You may elect to avoid, reduce, retain or transfer your risk of economic death.

Speculative Risk - gambling (a chance for gain or loss; created)

5. A rather impractical method of coping with risk is to *avoid it*. You could, perhaps, avoid the risk of illness by spending your life in a plastic bubble.

6. The first reasonable alternative is to *reduce risk* by living a healthier lifestyle or by living and working under safer conditions. For example, insurance companies would reward the professional rodeo rider who gave up that career to become a rancher by reducing his health insurance premiums.

avoid. . .

7. Another practical approach to risk is for you to *retain risk* by self-insuring or by accepting deductibles. A health insurance company will compensate the Policyowner who carries a high deductible by charging a lower premium. Your willingness to retain some of the risk reduces the company's exposure and allows the subsequent rate reduction.

. . . reduce. . .

. . . retain. . .

8. A majority of people prefer to *transfer risk*, or at least part of it, to a professional risk-bearer and pay for the privilege accordingly. The primary concern of this text, of course, is to examine the processes by which you can transfer the risk of economic death to an insurance company.

TRANSFER!

Risk

9. You will learn that we have bundled the risk offset by life and health insurance into an artificial package called economic death. In reality, things are far more complicated. There are several **perils (causes of loss)** which life and health policies might specifically address. Life policies obviously protect against the peril of death, but some pay more for the peril of **accidental death**. Health policies may cover only the peril of accident, but most cover two perils - accident and sickness.

To control the level of risk it assumes, insurance companies are concerned about
1 **hazards** which increase the likelihood that a peril will strike or increases the potential severity of the loss.

- **Physical Hazards** - tangible circumstances such as a heart condition or a high-risk hobby which might cause a company to decline a risk.

- **Moral Hazards** - are intentional losses, such as fraudulent claims, which companies try to screen out with probationary periods, exclusions and other underwriting devices.

- **Morale Hazards** - occur when an Insured ignores the financial impact of a loss because the company pays for it. Companies control this hazard with deductibles, coinsurance and other Policy limitations.

How Do You Transfer Risk?

Although it's simple to say that most people prefer to transfer their risk of economic
2 death to an insurance company, a little thought is required to understand exactly how it is done. The basic concept is not that difficult. Many insurance historians trace the basic concept of insurance back many centuries to the Chinese. In a principally agrarian society, Chinese farmers were faced with the problem of getting their crops to market. Most of them simply loaded their crops on a boat and used the rivers as transportation. Occasionally though, a boat would overturn and an entire harvest would be lost. The farmers began to transfer this risk to other farmers in a brilliantly simple way. Ten farmers from one area would get together at harvest and load the boats by putting one-tenth of every farmer's crop on each boat. If a boat sunk, each farmer lost a little, but no one lost everything.

Risk = Exposure

3 This concept of **sharing risk** is the basis of all insurance products. A modern-day Policyowner trades a small known loss (premium) for the insurance company's promise to pay for a large, unknown loss should it occur. All of the Policyowners lose a little, but no one has to take the risk of losing everything.

That fortune cookie was right again!

4 A slightly more traditional definition would say that **insurance is a device which provides for the transfer of individual risk to a company which, for consideration, assumes losses suffered by the Insured to a predetermined limit**.

TRANSFER RISK

share with other Policyowners

THREE TYPES OF ECONOMIC DEATH

1   As we have seen, economic death occurs when a breadwinner loses the ability to earn. If the breadwinner's risk has been transferred to an insurance company, the company pays a claim for this economic death or loss. It is worth noting that the emphasis is on the word *economic*. The insurance company cannot replace a human being like it can a car or a building, but it can replace the dollars that he or she could have earned had there been no disruption.

2   There are at least three ways in which economic death may occur.

1. Physical Death

A breadwinner dies during the earning period of life. All life policies are designed to provide for the contingency of premature physical death.

2. Retirement Death

A breadwinner (or two of them) reaches retirement without accumulating adequate cash to provide for a reasonable retirement income. Not surprisingly, many more people experience retirement death than premature physical death. Some life policies can help the Insured accumulate the funds necessary to reduce the possibility of retirement death, and many of the traditional retirement plans can be funded by products sold by life insurance companies.

3. Living Death (Disability)

This sounds worse than death and it probably is. If you are a single person and die, your income stops, but so do your expenses. It's not a desirable state, but it does balance. If you become disabled, you have not one problem, but several. Your income stops, your normal expenses continue, and on top of it all, you have a new layer of expenses in the form of medical bills. The two basic forms of health insurance are necessary to handle these problems. Disability Income policies can replace lost income and Medical Expense policies can pay for medical bills.

INSURANCE COMPANIES MAKE MONEY

1   Insurance companies exist for one reason: **to make money.** They are not charitable organizations.

2   Our definition of insurance tells us that companies assume risk for consideration. In its broadest sense, **consideration is something of value.** In insurance, from the purchaser's viewpoint, it is typically two items:

Consideration = something of value

- **money**
- **statements about the proposed Insured on the application**

3   Both of these are critical to the insurance company's purpose of earning money. The need for the money should be obvious, and the value of the proposed Insured's statements on the application should be nearly as obvious. If the medical exam portion of an application indicated that a proposed Insured would die within a month, no Policy would be issued. The company would not knowingly enter into a contract that would cause it to lose money. If the proposed Insured lied on the application, a company could contest (at least for a while) the validity of the contract they issued in good faith. The company would certainly contest counterfeit money. Likewise, they would contest a *counterfeit application*.

Two elements

4   Our definition of insurance contains two more words that point toward the capitalistic intent of insurance companies: *predetermined limit.* If I am Insured for $100,000 and I die, the company will pay $100,000. My wife can proclaim loudly that I was in the prime earning years and that my death will cost my family $200,000 in lost earning power, but the company will only pay $100,000. When the insurance company entered into its contract with me, it knew that its obligation was limited to $100,000. Without that knowledge, the company could never have established the amount of premium I should pay. If I had listened to my wife and purchased $200,000 of life insurance, I would have paid about twice as much in premium.

The Law Of Large Numbers

5   For the insurance company to make money, it must not only know how much it is on the hook for, it must know how much risk it is accepting. What is the chance of loss? If an insurance company issues a Policy on 40-year-old Joe Insured, a non-smoking male in a low risk occupation who is in excellent physical shape, the company has absolutely no idea when Joe will die. He could die tomorrow, he could die at age 72, or he could live to be 102. It is impossible to accurately predict what will happen to one particular person. However, **the Law of Large Numbers says that what will happen to a large group of similar individuals (or homogeneous exposure units) is very predictable.** If the company Insured Joe along with 100,000 other 40-year-old males who were in similar condition, the men would have an average life expectancy of another 32 years. Some would die earlier than expected and the company would lose by paying a death benefit after collecting only a few premiums. Most would die on schedule, and the company would pay as it expected. A few would live much longer than anticipated and the company would win by paying death claims much later than expected. Overall, the company would profit.

Law of Large Numbers
I. Large Numbers
II. Similar Risks

TYPES OF INSURANCE COMPANIES

1   As we pointed out at the beginning of this chapter, the first few centuries of insurance history were primarily concerned with insuring property. Life and health insurance as they exist today are essentially twentieth century developments. Before the Industrial Revolution, we had an upper class with enough inherited wealth to do without life and health insurance and a peasant class that could not afford insurance. It was the emergence of a strong middle class with a disposable income that set the stage for life and health insurance to become the large-scale national institutions we know today.

Lloyd's Of London

2   Probably the most startling fact about Lloyd's is that it is not an insurance company and does not issue policies. It merely provides a vehicle for associations of individuals to write insurance. The roots of this historically rich organization began in 17th century England when merchants gathered at the coffeehouses to do business and exchange ideas.

Lloyd's is not an insurance company

3   As you are aware, England has limited natural resources, and her growth depended in large measure on commerce that could be developed through shipping and trade. Her success in trade was due in part to the willingness of wealthy individuals to insure the ships and cargoes involved. An informal system slowly evolved in which the person seeking insurance would post a proposal in a coffeehouse, stating the amount of insurance required along with details of the risk involved, such as the ship's condition, name of the captain, nature of the cargo and the ship's destination. Those willing to assume a portion of the risk would write their name under the proposal and hence became known as underwriters.

4   The most enterprising of the coffeehouse proprietors was Edward Lloyd of Tower Street. He began making information available concerning weather conditions, ships, tides and captains. He even published a newspaper containing such data. While he was never directly involved in the business of underwriting, the most renowned insurance organization in the world still bears his name.

Ed Lloyd, Proprietor

NO CREDIT

SEA CAPTAINS WELCOME

1   Today's Lloyd's functions much as it did originally. However, substantial financial requirements are now placed upon the underwriters who are organized into syndicates (associations) controlled by managing Agents. Usually several of the over 250 Lloyd's syndicates are involved in underwriting a single risk. While the primary function of Lloyd's is to provide property and casualty coverage for normal exposures, it is most famous for underwriting highly unusual, one-of-a-kind risks.

2   Lloyd's most important contribution to our industry today is probably its ability to reinsure insurance companies around the world, thus spreading the risk and providing additional insuring capacity. In the same way an individual can transfer risk to an insurance company, that company may transfer some of its risk to still another insurance company. This process is called *reinsurance*. There are two types of reinsurance:

REINSURANCE

- **Facultative** - where reinsurance is negotiated on a Policy by Policy basis.

- **Treaty** - a blanket Agreement in which company B automatically reinsures 25% of all policies written by company A.

Stock Companies

3   A stock life company is a corporation that is organized to conduct the business of life insurance and is actually owned by its stockholders or shareholders. Shares of stock are sold to the stockholders to provide the capital (money) which the corporation needs in order to get started. This capital sustains the organization until it makes enough money to operate from current income. Since the stockholders own the company, they are entitled to share in the company profits, which are paid to them as a dividend — a return on their capital investment. On the other hand, individuals who have purchased insurance from the company, called Policyowners, do not participate in company profits and never receive dividends as they have no capital investment in the company.

Stock Companies are like General Motors or any other company

4   In short, a stock company may be characterized by the fact that:

- It is operated for the ultimate **benefit of the stockholders.**

STOCKHOLDER OWNED

- A portion of the earnings is paid to stockholders as dividends.

- The board of directors of the company is elected by the stockholders.

- **It does not pay dividends to its Policyowners.** The Policyowners do not participate in company profits, and stock companies are therefore referred to as *non-participating* companies.

STOCK COMPANY

STOCKHOLDER'S DIVIDEND TO J.P.STOCKHOLDER

STOCK CERTIFICATE

BENEFIT OF STOCKHOLDERS

Mutual Companies

1 The most important legal difference between a mutual company and a stock company is that a mutual has no stockholders and exists, therefore, for the benefit of the Policyowners. Because it has no stockholders, a mutual must be started in a different manner. The first step for a new mutual company is to find a required number of individuals willing to purchase a minimum amount of insurance from the company. Since most people would be reluctant to apply for insurance from a company that could only be formed if enough applications are taken in advance, it is almost impossible to start a mutual today. Most mutuals are now formed by mutualizing an existing stock company. Many of the huge mutuals with which you are familiar were formed in this manner.

Run for the benefit of Policyowners

2 Today's mutuals are technically classified as mutual legal reserve companies, which means that they meet the same state capital requirements that are placed on stock companies. Most states do require mutuals to incorporate, and the Policyowners control the corporation by voting for the board of directors which operates the company.

3 While the biggest legal difference between a mutual and a stock is that a mutual has no stockholders, the most visible difference is that **the mutual company pays Policy dividends to Policyowners** and the stock does not. It is important to note that these Policy dividends are not a return on investment in the sense of the dividends paid by stock companies to stockholders. In the truest sense, Policy dividends are a *return of premium overcharge*. In setting premium rates, a company makes many assumptions regarding mortality (death), anticipated earnings and expenses. Although **a Policy dividend is never guaranteed**, generally company projections are quite conservative, the company does better than anticipated, and a dividend is paid. While some money must be held as surplus in the event of adverse experience in the future, the excess surplus is returned to the Policyowner as **a dividend — a return of unneeded premium**. Because the Policyowners participate in the profits of a mutual company, the mutual company is often called *a participating company*. Interestingly enough, at one time Assessment Mutuals could assess Policyowners for additional premium if actual experience turned out to be worse than expected.

Policy Dividend- return of overcharge (NO TAX)

Key word: participating

DIVIDENDS NEVER GUARANTEED!

MUTUAL COMPANY

POLICY DIVIDEND TO JOE INSURED

BENEFIT OF POLICYHOLDERS

1 A mutual company, then, may be distinguished from a stock company by the following:

- It is operated for the ultimate **benefit of the Policyowners. It has no stockholders.**

- It generally **pays Policy dividends.** Since the Policyowners do participate in the profits of the company, it is called a *participating company.*

- There is no capital stock, so no stockholder dividends are paid.

- As there **are no stockholders**, the Policyowners elect the board of directors of the company.

Mutual - dividends to Policyholders

Stock - dividends to shareholders

Reciprocals

2 From the viewpoint of the Policyowner, a **reciprocal insurance exchange** operates like a mutual company. The biggest difference is structural. A reciprocal is an **unincorporated** entity managed by an **attorney-in-fact** generally offering homeowners or auto insurance to the public. Each Insured member is known as a **subscriber** and agrees to share in the other subscriber's Insured losses as they agree to share in his. It is from this *reciprocal promise* that the name is derived. In most jurisdictions, these not-for-profit organizations are regulated just like mutuals and must belong to the Insurance Guaranty Associations of the states in which they do business.

exchange of promises

Fraternals

3 In the late 1800's and early 1900's, waves of European immigrants began to land on the shores of this country. While they came for many reasons, they were welcomed as necessary labor in the factories of America which were operating at full capacity throughout the period known as the Industrial Revolution.

It's a club - when you join you get a lot of neat things - including insurance

4 These new city dwellers naturally grouped together in accordance with their ethnic and religious backgrounds and often formed fraternal societies to maintain their national heritage. Such religious and social fraternities began to provide small amounts of insurance, generally burial insurance, for their members.

5 They grew rapidly until the turn of the century. They have since declined in importance, although some very large fraternals still exist today, including the Aid Association for Lutherans, Independent Order of Foresters, Lutheran Brotherhood, Woodsmen of the World, Knights of Columbus and Modern Woodsmen of America.

6 Fraternals are not normally incorporated under state insurance laws as are insurance companies, and are usually subject to slightly different regulations than stock or mutual companies. They do, however, closely parallel mutual companies in their organization and operation. The biggest difference is that you must join the fraternity in order to buy fraternal insurance.

Service Providers

7 In Health insurance, service providers provide the medical services needed by its *subscribers* rather than providing claim dollars. The largest service provider is Blue Cross-Blue Shield, which generally operates on a not-for-profit basis. The Blues are discussed at length in Chapter 10 of this text. The new kid on the service provider block is the Health Maintenance Organization (HMO).

Self Insurers

1   **Self insurance** can appear in many forms from the very informal to the highly structured. Technically, a person who has no health insurance is self Insured. If Joe Insured calculates that his family would need $500,000 in the event of his death, he might buy only $250,000 in coverage if he already has $250,000 in the bank. He is self insuring for $250,000.

2   Most of us self insure in automobile insurance by selecting a deductible. When our car is worth less than the gas in the tank, we elect to self insure and drop collision damage coverage on our car.

3   Many large companies self insure their group health benefits. Rather than paying an insurance company, they set aside about the same amount they would have paid in premium and pay claims out of this fund. They then buy **stop loss** coverage from a traditional company to pay for losses which go beyond a specified limit.

Risk Retention Groups

4   Risk retention groups generally address commercial liability exposures and simply take self insurance to another level. Suppose our buddy Joe Insured owns a restaurant where he serves liquor. If he cannot buy Liquor Liability coverage, he might decide to self insure. If he joins a risk retention group comprised of all the other bar owners in his state they have the Law of Large Numbers working on their behalf.

5   Risk retention groups are generally not subject to the same regulations as an insurance company and normally do not belong to the state Insurance Guaranty Association.

Government Insurers

6   In terms of dollar volume and number of Policyowners, the federal government is by far the biggest insurance company on the face of the earth. Social Security and Medicare alone involve just about every U.S. citizen. In addition, programs are available for military personnel (Serviceman's Group Life) and their families (TRICARE).

7   The federal government also provides or subsidizes insurance for some catastrophic perils like flood. State government is involved in providing insurance for those who cannot buy through normal channels in the areas of medical expense, homeowners and automobile insurance. State government also plays an important role in Worker's Compensation insurance in most states.

OTHER WAYS OF CLASSIFYING COMPANIES ‡

1 While consumers are most likely to classify companies by structure - Stock or Mutual or Fraternal, there are several other important ways to classify companies.

BY ORIGIN (WHERE?)

2 In order for an insurance company to be granted a charter in a particular state it must have sufficient resources on hand to pay claims. The company anticipates that eventually enough policies will be sold to allow the Law of Large Numbers to work properly.

Domicile = home

3 Some states have exceedingly high requirements and others substantially lower. Therefore, knowing the state in which a company was formed (chartered) could tell you a lot about the financial resources of a company.

4 A company chartered in Illinois, for example, would be considered an Illinois **domestic company**. If a company is chartered in another state, territorial possession or Washington D.C., it would be considered a **foreign company.** Therefore, a company chartered in California would be a **foreign** company within the state of Illinois. A company chartered in another country would be viewed as an **alien** company.

Domestic = in state

Foreign = out of state, but in U.S.A.

5 Almost always, a company's home office is in the state in which it was formed - it is said to be *domiciled* there. Therefore, if we assume that we all live and work in Florida, a company domiciled in New York would be considered foreign. A company domiciled in Canada would be considered an alien company.

Alien = out of U.S.A.

BY AUTHORITY

6 A company is automatically granted the right to do business in its state of origin. If that company wants to do business in other states, it must apply to those states for approval as an **authorized (or admitted) company**. For example, a company domiciled in Indiana and authorized to do business in Kentucky, Ohio and Illinois is an authorized (or admitted) company in those states only. In any other state the same company would be an unauthorized (or nonadmitted) company.

Authorized = can do business

7 Requiring a company to be authorized before doing business in a given state gives that state's residents the assurance that their own state officials have approved the financial soundness, the method of operation and the policies sold by *almost* any company soliciting their business in that state.

8 The *almost* applies to a situation which rarely occurs in insurance - particularly on the life and health side of the business. It is possible to buy insurance from an unauthorized insurer in what is known as a **surplus lines transaction.**

9 Here's how it works. Suppose you are an Ohio resident and need an insurance Policy unavailable from any Ohio authorized company.

Loophole

10 If the coverage you need is available, say, from a Texas company unauthorized in Ohio, you do not have to fly to Dallas to purchase it. You could buy what you need through an Ohio-licensed Surplus Lines Agent. Typically, states grant this additional license only to individuals who are already Resident Agents in good standing and place some additional administrative requirements upon them.

BY FINANCIAL SOUNDNESS

fiscal health

1 One important task you have as an Agent is to make sure you are insuring your clients with policies from companies that are financially sound. This *due diligence* effort is particularly important if you are an independent Agent representing, say, 20 companies.

2 There are several independent rating services that assess the financial strength of insurance companies based upon that company's claims experience, investment earnings, level of reserves, management and other factors. Amongst these organizations are the A.M. Best Company, Moody's Investors Service, Standard and Poor's Insurance Rating services and others. One of the easiest ways to determine the financial soundness (or unsoundness) of an insurance company is to check them against the ratings they are given by one of these services.

3 For example, a superior company on the A.M. Best scale gets an A+. A grade of C or C- is considered marginal. A rating of D, E or F is below (or way below) minimum standards.

CONCLUSION

4 Life and Health insurance became important products as we began to recognize that the greatest asset of most individuals is their ability to earn. Since your earning power can be disrupted by economic death in the form of physical death, retirement death or living death, you must deal with that risk or chance of loss. Most of us try to transfer some or all of our risk to an insurance company which accepts our risk in order to make money. While no one — not even an insurance company — can predict what will happen to one person, the company utilizes the Law of Large Numbers which allows for a high degree of accuracy in predicting what will happen to a large group of individuals of the same age and sex with similar characteristics.

5 Today the two basic classifications of insurance carriers are stock companies and mutual companies. Stock companies are operated for the ultimate benefit of the stockholders and, historically, do not pay Policy dividends. Mutual companies are operated for the benefit of the Policyowners and do pay Policy dividends.

6 A company domiciled in your state would be known as a domestic company. A company domiciled in another state would be considered a foreign company, and a company domiciled in another country would be considered an alien company.

7 All domestic companies would be authorized to do business in your state; if a foreign or alien company seeks admission and meets the requirements, it too can become an authorized (or admitted) company. If a foreign or alien company does not meet the requirements of your state (or does not seek admission) that company is known as an unauthorized or nonadmitted company.

CONTRACT LAW

1 Would you purchase an expensive suit of clothes from someone who could not tell you whether the garment was made of wool or polyester? More importantly, would you try to sell another person a suit without this knowledge? The answer to both questions is (hopefully) "no!"

2 As an insurance Agent you will be selling insurance policies, and you must understand the components of your product, just as the clothing salesman should understand his. A "bad fit" in insurance coverage can be infinitely more devastating than a split seat in a pair of trousers.

3 In this chapter, you will discover the "fabric" from which policies are constructed. You will find that policies are legal contracts, and their provisions place certain obligations on the company and the Insured. To understand and explain these contractual obligations, you do not need the legal knowledge required of a lawyer — just like the clothing salesman who does not need the same knowledge as a clothing manufacturer. However, a basic understanding of contract law will be essential to ensuring your success as well as ensuring that your clients get a perfect contractual "fit."

4 The key points in this chapter which will help you develop this basic understanding are:

- The elements of a contract

- The significance of warranties, representations, misrepresentations and concealment

- How a Policy is put into force

- Important legal terms

WHAT IS A CONTRACT?

5 As we have already pointed out, **all insurance policies are contracts**. In its simplest form, a contract is nothing more than an Agreement between two or more individuals. In the course of your lifetime, you have probably entered into many such contracts — when you leased an apartment, bought a house or borrowed from a bank. For now, **a contract will be defined as an Agreement between two or more individuals or parties**.

Agreement

6 Although your experience with contracts may be limited primarily to two-party contracts, such is not always the case. There may be more than two parties involved in an Agreement. Interestingly enough, the parties do not even have to be "people." They may also be partnerships, corporations, associations or labor unions.

parties to a contract

© 2010 **Pathfinder Corporation**

1 Why is it necessary that an insurance Policy take the form of a written contract? When you consider the enormous sums of money involved as well as the duration of some insurance contracts (e.g., Whole Life), it is obvious that every effort should be made to avoid confusion and misunderstanding. The Policyowner must be made aware of what is being promised and what is not. The insurance industry decided early in its history that the best way to clarify the Agreement was to put it in the form of a written contract. As you may know, **oral contracts can be legally binding,** but since the industry's objective was clarity, insurance policies typically exist as written contracts.

ORAL CONTRACTS

WHAT IS AN INSURANCE CONTRACT?

2 While insurance contracts conform to the general rules of contract law, we will find in the *insurance specific* portions of the next section of this text that these contracts also have some characteristics which differentiate them from other contracts. Therefore, courts sometimes interpret insurance contracts differently than other commercial contracts.

3 The two broad principles which form the legal foundation of all insurance policies are the **Doctrine of Utmost Good Faith** and the **Doctrine of Reasonable Expectations**. The Doctrine of Utmost Good Faith says that to form an insurance contract, **each party must substantially rely on the integrity of the other** party. The normal rule of *let the buyer beware* does not always apply in insurance. It is presumed that both parties want the contract to work.

Basic doctrines. . .

Utmost good faith. . .

want it to work

4 For instance, if Joe Insured applies for coverage on his own life, the company will depend heavily on Joe's statements concerning his health in deciding if Joe's health makes him eligible for insurance. At the same time Joe must rely on the good faith of the company due to the complexity of the Policy which he is purchasing. And this leads to our second principle. The Doctrine of Reasonable expectations says that Joe's Policy **should do for him** and his beneficiaries **what he could reasonably expect** it to do. These two principles have nearly destroyed a common law doctrine known as the **Parol (Oral) Evidence Rule**. It is said that any discussions leading to the formation of the contract were assumed to be incorporated into the contract and were inadmissible in a lawsuit regarding the ambiguity of a Policy. Since 1920, courts have regularly allowed parol evidence in determining the intent of Policy language due to the Doctrines of Utmost Good Faith and Reasonable Expectations.

Reasonable expectations. . .

no surprises

ESSENTIAL PARTS OF A CONTRACT

OFFER

ACCEPTANCE } AGREEMENT

CONSIDERATION

LEGAL CAPACITY or LEGALLY COMPETENT PARTIES

LEGAL PURPOSE

Food for thought. . .

no contract = no coverage

All five elements needed for a contract. . . so. . . missing element = no coverage

1-2 **Agreement (OFFER AND ACCEPTANCE)**

1 Expanding upon our original definition, a contract is a legally enforceable Agreement, or a meeting of the minds, between two or more legally competent parties. To form a contract, there first must be an *offer* followed by an *acceptance*. One party must offer to do something, and the other party must accept that exact offer. For example, I may offer to purchase your automobile for a certain amount of money. If you accept my offer, we have an Agreement — the basis for a contract. Which party makes the offer is not really important. You could have offered to sell me your car, and I could have accepted your offer. But there must be an offer and an acceptance of that offer to establish a basis for a contract. The proposal that comes first is the offer and the acceptance of that exact proposal by the second party completes the Agreement.

Offer + Acceptance = Agreement

2 **INSURANCE SPECIFIC** — Normally, in insurance, the offer comes from the proposed Insured. As the Agent, you call on Joe, help him fill out the application and get a check from him. We have an offer. If Joe is acceptable to the company, they issue and deliver a Policy and that is the *acceptance*. However, it does not have to be that way. As you will soon learn, the offer can come from the company and it would then be up to Joe to accept or reject.

Application + $ = Offer

Issue + Deliver = Acceptance

3 **CONSIDERATION**

3 The third element necessary for the establishment of a contract is an exchange of *consideration*. In order for the Agreement to become binding, each party must give the other **something of value, such as money, promises, property or service. This is called consideration.** In our automobile example, I will pay you cash for your car. My consideration is the money. Your consideration is the automobile (or, more accurately, the title to the automobile). If one party fails to furnish the other with valid consideration, then the contract will not be enforceable.

Consideration = something of value

4 It is possible for the *consideration* in a contract to be the promise of future performance. If Joe hires a lawn care company to apply six treatments to his lawn from April to October, Joe's consideration is the money he pays. The lawn care company's *consideration* is the promise of future performance.

Company = promises

5 **INSURANCE SPECIFIC** — It is important to know what each side brings to the table in an insurance contract.

6 **COMPANY'S *CONSIDERATION* — The company's *consideration* is the promise contained in the Policy** to perform certain actions in the future. "If you die, we will pay $50,000 . . . ." It is important to note that only the company makes any legally enforceable promises. The Applicant might say he promises to pay future premiums, but the company could not take him to court and force him to do so.

7 **Applicant'S CONSIDERATION** — The Applicant's consideration consists of two items:

- **Settlement (payment) of the first premium and**

- **Statements made in the application.**

Applicant = $ + statement

© 2010 Pathfinder Corporation

Mirror symbolizes Joe's app - it gives us a picture of Joe.

1   The fact that the Applicant's initial premium payment is part of the **consideration** should not be surprising. But notice *that the Applicant's statements are also considered something of value.* Why? Well, logically, the physical condition, type of employment, lifestyle and hobbies of the Insured would be just as important in deciding if a Policy should be issued as the money he brings to the table. However, there is also an important legal reason to make the Applicant's statements part of the consideration. If important facts are misstated on the application, the company may contest the issuance of the contract on the basis of invalid consideration. The company will accept neither counterfeit money nor counterfeit statements.

2   Alright, to this point we have established the fact that statements on the application must be true or the company may contest the contract. But how do we define truth? Bette Midler once remarked, "I never know how much of what I say is true." While most of us do not make a living embellishing our experiences, most of us are not 100% accurate in our statements. Today there are two ways of defining truth in insurance contracts — warranties and representations. While both relate to the statements an Applicant makes to an insurance company for the purpose of getting that company to accept a risk, one definition is very strict and the other is very liberal. Let's start with the toughie.

Warranties

3   In the earliest days of insurance, statements made by an Applicant were considered to be warranties. To hold up legally, **these statements had to be absolutely true.** Although it seems harsh today, remembering a little history might make this approach a bit more understandable. If in 1750 a British merchant walked into Ed Lloyd's coffeehouse looking for insurance on his ship returning from the American Colonies, there was no way for the individuals insuring that risk to investigate the statements of the Applicant. They had to take his word for everything. If he said the ship was 247 feet long, and it was actually 274 feet long — there was no coverage. Important or unimportant, intentional or unintentional . . . any deviation from the truth was grounds for voiding the contract.

Warranty = the ABSOLUTE TRUTH

4   While certain statements made in Commercial Property and Casualty applications are still considered warranties, this doctrine has, for many years, been considered too strict for life and health insurance contracts. Except in cases of fraud, the doctrine of warranties no longer applies to life and health insurance. Instead, we have adopted the doctrine of representations.

Representations

5   **Representations are statements that are true to the Applicant's best knowledge and belief.** They are not necessarily the absolute truth, but they are what the Applicant *believes* to be the truth. For example, the company could ask an Applicant if he has cancer. If the Applicant actually had terminal cancer but did not know it, the company could only demand what the Applicant believed to be the truth — not what was actually true. The doctrine of representations is, therefore, far more liberal than the doctrine of warranties.

Representations = what you BELIEVE to be true

1   The illustration below shows Nero Joe stating that the world is flat like a pizza pie.

2   The truth of the matter, even in Roman days, was that the world was round.

FAILS AS A WARRANTY

3   Therefore, Nero Joe's statement about the world being flat would fail as a warranty because it was not the absolute or literal truth. However, his statement would hold up as a representation because Joe *believed* that the world was flat, as did everyone else at the time.

PASSES AS A REPRESENTATION

1 Now that you understand how we define truth in insurance, we need to explore the flip side to see how we define untruths. Since we were all children once, we know that there are hundreds of ways to avoid telling the truth. But in insurance, we group them into only two categories.

Misrepresentations

2 **Misrepresentations are plain, old-fashioned lies.** For example, the Applicant answers "no" to the question, "Have you ever had a heart attack?", knowing all the while that in fact he had had a heart attack.

Misrepresentations = lies
overt

Concealment

3 **Concealment is the failure to fully disclose all pertinent information.** For example, the Applicant is asked, "Have you been to see a doctor in the past five years?" The Applicant answers, "Yes, I went last year for the flu," but she intentionally fails to state that she also went to the doctor because of severe chest pains she was experiencing. The Applicant is guilty of concealing (hiding) the truth about her health. Telling a partial truth is concealment because a partial truth leaves something out. As Perry Mason said, *"The truth, the whole truth, and nothing but the truth."*

Concealment = hiding the truth

covert

The Truth . . . The Whole Truth . . .

4 For a misstatement or a concealment to be the grounds for voiding a Policy, it must be both of the following:

- **INTENTIONAL** — The Doctrine of Representations says that a statement is valid if the Applicant thought he was telling the truth. Therefore, only an intentional misrepresentation or concealment could jeopardize the contract. Note: A number of states have minimized or eliminated entirely the effect of *intent* by judicial action.

- **MATERIAL TO THE RISK** — In other words, important. A statement is material only if the company would have rejected the Applicant (or charged a different premium) had they known the truth from the beginning. If Joe's eyes are brown and he said they were blue on his application, we have an immaterial misrepresentation. It's a lie, yes, but not one important enough for the company to contest the contract.

INTENTIONAL MATERIAL

Know this

4 LEGAL CAPACITY

5 The fourth element necessary for the establishment of a contract is *legal capacity,* or said another way, legally competent parties. **The parties to the contract must be of legal age, sane, sober, of sound mind and under no legal handicap or duress.** Persons who might lack legal capacity are minors, people who are intoxicated or those adjudged incompetent.

6 While it is unlikely that you will want to sell much insurance to incompetents, you will probably want to be able to provide coverage for minors. Therefore, you should be aware of the special contractual circumstances that are involved when dealing with minors.

✗ 1 One of the privileges of adulthood is the ability to enter into contracts that are legally binding rather than voidable. A minor can enter into a contract that is binding on the other party but voidable on the part of the minor . . . a great disadvantage to the other party. You could sell your car to a minor and you are bound to the sale. However, the minor could later change his mind, and you could not hold him to the purchase of the car. Therefore, you cannot enforce a contract with a minor because he is not, under the law, a legally competent party.

2 **INSURANCE SPECIFIC** — This is of particular concern to insurance companies because providing life and health coverages for minors is a very important part of the insurance business. The usual solution is **to have the minor's legal guardian sign for the minor**. A guardian is an adult who is chosen to handle the legal affairs of a minor until the minor reaches the age of majority. Usually the guardian is the minor's parent(s). If there are no parents, the court appoints a legal guardian (usually a relative, a social worker or an officer of a bank).

guardian for minors

✗ 3 In your practice as an insurance Agent you will learn that there is no magic age of majority in insurance. Although each state has its own laws regarding minors and insurance, you might find that a person can purchase insurance in your state as early as age 15 or 16. However, they may not be entitled to receive payment as a Beneficiary directly from an insurance company until age 18.

5 LEGAL PURPOSE

4 The final essential element of any contract is legal purpose. The purpose of the contract itself must be legal. As an example, if you and I bet $500 on the outcome of the Super Bowl and I lost but refused to pay, you could not take me before Judge Wapner — gambling contracts are illegal in most states and therefore not enforceable through the courts.

5 **INSURANCE SPECIFIC** — Insurance contracts are generally considered to serve a legal purpose, but it is certainly possible for a mechanism like life insurance which pays one person upon another's death to be misused.

6 To eliminate the possibility depicted in the illustration above, two reasonably simple safeguards have been built into the laws governing the formation of an insurance contract.

- **Insurable Interest** — Something at Risk
- **Consent**

One is not enough

7 **INSURABLE INTEREST** — In order for an Applicant to insure someone else's life, the Applicant must have an insurable interest in that person. Simply, **the Applicant must be in a position to lose something of value if the Insured person should die**. The something of value could be financial support, love, debt repayment and so on. The purpose of requiring an insurable interest is to protect the Insured from bodily harm. Let's see how requiring an insurable interest can protect Joe Insured in the following example.

Insurable interest Something to lose

1 Jolene, the Applicant, is in a position to lose something of value — Joe's love and financial support — if he were to die. She, therefore, has an **insurable interest** in Joe because she is better off if Joe is alive. Thus, Jolene has no economic incentive to do away with Joe. This would not be the case if a stranger were allowed to buy insurance on Joe's life because the stranger could profit by Joe's death. Without an insurable interest, an insurance contract is not legally enforceable because it is against public interest.

2 Who has an insurable interest? Examples **are husbands and wives in each other, children in their parents, a creditor in a debtor, an employer in a key employee, and in business partners.** Each may stand to lose something of value if the other dies.

Who has it?

3 In life insurance, **the insurable interest need exist only at the time of application for the Policy, not at the time of the loss.** For example, one business partner, having an insurable interest in the other partner, could take out a Policy on the partner's life. If the partnership dissolved, the Policy would still be enforceable as long as the premiums are paid.

When. . . time of application

4 The law says that you have an unlimited insurable interest in your own life. You can purchase all the life insurance you wish on your own life, making the proceeds payable to anyone you wish. **The Beneficiary need not have an insurable interest in the Insured.** For example, you could buy a $1 million life Policy on yourself and name a charitable organization, a school, or the Texas Aggie Marching Band as your Beneficiary. Simply stated, **an Applicant must have an insurable interest in the proposed Insured to buy the Policy, but the Beneficiary need not have an insurable interest to be named.**

Beneficiary does NOT need it!

5 **CONSENT** — The second public interest safeguard is requiring the Insured's written consent to the issuance of a Policy. As the Insured, you must give your consent to have your life or health covered. This is accomplished on the application. If the Applicant is someone other than the Insured, then **the proposed Insured must also sign the application,** thereby giving consent. Why? Suppose Joe purchases a $1 million dollar Term Policy on his restaurant manager, Moe. If Moe was unaware of this, Joe could be tempted to serve Moe a bowl of French onion soup with salmonella if the restaurant begins to fail. Obviously, murdering Insureds is against public Policy and would not serve a legal purpose. In some states, consent is not required either for spouses insuring each other or their immediate family.

permission

Remember - you need both

OPTIONAL ELEMENTS OF A CONTRACT

6 To this point we have only discussed the five necessary elements of a contractual Agreement. There are two other elements that may occur prior to reaching an Agreement — **counter-offers and invitations to make an offer.** Either or both of these may occur, but they are not necessary to the formation of a contract. Let's first look at counter-offers.

counter-offers VOID what comes before them

7 COUNTER-OFFER — A counter-offer occurs after one party approaches a second party with an offer. If the second party will not accept the first party's offer, but instead makes an alternative proposal, the alternative proposal is referred to as a counter-offer.

1 For example, suppose I offer you $6,000 for your car but you don't think that is enough. However, you would sell it for $7,000, so you make a counter-offer of $7,000. I might make a second counter-offer of $6,500, and so forth. There is no limit to the number of counter-offers that we might make. The point to remember is that until there is a complete meeting of the minds, there is no contract. Also, an offer or a counter-offer is not binding (may be withdrawn) until it is accepted by the other party.

2 **INSURANCE SPECIFIC** — Counter-offers normally come about in the negotiation of insurance contracts in the following manner. As the Agent, you take an application and money from Joe. This is an offer. Your company will not accept Joe for the Specially Discounted Policy for the Super-Healthy that he applied for. However, they do issue a standard Policy at standard rates for Joe and send it to you. This is a counter-offer. You present the counter-offer to Joe, he pays the upcharge in premium and accepts the Policy. This is the acceptance.

3 INVITATION TO MAKE AN OFFER — The second optional element is an **invitation to make an offer.** An invitation to make an offer is not a true offer because some of the essential elements are missing. To have a true offer, all of the details must be complete, both parties must have full knowledge, and there must be consideration present. An invitation to make an offer is nothing but a signal that one party is open to offers. An example would be a "For Sale" sign on a house, or an advertisement for a product or service.

not specific enough

4 **INSURANCE SPECIFIC** — In the formation of an insurance contract, an invitation to make an offer could come from either party. The company could invite an offer through its advertising program. Or, if a proposed Insured submits an application for insurance **without any accompanying premium,** that is an invitation to make an offer because all of the consideration is not present. The first party is merely indicating that he or she is open to being approached with an offer. **If there is an invitation in the negotiating process, it will always come before the offer.**

5 You already know the sequence of the two essential steps in reaching a legal Agreement. First comes the offer and then the acceptance. If the two optional elements are present, they will fit into the sequence as shown below. Remember, the sequence must always remain the same.

- **Invitation To Make An Offer**   (Optional)
- **Offer**
- **Counter-Offer(s)**   (Optional)
- **Acceptance**

THE PROCESS FOR REACHING AN Agreement IN INSURANCE

6 One of the most important questions you will ever be asked as an Agent is, "When does my coverage start?" Before you can answer that question, you must first answer another question, "When will an Agreement be reached?" This sub-section will give you the information required to answer that preliminary question. Only when you are proficient in determining if an Agreement has been reached should you move to the next major section which will deal with the original question, "When does coverage start?"

BIG POINT: You can't have coverage without a contract; you can't have a contract without all five elements

1 The process for reaching an Agreement begins with you, the Agent, filling out the application with the help of the Applicant. The Applicant will then decide if the application is to be sent to the company with money (prepaid application) or without money (application only). **This decision primarily determines when Agreement is reached** because it normally dictates who makes the legal offer and who accepts the offer. (Remember, the Agreement is composed of the offer and the acceptance.) Let's examine the two possibilities.

1. APPLICATION ONLY (NO MONEY)

- The customer submits an application without payment of the first premium. This is an **invitation to make an offer.**

- The company issues and delivers a Policy and an invoice for the premium owed. This is the **offer**.

- The customer pays the first premium. This is the **acceptance**.

NO MONEY WITH APP

2. PREPAID APPLICATION (WITH MONEY)

- The customer submits the application along with settlement of the first premium. This is the **offer**.

- The company issues and delivers the Policy exactly as requested. This is the **acceptance**. If the company issued a Policy that was different than the one requested (say, rated), it would be a **counter-offer.**

PREPAID APP

2 **Recognize that either party can make the offer and that either party may accept the offer.** The only rule is that the sequence must remain the same. The offer always comes first, followed by the acceptance. **If counter-offers are involved, the last counter-offer before the acceptance is considered the legal offer.**

3 Now that you can determine when Agreement is reached, it is appropriate for you to learn when coverage begins.

WHEN DOES COVERAGE START?

4 For many years in the insurance industry this was an easy question to answer. Coverage began when the Policy was **physically delivered** to the Applicant by the Agent. The application had been submitted to the company, the underwriting decisions had been made, the Policy had been sent to the Agent who then had to manually deliver the Policy to the Applicant. At that point (and *only* at that point) did coverage begin.

Basic rule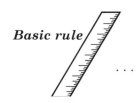

5 The time delay that existed from the date of application until delivery of the Policy was the obvious problem. While there are ways of accelerating coverage today, it may surprise you that the old system is still in use. Even now, **coverage will start when the Agent manually delivers the Policy to the Applicant unless both of the following factors are present:**

- **The application is prepaid** (company practices differ, but typically they require at least one month's premium) and

- **Some form of Interim Insuring Agreement is used** (e.g., Conditional Receipt, Acceptance Form of Receipt or Interim Term Receipt).

modified in the contract

1 Before we examine the methods for accelerating coverage, let's make certain that you know what will happen if one or both of the above factors is not present in the chain of events.

- When will coverage start if no money accompanies the application? The answer is when the **Agent manually delivers the Policy to the Applicant and collects the initial premium.**

- When will coverage start if the application is **pre**paid, but the company uses no form of Interim Insuring Agreement? **The answer is the same.** Coverage will not begin until the Agent delivers the Policy to the Applicant.

2 A Policy which does not take effect until delivery actually places one new responsibility upon the Agent. If, for example, you collected no money from Joe with the application, there is no coverage until you deliver the Policy and collect the premium. What if Joe has had three heart attacks since you took the application? Would your company want you to take his money and put the Policy into effect? Of course not. Your company wants you to verify that Joe is in essentially the same physical condition as he was when he completed the application. In fact, most companies require that the proposed Insured sign a **Statement of Continued Good Health** before accepting the premium.

Things haven't changed

3 Remember, *both* conditions (prepaid application and interim insuring Agreement) *must* be present, or the *old fashioned* delivery method is used to initiate coverage.

STATEMENT OF GOOD HEALTH

INTERIM INSURING AGREEMENTS

4 The reason for the Applicant's dissatisfaction with the delivery method is relatively obvious, but the solution to that problem is not so obvious. While the Applicant wants immediate (or near immediate) protection, the company must have the opportunity to completely check out the Applicant's health, reputation and financial status. This process takes a considerable amount of time.

speed up coverage

5 One way to fulfill the company's need to completely check out the Applicant and yet speed up coverage is by using an Interim Insuring Agreement. An Interim Insuring Agreement is an attempt at compromise . . . designed to *speed up coverage for the Applicant while still allowing the company the opportunity to check out the Applicant.* Don't forget though that for any of these Interim Insuring Agreements to be issued, the **application must be prepaid**. We will discuss three types of Interim Insuring Agreements, the most common of them being the Conditional Receipt.

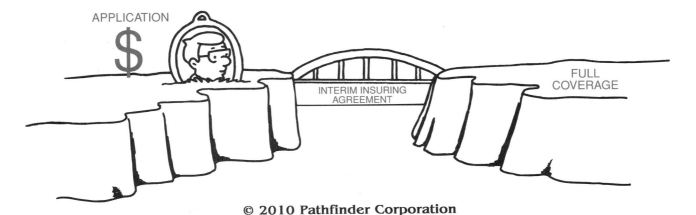

APPLICATION
$

INTERIM INSURING AGREEMENT

FULL COVERAGE

Conditional Receipt

1   The Conditional Receipt is used only when the Applicant submits a prepaid application to the company. You, the Agent, issue the Conditional Receipt to the Applicant, and the effective date of coverage is:

> **Either . . .**
>
> the date of the application, or
> the date of the medical exam . . .,
>
> whichever is **later** . . .,
>
> **IF** (and only if) the Applicant is insurable as applied for on that date.

Later of. . .
. . .Application. . .
or
. . .medical exam

2   This conditional promise focuses on the Applicant's insurability on a key date. But what is meant by *"if the Applicant is insurable . . ."*? In this instance, *"insurable"* means that the Applicant *is acceptable at the rates and risk category for which he applied according to the company's usual underwriting practices.* If the Applicant is not insurable at the rates and risk category for which he applied, then there will be no coverage under the Conditional Receipt. The company simply returns the premium to the Applicant.

3   For example, suppose that on January 1, you, the Agent, take a prepaid application and issue a Conditional Receipt to Joe. Joe completes his required medical exam on January 6. **If he is insurable at the rate category he applied for**, then his coverage will start on January 6. If Joe is uninsurable at the rate category he applied for, then there will be no coverage at all under his Conditional Receipt. The company will just refund the premium he paid.

4   The Conditional Receipt normally is attached to the blank application as a separate legal contract. It is completed and signed by the Agent and given to the Applicant.

5   It may take as long as six to eight weeks for the company to review all of the Applicant's information and conduct the credit and medical information checks. If the proposed Insured were to die in the interim, the critical question would be, "Was he insurable on the later date (either the application date or the date of the medical exam)?" If the answer is yes, the company must pay the face amount to the Beneficiary. If the answer is no, then the company simply returns the premium.

30 Day Interim Term Receipt

1 The biggest problem with the Conditional Receipt is that if an Agent is asked when coverage will start, there has to be an *if* in the answer. The use of a 30 Day (or 60 Day) Interim Term Receipt eliminates this problem.

2 Upon submission of a prepaid application for a more expensive form of life insurance than Term (e.g., Whole Life, Universal Life, etc.), the Applicant is automatically Insured for the next 30 days for the amount of the coverage requested. However, the interim insurance is in the form of Term life insurance. Therefore, if you took a prepaid application for Joe Insured on January 1 for a $100,000 Whole Life Policy, he would be issued a 30 Day $100,000 Term Life receipt with a start date of January 1. Most companies don't even make him wait until January 6 when he takes his medical exam to begin the Term coverage. The 30 days gives the company time to decide if they want to accept Joe or reject him. If Joe is acceptable at the premium rate he applied for, his $100,000 Whole Life Policy will be issued at or before the expiration of the 30 day Term. If he is not, the Term expires, and the premium he paid is returned.

No ifs!

3 While this appears to be a very risky proposition for the company, it truly is not. Let's suppose the worst. On January 1 when you take Joe's application, he has terminal cancer. He doesn't know it — he looks good and feels good. The cancer shows up on the medical exam, and the company declines to issue the Whole Life Policy. However, even in this worst case scenario, it is very unlikely that Joe would die in 30 days. If he looks good when he fills out the application, it is very likely that he will live beyond the 30 days. About all the risk the company is taking is that of an accidental death.

Acceptance (Approval) Form Of Receipt

4 A third type of interim insuring Agreement is the Acceptance or Approval Form of Receipt. Again, this requires a prepaid application. **Coverage starts on the date the application is approved at the company's home office.** That date is placed on the Policy as the Policy date, and therefore, delivery of the Policy is not important in establishing an effective date of coverage. The Acceptance Form of Receipt is used frequently in health insurance. Remember, the critical date is the date of approval by the company, not the date the home office receives the application in the mail.

Action taken at the home office

5 The chart on the next page summarizes what you should remember:

- The left hand column tells what the Agent has collected from Joe and if an interim insuring Agreement is in effect.

- The middle column tells when coverage will start.

- The right hand column will explain why.

WHEN DOES COVERAGE START?

 Manual delivery of Policy, and payment of premium

 Manual delivery of Policy

 Later of either the ...date of application, or medical exam

IF

the Policy is issued exactly as applied for.

 Application date

 Approval date at home office

THIS IS GOOD STUFF

Without money, the application is an invitation to make an offer, the issuance of the Policy is an offer and the **payment** upon delivery is the **acceptance**.

The prepaid application is the offer. The **issuance and delivery** of the Policy is the **acceptance**.

The prepaid application is the offer and the **issuance of the same Policy** is the **acceptance**. The Conditional Receipt serves to start coverage retroactively beginning on the date of the application or date of the medical exam IF ...

The prepaid application is actually two offers — one is for the thirty day Term insurance and the Agent, by merely taking the application, issues the acceptance immediately. The second is for the desired Policy and **issuance** is the **acceptance**.

The prepaid application is the offer. The language of this receipt causes the **approval** of the risk to be the **acceptance**.

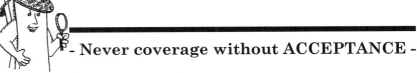

- Never coverage without ACCEPTANCE -

AGENT RESPONSIBILITIES AT TIME OF APPLICATION AND TIME OF DELIVERY ‡

1 As we have walked through the application-to-coverage process, the Agent's role has not been our central focus. To keep things simple, you the Agent have been portrayed as a high-priced mail carrier delivering applications to your company and policies to the Insureds. In truth, your role is far more important than carrier pigeon.

2 **At the Time of Application** - In addition to laws requiring that you keep your client's needs uppermost in recommending an insurance purchase, most states also have specific documents you must present to the client at the time of application. A *Buyer's Guide* is designed to educate the Applicant concerning the types of insurance available to better enable him to make an informed and appropriate choice. Additionally, if your company utilizes a Conditional Receipt, you should verify that the Applicant understands that interim coverage will not exist if the proposed Insured is not insurable under the Policy for which he applied.

Full disclosure

3 **At Time of Delivery** - While we have observed situations where delivery is no longer an important factor in starting coverage, delivery is always important in building client trust and rapport. Before you set the delivery appointment, double check the Policy to verify that everything was issued as required. The appointment should normally include both husband and wife if the Policy was purchased with the family in mind. This delivery appointment is an important opportunity to resell the contract, clear up misunderstandings and build future business.

Service doesn't stop with the sale

4 There are also some legal requirements that might well be important at delivery. We've already pointed out that if premium did not accompany the initial application or if a rated Policy is issued instead of the standard Policy applied for, you have several important tasks. You must collect premium, verify that the proposed Insured is in the same physical condition as before and have the Insured sign the Statement of Continued Good Health.

5 Additionally, most states require another consumer-protection document to be delivered called a *Policy Summary*. It highlights the critical parts of the Policy issued by your company and provides an easy way for you to review the coverages, riders, exclusions and costs of your product. Since many states now require a 10 or 20 day Free Look which gives the client a specific period of time to rescind the contract and recover his money, you might also need to obtain a signature for the delivery receipt which starts the Free Look countdown.

UNIQUE CHARACTERISTICS OF INSURANCE CONTRACTS

6 Insurance contracts have certain unique legal characteristics. You need to understand the basics of the following concepts.

7 **CONDITIONAL** — Insurance policies are conditional in nature because certain future conditions or acts must occur before any claims can be paid. For example, the Insured must pay the required premiums, suffer a loss, notify the company of the loss and provide adequate proof to support the claim. The company will verify the accuracy of the claim before paying it. **Conditional statements are "If . . ., then . . ."** in nature: "If there is a loss, then the company is obligated to pay."

If. . .

. . .then

1 **VALUED (STATED AMOUNT), REIMBURSEMENT AND SERVICE** —
Insurance contracts may provide benefits in any of three ways:

- **Valued or stated amount contracts pay a predetermined amount of money in the event of a loss** (regardless of the amount of the loss). Life insurance and Disability Income policies are valued contracts. They pay a stated amount for a loss, such as $50,000 upon the death of the Insured, or $800 per month upon the disability of the Insured.

Valued:
Face amount

- **Reimbursement or indemnity contracts, on the other hand, reimburse Joe Insured for his actual out-of-pocket expenses incurred because of a loss.** Medical Expense and Auto Collision policies are examples of reimbursement contracts. The concept is to return Joe Insured to the same financial condition that he was in before the loss. How much he is paid is determined by how much he loses.

Reimburse-ment:
make whole

- Unlike the two previous methods of providing benefits, a true **service contract** never pays money to the Insured or a Beneficiary. Under this arrangement, **the Insured is simply provided with whatever services are needed at the time of loss**. Service contracts are generally found in health insurance. The traditional Blue Cross plans and Health Maintenance Organizations (HMOs) are excellent examples.

Service:
Does the job

2 **UNILATERAL** — Insurance contracts are unilateral in nature because **only one party, the insurance company, makes any legally enforceable promises**. The Policyowner promises nothing, not even to pay the premiums. If Joe Insured fails to pay the premium, the Policy will simply lapse. **Unilateral – one promise.**

Uni = one
Lateral = side

one sided

3 **ADHESION** — Life and health policies are considered contracts of adhesion. Joe Insured is simply offered the contract on a take it or leave it basis. He has no input into the writing of the contract. Therefore, any ambiguity in the contract will be decided in Joe's favor. The company wrote it; they are stuck with it; they must adhere to it. **Adhesion – one author.**

We wrote it:
we're stuck
with it.

4 **PERSONAL** - As we saw in our discussions concerning insurable interest, insurance contracts are **personal** in nature. I could not insure Joe's life as I would lose nothing in the event of his death. In many respects, Jolene is not insuring Joe's life so much as she is **insuring her loss upon his death**.

It's you, babe.

5 **ALEATORY** - Aleatory contracts are contracts in which both parties realize that one party may obtain far greater value than the other party under the Agreement, and in which payment depends upon future events. For example, Joe Insured could pay the first premium, die, and his Beneficiary, Jolene, would receive $50,000. With insurance, there normally is an **unequal exchange of values**.

not always
balanced

OTHER IMPORTANT CONTRACT TERMS

1   There are a couple of other legal terms that are important in the insurance industry with which you should be familiar.

2   **WAIVER** — A waiver is the intentional and voluntary relinquishing of a known right or privilege. In an insurance contract, either party can waive such a right. For example, the company can waive the right to receive the premium under certain circumstances (such as a Waiver of Premium rider). Or, Joe's bad knees could make him uninsurable unless he is willing to accept a Policy rider that excludes coverage for future knee problems. This waiver is called an Impairment Rider. In this case, Joe has waived his right to receive payment for losses caused by future knee problems.

Waive goodbye to a right

3   Another important example of a waiver of legal rights concerns the completion of the application form. Suppose a question on the application is not answered by the Applicant and the company issues and delivers the Policy anyway. Is the Policy voidable? No, because legally the company is deemed to have **waived its right** to receive an answer to that question. After the Policy is issued, the company cannot force the Policyowner to answer further questions, nor can it modify the Policy in any way.

4   **ESTOPPEL** — Estoppel is little more than the legal consequence of a waiver. Under this doctrine, one party to a contract may be estopped (stopped) by his past words or actions from asserting a right granted to him in the contract.

5   For example, let's suppose that Joe Insured purchases a Term Life Policy with a 30 day grace period for premium payment. For several years the company has accepted Joe's premium 5 to 10 days after the expiration of the grace period. If at this point the company embarked on a new *get tough* attitude and tried to cancel Joe's Policy at the end of a grace period, it would probably be estopped from doing so. The theory is that the Policyowner was led to believe by the company's past actions that late payment was OK. The company had waived its rights so frequently that it could no longer enforce them.

Waived rights may NOT be enforced

1 **FRAUD** — Fraud is an act of deception or cheating in order to financially benefit yourself at the expense of another. For example, Mr. Ripoff has a $100,000 yacht Insured by Noah Insurance Company. Without telling the company, Ripoff sells his yacht, pockets the cash, and then buys an old junk boat about the same size as the yacht. He then intentionally sinks the old boat in deep water and claims a $100,000 loss to the company. Ripoff is guilty of fraud — material misstatements and acts designed to mislead another for his own advantage.

fraud is the result of a lie

2 Fraud can work in many different ways. It is possible for the Insured to defraud the company, the company to defraud the Insured, or the Agent to defraud either the Insured or the company.

INSURANCE LAW AS IT PERTAINS TO THE AGENT

3 Insurance is underwritten by companies, not individuals. These companies, however, normally market their products through individuals (such as yourself) who are its legal representatives. The law allows a company to appoint legal representatives to act in its place. **The company is referred to as the principal**, and its representatives are called Agents. The Agents have various legal powers and duties. A failure to fully comprehend those responsibilities can result in unnecessary hardship, economic loss, and confusion to your company and your customers, as well as to yourself. This confusion could quite possibly result in an unnecessary lawsuit.

4 **THE AGENT** — As an Agent, you are the **legal representative of your insurance company.** Your legal obligation is to serve your company. As an Agent, you solicit insurance business on behalf of your insurance company. Your words or acts are binding on the company because legally, **you are the company** in that you have been authorized to act on its behalf, subject to certain rules. However, you are morally obligated to serve the interest of your clients as well. As a **fiduciary**, you are in a position of financial trust. Failure to submit Policyowner premiums to your company or put these monies to your personal use could constitute **embezzlement**. In fact, mixing client funds with your own is considered **commingling** and is illegal in most jurisdictions. In today's lingo, an Agent is known as a **producer**.

Agent represents the company

5 **AGENCY AGREEMENT OR AGENCY CONTRACT** — You and your company will enter into a contract, called **an Agency Agreement**, which will tell you specifically what you can and cannot do, and how you will be compensated. For example, the Agreement might state that you can collect the first premium payment along with the application, but that you cannot collect past due premiums (which could reinstate coverage on a lapsed Policy which might injure your company). Your relationship with your company will be framed by this Agreement, so study it carefully.

Expressed Authority

6 **AN AGENT CAN EXTEND THE COMPANY'S LIABILITY** — Your actions as an Agent may extend the company's liability if you act outside the authority specifically granted to you in the Agency Agreement. Your words and actions are the company's. If you say or do something beyond the scope of your authority, the company is bound by your actions. For example, if you state that coverage will start prior to the time insurability is actually determined, your company will be bound by your statement.

Apparent Authority

7 **AGENT'S KNOWLEDGE** — Your knowledge as an Agent is deemed to be the knowledge of the company because legally you are the company. Therefore, be certain to pass along all of the relevant information given to you by your clients.

you're the company's eyes and ears

MEDICAL EXAMINERS — The physicians who conduct medical exams for the insurance company are also legal Agents of the company. Their knowledge is deemed to be the company's knowledge, and their failure to properly classify an Applicant as uninsurable is not a defense for the company's refusal to pay a claim.

company's doc

SOLICITORS - Some states license an individual as a Solicitor who contracts with an Agent to represent that Agent's product line to the public. Normally, a solicitor is not empowered to obligate the company in any way.

represent Agents, not companies

BROKERS — The term *Broker* is one of the most misused and misunderstood terms in the insurance industry. You will hear *Broker* used in many different ways such as, "He Brokered the business to another Agent," or "She is a licensed Broker." In each example, the word *Broker* has a different meaning. While, in time, you will learn all the different ways that the term can be used in insurance jargon, first learn the legal definition of a Broker.

represent Insureds

You know that **as an Agent, you are the legal representative of the company.** On the other hand, if you are an insurance Broker, your legal responsibility is just the opposite. **As a Broker, you are the legal representative of the client.** A Broker determines the client's needs and then seeks to find the best product offered on the market by the numerous insurance companies that provide such products. As a Broker, your legal obligation is to your client, not to the companies providing the products.

AGENT   BROKER ← COAL ?

REPRESENTS THE COMPANY   REPRESENTS THE CUSTOMER

Agent = producer

broker = producer for the Insured

As an Agent you have an Agency Agreement with the company that you represent. Legally, you can represent more than one company, but for each company that you represent, you will have a separate Agency Agreement. On the other hand, as a Broker, *you would not have an Agency Agreement* with any company. There is a significant legal difference. As a Broker, your words and actions are not legally binding on the company.

Because of the confusing terms and the difficulty in establishing legal responsibility, there is currently a trend in some states to no longer issue Brokers licenses. The states that still allow Brokers generally refer to them today as **producers for the Insured**.

No brokers in some states

Powers Of Agency ‡

As we have discussed, your authority as an Agent is specifically stated in your Agency Agreement. As we have mentioned, your actions outside this Agreement can extend your company's liability. As an Agent, you have three types of power or authority. They are **Expressed, Implied** and **Apparent.**

- **Expressed Authority** - Expressed Authorities are the ones *specifically granted* to you in your Agency Agreement, such as the power to collect the first premium. You must strive to operate within the scope of your Expressed Authority.

in writing

- **Implied Authority** - The Agency Agreement cannot cover every last detail of your duties. Implied Authority covers the powers that are *not* specifically given to you in your Agency Agreement, but *they are the powers that you can imply or assume that you must have* in order to do your job. For example, medical exams are a necessary prerequisite to the purchase of many life and health policies. Therefore, you can *imply* that you have the authority to schedule medical exams for new Applicants.

got to have it to do your job

- **Apparent Authority** - The two types of authority discussed above concern the relationship between you and your company. Apparent Authority concerns the relationship between you, *your customers,* and your company. As long as you act within you contractual powers (your Agency Agreement), you will have no problem.

Reasonable expectations

1   But, if you should say or do something you are not authorized to do, and the public could logically assume that an insurance Agent might have such powers, then your company will be bound by your actions. For example, the public could logically believe that you have the power to place small value life policies in force without a medical exam or home office approval. Therefore, if you state that a person is covered, then that person may, in fact, be Insured. Even though you did not have the authority to bind the coverage, your company could be liable for the risk because your word is the company's word. The company would, however, have a valid cause of action against you. You can avoid these problems by operating within the scope of your Agency Agreement.

CONCLUSION

2   The purpose of this chapter has been to acquaint you with the fundamentals of Contract Law. You should (a) have a working knowledge of the parts of a contract and how a contract of insurance is formed, (b) know when insurance coverage starts, (c) understand the differences between warranties, representations, and concealment, and (d) understand the legal relationship between a company and its Agents or between a customer and a Broker.

3   A contract is a legally binding Agreement between two or more legally competent parties. The necessary elements are: **an offer, followed by an acceptance (the Agreement), consideration (an exchange of values), legally competent parties and a legal purpose**. The negotiations may include an invitation to make an offer and/or counter-offers. A contract cannot be formed until there is a complete "meeting of the minds" (Agreement) between the parties involved, and once the contract is formed, no party can coerce the other into modifying it.

4   No contract can be formed without an exchange of values, called consideration. The company's consideration is the promise contained in the Policy. The Applicant's consideration is *both* the settlement of the first premium *and* the statements made on the application.

5   When insurance coverage starts is a key question because it determines whether or not any benefits will be received if a loss occurs.

1   If Joe submits an application with no money, coverage won't start until the date his Agent delivers the Policy to Joe and Joe pays the premium.

2   If Joe submits a prepaid application, we must determine whether an interim insurance Agreement was used, and if so, what type. If none was used, then coverage starts on the delivery date of the Policy.

3   Interim insuring Agreements are attempts by the company to speed up the effective date of coverage while still preserving the right to reject poor risks. While the 30 Day (60 Day) Interim Term Receipt is used by a few companies, most use the Conditional Receipt. For a prepaid application, this receipt is detached from the application form, completed, and given to the Applicant. **The Conditional Receipt states that coverage will start on the date of application, or the date of the medical examination, whichever is last, if, and only if, the Applicant (Insured) is insurable for the Policy for which he applied on that date.**

4   **Insurable interest must exist for one person to insure the life or health of another.** This means that the first person must lose something of value if the other person (the Insured) dies or becomes disabled. In addition to having an insurable interest in their life, **you must also normally have their written consent** to buy life or health insurance on them.

5   The insurance company is vitally concerned with the accuracy of the statements made on the application by the proposed Insured because the company will decide whether to issue the Policy based on those statements. But there are two different levels of "truth," such as the absolute or perfectly accurate (literal) truth, as compared to what someone believes to be the truth. **A warranty is the absolute truth.** This very strict interpretation is no longer used in life and health insurance except in cases of fraud. Instead, we consider the Applicant's statements as **representations, which means that they are taken as true and accurate to the best of the Applicant's knowledge and belief. Lies on the application are misrepresentations** which is grounds for voiding the Policy if material to the risk. If the Applicant hides the truth or tells a partial truth **(partial hiding of the facts), it is called concealment.**

6   Insurance contracts have certain unique characteristics with which you should be familiar. They are **personal** contracts. They are **conditional** contracts, and may be either the **stated amount** type, the **reimbursement** type or they may be **service** contracts. They are **unilateral** in nature because only one party makes any promises. They are also **aleatory** in nature because both parties recognize that there will likely be an unequal exchange of values.

7   As an Agent you will enter into a contractual Agreement with each insurance company you represent. This contract is called an **Agency Agreement**. It spells out your **expressed authority** and suggests your **implied authority**. Your actions are the company's actions since you legally are considered the company. In fact, your actions could obligate the company even if you are doing something outside of your legal authority. If the client concludes that your actions could reasonably be within the framework of an Agent's powers, the doctrine of **apparent authority** would bind the company.

8   A Broker is legally very different from an Agent. As a Broker, you do not represent the company. The Broker represents the customer and is legally bound to look out for the best interest of that customer.

9   In the next chapter we will focus on underwriting — how do the insurance companies determine whom to insure and how much premium to charge. It will provide you with the background necessary to more easily understand life and health insurance.

3

UNDERWRITING BASICS

1 From the last chapter you learned what insurance policies are and how they are placed into force. Next, you need to understand how insurance companies underwrite risks — determine whom to insure and how much to charge.

2 **Underwriting is the process of selecting and classifying risks** ... who is eligible to be Insured, what will be the criteria for their selection, how similar risks will be grouped together and what rates will be charged.

3 This chapter will provide you with an understanding of the basics of underwriting. Obviously, the more aware you become of how the underwriting department accepts or rejects risks, the easier it will be for you to locate acceptable risks, place business on the books, and earn commissions.

Origin Of The Word Underwrite

4 As previously discussed, the word *underwrite* originated from the process by which the first policies of insurance were drafted and accepted. English merchants, seeking to insure their ships and cargo, would post letters of Agreement describing the risks in the coffeehouses along the London waterfront. Those interested in accepting part of the risk would sign their names under the risk, thus *underwriting* the risk. The term **underwrite**, although modified in meaning, is still with us today.

Underwriting Characteristics

1 As we have seen, not all risks are insurable. Those that are share several important characteristics.

- There must be a large number of homogenous (similar) risks for the **Law of Large Numbers** to work.

- **Uncertainty** is insurable whereas intentional losses are typically excluded.

- The loss must be **economically significant to the Applicant**. You would not insure a disposable lighter because it is economically insignificant. You could not insure a stranger's life; his life would be economically significant to his family, but not to you.

- **Catastrophic losses** which impact many Insureds simultaneously are excluded in most forms of insurance. If the Martians declare war and invade your neighborhood, your house and car would not be covered. However, you will be relieved to know that your injuries or your death would be covered by your life and health policies.

- Losses must be **measurable in dollars**. Each Insured must contribute premium in accordance with the dollar amount of risk that he or she wishes to transfer.

Know these. . . they allow insurance to work

calculable

2 It is this final characteristic which requires the company to develop an equitable system of selecting and classifying and pricing risks.

Why Underwriting Is Necessary

3 The first step in determining the premium rate to charge a specific risk group is to estimate the annual cost of claims for that group. How much will the company have to pay out each year in total claims? Since it is impossible to predict what the losses will be for each individual member of the group, the loss experience of the group as a whole is used, which is predictable. Thus, it is important for the company to group similar or like (homogeneous) risks together in groups, and then predict the losses of the total group. This estimated loss is the basis for generating a premium rate to be charged to each member of the large group. The larger the group, the more accurate the prediction.

Pay only your fair share

4 Insurance companies have compiled data on hundreds of thousands of lives in order to predict the probability of death and the probability of disability due to accident or sickness. This data covers groups of people of each age, sex, occupation and so on. It is formalized into tables: **mortality tables, which predict the probability of death for each age group, and morbidity tables, which predict the incidence of sickness or accident for each age group**. For example, the mortality tables permit an actuary to determine, with reasonable certainty, how long a male or female of a given age can be expected to live. This is obviously one of the basic calculations necessary to generate a life insurance premium rate.

mortality = life insurance

morbidity = health insurance

SOURCES OF INSURABILITY INFORMATION

1 Where does the insurance company collect all of the information on a proposed Insured which is necessary to determine whether to accept or reject him as a risk? There are several common methods of obtaining the insurability information. Their use will vary depending upon the age of the proposed Insured and the size of the case submitted. Since the company bears the cost of collecting this information, there are sources that are used almost always, others that are used frequently and some that are almost never used. The company cannot afford to spend much to screen a 20-year-old non-smoker buying a $10,000 Policy. However, the same company can ill-afford not to spend the money necessary to collect information on a 50-year-old smoker buying a $500,000 Policy.

2 A great deal of the information the company may want can be recorded on the application. Most applications contain six separate parts:

- Part I (General Information)
- Part II (Medical History)
- Agent's Report
- Medical Examiner's Report
- Two Disclosure Statements
- Any of the Interim Insuring Agreements (See Chapter 2)

3 Depending on the nature of the case, we may use all of these or only a few. Let's begin with the ones that are almost always used.

APPLICATION (PARTS I AND II)

4 As previously discussed, most individual policies of insurance require the submission of an application. Part I includes general information on the proposed Insured: name, address, occupation, date of birth, marital status, Beneficiary and relationship to the Insured, amount of life insurance already in force, refusal of insurance, aviation activities, avocations, and any plans for foreign residence. Part II (often called the Non-Medical) contains the Insured's medical history: past illnesses, diseases, surgical operations, doctors visits in the past five years, present physical condition, parents' medical history and usage of alcohol and drugs. As an Agent helping a client complete the application, you may ask if he has had a heart attack, but you cannot examine his heart to assess its condition. Hence, this part of the application is filled out by two *"non-medical"* people and for that reason, it is referred to as a *non-medical application*. When policies are issued on a non-medical basis, this is all the medical information the company receives.

non medical = no M.D.

5 The Applicant must sign the application, attesting to the fact that the statements are true and accurate to the best of his or her knowledge and belief. Therefore, the signature is an important part of the application as it holds the Applicant to the statements made. **If the proposed Insured is a person other than the Applicant, both the proposed Insured and the Applicant must sign the application form.** For example, suppose Joe is the proposed Insured and his wife, Jolene, is the Applicant. Jolene signs as the Applicant, and Joe's signature is required to indicate his *consent* to the insurance. Once completed, the signed application is attached to the Policy and made a part of the contract. As we have learned, any material misrepresentation or concealment made by the Applicant can cause the company to contest the validity of the contract. While most companies require the Agent who solicited the insurance to sign the application, the legally significant signatures are those of the Applicant and the proposed Insured.

SIGNATURES

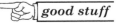
good stuff

★
1   If the company receives **an inaccurate or incomplete application**, it must be returned to the Applicant for completion. If the Agent physically enters the necessary information, the Applicant must initial those changes. On the other hand, **if the company receives an incomplete application and issues and delivers a Policy anyway, the company must honor the contract.** Legally, the company has waived its right to receive those answers and must live with it.

MEGA important

AGENT'S REPORT OR STATEMENT

2   Certainly, Parts I and II of the application are an inexpensive way for the insurance company to collect insurability information. Another inexpensive method is through the Agent's Report or Statement. These are questions on the application which are answered by you, the Agent. Typical questions concern how long you have known the Applicant, whether replacement of insurance is involved, and whether or not you recommend the Applicant as a good risk.

your observations

MEDICAL INFORMATION

3   As soon as the company begins to collect medical information, the cost of gathering information increases dramatically. We will begin with the least expensive sources of medical information and progress to the most expensive.

INTER-COMPANY DATA

4   Insurance companies share medical data through an organization called the **Medical Information Bureau (MIB).** The MIB is a not-for-profit association designed to allow member companies to share data on health risks and to uncover misrepresentation and prevent concealment. Since insurance companies will sell small amounts of insurance on a non-medical basis, they can be easily victimized by an unscrupulous client. For example, suppose that Bunko Joe applies for $500,000 of life insurance from Company A. The medical exam reveals that Bunko is already dying from an incurable disease, so Company A rejects him. Bunko then finds out that most companies would issue him $20,000 of life insurance on a non-medical basis so he then applies for five $20,000 policies at five different companies.

MIB

SHARE DATA BETWEEN COMPANIES

5   To protect against such abuse, the insurance companies started the MIB. Referred to as **inter-company data**, information on Applicants is pooled by computer and made available to any of the subscribing companies. Member companies are required to report any specific impairments they might find. **Claim information or the amount of insurance applied for is not reported to the MIB.** In addition to medical information, other relevant underwriting data from the application is also reported such as **reckless driving habits, aviation or hazardous sports activities**. Therefore, the five companies from which Bunko selected to buy smaller policies would be protected by getting the information from the MIB without ever conducting a medical exam.

6   Obviously, this system could misfire and cause a perfectly insurable person to be denied insurance. Therefore, many safeguards are built in to protect the consumer. First of all, we should point out that all of this information comes from a physical exam that the company pays for. Your doctor does not sell your file to the MIB. In a very real sense, the information belongs to the insurance company as they paid to collect it.

1 However, the company must advise the client of several facts:

- The company will check the information held by the MIB.

- Information collected by the company will be shared with other companies through the MIB.

- Most information held by the MIB can be checked by the individual. However, sensitive medical information will only be released to the individual through his or her family physician.

2 The following disclosure statement addresses each of the safeguards we've mentioned and is printed in most life and health insurance applications.

Medical Information Bureau Disclosure

Information regarding your insurability will be treated as confidential. This insurance company may, however, make a brief report thereon to the Medical Information Bureau, a non-profit membership organization of life insurance companies which operates an information exchange on behalf of its members. If you apply to another Bureau member company for life or health insurance coverage, or a claim for benefits is submitted to such a company, the Bureau, upon request, will supply such company with the information in its file. Upon receipt of a request from you, the Bureau will arrange disclosure of any information it may have in your file. (Medical information will be disclosed only to your attending physician.) If you question the accuracy of information in the Bureau's file, you may contact the Bureau and seek a correction in accordance with the procedures set forth in the Federal Fair Credit Reporting Act. The address of the Bureau's information office is Post Office Box 105, Essex Station, Boston, Massachusetts, 02112. This insurance company may also release information in its file to other life insurance companies to whom you may apply for life or health insurance, or to whom a claim for benefits may be submitted.

---

3 As the amount of insurance climbs and the age of the proposed Insured increases, the company is taking on greater amounts of risk and is, therefore, more willing to pay money to screen out bad risks. The company will typically use an Attending Physician's Report if a question arises over the information gathered in the application, the Agent's Report or the MIB report. A medical exam is usually *not required* unless a proposed Insured requests an above average amount of life insurance.

ATTENDING PHYSICIAN'S REPORT

4 This is used if information collected on an application requires follow-up. For example, if Joe Insured indicates that he saw a doctor 12 weeks ago for chest pains but the doctor said it was gas and prescribed an antacid, the company might want to write to that doctor (the attending physician) just to verify that there was no evidence of a heart condition. This would be considerably cheaper than conducting a full-blown medical exam. This device is also frequently used in health insurance to determine the likelihood of future claims for a condition that has been treated in the past. For example, an insurance company wanting to sell medical expense insurance to Joe Namath, the famous former New York Jets quarterback (who has bad knees), probably would ask the attending surgeon who performed Namath's previous knee operations for a detailed status report — an Attending Physician's Report.

MEDICAL EXAM *avoided if possible = costly to co.*

1 From the company's viewpoint, one of the major costs of adding a new Policyowner is the expense of a medical exam. Therefore, "medicals" are avoided if possible. If required, they range from the very minimal to the very extensive depending on the age of the Insured and the amount of insurance requested. Today, a medical exam could fall into one of three categories:

- **Laboratory Screen** — Blood and urine samples are collected from the proposed Insured and sent to a medical lab. The blood screen is primarily concerned with HIV, cholesterol levels, and liver and renal functions. The urinalysis can show a variety of medical conditions as well as screen for nicotine and illegal drug use. The laboratory screen is used for individual Insureds in situations where the company needs some medical information but the amount of insurance does not merit a full physical exam. Lab screens are also commonly used in group insurance.

- **Paramedical Exam** — Some of the essential facts about a proposed Insured's health (height, weight, pulse rate, blood pressure) can be obtained much more economically by using a paramedic rather than a doctor. For certain cases, this may be all the company needs to make an underwriting decision.

- **Medical Exam** — This is the expensive one. Here, as in a laboratory screen and a paramedical exam, the insurance company conducts a physical exam and takes blood and urine tests. However, it is done by a *medical doctor or a registered nurse*, so a great deal more credibility is given the information. Depending on the amount of insurance requested, the exam could be more extensive and include X-rays, a complete blood profile and medical tests such as an EKG.

company doctor's input

CREDIT REPORT

2 Although most insurance companies routinely get the Applicant's permission to investigate his or her credit report, they rarely utilize this source of information. For the most part, a credit report is only used in business insurance situations where the business is insuring a key employee or the insurance is funding a buy-sell Agreement. The insurance company is primarily concerned with the value of the business purchasing the insurance and if the amounts of insurance are in line with the value of the business.

3 In order to get a customer's credit report, the insurance company must comply with the federal **Fair Credit Reporting Act**. This law requires that any Applicant for insurance be **notified in writing that an investigative consumer report (credit report) is being made**. This notification is frequently a part of the application form itself (see the sample Fair Credit Reporting Act Disclosure Statement shown below). This law also gives every consumer in the United States the **right to question the validity and source of any credit information** collected and retained on file. If the consumer questions such information, the credit bureau must reinvestigate the case. If the consumer believes the credit bureau has sent any inaccurate information to an insurance company within the past six months, the credit bureau must check the accuracy of the information and forward the corrected data to the receiving company. If the data was not truly incorrect but somewhat one-sided, the bureau must include the consumer's side of the story in the file.

FAIR CREDIT REPORTING ACT

Federal law

While the Act provides the consumer with many additional rights concerning credit information, the thrust of the law is to give insurance Applicants the right to review their credit report, to know who has the data, and to **have incorrect data updated and corrected**. The Act also limits the retention of data to **7 years** (10 years on bankruptcy information).

Fair Credit Reporting Act Disclosure

This is to inform you that as part of our procedure for processing your application, an investigative consumer report may be made whereby information is obtained through personal interviews with third parties such as family members, business associates, financial sources, friends, neighbors, or others with whom you are acquainted. This inquiry includes information as to your character, general reputation, personal characteristics, and mode of living, whichever may be applicable. You have the right to make a written request within a reasonable period of time to this insurance company for a complete and accurate disclosure of additional information concerning the nature and scope of the investigation.

2nd Disclosure statement

INSPECTION (CONSUMER INVESTIGATIVE) REPORT

Although *rarely* used today, there are circumstances where an insurance company may hire an investigative company such as Equifax to conduct an inquiry into the character, personal habits, vocational duties and avocations of a proposed Insured. Sometimes these companies utilized a pretext interview where the purpose (and even the identity) of the interviewer was disguised. Up until 1970, this kind of insurability information was commonly used but since then, federal law has placed such massive restrictions upon what kind of data can be obtained, how it can be obtained and how it can be used that most companies rarely utilize this tool today.

Now that you know *where* the insurance company gets insurability information on the proposed Insured, let's look at *what* data is collected.

SELECTION AND CLASSIFICATION FACTORS

In order to treat all Policyowners equitably and to maintain the financial well-being of the insurance company, companies give careful consideration to a number of significant factors for each application for insurance. The information the companies obtain relating to these factors aids the underwriters in determining the extent of the risks involved. In other words, the company will **discriminate** in favor of good risks and to the disfavor of poor risks. Obviously, we cannot **unfairly discriminate** by using factors such as race or national origin. The key factors we can use are:

Key word: UNFAIR

AGE — The probability of death or disability increases as a person grows older. Surprisingly enough, an Applicant is not required to furnish proof of age at the time of application.

GENDER — Statistically, women outlive men by three to five years. However, women submit 40% more health claims. Therefore, women's premiums for life insurance are less than men's, but their health premiums are higher than those charged to men. Interestingly enough, some states view gender in rating to be unfairly discriminatory and have forced unisex rating in their jurisdictions.

Life: men pay more

Health: women pay more

1 **TOBACCO USAGE** — Today this is as big of a factor as gender in rate determination. A 40-year-old male who smokes a pack a day will pay about 20% - 50% more for insurance than he would if he were a non-smoker.

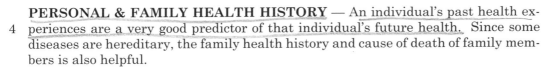

2 **BUILD** — Build includes height, weight, and distribution of weight. Experience has shown that being overweight significantly increases the life and health risk at all ages.

3 **PHYSICAL CONDITION**—The physical condition of a proposed Insured's cardiovascular, nervous, digestive, and glandular systems is obviously very important. The insurance company will screen out **pre-existing conditions**—physical defects that already exist, such as a heart condition, nervous disorders, ulcers, hernia, and chronic illnesses. This information can be obtained through a medical exam.

4 **PERSONAL & FAMILY HEALTH HISTORY** — An individual's past health experiences are a very good predictor of that individual's future health. Since some diseases are hereditary, the family health history and cause of death of family members is also helpful.

5 **OCCUPATION** — Hazardous occupations obviously increase the risk. Coal miners or race car drivers are exposed to much more risk than schoolteachers or office workers. Less obvious is the danger of working in dusty or poorly ventilated spaces, or being exposed to poisonous air or fumes.

6 **PERSONAL LIVING HABITS** — The concern here is with the use of drugs and alcohol. If the Applicant drinks heavily or takes illicit drugs, then the company may rate the Applicant as substandard or decline the risk altogether.

7 **MORAL HAZARD** — An Applicant's character, personal reputation, living habits, and financial status are of prime importance to the insurance company. Information concerning the Applicant's character includes business as well as personal activities. The Applicant's reputation for meeting obligations, and fairness in business and personal dealings indicates the type of moral risk involved. Also of interest is the total amount of insurance in force because overinsurance can increase the risk.

8 **AVIATION** — It is customary to ask about participation in either private or military aviation, which, not surprisingly, increases the risk. If so, the company can either charge an extra premium to compensate for the aviation risk or exclude it entirely from coverage. If the risk is excluded and if death occurs from an aviation accident, then the company is liable only for the return of premiums paid.

9 Flying on regularly scheduled commercial flights as a fare-paying passenger (for example, Soutwest Airlines Flight #402 to Indianapolis) does not significantly increase an individual's risk and, therefore, is usually not excluded from coverage or cause an increase in premium.

MILITARY SERVICE — Military service also increases the insurance company's
1 risk. In the past, the military service problem was usually handled by a military service clause, or war clause. This clause limited the company's liability to the return of premium plus interest if the Insured died while on active duty. Today, in the absence of major hostilities, most life policies are issued with no military service exclusions or limitations. However, in the presence of potential hostilities, underwriters would probably either: (a) reintroduce the military service clause in future policies, (b) place a limit on the amount of insurance each individual could buy or, (c) waive this clause in exchange for increased premium.

2 Most health policies contain a clause stating that the Policy will not pay benefits if the loss is covered by a federal or state government medical plan (such as is provided by the military).

OTHER FACTORS — Other important factors to underwriters include residence
3 outside the U.S. or Canada (due to increased mortality rates as the result of disease and lack of quality health care providers), and hobbies or avocations. Activities such as sky-diving, scuba diving, skiing, snowmobiling, mountain climbing, and competitive automobile racing are normally handled either by charging a flat extra premium or by attaching a rider to the Policy excluding death or disability as the result of participation in such activities.

Hobbies that you see on the X-Games

AIDS, HIV AND UNDERWRITING

4 Obviously, the disease known as Acquired Immune Deficiency Syndrome, or AIDS, has and will continue to have a huge impact on the underwriting of Life and Health insurance. Blood tests to detect the presence of HIV (Human Immunodeficiency Virus) are becoming commonplace. However, laws have been passed in most states to protect the privacy of the Applicants, to prohibit unfair discrimination and to provide full disclosure of the purpose and use of these test results.

5 Though some variation exists from state to state, most laws regarding AIDS testing include the following:

- While questions on the application can seek *medically specific* information regarding AIDS and HIV, no **information can be sought directly or indirectly concerning an Applicant's sexual orientation.**

- Companies may not use the fact that an individual has previously sought **AIDS testing or counseling** to trigger an AIDS test to obtain insurance.

- The companies at their own expense **can require AIDS testing.**

- Applicants must be informed as to the testing methodology to be used and must **give written permission for such testing.**

- The test results must be **kept strictly confidential.**

- The company may only report to the MIB that the individual has **abnormal blood test results**, but **not the presence of AIDS antibodies.**

- A company **may choose to deny coverage** to an individual with AIDS. However, if a Policy is issued, it **cannot contain exclusions** for AIDS-HIV losses, nor shall it contain any specific benefit limits for AIDS-related claims.

SELECTION OF RISKS

1 We have now determined the type of information that is collected on a proposed Insured and the sources of this information. Once the data is collected, the company decides whether to reject or accept the Applicant. Those which are rejected are considered to be **declined risks**. If the company accepts the Applicant, the company will classify the Applicant as **preferred, standard or substandard(extra)**. The preferred and standard groups in life insurance cover 90-95% of all Applicants. These are the "normal" groups.

*PREFERRED =
Good risk*

*STANDARD =
Average risk*

*SUBSTANDARD =
Poor risk
(Rated Policy)*

2 It would obviously be unfair to those in the *normal* groups to allow higher risk people to join. Therefore, in order to maintain equity between Insureds, the company places Applicants whose health, habits, or occupations make them higher than normal risks into substandard groups and charges them additional premium to compensate for the increased risk. **The policies issued to substandard risks are referred to as rated policies.** Although there are a number of factors that may cause an Applicant to be rated, about 75% are rated because of physical defects, such as heart murmurs, obesity, or high blood pressure.

*substandard
risk gets a rated
Policy*

Rated Policies — Special Class Risks

3 Applicants who cannot qualify for insurance at the standard rate may be accepted for insurance on a *rated* or *extra premium basis*. This extra premium can be calculated in many different ways. For example, if the rating stems from a hazardous hobby, most companies simply add a flat extra premium (like $2 per thousand) to the existing rate. If the rating arises from a physical impairment like high blood pressure, most companies utilize the extra percentage table ratings. Table ratings are based on a percentage increase over the standard rates.

4 If an Applicant cannot be accepted even with a rated Policy, then the company will decline the risk.

Adverse Selection (Anti-Selection)

1 Mama always said, "Don't buy groceries on an empty stomach." People who are hungry tend to buy more food. Similarly, when an individual has the freedom to buy or not to buy insurance, there is a **tendency for poor risks to buy insurance** and the people in excellent health not to buy. This process of natural selection is called adverse selection or anti-selection. The *adverse* or *anti* part of the term comes from seeing this self-selection process through the company's eyes.

You often don't realize that you need it until it is too late

2 The individuals who buy insurance from the company, when viewed as a group, are worse than average risks as compared to the U.S. population. If, for example, 90% of all Americans are healthy, then only 10% are unhealthy. But, a company selling individual health insurance might find that only 20% are healthy and 80% of its Policyowners are unhealthy.

3 Certainly, one way to deal with bad risks is to screen them out and not issue any insurance to them at all. Therefore, the application (including its non-medical section, Agent's report and medical examiner's report) is the biggest underwriting safeguard of them all. However, it's possible to issue a life or health insurance Policy to a perfectly insurable individual who then abuses the Policy in some way after it is issued. For instance, a perfectly insurable Joe Insured could buy a life Policy and then take his own life with the intention of making Jolene a wealthy woman. Or, a perfectly healthy Jolene could buy health insurance and then collect an amount which greatly exceeds what the company anticipated because she calls an ambulance to take her to the hospital every time she sneezes. In situations such as these, the company needs additional underwriting safeguards such as exclusions and deductibles. You will learn about these and more when we study the life and health contracts in detail.

Adverse Selection makes everybody pay more

PREMIUM DETERMINATION

1 Once the insurance company has collected all the necessary data on the proposed Insured, rejected the uninsurable, written policies which provide all the underwriting safeguards against adverse selection we've discussed, and then made provisions to upcharge the substandard risks, how does the company determine the premium rate to charge the standard risks? There are three factors or elements which the company considers: risk, expenses and interest.

- **RISK** — Risk is normally defined as the **chance of loss**. The first step is to determine the expected claims costs . . . how much the company will have to pay in claims, and when they will have to pay those claims. The basis for these estimates, in life insurance, is the **mortality** table; in health insurance, it is the **morbidity** table.

  mortality and morbidity

- **EXPENSE** — Insurance companies compute the total operating cost of their business for each $1,000 of insurance in force. These expenses include sales commissions paid to Agents, salaries, rent, postage and utilities. If the operating costs of XYZ Mutual are computed to be $2 per $1000 of coverage in force, then this cost is added (or "*loaded*") to the premium cost of each new Policy issued.

  Agent commissions, etc.

- **INTEREST** — Because insurance premiums are paid in advance and because insurance companies invest the money to earn interest, Policyowners do not have to pay the entire amount necessary to cover the risk and the expenses. The Policyowner pays the bulk of the money in the form of premium and the company earns the balance in interest. For instance, assume Joe purchases a Policy for which the company calculates the risk factor to be $8 per thousand. Further, assume that the company's expense factor is $2 per thousand. If Joe bought a $100,000 Policy, he should pay 100 x $10 (or $1,000) for the Policy this year. However, because the company can earn 5 1/4% on his money, Joe would only pay about $950 for the Policy as the company would earn the other $50 in interest.

  money makes money. . .

GROSS AND NET PREMIUM

2 The calculation we just completed is the method the company uses to calculate the premium charged the Policyowner — the gross premium. For a $100,000 Policy, our numbers would follow the following formula:

RISK + EXPENSES - INTEREST = GROSS PREMIUM
$800 + $200   - $50   = $950

Risk
+ Expense
- Interest

Gross Premium

3 Although most insurance is sold on a ***gross*** **premium** basis, companies will often allow existing Policyowners to buy small additional amounts of insurance on a ***net*** **single premium** basis. As you will see momentarily, the expense factor is not loaded into a net premium calculation. The formula for calculation of the net premium is:

RISK - INTEREST = NET PREMIUM

Risk
- Interest

Net Premium

4 Therefore, on a net premium basis, Joe's cost for additional amounts of insurance would be about $8 per thousand. This would obviously be a good deal for Joe, but it would generate no commission for the Agent because the Agent's commission is a part of the expense element of the premium calculations.

PREMIUM MODE

1 **How frequently a Policyowner pays his or her premium is called the premium mode.** The premium mode can be annually, semiannually, quarterly, monthly, or weekly. Usually, the company calculates the premium rates on an annual basis (paid in advance) and then increases the premium for delayed modes of payment. Therefore, the premium for a monthly premium mode will cost more than an annual premium mode. For example, if Joe's premium is $950 per year on an annual premium mode, he might pay a total of $984 per year for the same exact Policy if he pays on a monthly premium mode. This increase is due to two factors:

Frequency of premium payment

- **Lost interest** — The company did not have Joe's money invested all year.

- **Higher expenses** — It's more expensive to collect money twelve times a year than one time each year.

The more often the premium is paid. . .

2 As with any installment purchase, the longer the company waits for its money, the more it will cost the customer.

. . . the higher the cost

INSURANCE DISTRIBUTION SYSTEMS ‡

- **Independent Agency System** - An Independent Agent is appointed on a **non-exclusive** basis by several insurance companies. He or she is paid a commission on personal sales and takes an override on sales by other producing Agents in the office. Independent Agents own the expirations of their policies and can place the renewal of the business with any company he or she represents commensurate with the best interests of the clients. Typically, little financial support except commissions is paid by the appointing companies.

- **Exclusive or Captive Agency System** - Similar to the Independent system in structure with one important difference. These **career Agents** and the Agents who work from their office are appointed by one company on an **exclusive** basis. Again, they are paid on a purely commission basis.

- **General Agency System** - An insurance company contracts with a **General Agent** usually on an exclusive basis. An allowance may be paid for office expense, advertising and staffing. The General Agent is paid a commission on personal sales and earns an override on those of his Agents.

- **Managerial System** - Both manager and Agents are actually **employees** of the insurance company and may be paid a salary or a commission or both.

- **Direct Response Marketing System** - The company advertises for clients to mail their applications directly to the company which bypasses the Agent altogether. Others solicit inquiries in which case a licensed Agent on a salary (maybe plus commission incentive) completes the transaction by telephone.

- **Others** - Including non-insurance sponsors like banks and others in the financial services industry. Could even include vending machines in transportation terminals used to distribute Travel Accident policies.

Here's how the company gets to the public

CONCLUSION

1 Underwriting is the process of selecting risks and classifying them into groups, such as standard or substandard. Insurability sources include the application, Agent's report, medical exam, inspection report, credit report, attending physician's report, and inter-company data (MIB information). Classification factors include the proposed Insured's age, gender, build, physical condition, personal health history, occupation, habits, personal reputation, military status, and engagement in dangerous hobbies.

2 The basis for rate-making starts with the mortality (death) and morbidity (disability) tables and records. From this data, the actuaries project the estimated cost of claims (the risk factor). The cost of operating the business (the expense factor) is added to the estimated cost of claims and the total is adjusted for the fact that premiums are collected in advance and invested to earn income until the claims must be paid (the interest factor). The total of these three items is the gross premium charged to the Policyowner.

3 Insurance companies use a number of underwriting safeguards to control and limit risk. The most common safeguards are exclusions, definitions, deductibles and the perils covered. If any of the terms used in this conclusion are unfamiliar to you, review the appropriate sections of this chapter.

4 The next chapter will begin our discussion of life insurance. The subject of health insurance is covered later in this text. A good understanding of the insurance basics contained in these first three chapters should have prepared you well for your studies ahead.

Part II
LIFE INSURANCE

FUNDAMENTALS OF LIFE INSURANCE AND ANNUITIES

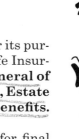

1   Understanding Life Insurance necessarily entails examining the purpose for its purchase. The next few chapters in this text will discuss the various uses of Life Insurance. Life Insurance has evolved from a product that simply paid for the **Funeral of the Insured** to a product that potentially can provide **Survivor Protection, Estate Protection, Estate Creation, Living Values and Accelerated Death Benefits.**

2   From simply paying a death benefit, to buying enough insurance to pay for final expenses (**Survivor Protection**), or to leave an inheritance to children (**Estate Creation**), Life Insurance has been able to fit the changing needs of individuals in contemporary America. By building accessible cash value (**Living Values**), paying an amount sufficient to cover estate taxes (**Estate Protection**) and allowing access to a portion of the death benefit before death (**Accelerated Death Benefits**), Life Insurance has proven itself to be a versatile player into today's financial planning portfolio.

Why life insurance?

In Chapter One of this text, we somewhat oversimplified by saying that life insurance offset the problems of **premature physical death** and **retirement death**. As we've

3   just noted, life insurance can provide many more benefits than those two. However, it remains true that most life insurance is purchased with one of these two intentions in mind. We want a contract that offers **death protection** or **cash accumulation**, or, maybe, a contract that offers **both**.

1   Although today's insurance marketplace is crowded with scores of specialized products, most are variations, permutations, or combinations of four basic contracts which have served the life insurance industry for several hundred years. These basic building blocks are **Term, Whole Life, Endowment and Annuities**. Two may be easily categorized. Term insurance offers death protection only and the principal use of an Annuity is cash accumulation.

DEATH PROTECTION   CASH ACCUMULATION
Term   Annuities

2   The two remaining products are not as easily categorized. Both Whole Life and Endowment offer death protection and some cash accumulation potential. On the Death Protection/Cash Accumulation spectrum, they should be positioned as follows:

DEATH PROTECTION   CASH ACCUMULATION
Term   Whole Life   Endowment   Annuities

*Death
protection
or
Cash value
or
Both*

3   A common characteristic of Term, Whole Life and Endowment policies is that each offers (in varying degrees) death protection. The fourth product, the Annuity, does not. Annuities are sold by life insurance companies, but they are not technically life insurance because *they have no death benefit*.

4   To organize our discussion of these four fundamental products, we will discuss those that have a death benefit first, and leave the one without a death benefit (the Annuity) for last.

How Much Life Insurance Should an Applicant Purchase? ‡

1   When an Agent sits down with Joe and Jolene to help them assemble an appropriate life insurance program, the Agent today will probably take one of two possible approaches - the **Human Life Value** approach or the **Financial Needs** approach. To illustrate each, let's assume that Joe and Jolene have no existing policies and that we are concerned at this point with insuring Joe's life. (The same process would then be followed for insuring Jolene's life.) Both spouses work, each earns $25,000 a year, and both are 40 years old.

2   **Human Life Value Approach** - The human life value approach totally focuses on what Joe reasonably anticipates earning and contributing to his family as a breadwinner. Currently he makes $25,000 in his restaurant and anticipates no change for 5 years (5 x $25,000 = $125,000). At that time, the mortgage will be fully paid on the business and his income will go to $50,000 a year. His earnings will stay at about that level from age 45 to 55 as he opens a second restaurant (10 x $50,000 = $500,000). From age 55 to 65 he will operate both restaurants with an income of $100,000 a year (10 x $100,000 = $1,000,000). At 65 he plans to sell both restaurants and pocket $300,000 after taxes for retirement. If Joe lives to fulfill his plan he would earn $1,925,000 over the next 25 years or about $40,000 a year. We might further calculate that Joe contributes in various ways around the house. He mows the yard, washes the car and does minor carpentry and painting. If we assume that Jolene would pay to have those things done, Joe's contribution to his family might average $45,000 a year.

3   At this stage, Joe and Jolene need to make a decision. They could buy a $1 million dollar Policy on Joe's life which could easily be invested to earn $45,000 a year. With this approach, the $1 million would never be spent (**retention of capital**) and could ultimately be given to the children following Jolene's death. Alternatively, they could buy $850,000 in insurance which could be used as a single premium to purchase a life income of $45,000 a year. With this approach all principal and interest would be spent (**liquidation of capital**) by Jolene's death.

How much do they need?

4   **Financial Needs Approach** - The focus of this approach is not on Joe but on the needs of his surviving family. Several elaborate manual or computerized needs analysis worksheets are in use which help pinpoint the amount necessary to meet the family needs. For instance, Joe's income will no longer be available, but the need for two cars will disappear. Their eldest son has three years left at college, but daughter Betty Jo plans only on two years to train as a dental hygienist. Jolene's income covers only a portion of the family need at this time, but she expects significant increases in earnings in the future. There will be costs associated with Joe's death (**post mortem expenses**), but he will not be a factor in future family expenses.

5   Another important factor would be other sources of income - like Social Security. If Joe dies with minor children living at home, Jolene would receive a check for the children until the youngest is 18 and she is 50. She would not be eligible for Joe's retirement income until retirement age. Therefore, this **Social Security "blackout" period** would have to be taken into consideration.

To get really picky, the check is made out to Jolene until the child is 16, then it is made out to the child from ages 16-18

6   Let's assume that after final expenses are paid, the family would be about $10,000 a year short of what they need. Under this scenario, a Policy of about $200,000 would earn the difference and preserve the capital. Using the liquidation approach, a death benefit of $190,000 would provide Jolene an income of $10,000 a year for life.

Individual (Ordinary) Life Insurance

1 Ordinary Life insurance is quite simply a Policy sold to an individual by an Agent who may collect the first premium with the application but who does not return regularly to collect additional premium installments. Premiums after the first are mailed directly to the home office of the company that issued the Policy.

The Ordinary Life Marketing System has traditionally included three basic Policy types:

2
- **Term**
- **Whole Life**
- **Endowment**

3 An interesting starting point is to observe the cost differences that exist between the various Ordinary life policies. As we will see, a forty-year-old male like Joe Insured can purchase $50,000 worth of protection for $125, $150, $1,850 or even as much as $2,250 per year.

4 Since all the policies in this example give Joe Insured $50,000 worth of protection from the same company, it should be obvious that there are several variables which affect the price. By the end of this chapter you should be able to understand what these variables are and how they do affect the price of a Policy.

5 Note to the Student:

In order to help you to differentiate the various Policy forms, we have indicated sample prices for many of the products described in this and subsequent chapters. While these figures will prove most helpful for comparison purposes in this text, it would be highly inappropriate to compare these examples to the actual premiums of any one particular company. Comparing policies on the basis of price alone is very misleading. Many other features must be considered to make a proper evaluation.

TERM INSURANCE

1 Term insurance is designed to provide death protection for a definite and limited period of time such as One Year Term, Five Year Term or Term to 65. If the Insured dies during the term, the Policy **matures** and the insurance company pays the face amount of the Policy to the Beneficiary. If the Insured doesn't die during the term, the Policy **expires**.

TERM . . .

2 The second important characteristic of Term insurance is that it is **pure protection.** As long as you pay the premium during the Policy period your family is afforded a death benefit - pure protection.

MOST PROTECTION FOR THE SMALLEST $

3 Since there are no promises of forced savings or cash value attached to the Term contract, it is designed to provide the greatest possible protection for the lowest possible cost. Therefore, the two key points to remember about Term insurance are that it offers (1) **protection only** for (2) a **specified period of time.**

4 One of the most widely marketed forms of Term insurance is Annually Renewable Term (ART). The company grants the Insured the right to renew the Policy each year (to a stated date or age), but the cost goes up each year. This is because the rates are based on the Insured's **attained (current) age.** For example, the cost per thousand for Joe at age 40 is $3.00. By age 50, the cost has risen to $6.50 per thousand, and by age 65, the cost has sky-rocketed to $30.00 per thousand. As an individual gets older, his or her risk increases, so the cost for the same amount of insurance also goes up. The cost curve is directly related to the mortality (death) rate, which increases with the individual's age.

PURE PROTECTION

*cost goes up
with age*

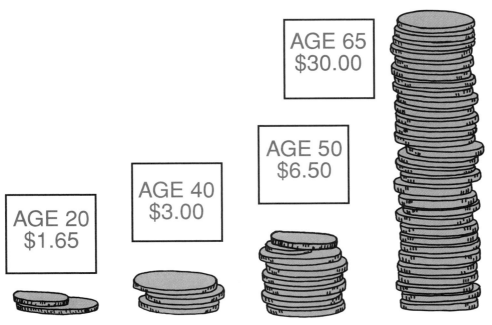

AGE 65
$30.00

AGE 50
$6.50

AGE 40
$3.00

AGE 20
$1.65

1 While it is quite logical that this yearly increase in the risk of death leads to an annual increase in the premiums an individual pays, these increasing prices can present a real problem for the insuring public. One Term product that offers at least a partial solution to the problem of rising costs is **Level Premium Term**. With a Term Policy of long duration (like Term to 65), the payments may be leveled out over the life of the Policy to create Level Premium Term.

Level Premium Term

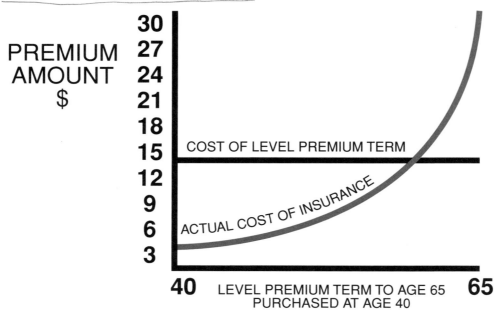

2 During the early years of the Policy, the Policyowner overpays the actual cost of insurance, and this overpayment and the interest it earns is used to make up the deficit caused by the owner's underpayment in the later years. The fundamental idea is that the company calculates a level premium that is the mathematical equivalent of the total of the increasing premiums of an Annually Renewable Term Policy. Level Premium Term to Age 65 would cost Joe Insured at forty years of age $12.00 per thousand. Annually Renewable Term would start at $3.00 per thousand and rise to $30.00 per thousand by age 65. Including assumptions made about the interest to be earned, the level premiums are the mathematical equal of the Annually Renewable Term premiums.

Term = most death benefit for the money

3 Term insurance, then, in any of its many forms, is the **most affordable** protection available for the premium dollar. It is particularly suitable for a person who has only a temporary need for insurance, for a person who may want permanent insurance in the future, or for **the person who has the discipline to buy Term** and *really invest the rest*.

1   We will examine five important types of Term insurance.

- **Level Term**
- **Decreasing Term**
- **Increasing Term**
- **Renewable Term**
- **Convertible Term**

Level Term Insurance

Face Amount

2   This type of Term insurance <u>provides for a **specific and constant amount of insurance throughout the life of the contract.**</u> For example, a Five Year $10,000 Level Term Policy provides $10,000 of protection for five years. Likewise, a very long Level Term Policy (such as Term to 65) provides **the same face amount of coverage throughout the life of the Policy.**

Level

3   Notice that ***the Policy element which remains level is the face amount (or death benefit).*** The premium could increase each year like the red line in the previous illustration, or it could remain level like the black line in the same illustration.

Decreasing Term Insurance

Face Amount

4   The face amount of a Term insurance Policy need not remain level during the life of the contract. If the insurance needs of the Policyowner decrease over time, it would be appropriate for the **death benefit to decrease** as well. The most common use of Decreasing Term insurance is to provide **Mortgage Protection.** A Level Term Policy would not be necessary if a family's sole need for insurance is to pay off the mortgage if the breadwinner dies. In the following illustration, the original mortgage is $50,000. A Level Term Policy would soon provide *excess insurance*, which would mean *excess cost* to the Policyowner (see illustration below).

Decreasing

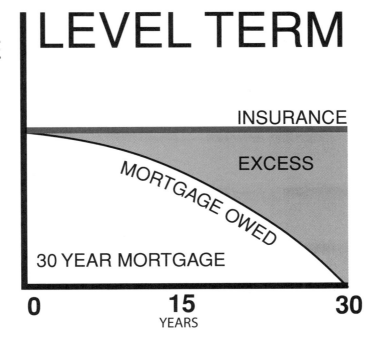

MORTGAGE AMOUNT $50,000

LEVEL TERM

INSURANCE

EXCESS

MORTGAGE OWED

30 YEAR MORTGAGE

0   15   30

YEARS

1 It would be more economical to provide **Mortgage Protection** with Decreasing Term so that there is no excess insurance. The illustration below shows how the Term insurance decreases as the mortgage obligation decreases.

MORTGAGE AMOUNT BALANCE

DECREASING TERM

30 YEAR MORTGAGE

0   15   30

YEARS

Mortgage protection

Decreasing Term

2 As you can see, **Decreasing Term consistently has less total insurance in force over the Policy period,** so its price is correspondingly less than that of Level Term. However, its *price* may not be decreasing. With Decreasing Term, the **death benefit decreases** — the premium could decrease as well, but it usually remains level.

Don't have more than you need

3 Decreasing Term is an appropriate coverage in any situation in which a financial obligation decreases. In some cases, the obligation decreases more rapidly at the end of the time period than at the beginning (such as a mortgage) but in some cases, a financial obligation decreases at a constant rate. In this situation, the amount of term insurance would also decrease at a constant rate.

Typifies "pure protection"

Increasing Term Insurance

4 Just as Term insurance death benefits can decrease each year, they may also **increase each year.** As the name implies, Increasing Term can be used when there is an increasing need for insurance. While virtually no company sells Increasing Term as a separate contract, theoretically, it would be more expensive than Level Term because there would be more and more protection in force over time.

5 Probably the most common use of Increasing Term is in the construction of two types of Policy *riders* (extra Policy benefits purchased for extra premium dollars) — the **Return of Premium Rider** and the **Return of Cash Value Rider**. You will see in the portion of the text dealing with riders that these two riders promise an increasing settlement amount to the Beneficiary each year. Increasing Term is used to meet this increasing obligation.

Return of cash value rider

Renewable Term Insurance

1 For a small amount of additional premium ($.50 per thousand at age 40) you can make a Term Policy **renewable**. In addition to the normal benefits found in a Term Policy, you would be purchasing the **right to renew the Policy without showing proof of insurability**. Renewable Term is always limited by the number of times it can be renewed, or by setting an age after which it cannot be renewed. Common forms are Five Year Renewable Term (for one more period of five years) or Annually Renewable Term to 65. The premium **will remain level during the Policy period** (e.g. 5 years or 1 year) but **will increase at renewal** due to the Insured's newly attained age. Renewable Term does not guarantee renewal with the same *premium*. It merely guarantees that *the Policy can be renewed, regardless of the Insured's health*, to a predetermined date or age. Since the number of renewals is limited, Renewable Term does not guarantee insurability beyond the period specified by the Policy.

2 Though not widely popular, one approach to Renewable Term was called **Life Expectancy Term**. If at age 40, Joe was expected to live to age 76, then he was sold Annually Renewable Term to 76.

Convertible Term Insurance

3 With this form of Term insurance comes **the right to convert a Term Policy to any form of permanent protection** (e.g., Whole Life) **without having to show proof of insurability**. Most companies stipulate the length of the period in which this privilege may be exercised. If the Insured fails to convert before this deadline, the Term coverage can be continued, but the right to convert is lost forever. Since the company must allow the conversion for even a terminally ill Policyowner who wishes to convert, the cost of Convertible Term is slightly higher than Term without this privilege.

4 **When the conversion is made, the premium will increase.** This is because permanent forms of insurance are more expensive than Term and also because the new premium will be based on the attained age of the Insured. Convertible Term is normally sold to people who may want permanent protection in the future, but have other priorities at the present time. It provides the greatest protection for the dollar today, and leaves their options open for a specified time into the future.

BREAK GLASS
WHEN READY

CASH VALUE

CONVERTIBLE TERM

Maturity

5 Finally, it is important to remember how a Term contract reaches maturity. **Maturity occurs in any life Policy when the face amount is paid out.** Therefore, a Term Policy can only mature upon the death of the Insured during the Policy period. If the Insured *lives beyond the designated period of coverage*, the contract has not matured; it has *expired*.

6 When a Term Policy matures, the face amount is paid to the designated Beneficiary. It is at this point that you should recognize the first major tax advantage the law gives insurance policies. **The death benefits are not considered to be taxable income to the Beneficiary.** This is true not only for Term policies but also for the death benefits paid out by *any* life Policy.

WHOLE LIFE INSURANCE

1 The second category of Ordinary Life insurance is Whole Life. Probably the first thing we notice about Whole Life insurance is that its premiums are higher than Term insurance premiums. In exchange for this increased premium, Whole Life offers additional features.

- Whole Life policies provide **coverage for the whole of life.**

- Whole Life policies **build cash value.**

- Whole Life **premiums never increase.**

2 You will also learn the different methods of purchasing a Whole Life Policy as well as the conditions under which a Whole Life Policy matures. Let's begin our discussion of Whole Life by examining its important characteristics.

Permanent Protection

3 Unlike Term insurance, Whole Life contracts provide permanent protection — protection for the whole of life. A higher premium is required because the company is not so much promising to pay *if* the Insured dies, but rather *when* the Insured dies. In a very real sense, the company is not underwriting a possibility (a contingency), but a certainty.

4 For example, with a Term to Age 65 Policy, Joe Insured (at age 40) is statistically expected to live to age 72 and never become a death claim to the company. However, we know for a certainty that Joe will die at some time, and if he owns and keeps his Whole Life contract, the face amount will be paid. The death question is not *if*, but *when*. By paying a higher premium, Joe is essentially using his Whole Life insurance to relieve the uncertainty of the timing of his death.

WHOLE LIFE . . .

PROTECTION + LOCKED IN CASH VALUE

Cash Value

5 Whole Life insurance offers the protection of Term insurance and another feature as well. With **the Whole Life contract there is a build up of equity or cash value within the contract.**

6 The cash value in a Whole Life Policy begins to grow about the third year after purchasing it and continues to build throughout the life of the Policy. Whole Life is normally guaranteed to produce **a cash value equal to the face amount of the Policy at the time the Insured would reach age 100.** Recognize that *unlike* dividends which may or may not be declared and paid, **cash value is absolutely guaranteed** by the Policy. Further, recognize that **the cash value is not a return of premium paid.** The table following is a lift from a Whole Life Policy. As you see, the table reflects the guaranteed cash values for each $1,000 of face amount of the contract. If you purchased a $100,000 Policy at age 25, the table promises that your cash value at the end of five years would be $35 per thousand, or $35 x 100 = $3,500. (Remember, you own 100 thousands.) At the end of the sixth year, it would be $4,900.

cash value is locked

Table of **Guaranteed Cash Values** Per Thousand

ISSUE AGE 25				END OF YEAR
CASH VALUE	PAID UP	EXTENDED TERM INS.*		
		YEARS	DAYS	
0	0	0	0	1
0	0	0	0	2
9	27.30	3	137	3
22	65.21	8	69	4
35	101.37	11	362	5
49	138.66	14	327	6
63	174.17	16	363	7
77	207.97	18	188	8
92	242.76	19	284	9
107	**275.82**	**20**	**260**	**10**
121	304.72	21	107	11
136	334.61	21	292	12
150	360.59	22	23	13
165	387.60	22	107	14
180	413.26	22	155	15
196	439.87	22	199	16
211	462.98	22	188	17
227	487.07	22	178	18
243	509.97	22	145	19
260	533.79	22	115	20
				AGE
420	702.30	19	51	55
502	766.73	17	74	60
581	**818.50**	**15**	**53**	**65**

CASH VALUE FACTORS:	YEARS 1-10	14.34352
	YEARS 11-20	12.94134
	YEARS 21-	11.89244

Guaranteed cash values

1 It doesn't matter how many people in your insuring class die, how high the company's expenses may be or how well (or poorly) your company's investment department performs — you are **guaranteed a cash value** of $3,500 after the fifth year and $4,900 after the sixth year.

2 In fact, you might view the Whole Life Policy as a contract which makes you an either/or promise. Either your Beneficiary will collect the death benefit or you will get your guaranteed cash value, **but you don't get both**.

Either

the company will pay the face amount to your designated Beneficiary when you die,

Or

NOT BOTH!

the company will return your guaranteed cash value at any point in your lifetime if you surrender the Policy.

1   In order for the company to make this either/or promise, they must charge a much higher premium than what they would for Term. This is because with a Whole Life Policy, the company is dealing with a *certainty* — they know they will have to pay out either a death benefit or the cash value. With a Term Policy, the company is only dealing with a *contingency* — they may never have to pay out the death benefit.

2   As you recall, the first major tax advantage given insurance policies is that death benefits paid to a Beneficiary are not considered to be part of the Beneficiary's taxable income. The second major advantage given insurance policies under current tax law is this:

> **The growth of your Policy's cash value is not subject to taxation while the Policy is in force.**

3   If you **surrender your Policy for cash,** however, you **would have to pay income taxes on the amount the cash value exceeds the total premium paid.**

4   The uses you can make of your Policy's cash value are quite extensive and will be explained in detail later in this text. For now, let's turn to the third major reason that Whole Life policies require a higher premium than Term contracts.

Guaranteed Premium

5   One of the most important features of Whole Life insurance (and one of the most overlooked) is that premiums are established for life — they can never be increased for any reason. At age 40, Joe might consider purchasing one of the following three insurance products:

- Annually Renewable Term to Age 65 at a premium of $3 per thousand increasing to $30 per thousand by age 65.

- Level Premium Term to Age 65 at a cost of $12 per thousand.

- Whole Life insurance at a premium of $25 per thousand.

6   Suppose Joe purchases one of the Term policies and lives to age 66. In the unlikely event that he *still has a need for the same amount of insurance*, he will have to start paying at the rate of $30 per thousand for the protection of a new Term Policy. Had Joe selected Whole Life at age 40, his premium would forever be guaranteed at the rate he paid originally, $25 per thousand — regardless of his health.

7   As we learned with Level Premium Term, creating a constant premium over long periods of time requires an *overpayment* in the early years to offset the *underpayment* in the later years. With Whole Life this characteristic is taken to its extreme (a lifetime of payments), and it definitely impacts the price in the early years particularly.

1 We started this section on Whole Life policies by pointing out that Whole Life contracts require a higher premium than Term policies and set out to understand why this is so. Before the discussion progresses any further, it would be well to remind you of the important features Whole Life provides in exchange for the higher premium charged.

- **Whole Life policies provide coverage for the whole of life.**

- **Whole Life policies build cash value.**

- **Whole Life premiums never increase.**

2 Now that you understand these three distinguishing features of Whole Life policies, it should not surprise you to learn that Whole Life policies are sometimes informally referred to as *cash value policies* or *permanent policies*. While the use of either of these slang terms for Whole Life insurance is not recommended, the promise of permanent coverage and the optional uses of the Policy's cash value give the Whole Life contract one of its most important characteristics — *continuity*.

3 In fact, there are only two events that can affect the continuity of a Whole Life Policy — non-payment of premium and maturity of the Policy. **Maturity of a Whole Life Policy can occur in one of two ways:**

- **death of the Insured** (same as Term insurance), or
- **attainment of age 100.**

4 In each case, the face amount of the Policy would be paid. In the case of death of the Insured, the face amount would be paid to the Beneficiary as a death benefit. In the event the Insured attains age 100, the face amount would be paid to the Policyowner and would be called an Endowment at Age 100. (To call it a *death benefit* might be a bit unseemly since the Policyowner is still living.)

Purchasing The Whole Life Contract

5 In this section you will find that there are three basic methods available for purchasing a Whole Life Policy. But no matter how the Policy is purchased, do not lose sight of one of the principles of Whole Life you have already learned — **Whole Life protects the Insured for the whole of life**. Regardless of the length of the premium payment period, the period of coverage is for life.

Single Premuim

6 **SINGLE PREMIUM** — Certainly the simplest way to buy a Policy would be to pay for it in one lump sum. Under the Single Premium plan, the Insured pays a single premium at the inception of the Policy and the Policy is fully paid. Joe Insured, at age 40, would pay $360 per thousand, or $18,000 for a $50,000 Policy if he were to purchase the Policy with a single premium. While it might seem like a bargain, recognize that the company does not expect Joe to die until age 72. Therefore, the company has over 30 years to invest Joe's $18,000 to increase it to the total premium amount required for the death benefit payment, as well as to generate a profit for the company.

Buy now

Die later

1   For many years this was the least popular method of purchasing a Whole Life contract. Most people didn't have $18,000 to plunk down on life insurance, and even those that did were not too inclined to do so. The normal thought process went like this: "Suppose I pay $18,000 and my twin brother pays only a minimum premium deposit of, say, $250. If we both die tomorrow, each family will receive $50,000. My brother's family will have profited $49,750 and mine will have profited only $32,000."

2   While it is still true that anyone who plans to die tomorrow should not purchase Whole Life with a Single Premium today, this purchase plan has become far more attractive than it once was. With policies issued since 1980, it is not at all unusual to see cash value grow at annual rates of 5% to 8%. Coupled with the deferral of taxes on the growth of cash value and the possibility of escaping income taxes altogether in the event of death, these competitive rates of return have caused many higher tax bracket investors to purchase Single Premium Whole Life contracts.

3   **LIMITED-PAY** — Whole Life policies, like most products, can be bought over time. Under the Limited-Pay method, payments are made over a given period of time (such as 20 years) or until a certain age is attained (often 65).

Limited Pay

4   Though Limited-Pay Whole Life policies are commonly referred to in terms of their payment period — such as **20-Pay Life** or **Life Paid at 60,** you should still immediately translate these names to mean **Whole Life sold on the installment plan.** As with any installment purchase, there is a charge made for taking advantage of time payments. In other words, if all payments made over the twenty-year period of a 20-Pay Life Policy were totaled, they would greatly exceed the amount of the Single Premium payment just discussed. Please remember that even if the Whole Life Policy is *paid-up* at a specified age, the *coverage continues for the whole of life*.

NOTE: Limited payment period NOT limited coverage period

5   **STRAIGHT LIFE (CONTINUOUS PREMIUM)** — The final and most popular premium payment plan takes the installment theory to the extreme. Under Continuous Premium (Straight Life), the Insured makes payments until death or until age 100, whichever comes first. This purchase plan is sometimes inaccurately referred to as Ordinary Life. The term Ordinary can create confusion as Ordinary Life is more accurately a system of marketing Term, Whole Life and Endowment insurance to individuals. For purposes of clarity, this text will not refer to Continuous Premium Whole Life policies as Ordinary Life.

"STRAIGHT"

pay, pay, pay, pay, etc., etc.

---

6   Now that you understand the methods of purchasing a Whole Life Policy, it is important to observe how they impact our client, Joe Insured. As you would probably guess, **the shorter the payment period, the higher the annual premium**. Obviously, the reverse is also true — the longer the payment period, the smaller the annual premium.

7   For instance, Joe would pay $25 per thousand for a Straight Life Policy and $37 per thousand for a 20-Pay Life Policy. **You can see that the premium is higher for the shorter payment period.** But there remains another question. If Joe lives to his statistically designated age of 72, under which payment method would he **pay the most in total premium?** Relax, you do not have to be a math wizard to figure the answer.

Time value of money

1   If you were Joe's insurance company, under which plan would you charge the most?

- 20-Pay Life under which you, the company, get all of Joe's premium dollars in 20 years?

or

- Straight Life under which you have to wait 32 years (remember Joe is 40) to get all that you expect of Joe's premium?

2   If Joe lives to his statistically determined age of 72, he would pay more in premium under the Straight Life method. The point to remember is that with 20-Pay Life, the company has more of Joe's money sooner and can invest it to earn more money.

3   All other things being equal (same Insured, company, Policy and face amount), **a higher premium per thousand means** two things:

- **A shorter premium payment period.**

- **A faster growth of cash value.**

4   The first point should be readily apparent by now, but let's develop the second a little further. If (all other things being equal) a higher premium per thousand means a faster growth of cash value, then the Single Premium payment method would generate cash value faster than either of the two installment purchase plans. It would also follow that the Limited-Pay method would build cash value more rapidly than Straight Life.

5   Practically speaking, the Straight Life payment method probably would never build cash values equal to those of an equivalent Limited-Pay Policy. With equal face amounts, the build-up of cash value in the Straight Life Policy would not equal the Limited-Pay Policy until the owner paid the final installment at age 100 — a rather unlikely event. Since it is so unlikely, you may wonder what happens if the Policyowner is forced by circumstances (or by choice for that matter) to stop paying premiums. Understand that while Joe may pay premiums until death or age 100, he is not obligated to do so. As you will see in the section of the text devoted to nonforfeiture options, Joe may stop paying premiums at any time and not forfeit his equity in the contract. He may choose to take the cash value of the Policy, a paid-up Policy of a lesser amount, or perhaps continue the full face value protection of his current Policy for a fixed period of time.

6   These are called *nonforfeiture options* and they contribute greatly to the flexibility of a Straight Life Policy. This flexibility and the very competitive price in the early years of premium payment have made Straight Life the most popular of all the Whole Life premium payment forms. In fact, it is common to see references to Whole Life policies in textbooks, sales brochures and even state insurance exams in which the payment method is not specifically designated. If this happens, **you should assume that the payment method for the Whole Life Policy mentioned is Straight Life** (Continuous Premium). That might seem a bit confusing at first glance, but when you recognize that the vast majority of Whole Life contracts are sold on a Straight Life (Continuous Premium) basis, the logic becomes a bit more obvious.

HIGHER PREMIUM =

SHORTER PAY PERIOD
+
LOWER TOTAL COST
+
FASTER GROWTH OF CASH VALUE

Notes

ENDOWMENT INSURANCE

PAYS IF YOU MAKE IT   PAYS IF YOU DON'T

JOE INSURED

$50000----

ENDOWMENT PERIOD

1   While the Tax Reform Act of 1984 virtually elimi-nates the future marketing of Endowment policies for reasons which will be addressed later in this section, you should still be familiar with the Endowment Policy as many of your prospective clients may own Endowment contracts purchased prior to 1984 which are unaffected by this legislation.

2   Like the Term and Whole Life policies previously discussed, an Endowment Policy will pay if the Insured dies within the Policy period. However, an Endowment Policy will also pay if the Insured lives to the end of the Policy period. Like Whole Life, Endowment contracts combine the features of equity growth and protection, but the emphasis is placed primarily on the *build-up of equity or cash value*.

3   Said another way, an **Endowment contract can mature (pay out) in either of two circumstances**. It will pay a death benefit (the face amount) if the Insured dies within the endowment period, or it will pay the cash value of the contract (the equivalent of the face amount) if the Insured lives to the endowment date. Therefore, the cash value of an Endowment Policy must build at an accelerated rate, **so that at the end of the Policy period, the cash value equals the face value and is payable to the Insured**.

4   Endowment insurance, then, provides for the payment of the face value of the Policy upon either the death of the Insured during the endowment period or at the end of the endowment period should the Insured survive.

Another way of looking at it

5   Prior to 1984, most Endowment policies were written with a maturity date which coincided with an event which required a large sum of ready cash (e.g., retirement or college). In fact, Endowment policies were categorized by the way this maturity date was expressed. There were Endowments that matured at a specified age (Endowment at 55, 60, or 65), and there were Endowments that matured at the end of a specified period of years (10, 20, or 30-Year Endowment). The premium for Joe, as a 40-year-old male buying a 20-Year Endowment Policy, would have been $45 per thousand and would have endowed at his age 60. An Endowment at Age 65 would have cost Joe $42 per thousand.

6   Some companies marketed Endowment policies by combining the two standard methods of expressing the maturity date. For example, Joe (at age 40) could have bought a 20-Year Endowment at Age 65 Policy which would mean that he would pay premiums for 20 years (until age 60) and the Policy would mature when he became 65.

Died in 1984

7   To reinforce your understanding of Endowment contracts, let's compare a 20-Pay Life to a 20-year Endowment Policy, either of which Joe could have purchased prior to 1984 in the amount of $50,000.

1 For each alternative, Policy payments would be over a 20 year period, but that is the only similarity. Whole Life purchased on a limited pay period of 20 years would cost Joe $37 per thousand, and the 20 Year Endowment would cost him $45 per thousand. At the end of twenty years (age 60 in this example), the Endowment Policy would pay Joe $50,000 and, since the endowment period was over, he would no longer have life insurance coverage. The 20-Pay Life Policy, on the other hand would simply be stamped as paid-up when Joe turns 60. He would not have to make any further premium payments. His life insurance coverage would continue, but he would not be paid the face value of the contract as would the Endowment Policyowner. He could surrender the Policy for the cash value designated in the Policy table, but it would be far less than $50,000.

2 The traditional Endowment had several major advantages:

- Rapid growth of cash value.

- Deferral of taxes on cash value growth.

- The possibility of escaping income taxes altogether if the Insured died and the proceeds were paid as a death benefit.

3 But it also had some major disadvantages:

- High cost.

- Immediate tax liability if the Insured lived to the endowment date or age.

CV not exceed face before age 95

1 It was the accelerated growth of cash value and the tax treatment thereof that caused the Tax Reform Act of 1984 to impact unfavorably upon the Endowment contract as well as a few other life policies. Insurance policies have always received special tax treatment because they are *insurance* policies. The Endowment Policy placed so much emphasis on the accumulation of cash and relatively so little emphasis on death protection (particularly so for Endowments of a very short duration), that it was viewed more as an investment contract than as a life insurance Policy. **The '84 Act states** that if any insurance contract is to enjoy the two major tax benefits historically accorded insurance products (i.e., the cash value growth is not subject to taxation while the Policy is in effect, and death benefits are received income tax-free by the Beneficiary), then **the cash value in the contract can build no faster than to equal the face value when the Insured reaches age 95**. If any life Policy builds cash value more rapidly than this benchmark, it loses most (if not all) of its tax advantages - tax deferred growth and no income tax on death benefits paid a Beneficiary.

MODIFIED ENDOWMENT CONTRACT

2 No sooner did the '84 Act eliminate the original Endowment Policy than some companies began marketing other cash value contracts which allowed for heavy deposits of premium in the early years to individuals with a need to escape taxes. The cash values grew at very competitive rates on a tax-deferred basis. If the Policyowner needed the cash quickly, he could borrow against the cash value without any tax liability.

MEC

10% Penalty

3 It only took Congress until 1988 to pass the Technical and Miscellaneous Revenue Act (TAMRA), which slammed the door on this idea. This legislation said that if a Policy creates cash value at a rate **faster than that of a Seven-Pay Whole Life Policy, then it is a Modified Endowment Contract**. When the IRS deems a Policy (Whole Life, Universal Life, whatever) to be a Modified Endowment Contract (MEC), any loan or withdrawal must be made with the understanding that the taxable dollars come out first, then the return of premium (already taxed) dollars. Furthermore, there is a **10% tax penalty** in addition to any taxes due on all withdrawals made prior to age 59 1/2.

A "material change" in a MEC is defined as any increase in death benefits

4 Notice, the only problem with a MEC is if you disturb the cash value. Suppose Joe bought a Single Premium Whole Life Policy on himself, named Jolene and the kids as beneficiaries and did not disturb the cash value during his lifetime. Upon his death the face value would be paid as usual and the benefits would not be subject to the income tax.

MEC Summary:

1. The Cash Value may not exceed the face amount prior to age 95.

2. 7-pay Whole Life Rule

3. MEC surrender prior to age 59 1/2:

- 10% penalty

- Tax on profits

ANNUITIES

WHAT IS AN ANNUITY?

1 **An Annuity is a tax deferred investment that has multiple payback options.**

WHAT PURPOSE DO ANNUITIES SERVE?

2 There is a major difference between **Life** insurance and an **Annuity**. Simply put, the basic difference lies in **who benefits from the Policy**. Life insurance is traditionally purchased **for the benefit of a loved one/your family**. You as the Policyowner purchase a Life insurance Policy at your expense, name yourself as the Insured person, and name a **Beneficiary**, which is the individual that will receive the death benefit when you die. Again, the primary purpose of Life insurance is to **benefit loved ones**, as opposed to benefitting yourself.

Who benefits?

3 The **purpose for an Annuity contract** is the *Polar Opposite*:

4 The primary purpose for purchasing an Annuity contract **is for your own benefit**. It is **a tax deferred investment account**. As with the Cash Value feature of a Life insurance Policy, you pay no taxes from year to year on the interest earned in your Annuity contract. This feature allows you to accumulate money over time **on a tax advantaged basis**, generally to be used to accumulate funds **for your own retirement**.

This one is for YOU!

5 To summarize, Life insurance protects your family against your premature death. Whereas an Annuity is a contract **you** purchase to accumulate wealth during **your** own lifetime for **your own benefit** during your retirement years. Life insurance provides protection **when life is cut short. Annuities provide for** *long life*.

$$ to live a long life

WHY ARE ANNUITIES CHALLENGING TO UNDERSTAND?

6 Details. Details. Details. *The devil is in the details.*

7 Some folks find understanding Annuities challenging because of the myriad of details. For example:

1. An Annuity contract has **two lives**, or phases: (1) **putting the money in**; and (2) **taking the money out**. If you get confused about which life/phase you are referring to, you can easily draw the wrong conclusion.

2 Lives

2. Annuity contracts have a myriad of **options** for putting the money in/investing in the contract. Are you purchasing your Annuity with **one lump sum**, or are you investing in it **over time**?

3. There is a multitude of **funding vehicles**. Is this a **Conventional Annuity** that guarantees a fixed rate of return, or is it a **Variable Annuity** where your money is invested in the **stock market**?

4. There are **multiple payback options**. Do you want your money in **Cash**? Or would you like a **Fixed Period** of income payments? Or would you prefer a **Life Income**?

5. **Taxation** gets to be a challenge. Unlike a Life insurance death benefit, which is NOT taxed, the profits earned by an Annuity **are always taxed**.

6. Annuities can be used as **funding vehicles** for **Qualified Pension plans** which change most of the tax rules.

7. Another source of confusion comes from ***terminology***; in this case, the definitions of the words ***Policyowner*** and ***Annuitant***. If the Annuity contract is in **Phase One : The Pay In Phase**, when you are investing in the contract, you are called the ***Policyowner***. However, if you ***annuitize*** your contract and go into **Phase Two : The Pay Out Phase**, you will now be called the ***Annuitant***. Said another way, **Policyowners are putting money into their Annuities, and Annuitants are taking money out of their Annuities.**
    It is still you/ the same person, but your title changes to reflect the different phase of your Annuity.

1   So let's sort out the details to facilitate your becoming an Annuity Expert.

PHASE # 1: THE *ACCUMULATION* OR *PAY IN* PHASE

2   There are numerous different ways that you can put money into an Annuity as follows:

1. **Single Premium**

2. **Fixed Premium**

3. **Flexible Premium**

Your Annuity Takes Wings

3   **First**, you could purchase an Annuity with a **one lump sum payment**. For example, you could sell your house or your business, or receive a death benefit from a deceased family member, and take this money directly to an insurance company and purchase an Annuity with a one lump sum payment - a **Single Premium Annuity**.

1 A **second** way to purchase an Annuity would be with regular periodic premium investments over time, which is referred to as **Fixed Level Premium Payments**. The amount of time can be for any duration that you choose, and the amount of money can be any amount that you wish. The focus here is more on **the dollar amount** of the monthly payments (what you can afford to save each month) as opposed to how long you wish to continue to save money.

#2 Fixed

2 The **third** way to invest in/purchase an Annuity is to use **Flexible Premium Payments**. In this strategy you would make investments into your Annuity any time you want, in any amount that you want, as you have additional funds to save/invest.

#3 Flex

3 Unlike Life insurance, investments in an Annuity do not necessarily have a set target monthly premium, or a set total dollar goal. During the **Accumulation Phase**, you may invest as much or as little money as you choose.

4 While a Fixed Monthly Payment may be a way of **establishing a discipline** for making your payments, it is absolutely **voluntary**. It is not like paying a monthly mortgage where you must make the monthly payments, or you are contractually in trouble/in default. And there is **no set period of time** for the accumulation of your wealth. When you start saving money in an Annuity, you do not have to have a specific number of years in mind. **You can accumulate money for about as long as you wish**. And you can accumulate as much money as you wish. **No limits!**

No dollar limits

ANNUITY UNDERWRITING & ELIGIBILITY

5 Unlike Life insurance, which requires a major screening, underwriting, and acceptance process, **virtually any one can purchase an Annuity**. Said another way, there is **almost no underwriting required** for Annuity Applicants. And the reason should be obvious once you fully understand Annuities: **the insurance company has nothing at risk**. All the insurance company has at risk is **to give back the Policyowner's money**, either if the Policyowner doesn't want to continue with the contract, or if the Policyowner dies while accumulating money. Basic Annuity contracts **DO NOT HAVE DEATH BENEFITS!** So the insurance company has virtually nothing at risk. An individual can be **uninsurable** for a Life insurance Policy, and still invest $10 million in an Annuity!

For sale to sickies

DEATH DURING THE *PAY IN* PHASE

6 If you, as the Annuity Policyowner, should die during the Pay In Phase, the insurance company's only obligation is to simply **return the Value of your Account (VA / Cash Value)** on the date of your death back to your estate. There is no difference between an Annuity contract, a savings account in a bank, or a securities account with a Broker/Dealer. Upon the death of the Policyowner, the institution determines the value of the account (VA), and returns that value to the estate of the Deceased. Then the estate **will pay the taxes**, and distribute the balance of the contract money according to the Deceased's will. Remember that an Annuity contract is **NOT** a Life insurance Policy (no death benefit), and that the **proceeds of the Annuity Policy ARE taxable**. We will discuss taxation later.

No death benefit! Therefore, taxes.

ANNUITY *SURRENDER* DURING THE PAY IN PHASE

1 You, as the Policyowner, can **surrender** your Annuity **at any time for any reason** during the Pay In Phase. However, there may be substantial adverse consequences for **premature/early surrender**, as follows:

1. **Pay The Taxes On The Profits** – Since the **profits** on your investment have been **Tax Deferred** (no taxes are payable as you earn profits from year to year), the taxes are now due upon the **surrender** of your contract, as we will discuss below.

Pay taxes

2. **10% Penalty For Early Surrender Prior To Age 59½** - The IRS charges a **10% penalty** for surrendering an Annuity **prior to Age 59½**. The same rule applies to most Qualified Pension plans as well, as we will see in Chapter 8. Obviously there are certain extenuating circumstances where the Policyowner can obtain money out of their contract without paying the penalty, such as suffering a Permanent and Total Disability. But normally, surrender prior to age 59½ will have adverse tax consequences. **This 59½ Rule** fundamentally relegates the usage of Annuity contract to a retirement vehicle.

10% Penalty

3. **Lawful Surrender Charges** – Insurance companies are in business to **make a profit**, which is accomplished by investing your Annuity money at a higher rate of return than they pay you. The insurance companies also have acquisition costs and commissions paid to recover. Therefore, the insurance company wants to discourage the early surrender of your contract. The longer the company can continue to invest your money, the greater its profits. Therefore, in order to **discourage early surrender**, the company may impose **surrender charges/fees for early withdrawal** of your money prior to a certain number of years, such as six or seven years. Sometimes the fees are referred to as a "Back End Load".

POLICY YEAR	SURRENDER PENALTY
1	6%
2	5%
3	4%
4	3%
5	2%
6	1%

2 To summarize, it is probably disadvantageous to surrender an Annuity Policy prior to age 59½: (1) **Taxes** have to be paid; (2) there may be a **10% penalty** for early withdrawal, and (3) the insurance company may impose **surrender charges**.

IMMEDIATE VERSUS *DEFERRED* Annuity – *NOW* or *LATER*

3 Two terms that you need to remember are *Immediate* and *Deferred*. If you make a **single premium** payment to purchase an Annuity, one of your choices is to **immediately** go into **Phase Two: The Pay Out Phase**. If you select this option, it would be called an *Immediate Annuity* because you are immediately going into Phase Two which is the **Pay Out/Income Phase**. Invest your money this month. Start receiving your income **NOW = *Single Premium Immediate Annuity***.

Immediate

4 The other option is to place your money into the Annuity today, and start the payout period **sometime in the future/LATER**. This is called a *Single Premium Deferred Annuity*.

Deferred

PHASE # 2: TAKING THE MONEY OUT / THE *INCOME PERIOD*

One strange characteristic when you purchase an Annuity is that you really do not need to have a set time in mind for when you are going to withdraw your money. It is somewhat similar to deciding today about when you want to retire. You may have a retirement goal/age in mind, but your plans will probably change many times as your life progresses.

So when you purchase a (Deferred) Annuity, your goal is to accumulate money over time on a **Tax Deferred basis**, but you may not have a firm grasp on how or when your money will ultimately be used. It is up to you to decide in the future what to do with your monies in your Annuity account, and when. Your **choices are very flexible**, as follows.

Surprising to many individuals, **there is no contractual requirement for you to annuitize your contract** (moving from the "Pay In" phase to the "Pay Out" phase is referred to as "annuitizing"). In other words, you contractually **DO NOT NEED TO** enter into Phase Two, because one of your choices is **to surrender your Policy for its Cash Value**. You must pay your taxes, but then you are free to use the remaining money any way you wish. You do **NOT** have to annuitize your contract.

Your choices/options are as follows:

1. **Surrender** your Policy for **Cash**

2. *Annuitize* your Contract, and select one of the following options:

    A.   **Annuity Certain**
    B.   **Life Annuity**

1. SURRENDER THE Policy FOR CASH

Cash Out

Take the Money / Surrender for CASH

At any time, you can notify your insurance company that you wish to **surrender** your Policy for **cash**. The insurance company writes you a check for the value of the account (Cash Value), and you pay the taxes.

Remember: If you surrender your Policy before age **59 1/2**, in addition to the taxes, you will **suffer a 10% penalty**. So as you start making your decisions about your retirement and the use of your Annuity, one option is to just cancel your contract, take your money and use it for any purpose you wish. Buy a boat. Take a trip around the world. Educate the grandkids. Go to Vegas. Whatever......

2. ANNUITIZING THE CONTRACT *Entering a new Phase*

1 Your other option is to keep your contract and enter into **Phase Two/The Pay Out Phase**, which requires you to *"annuitize"* your contract. Up until this point, the money in your account (Cash Value) **has clearly been your money.** As stated above, you do not need to annuitize your contract. You can just surrender your contract, take your money and walk away. But if you do choose to annuitize your contract, **the nature of your relationship with your insurance company changes dramatically.**

Annuitize

2 NOTE: Remember: *Policyowners* **are putting money into their Annuities, and** *Annuitants* **are receiving income benefits out of their Annuities.**

3 *Annuitizing* **your contract** effectively **transfers** the value of your account (its Cash Value) to your insurance company **in exchange for a promise** to pay you **income benefits over time.** Your account **NO LONGER HAS ANY CASH VALUE!**

ZERO CASH VALUE

4 There are multiple pay back choices/options. Select the option which best fits your future financial needs. Once you select an income option, you contractually agree that, in exchange for the value of your account (Cash Value), the insurance company agrees to pay you money/income benefits over time according to that plan. But once you have contractually agreed to your payout plan, **you cannot change your mind!** Again, your contract now has **NO Cash Value** as your money has been transferred to the insurance company in exchange for their promise to pay future income benefits. So you can no longer back out of the Agreement.

PLEASE REMEMBER: *ADVERSE SELECTION*

5 **Changing Your Mind Is Not An Option** – Be very careful in selecting which Annuity option will work best for you, because once you have contractually agreed with the insurance company to that option, **you cannot ask for changes or modifications.** The **reason** for not allowing any changes is **Adverse Selection.** If your life situation changes in the future, you would want to select a different pay out option to better fit your new situation, which would probably be to the insurance company's disadvantage. Said again, **once you start receiving pay out benefits,** you cannot change your selection!

6 For example, suppose that income benefits were being paid to both you and your spouse for as long as either of you live. Also assume that both of you are age 68. You get a divorce, and you now want to name your new spouse, age 28, as your new Annuitant. Is it fair to your insurance company to replace a 68 year old Annuitant with a 28 year old Annuitant? Obviously not, as the 28 year old Annuitant will probably live 40 years longer than the 68 year old Annuitant. This is a case of Adverse Selection, and is why your insurance company will **NOT** allow you to change your mind once you have contractually agreed to a Pay Out plan.

it's a blonde moment

TWO BASIC ANNUITY PAYOUT TYPES: *CERTAIN* v. *LIFE*

1   If you decide to annuitize your Policy, you have two basis Pay Out choices: (1) an **Annuity Certain**, or (2) a **Life Annuity**. As there are two categories of human beings, males and females, there are two categories of Annuity Pay Outs: the Annuity Certain, and the Life Annuity. While they are both Annuity payout plans, they have very different characteristics, and you must be able to differentiate between them. The *Certain* just pays you for **a designated period of time**, whereas the *Life* pays you for **the rest of your life.**

OPTION 2A: ANNUITY CERTAIN   *A BRIDGE*

2   An *Annuity Certain* promises to pay you as the Annuitant a **known amount of money for a known amount of time without regard to your mortality** (estimated remaining length of your life). It simply pays you so many **dollars** per month/year for so many **months**/years.

3   You as the Annuitant can select **how many dollars** per month you want to receive, and the insurance company will calculate **how many months the money will last**. Or you as the Annuitant can select **how many months** you want to receive benefits, and the insurance company will calculate the dollar amount it can pay each month. **There is no regard for mortality in these calculations** because your payments have nothing to do with your living or dying.

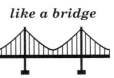

4   The insurance company is simply **looking at time and dollars** (as well as interest rates, because the insurance company is still paying you interest on the unpaid balance).

5   There are two major choices under the **Annuity Certain**:   *Time* or *Dollars*

- **Fixed Period** – Under the Fixed Period choice, you as the Annuitant selects the **period of time** over which you would like to receive your payments (for example: 10 years), and the insurance company calculates the dollar amount that can be paid to you each month for the next ten years.

- **Fixed Amount** – You as the Annuitant select the **amount of dollars** that you want to receive each period (for example: $50,000 per year), and the insurance company calculates how many years of payments they can make to you.

6   With the selection of Fixed Period or Fixed Amount, the **Annuity Certain** option will pay a **known amount of money for a known amount of time** to the Annuitant regardless of whether the Annuitant is alive or dead. In other words, there is no consideration for mortality in Annuity Certain pay out plans.

7   **An *Annuity Certain* is like a BRIDGE: A definite start point, and a definite stop point.**

OPTION 2B: LIFE ANNUITY / LIFE INCOME

1 If you decide to annuitize your Policy, the **second option** you have is to select a **Life Income / Life Annuity**. While there are many versions of this choice, the most important characteristic for all the choices is that **each will pay you an income for the rest of your life! You cannot outlive a Life Income!** It may outlive you, but you cannot outlive it. So if you live to age 89, a Life Income will pay you through age 89. If you live to age 129, a Life Annuity will pay you an income through age 129. Please do not forget that the fundamental promise of a Life Income is **to pay you an income for the rest of your life!**

An income for the rest of your life!

Making a safe landing in retirement

Making a Safe Landing in Retirement

Who Would Want a *Life Income*?   Living Too Long

2 You might ask, who would consider trading their entire Cash Value in their Annuity for a promise to receive an income for the **remainder of their life**? The answer is that if you are a senior citizen, in excellent health, but with limited assets, you may be concerned about **outliving your assets**, and running out of money (this is when *Miller Time* becomes *Alpo Time*!). So, if you anticipate living a long life, and your net worth is not in the millions of dollars, perhaps you should seriously consider buying a **guaranteed income for the rest of your life**, which is the Life Income/Life Annuity pay out option.

Factors Necessary to Calculate a Life Income

3 The amount of money that the insurance company can pay you each month for the rest of your life will primarily depend upon the following factors:

1. The **value of your account**/Cash Value at the time you chose to annuitize your account.
2. The **type of pay out plan** that you elect as discussed below.
3. Your **age**.
4. Your **gender**.
5. The **number** of Annuitants.
6. The **interest rate/rate of return** being paid on the balance of your account during the payout period.

Life Annuity Options

1   There are **four** major categories of options for the Life Annuity as follows:

    1. **Straight** Life Annuity
    2. Life Annuity With **Period Certain**
    3. Life Annuity with **Refund** / Refund Life Annuity
    4. **Joint And Survivorship** Life Annuity

1. Straight Life Annuity
WIN / LOSE

2   Under a **Straight Life Annuity** pay out plan, the insurance company will pay you a known amount of money every month **until you die**. The good news is that the Straight Life option will **pay the largest monthly income** because it is the **lowest risk to** the insurance company. The bad news is, if you die prematurely, you will not receive the full value of your contract. Live to age 129, and you are a big winner! You received far more in income benefits than the original value of your account. But if you die three months after you annuitize your contract, **your income benefits stop**, and you do not receive benefits equal to the original value of your account. (The insurance company will use what they saved on you to pay the Annuitant who lived to age 129.) The insurance company actuaries do the calculations as follows.

3   The actuaries calculate the risks associated with paying you an income for the rest of your life **according to your *Risk Group*** (which is your group of Annuitants that are your same age and gender). Under a Straight Life Annuity, the insurance company calculates the predicted average age to which the individuals in your Risk Group will live, and calculates your benefits accordingly. If you die prior to reaching the predicted age, the insurance company **will stop paying you benefits**. In this circumstance, you would not get back the original value of your plan. However, if you outlive your Risk Group age, you clearly would get paid benefits beyond the value of your original investment. In that sense, the **Straight Life Annuity is a win/lose proposition**.

4   The **Social Security Retirement Income** plan is an example of a Straight Life Annuity. Once you start receiving your Social Security income benefits, the government will pay you **an income for the rest of your life**, which is a **Straight** Life Annuity. If you die two years after you retire, you will not receive back the full value of your original retirement account. But on the flip side, if you live until age 110, you clearly will be paid back more in benefits than you paid into the plan. **Win / Lose**.

2. Life Annuity With Period Certain
TIME Guarantee

1 While the value of the first option, the **Straight** Life Annuity, is that it provides the **largest monthly income**, the downside risk is that if you die prematurely, you have NOT received back the full value of your account. One way to hedge your bet at the cost of a **small monthly decrease in benefits**, is to build in a **"Period Certain" Time Guarantee** into the pay out Agreement. This is called a **Life Annuity With Period Certain**. This option is appropriate for the Annuitant that needs to **guarantee payments for at least a minimum period of time**.

2 You as the Annuitant select your desired **"Period Certain"**. Common lengths of time are 5 years, 10 years, or 15 years. Some of your major considerations in selecting the appropriate *Period Certain* are your future financial obligations, such as retiring debt, paying estate taxes, health care costs, and providing liquidity to your estate.

3 Let's suppose that you select a *Life Annuity With 10 Years Certain*. The fundamental promise remains the same: the insurance company is going to pay you until you die. However, **if you die before the end of 10 years**, the insurance company will **continue your payments** to your estate **through the end of 10 years**. Example: You annuitize your contract at age 68. You select the Life Annuity With 10 Year Certain option. If you die at age 70, the insurance company would continue to pay your same benefits to your estate (or you could name a Beneficiary) for an additional eight years (for a total of 10 years of payments).

Two promises:
1. Til death
2. But not less than XX years

4 However, **if you live beyond the 10 year Period Certain, the insurance company will continue to pay you until you die. Remember: You cannot outlive a Life Income!**

So we have two promises running simultaneously: (1) the insurance company **agrees to pay you until you die**, but (2) **not less than 10 years**.

3. Refund Life Annuity
Money Back Guarantee

5 Under the **Refund Life Annuity** plan, you as the Annuitant are primarily concerned with **getting all of your original Cash Value back**. For example, imagine that the **value of your account (VA)** when you annuitized your contract is $800,000. If you are concerned about getting back your entire $800,000, the **Refund Life Annuity** is for you.

All your money back

6 Under the Refund Life Annuity, the insurance company **promises to pay you back at least your $800,000**. If you annuitized your contract, and had received $500,000 in income benefits and then died, the insurance company would *REFUND* the remaining $300,000 back to your estate (or you could name a Beneficiary). This could be done either as one lump sum, called a **Cash Refund Life Annuity**, or in installments which would be called an **Installment Refund Life Annuity**. Under the Installment plan, the insurance company would simply continue to pay your monthly payments until the balance of the $800,000 has been paid.

7 Remember, if you are still alive after you have received $800,000 in income benefits, the insurance company is going to **continue to pay you until you die. Remember: You cannot outlive a Life Annuity!**

4. Joint and Survivorship Life Annuity
Spousal Guarantee

1 In insurance terminology, *Joint* means *Two or More*.

2 *Survivorship* means *there are no remaining survivors: They are all deceased.*

3 Under the *Joint and Survivorship Life Annuity*, there are **two or more Annuitants (= *Joint*), and the insurance company is going to pay income benefits until all of the Annuitants are deceased (= *Survivorship*)**. The most common arrangement is for both you and your spouse to be the Annuitants.

4 Obviously, **two individuals will statistically outlive one individual**, so the insurance company is going **to slightly reduce your monthly income benefit** accordingly, to pay for this increased risk. In addition, the insurance company is concerned with the **age** of **both** Annuitants. The younger you are, the less money you will be receiving each month, because the insurance company will be required to pay benefits for a longer period of time. **Gender** is also an underwriting factor, because women, on average, will statistically outlive men by four or five years.

5 So what happens if your spouse dies first? The insurance company will **continue to pay you the same dollar amount of income until you die as well. Remember: You cannot outlive a Life Annuity!**

6 There is also another version of the Joint and Survivorship Life Annuity which is called the **Joint and Two-Thirds Survivorship Life Annuity**. Under this option, the insurance company will pay a little bit more to you and your spouse while you are both alive, but will reduce the payments upon the death of the first person to **2/3** of the original monthly payment.

7 **NOTE:** It is also possible to add a **Period Certain** *Time Guarantee*, or the **Refund** *Money Back Guarantee* to the Joint & Survivorship Life Annuity Pay Out plan. Such plans would be called **Joint & Survivorship Life Annuity With Period Certain**, or **Joint & Survivorship Life Annuity With Refund**. Lots of choices!

PHASE #1
ACCUMULATION PHASE
"PAY-IN"

SINGLE PREMIUM
- IMMEDIATE
- DEFERRED

OR

INSTALLMENTS
- LEVEL/FIXED
- FLEXIBLE

PHASE #2
INCOME PHASE
"PAY-OUT"

CASH

OR

ANNUITIZE THE CONTRACT

ANNUITY CERTAIN
1. FIXED PERIOD
2. FIXED AMOUNT

OR

LIFE ANNUITY
1. STRAIGHT LIFE
2. LIFE W/ PERIOD CERTAIN
3. LIFE W/ REFUND
4. JOINT & SURVIVORSHIP LIFE

ACTUARIES & MORTALITY : HOW LONG WILL YOU LIVE?

1   In all four of the above **Life Income** pay out plans, the insurance company's actuaries are using the **age/mortality** of the Annuitant(s) because the insurance company is going to pay benefits until the Annuitants are deceased. And obviously the younger the Annuitants are, the longer statistically they should live, and therefore the less the insurance company could afford to pay each month (because the money has to be stretched out over a longer period of time). Or said another way, the older the Annuitants are, the more the insurance company can afford to pay each month in benefits.

AGE

2   **Gender** is also important, because females are statistically predicted to outlive males by four or five years. Therefore, the monthly/periodic payments made to female Annuitants will be somewhat less than the payments made to the equivalent age male Annuitant. **The longer the predicted payment period, the smaller will be the monthly benefits paid**.

GENDER

Surprising to some, *Health* is NOT an Annuity underwriting consideration! The sicker you are, the more the insurance company likes you as an Annuitant! Think about it!

RATE OF RETURN ON YOUR INVESTMENT   *ROR*

3   Another confusing aspect of Annuities is that there are multiple ways for the insurance company to pay you **interest/rate of return (ROR)** on your invested money. Some of the more common methods are:

1.   **Fixed Dollar / Conventional with Fixed Interest Rate**
2.   **Fixed Dollar / Conventional with an Interest Sensitive Rate**
3.   **Equity Indexed**
4.   **Variable / Securities**

1. Fixed Dollar / Conventional Annuity with Fixed Guaranteed Interest Rate

4   Under the Fixed Dollar / Conventional Annuity **with a Fixed Interest Rate** the insurance company pays a **fixed guaranteed rate of return** on your invested capital. Typical rates of interest paid are between 4% and 6% of the existing value of your account (your Cash Value) paid on an annual basis. This rate of return is **guaranteed** by the insurance company for the life of your contract. So, if the insurance company is earning less on your invested funds than they've guaranteed to you, the insurance company makes up the difference at their expense.

FIXED ROR

5   On the other hand, if interest rates are high, and the insurance company is making a high rate of return on your investment, you are not benefitting from these higher rates of return. You could be earning more money with a different contract, but you are safe because you have a guaranteed fixed rate of return.

GENERAL ACCOUNT
Insurance Company Guarantees the Rate of Return

In all forms of **Conventional** Annuities, your monies are in the insurance company's **General Account**. Under the General Account, the insurance company is responsible for investing the money, and they **guarantee a rate of return** to their Policyowner/Annuitants. So you as the investor are NOT taking to risk on earning interest on your money. **The insurance company is taking that risk.**

GENERAL ACCOUNT

2. Interest Sensitive   Guaranteed ROR, Plus

The second, and more progressive, way of paying interest in a **Conventional** Annuity is called *Interest Sensitive*. Under the Interest Sensitive arrangement, the insurance company **guarantees a certain minimum rate of return**, such as 4%, and then **pays higher interest rates** if the insurance company is earning higher interest rates in the financial markets. In an Interest Sensitive plan, you benefit from having a **guaranteed minimum interest rate**, but you also benefit from periods when the insurance company is earning higher interest rates. So there is no downside risk for you, but there is **upside potential**. Obviously the Interest Sensitive contract may be more lucrative to own because you have the best of both worlds: **A guaranteed minimum rate of return, plus upside potential for higher rates of return on your investment, based on current interest rates.**

Invested monies paying interest on an Interest Sensitive basis are still invested in the insurance company's **General Account**.

INTEREST SENSITIVE

3. Equity Indexed   S & P 500 Index

A third way of paying you a rate of return in a **Conventional** Annuity is on an *Equity Indexed* basis. Under the Equity Indexed plan, the insurance company again **guarantees a minimum rate of return**, such as 4%, but then potentially pays a higher rate of return on your money based on the performance of a **stock market index**. This is still considered to be a **Conventional** Annuity (the invested money is still in the **General Account**), but with a stock market twist! The stock market index that is most commonly used is the **Standard & Poor's 500, or the S&P 500** as it is commonly called. So, when the stock market is down, you would **still be guaranteed your 4% rate of return**. However, if the stock market is performing very well, you will earn excess interest/rate of return on your money according to a relationship with the S&P 500 Index. Please note that your money is NOT directly invested in the stock market. Instead, your Rate Of Return is **indirectly** dependent on the performance of the stock market.

HYBRID:

Conventional promise, but with Stock Market Potential

Again, with an **Equity Indexed** contract, you have the best of both worlds: A **guaranteed minimum rate of return** on your investment, as well as the upside potential for higher rates of return. But this time, the upside potential is tied to a **stock market index** instead of to the interest rate markets.

To date, **Equity Indexed contracts are NOT considered to be securities investments. Therefore, Life insurance Agents do NOT need a Securities license to sell Equity Indexed products.**

Quasi Security

NOTE: The Standard & Poor's 500 Index is a collection of 500 top named stocks, such as Microsoft, Ford Motor, Proctor & Gamble, Eli Lilly, John Deere and Caterpillar Tractor. For a full list of the companies contained in the S&P 500, visit WWW. STANDARDANDPOORS.COM.

4. Variable   Stock Market & Separate Account

1   The fourth investment plan is called the **"Variable Annuity"**. The word **"Variable"** in insurance terminology means **"stock market"**. In other words, in a Variable contract the insurance company invests the value of your account **directly** in the stock market. The normal investment vehicles are **mutual funds**. We will talk extensively about **Variable** contracts in Chapter 9, but for the interim, please remember that with **Variable** contracts your money is placed in the **Separate Account**, which is short hand for stating that your money is invested in the stock market. Agents selling **Variable** contracts must have a **Securities license** *in addition to their Life insurance license.*

2   One of the unique features of Variable Annuities is that the Value of your Account is expressed in terms of UNITS, and NOT in terms of dollars. You accumulate UNITS during your Accumulation/investment period. Think about the process this way: Each time you invest money, your dollars are used to purchase shares of Mutual Fund stock. And since the price per share changes daily as the stock market fluctuates, the number of shares that can be purchased per dollar will fluctuate every day as well.

Separate account

3   At the end of your Accumulation Period, you will have accumulated so many thousands of shares/ Accumulation Units. You can now surrender your units/ shares of stock for cash, and walk away. Or you can annuitize your contract.

4   If you choose to annuitize your contract, you can select either a Conventional payout, as discussed above, or you can select a Variable payout. The logic for a Variable payout is to keep up with inflation. Or even better, perhaps your monthly incomes will grow faster than the rate of inflation, as the stock market has traditionally grown at a rate of about four times the rate of inflation.

Securities License Required

5   If you select a Variable payout, your Accumulation Units/shares of the Accumulation Mutual Fund stock will be converted to a FIXED NUMBER of Income Units of the payout Mutual Fund stock. The number of your Income Units now will never change! But your monthly income benefit will fluctuate depending upon the performance of the underlying investments and the stock market.

TAXATION   THE *BITE*

6   For the moment, let's talk about the taxation of **individually owned** Annuities. In Chapter 8 we will talk about the taxation of Annuities that are purchased through **Qualified Pension plans**. But for the moment let's keep it simple by talking only about individually owned Annuities.

7   In an individually owned Annuity, you are investing **after-tax money** into your Annuity. In other words, you first pay your income taxes on your income, and then invest the remainder (which is now after-tax money) into your Annuity contract. So you have already paid your taxes on your invested capital.

1   Your **after–tax investment(s)** creates your **"Cost Basis"**, which is your **Principle (invested capital)**. In the future, when your Cost Basis money/Principle is paid back to you, there will be **no taxation on this money** because you have already paid the taxes. For example, assume that you originally invested $100,000 into your Annuity. Your **Cost Basis** is therefore $100,000. In the future, when you receive money back, **your original $100,000 will NOT be taxed**, because it already has been taxed before you invested it. So please remember: individually owned **Annuities are funded with after tax money**.

2   As you know, you as the Policyowner of an Annuity are earning interest/profits on your investment on a **Tax Deferred Basis**. Therefore, **no matter when or how you take your money out, you are going to owe the taxes on the interest/profits earned in your account**. This is true whether you take your money out as a lump sum surrender, or if you annuitize your contract for an income over time.

3   If you **surrender** your Policy, the **taxes will be due in the year that you surrender your Policy**. If you **annuitize** your contract, some part of every income payment that you receive will be the return of your **Principle**, and therefore **not taxed**. The remainder of each income payment will be the **interest/profits** that you earned on your money, which is **taxable as ordinary income**. The reason why the entire profit portion is all taxable is because your Annuity allowed your profits to accrue year after year on a Tax Deferred basis, so you have never paid taxes on your profits/gains/earnings. Now is the time!

Exclusion Ratio = $$\frac{\textbf{\$\$s Invested}}{\textbf{Value of Your Account}}$$

4   The amount of taxes payable will be based on the **Exclusion Ratio**. The Exclusion Ratio is the ratio of how much of your Cash Value is Principle (after tax money), and how much of your Cash Value is interest/profits. For example, if you invested $100,000 in after tax money into your Annuity, and the value of your Annuity is $300,000 when you annuitize your contract, the **Exclusion Ratio** would be $100,000/$300,000 or 1/3. Said another way, 1/3 of every dollar coming back to you will be excluded from taxes (a return of your Principle), and 2/3 of every dollar paid back to you will be taxable as ordinary income (your profits).

10% Penalty for Premature/Early Surrender

5   As you recall, if you **surrender** your Annuity Policy **prior to Age 59 ½** (with certain exceptions), there is an **additional 10% penalty**. The IRS is essentially saying they want you to keep your money in your Annuity contract until you are close to being a senior citizen, which makes Annuities more of a retirement vehicle than a mid-life savings vehicle.

6   NOTE: While you cannot **surrender** your Annuity contract prior to age 59 ½ without the 10% penalty, you CAN **annuitize** your contract prior to Age 59 ½ **without penalty**. Early retirement, anyone?

Qualified Pension Plans

7   As you will see in Chapter 8, it is possible to use Annuities as funding vehicles for Qualified Pension plans. The taxation of such programs is essentially controlled by the taxation rules for Qualified Pension plan, and not by the underlying funding vehicles themselves. Stay tuned.

A Practical Example

At age 65, Joe and Jolene inherit $1,000,000. They decide to buy an Annuity that will begin paying at once and will continue to pay full value as long as either is alive. They are frightened of the impact of inflation and decide to receive benefits based on the value of Annuity units. Hopefully, the value of the Annuity units will increase at a rate equal to inflation. Since the children are no longer dependent, Joe and Jolene decide that no minimum guarantee is necessary. When both have died, the Annuity will stop paying.

1

Remember the classification questions.

Accumulation	Income
How are the premiums paid? Once... Single Premium More than once. Level Premium Flexible Premium	**When do benefits begin?** Now... Immediate Or later. Deferred **How long are benefits paid?** Life... Straight Life Annuity Or longer. Life Annuity with Period Certain Refund Life Annuity **How many lives are covered?** One... Life Annuity Or more than one. Joint Life Annuity Joint and 2/3 Life Annuity **Are benefits guaranteed?** Yes... Conventional Annuity Or no. Variable Annuity

Your description of Joe and Jolene's Annuity.

_____

_____

_____

Answer To Exercise

Joe and Jolene purchased a Single Premium $1,000,000 Immediate Joint and Survivor Variable Straight Life Annuity (or equivalent answer).

CONCLUSION

1 Insurance companies have traditionally marketed their products in three different ways: Industrial, Group, and Ordinary. The focus of this chapter has been on Ordinary (Individual) Life. Ordinary Life has traditionally included Term, Whole Life, and Endowment insurance. We examined these three forms of life insurance in this chapter and also looked at the Annuity, which is not, strictly speaking, life insurance because it has no death benefit, but it is sold by life insurance companies.

2 Term life insurance is a contract in which the insurance company agrees to pay a death benefit if the Insured dies during the term of the Policy. The term is a specific period of time, such as one year, five years, until age 65, etc. If the Insured dies during the specified period of time, the Policy matures and the insurance company pays the face amount. If the Insured does not die during the term, the Policy expires. For this insurance coverage, the Policyowner must pay premium. Because the risk of death increases with age, the premium for this death protection will also increase with age. Therefore, Term life insurance premiums are based on the Insured's attained (current) age. As the Insured gets older, the cost of insurance increases.

3 Term life insurance comes in different varieties. The face amount (death benefit) may increase over time (Increasing Term), decrease over time (Decreasing Term), or remain level throughout the term (Level Term). One of the most common usages of Decreasing Term is for mortgage protection. Regardless of the face amount, the term Policy may also be renewable and/or convertible. If it is Renewable Term, the Policyowner has the right to renew the Policy up to some predetermined date or age without having to show proof of insurability. Likewise, proof of insurability is not required to convert the Term to Whole Life in a Convertible Term Policy.

4 Whole Life insurance is different from Term because it offers death protection but for the whole of life. It also differs from Term in that it builds cash value . . . or equity in the Policy. The cash value is absolutely guaranteed to build at a rate which will cause it to equal the face amount of the Policy when the Insured would reach age 100. With Whole Life, the insurance company makes an either/or promise. The company will either pay the face amount upon maturity (the Insured's death or attainment of age 100, whichever comes first) or return the guaranteed cash value if the Policyowner surrenders the Policy or stops paying premium.

5 There are three ways to purchase a Whole Life Policy: Single Premium, Limited Pay, and Straight Life (Continuous Premium). The method the Policyowner chooses will affect the growth of cash value. The rule of thumb is, "The higher the cost per thousand, the faster the growth of cash value." Therefore, a Whole Life Policy purchased with a Single Premium will build cash value faster than the same Policy purchased over a period of time, such as 20 Pay Life. Likewise, the 20 Pay Life will build cash value faster than the same Policy purchased as Straight Life.

6 The third traditional Ordinary Life product was the Endowment Policy. An Endowment contract offered life insurance protection for a specified period of time (such as 10 years, 20 years, until age 65, etc.) and an accelerated growth of cash value. If the Insured died during the endowment period, the Policy would pay a death benefit. If the Insured didn't die, but lived to the endowment date or age, then the Policy would endow (pay) the face amount. In other words, the Endowment Policy could mature in one of two ways: death or reaching the endowment date or age. It was designed so that the cash value would equal the face amount at the endowment date or age and, therefore, required a much higher premium than Whole Life. But, because of the higher cost per thousand, it had a faster growth of cash value.

1   Life insurance products offer two important tax benefits:

(1)   Death benefits paid to a Beneficiary are not subject to income taxes.

(2)   The growth of cash value is not subject to income taxation as long as the Policy is in force.

2   This first tax benefit applies to Term, Whole Life and Endowment. Under current tax law regarding these three traditional policies, the second tax benefit only applies to Whole Life. This is because Term, as a general rule, does not build cash value, and the traditional Endowment has not been marketed since the Tax Reform Act of 1984.

3   The last product we looked at in this chapter was the Annuity. An Annuity is not truly "life insurance" because of one important difference: an Annuity has no death benefit. Annuities do enjoy a tax deferred accumulation of cash value though and are sold by life insurance companies.

4   An Annuity is a contract under which the insurance company agrees to pay the owner (the Annuitant) a guaranteed income for either a set period of time (an Annuity Certain) or for life (a Straight Life Annuity). A Straight Life Annuity can be beefed up with additional guarantees, but the cost will reflect these additional promises. Examples of Annuities with beefed up promises include: a Life Annuity with Period Certain (which pays out for a set amount of time or for the life of the Annuitant, whichever is longer); a Refund Life Annuity (which pays out the full amount the annuitant paid for the Annuity or for the life of the annuitant, whichever is longer); a Joint and Survivor Life Annuity (which pays out to two or more annuitants for as long as either annuitant lives).

5   Annuities have two phases: an accumulation (pay-in) phase and an annuity (pay-out) phase. During the accumulation phase, the owner pays premium and the annuity builds cash value on a tax deferred basis. This pay-in can be accomplished with a Level Premium, a Flexible Premium, or a Single Premium. Either immediately or sometime in the future, the insurance company, at the annuitant's direction, will begin the annuity phase. If the pay-out stage begins immediately, it's called an Immediate Annuity. If the income stage is put off until a later time, it's called a Deferred Annuity.

6   Once the annuity (pay-out) phase begins, the insurance company begins paying the Annuitant a regular income. The income will continue for as long as the Annuitant lives (Straight Life Annuity) or possibly longer if the Annuitant purchased a beefed up Annuity, such as a Life Annuity with Period Certain, a Refund Life Annuity, or a Joint and Survivor Life Annuity.

7   The insurance company determines the income amount based on:

- the amount of premium/cash value the annuitant has accumulated
- the type of plan selected
- the frequency of the payment (monthly, quarterly, annually)
- the interest rate
- the age and gender of the annuitant(s)

8   The longer the Annuitant is expected to live, the smaller the income installments will be. The insurance company projects the annuitant's life expectancy based on the Law of Large Numbers and the mortality tables. So, the older a person is (the greater the risk of death), the greater the income check will be.

1 The insurance company may pay out the income benefit in a fixed dollar amount (a Conventional Annuity) or in units based on the stock market (a Variable Annuity). Each has its own risks: a Conventional Annuity carries with it the risk of inflation; a Variable Annuity carries the risk of investment in the stock market. It's up to the Annuitant to make the choice. If you wish to sell any Variable product, such as a Variable Annuity, you must become licensed not only in life insurance, but also in securities. In order to obtain your securities license, you must first be approved by the National Association of Securities Dealers (NASD / FINRA).

2 Upon answering the following five classification questions, you will be able to completely describe any Annuity:

- How are the premiums paid?
- When do benefits begin?
- How long are benefits paid?
- How may lives are covered?
- Are benefits guaranteed?

3 In this chapter we have examined the fundamental building blocks of the life insurance business: Term, Whole Life, Endowment, and the Annuity. An understanding of these key products will provide you with the firm footing you will need in finding your way through the maze of newer products developed and to be developed in the future.

LIFE INSURANCE REGULATION AND POLICY PROVISIONS

1 As discussed in Chapter Two, insurance contracts are contracts of *adhesion* . . . written by insurance companies and offered to the public on a *take it or leave it* basis. Because insurance companies write the contracts and because they enjoy greater financial and legal resources than the typical Policyowner, the companies would hold an unfair advantage in the formation of these contracts if the process were totally unregulated. The task of governing these potentially one-sided agreements is the responsibility of each state's insurance regulators. The **McCarran-Ferguson Act of 1945** (Public Law 15) said that it is the federal government's right to regulate insurance, but they would not do so as long as the individual states did an adequate job of regulation.

2 In recent years, there are two important areas where the Federal Government did feel compelled to enact legislation. Concerns about Insurance Fraud and potential money laundering from subversive or terrorist elements lead to the passing of both **The Violent Crime Control and Law Enforcement Act** and **The Patriot Act**.

The Violent Crime Control and Law Enforcement Act

3 The Violent Crime Control and Law Enforcement Act was passed into law by congress in 1994. It is the largest crime bill in history. The bill was wide ranging, but of particular interest to the insurance industry is the **Insurance Fraud Prevention Act** that specifically prohibits people convicted of felonies involving breach of trust or dishonesty to work in any capacity in the field of insurance without a written waiver. The waiver must be obtained from the Office of the Insurance Commissioner in the state in which the Applicant works. The act requires producers, their managers, and even administrative personnel who have been convicted of such felonies to obtain the waiver. If an individual has been convicted of the felonies listed above and is found to be willfully working in the insurance field, that person can be fined and imprisoned for up to five years.

The Patriot Act

4 As a result of the terrorist acts committed on American soil on 9-11-01, Congress passed the USA Patriot Act into law. The USA Patriot Act is actually an acronym for **Uniting and Strengthening America by Providing Appropriate Tools Required to Intercept and Obstruct Terrorism Act of 2001.** The Act requires all insurers who issue policies which contain cash value (Whole Life, Annuities, etc.) to develop procedures, furnish training, and designate a Compliance Officer to ensure that such policies are not being used by individuals to launder money that could eventually end up in the hands of terrorist entities. The Act only applies to cash value bearing insurance policies and not policies such as Term Life or Property and Casualty policies.

9-11

© **2010 Pathfinder Corporation**

1   Not surprisingly, many minor differences exist in the regulatory apparatus from state to state. In most states, the regulatory jurisdiction belongs to the Insurance Department headed by an Insurance Commissioner. In other states, this could be the Insurance Bureau run by the Insurance Superintendent. But, it is equally unsurprising that the laws and regulations in most states are remarkably similar in scope and intention. Some of the more important regulatory areas include the following.

- Communications with the public
- Assurance of company solvency
- Consumer privacy
- Policy content

COMMUNICATIONS WITH THE PUBLIC ‡

2   Most states have labeled any communication with the public as **advertising**. Whether it is traditional advertising (radio, TV, billboards, direct mail) or communication we would normally not call advertising (an Agent's presentation, Policy illustration, needs analysis worksheet), the laws in most states label everything *advertising*.

written. . .

printed. . .

electronic. . .

oral. . .

3   As you would guess, the laws regarding insurance advertising require honesty and full disclosure. You cannot mislead the public by telling lies nor can you lie by leaving out relevant information. Exclusions and limitations must be given as much prominence as positive features. And, it must be clear that company spokesmen are being compensated.

IT'S ALL ADVERTISING

4   **Illustrations** must not be deceptive. In the two graphs below, growth of cash value is represented. In both, the cash value is $2000 after 4 years. However, by recalibrating the vertical axis in chart A, it is made to appear that cash value is growing more rapidly in A than in B.

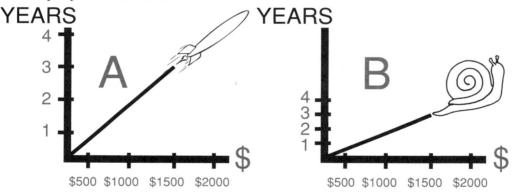

Pictures can lie

5   And, by drawing a rocket on the line in A and a snail at the end of line B, the illustration is even more deceptive.

6   **Cost Comparison Methods** can also be use to misinform the public. The **traditional net cost comparison** simply totals the premiums paid and from that number subtracts the accumulated dividends and cash value of the Policy to produce a net cost. This traditional approach totally ignores **the time value of money** and is outlawed in many states. It is like saying that if I give the insurance company $1000 today and have a cash value of $1000 after 10 years, my cost was zero! (Invested at 7.2% for 10 years, $1000 would become $2000.) An **interest adjusted net cost comparison** would be a far more valuable tool.

Two of the more useful **interest adjusted** indices are the **Surrender Cost Index** and the Net Payment Cost Index. The first is particularly helpful to a Policyowner who is primarily concerned with the growth of cash value. It is a valid measure of cost if the Policy is to be surrendered for cash in, say, 20 years. The **Net Payment Cost Index** is more for people whose main concern is death protection and the cost of death protection over an extended period of time.

Another popular way to assess cost is known as the **Comparative Interest Rate method**. With this approach (sometimes called the internal rate of return) you simply compute an interest rate based upon premiums paid versus cash developed under the contract. For instance, if the premium for a Policy is $1000 and the cash value developed and dividends paid in a given year total $80, the rate of return is 8% for that year. If a competitive Policy shows a 9% rate of return, then it is the *better* Policy given the rather narrow comparison we are making to illustrate the point.

ASSURANCE OF COMPANY SOLVENCY ‡

Another important responsibility of each state's Insurance Department is to monitor the financial well-being of the companies operating within its borders. Most states require that the Commissioner examine all admitted companies at least every 5 years and give him further authority to examine any authorized company at any time he feels it prudent to do so.

keep companies healthy

The Commissioner is also given the power to *rehabilitate* financially-troubled companies. Normally, this means that the Department will actually take over a problem company and operate it until it is solvent again.

Guarantee Associations

State Life and Health Guaranty Associations are to aid Policyowners of companies that cannot be saved. Operating somewhat like the FDIC which guarantees bank deposits, these organizations aid Policyowners of insolvent companies, within certain limitations.

protect the Policyholders

Normally every company selling Life and Health insurance in a given state must belong to the Guaranty Association. If a company goes bankrupt, then all the other companies must contribute financially to help the Policyowners of the problem company. Normally, the healthy companies are assessed by size. For example, if Cosmo Mutual sells 5% of all the life insurance in a given state, Cosmo will pick up 5% of the bill. Smaller companies writing 1% of the business would be assessed 1% of the cost.

Unfortunately, this consumer protection device has been misused by some in our business. If it is advertised that the financial health of your company is irrelevant due to the Guaranty Association, you have been severely misled.

Some states even require a **Guaranty Association Disclaimer** which strongly expresses the limitations of the Guaranty Association. For example, most states limit the amount that any one Policyowner can recover to $300,000 in death benefits and $100,000 in cash value. Health benefits are frequently capped at $100,000. Further limits restrict how much any company could be assessed in any one year. Obviously, it would make little sense to jeopardize ten more companies in an attempt to rescue one.

has its limits

CONSUMER PRIVACY ‡

1   With the computer data banks now available, consumer privacy has become a large issue in many businesses, and insurance is no exception. As you have learned, insurance companies collect very personal information on proposed Insureds, and many insurance regulators now limit the kind of information that can be collected and how it is disseminated.

2   In addition to the Fair Credit and the Medical Information Bureau disclosure statements already discussed, many states require life and health companies to give **written notice** outlining their **information practices** regarding personal information requested in an insurance transaction. The specifics vary somewhat from state to state, but generally follow the **Information and Privacy Protection** model law written by the National Association of Insurance Commissioners. Often, **written disclosure authorization forms** must be signed by a proposed Insured before any such information can be collected and used. These forms list the kind of information which may be collected, why it is being collected and how it will be utilized. The company, of course, must then protect any sensitive information in accordance with the procedures outlined in the form.

protect privacy

Policy CONTENT & PROVISIONS

3   Perhaps the simplest way to assure the fairness of an insurance contract would be for the insurance regulators to dictate the Policy provisions to the companies word-for-word. While this method has been used in several areas of insurance (most notably in property insurance with the Standard Fire Policy), it is not the regulatory approach taken in life insurance. Life insurance companies are allowed to fulfill their statutory obligations and still retain some flexibility in Policy design. This is accomplished by regulating the formation of life insurance contracts with the following two types of provisions:

> **REQUIRED PROVISIONS** — *must* be found in the Policy.

> **DISCRETIONARY PROVISIONS** — *may* be included in the Policy if the company wishes.

4   This chapter will deal primarily with these two types of provisions. We will also look at some additional provisions relating to beneficiaries.

5   Since there are no *word-for-word provisions* required in all life policies in all states, the companies have great flexibility in writing insurance contracts. Thus, you, as a life Agent, have a more difficult task before you. It ultimately becomes *your* responsibility to learn the provisions found in your company's policies as required by the laws of *your* state. But that is not as big a chore as it might seem at first. Most states have enacted the Uniform Standard Policy Provisions Model Law (recommended by the National Association of Insurance Commissioners) which governs the *intent* of life insurance contracts. The result of this first step towards uniformity is that the *intent* of corresponding policies issued by different companies in different states is remarkably similar. Even the *wording* of these policies has gradually become more consistent due to the states' insistence that Policy language comply with the intent of the statutory regulations. The variations that still persist from state to state and company to company are not many, and they are not difficult to learn once you have mastered the basic Policy provisions which will be fully explored in this chapter.

REQUIRED PROVISIONS

1 The first group of provisions found in the laws of most states are the required provisions. They tend to protect the *Policyowner*.

2 As you learned earlier, conformity to the exact phraseology of the law is not required; companies need only comply in substance with the state statutes. For this reason, the example provisions used in this section of the text may not be word-for-word the same as your company's policies. However, there probably will be substantial similarities since they are typical of the policies of most companies doing business in most states.

General Rule protects the Policyholder

ENTIRE CONTRACT (CONSIDERATION) CLAUSE

3 This clause declares that the **entire contract** or agreement that exists between the Policyowner and the company is the **Policy** and the **application** if attached to the Policy.

Policy + Application = Entire Contract

> *This Policy and the application attached hereto constitute the entire contract between the parties and the Company.*

4 The next portion of the clause points out that the statements made by Joe on the application are not considered to be the absolute truth, but the truth as he believes it to be, to the best of his knowledge. In other words, **statements made in the application are taken to be representations,** not warranties.

> *All statements made in the application for the Policy of insurance shall, in the absence of fraud, be deemed representations and not warranties.*

5 In Chapter Two, there was a detailed exploration of the differences between representations and warranties. A quick review will clarify that distinction if you find it necessary.

Representations

6 The final portion of the Entire Contract clause indicates who has the power to make changes in the contract.

> *Only the President, a Vice President, Secretary or Chief Attorney has the power on behalf of the Company to modify this contract of insurance, and then only in writing above the signatures of the authorized officers, and the Company shall not be bound by any promise or representation heretofore or hereafter made by any other person.*

Only Executive Officer can make changes. . .

7 While the specific Officers that are authorized to make Policy changes differ from company to company, this responsibility is normally restricted to just a few people. With this clause, companies have attempted to limit their responsibilities if an Agent should make an unauthorized verbal change to a life insurance Policy. Very simply, the Policy states that **an Agent cannot modify the provisions of a Policy**. The courts, however, could very well require a company to stand by an *unauthorized* change made by an Agent.

NOT an Agent

© 2010 Pathfinder Corporation

INSURING CLAUSE

1 The essence of the **promise** that exists between the company and the Policyowner is the **Insuring Clause.**

the Heart of the Policy

> *The Company agrees to pay, subject to the terms and conditions of this Policy, the sum Insured to the Beneficiary immediately upon receipt of due proof of the Insured's death.*

2 Simply put, the **company promises to pay the amount designated in the Policy to the Beneficiary immediately after receiving proof of death** (i.e., a copy of the death certificate).

PREMIUM PAYMENT CLAUSE

3 The law normally provides that all premiums, after the first, are payable **in advance** to the home office of the company. The first premium is, of course, usually collected by the Agent and submitted with the application or is paid to the Agent when the Policy is delivered and accepted by the Policyowner.

pay in advance

> *Premiums are payable in advance at the Home Office of the Company or to an Agent of the Company.*

4 Although this provision makes allowance for the Agent to collect the premium, this right is normally exercised only on an exception basis (e.g., when an overdue premium might be collected by the Agent).

INCONTESTABLE CLAUSE

5 The Incontestable clause **prohibits the company**, after a certain period of time (usually one or two years) **from denying or contesting the payment of a death claim on the basis of statements made in the original application**. In many respects, the Incontestable clause could be viewed as an attempt to balance the rights of the company and those of the Policyowner in regards to misstatements on the application.

6 From the company's viewpoint, misrepresentation, concealment or fraud on the application should be grounds for legally contesting the payment of a claim. Suppose Joe Insured knows that he has terminal cancer, purchases a Policy with a death benefit low enough to avoid a medical exam and then lies on the application. The company should have the right to contest payment of the death benefit on the grounds that Joe gave them invalid consideration when the contract was originally formed. Under the circumstances outlined, the company would have a valid point. With most contracts, the law provides that if fraud existed in the original agreement, the contract can be contested at any time.

limited time to "scope out" the app

7 But, life insurance contracts are different. Normally, death of the Insured occurs many years after the purchase of the Policy. If companies were allowed to contest payment in court on the basis of statements made in the original application, the **Beneficiary would be at a decided disadvantage.** Each day the case is delayed in court is another day the Beneficiary is without the Policy benefits. Since the company can usually afford greater legal talent than the Beneficiary, this delay could be lengthy.

1 Perhaps the greatest disadvantage facing the Beneficiary is that in all likelihood, the **individual who completed the application is dead** and, therefore, not in a position to defend the statements he made.

2 The regulatory response to this problem has been to rule that the company has only one or two years to investigate applications and contest any misrepresentations or concealments. If the Insured dies after this one or two year contestable period, the company may not contest the claim on the basis of fraud, misrepresentation or concealment in the application.

> *This Policy will be incontestable after it shall have been in force during the lifetime of the Insured for a period of two years from its date of issue, except for non-payment of premium.*

MUST CATCH ANY LIES QUICKLY

3 There are two types of claims, however, which the company does have the right to investigate after the expiration of the incontestable period. These are claims resulting from policies which contain total disability or accidental death benefits as may be seen in (b) and (c), following.

> *This Policy shall be incontestable after two years from its Policy date except: (a) for non-payment of premium, (b) as to any accidental death benefits and (c) as to any benefits in the event of permanent and total disability.* (Surprise! Life insurance can pay more for accidental death and can pay disability income benefits.)

4 With this clause, the company protects its rights to challenge claims concerning accidental death benefits or disability benefits. These types of claims lend themselves easily to fraud, and the company must retain its right to determine their validity.

5 How is incontestability handled on policies that have been reinstated? Suppose a Policy has been in force for two years before it lapsed and then it was reinstated. Should the contestable period begin again? Generally, the contestable period starts again for the statements made in the reinstatement application. However, the statements made exclusively in the original application are incontestable once the original time period has expired. On the other hand, policies like Renewable Term are renewed without a new application, and the contestable period would not, therefore, begin anew.

MISSTATEMENT OF AGE AND GENDER (SEX) CLAUSE

6 There are two errors which are so commonly made on life insurance applications that the **Incontestable clause simply does not apply.** They are the **Misstatement of Age** and the **Misstatement of Gender.** Since these two factors are extremely important in correctly calculating the premium, the **company is not forced to accept misstatements in these areas,** no matter how long the Policy has been in force. Alternatively, the Policyowner should not be totally denied coverage because of a common mistake made on the application. To correct for these errors, the **face amount of the Policy is simply adjusted** to **the amount of coverage the premiums paid would have purchased had the correct information been given originally.**

Misstatement of age. . . sex. . . MAKE IT RIGHT

> *If the age or sex of the Insured is misstated, any amount payable hereunder shall be such as the premium actually paid would have purchased on the Policy date on this plan of insurance at the correct age or sex of the Insured.*

1 For example, if Joe understated his age so that he paid $8.00 per thousand for a $100,000 Policy that should have cost him $10.00 per thousand, he has paid only 80% of what he should have paid. In this situation the company would multiply 8/10 times $100,000 and pay a death benefit of $80,000.

GRACE PERIOD CLAUSE

2 A grace period is a prescribed **period of time after the premium due date during which the contract remains in force without payment of the premium.** A period of one month (30 or 31 days) is mandated by most states to protect life insurance Policyowners against an accidental lapse of the contract. **The Policy remains in effect during the Grace Period, and as long as the overdue premium is paid before the Grace Period** has expired, no new proof of insurability can be required by the company. Though state laws normally give the company the option of charging interest on any late premiums received during the grace period, not all companies exercise the right to do so.

LATE PAYMENT

> *A Grace Period of thirty days with the interest at the rate stated in the Policy will be allowed for payment of a premium in default, during which time the insurance under this Policy will remain in force. If death occurs during the grace period, any overdue premium and interest will be deducted in settlement of this Policy.*

3 The second portion of the Grace Period clause outlines the procedure to be followed if Joe Insured dies during the grace period. In this case, Jolene would receive a check for the death benefit **minus the overdue premium and any interest charged**.

REINSTATEMENT CLAUSE

4 In Chapter Four you learned that certain types of life policies develop equity or cash value. As will be discussed later in some detail, the **Policyowner has the right to surrender the Policy** for cash, or *to recover the equity in the form of continued insurance coverage* if premiums are discontinued. The duration of this coverage and the amount of coverage depend on the amount of the Policy's cash value and the particular option the Policyowner selects. The details of this procedure will be explained later. For now, it is sufficient to know that *even if the Grace Period passes without payment of the past due premium, a Policy which has cash value can still remain in effect for some time.* If Joe Insured defaults on his premium payments, the law requires that the company reinstate him, if he desires, to his original position before default, as long as he meets certain conditions.

Know this

back premium + interest + proof

5 The **reinstatement** conditions are that the Insured must **pay the overdue premium with interest, repay any outstanding Policy loan, and submit proof of insurability within the allotted period.** The period is set by state statute, and it varies from three to five years.

6 Companies are aware that the most likely candidate for reinstatement is a person whose health has recently declined; hence, the requirement for proof of insurability. To *not* require this proof would be unfair to the *healthy* Policyowners that fall into the same risk category who have kept their premiums current.

*If this Policy shall lapse due to nonpayment of premium and shall not have been surrendered for its cash value, it **may be reinstated at any time within three years** of default in premium payment upon presentation of **evidence of insurability** of the Insured satisfactory to the Company, and **payment of all past due premiums with interest** compounded annually from the date of default at the same rate as hereinafter provided for Policy loans.*

1   As noted previously, the incontestable period begins anew only for those statements made in the reinstatement application.

OWNERSHIP CLAUSE

2   Up to this point in the text, most of our examples have portrayed that the person Insured by a life Policy is also the Policyowner. While this is probably the most common situation, it is certainly not always the case. Third-party ownership (the first two parties being the Insured and the company) is certainly possible and in some cases necessary. For instance, Jolene could own a Policy on Joe's life — she has insurable interest and could gain his written consent. "But," you say, "if she's the Beneficiary, nothing changes. If Joe dies, she gets paid. What possible difference would the question of ownership make in the great scheme of things?"

3   Well, the question of ownership is most important since **the Policy rights rest with the Policyowner** and *not* with the Insured or the Beneficiary. Ownership privileges include the right to name and change beneficiaries, to change ownership, to select any options available under the Policy and to receive any cash value, loans or other financial benefits from the Policy.

During the Insured's lifetime the right to receive all cash values, loans, dividends and other benefits, to change the Beneficiary, to assign this Policy, to exercise all privileges and options, and to agree with this company to any release, modification or amendment of this Policy, shall belong exclusively to the Owner.

4   Okay, okay, it's important. But under what circumstances does third-party ownership make sense? Actually, there are several circumstances where someone *other* than the Insured should be the owner of the Policy. Policies written on the lives of children would in all likelihood be owned by the parents. A creditor could require collateral from a borrower which might be satisfied by the borrower temporarily transferring ownership of a Policy. If a business buys insurance on its key employees, the business would be the owner of the Policy.

ASSIGNMENT CLAUSE

5   The owner of a Policy may assign ownership interest to another party, subject to the contractual limitation of the Policy. The most customary limitation is that the assignment must be filed with the company for it to be honored.

Any assignment of this Policy must be executed in duplicate on a form acceptable to the Company and one copy filed with the Company at its Home Office before it shall be binding on the Company.

1   It is important to note that as the owner of the Policy, Joe may permanently assign or temporarily assign his rights to another party. The distinction between the two types of assignments is based on the extent of the transfer. If Joe permanently gives up his ownership rights, the classification is **absolute assignment**. Absolute assignment conveys all of Joe's rights as owner of the Policy to the assignee. If Joe absolutely assigned his Policy to Jolene, then she would permanently enjoy all of the privileges of ownership provided in the Ownership clause. On the other hand, if Joe only temporarily assigns his interest, it becomes a **collateral, (or temporary) assignment**. This is the most common use of the Assignment clause.

Absolute = permanent

Collateral = temporary

2   Collateral (or temporary) assignment is frequently used in circumstances where a creditor requires insurance as part of the security for a loan. If Joe were to borrow $5,000, he might be required to make a collateral assignment of $5,000 to the creditor. If Joe dies before repaying the loan, the $5,000 would be deducted from the insurance proceeds to pay off the loan before payment would be made to the Beneficiary. If Joe does not die before the loan is repaid, then once the loan is repaid, the collateral assignment would be canceled, and all Policy rights would revert to Joe as the owner.

3   If a Policy is *absolutely* assigned, *all* ownership rights are permanently transferred to the new owner. If a *collateral* assignment is made, most of the ownership rights are *temporarily* transferred to the creditor (assignee). Questions often arise over which rights Joe retains as a Policyowner and which rights he gives up by collateral assignment. The standard assignment form approved by the American Bankers Association (ABA) specifically lists the rights kept by the Policyowner and those transferred to the lender.

4   One more important reason to transfer ownership of a Life Policy does not affect most of us. The concern is estate taxes. The reasons most of us are not impacted are two:

- Assets passing to a spouse following death are not subject to this tax.

- Only assets in excess of $1.5 million are taxable (This number is increased each year until it reaches $3.5 million in the year 2009).

5   Therefore, if Joe is a widower with a $5 million dollar estate and a Life Policy in the amount of $10 million naming the children as beneficiaries, he is considered to have a $15 million dollar estate. **Owning a Life Policy is like owning any other asset.** If someone else (like the children) owned the Policy for at least 3 years before Joe's death, his estate would be only $5 million and the taxes would be substantially less.

Policy CHANGE PROVISION (CONVERSION OPTION) ‡

6   With some companies, a life Policy may be exchanged for another Policy form *with the same face amount* as long as certain conditions are met.

> *Subject to the Company's approval and such requirements and payment, if any, as the Company shall determine, the Owner may exchange this Policy for a Policy on another plan of insurance for an amount not exceeding the sum Insured by this Policy.*

7   The Policy conversion can bring about one of two possible results.

> Change to a *higher* premium form — If Joe selects a Policy type which has a higher premium-per-thousand, the conditions of the change would require simply that Joe *pay the higher premium*.

Higher cost - no proof

Change to a *lower* premium form — If Joe converts his Policy to one with a lower premium-per-thousand, the company could suffer as a result. Suppose that Joe discovers that he has only two more years to live. He would, of course, convert his more expensive Whole Life Policy into a less expensive Term Policy to reduce his premium while keeping the same amount of death protection.

Lower cost - proof

1 The company can resolve this adverse selection by requiring that Joe take a physical if he converts to a lower premium form. Thus, **proof of insurability is the required condition for conversion to a lower premium form.**

2 **Tax Note - Section 1035 Policy Exchanges** - Since insurance is considered property, it is possible that a gain or loss could occur in an exchange of policies. Section 1035 of the IRS Code says that no gain or loss will be recognized on the following types of changes:

- A Life Policy exchanged for a Life Policy
- A Life Policy exchanged for an Annuity
- An Annuity exchanged for an Annuity

If going from Company A to Company B, it is advisable for Company A to transfer the value of the first contract directly to Company B

LOAN VALUES

3 It's possible for Joe to borrow the cash value of his life insurance Policy without canceling or surrendering the Policy and **with no negative tax ramifications**. State laws require that cash value policies give the Policyowner the right to borrow up to the amount of the cash value with the Policy as sole collateral. Sometimes this is called a *partial surrender*.

borrow up to cash value. . .

4 Since this is a loan, the company charges interest - and this leads to the outraged question, "Whaddya mean? Why do I have to pay interest to borrow my own money?" Let's explore that. In a Whole Life Policy, the company has guaranteed the premium, the face value and the growth of cash value. One assumption important to all three is the *interest factor* we discussed as an element of premium determination. The company assumes that it will earn at a certain rate on a predictable amount of cash value. If you take the cash value out, the company must modify one of its guarantees or charge interest, and charging interest has been the norm for several hundred years.

. . .but

5 Most policies stipulate that **interest is charged in advance**. They must further stipulate whether the interest rates are *fixed* or *adjustable*. Although most policies today are written with fixed rates of 8% or less, all states do allow for policies with adjustable rates. Even the adjustable loan rates are somewhat controlled as most state laws tie them to some well known index such as Moody's Corporate Bond Yield Average.

6 As the interest is charged in advance, most frequently the maximum loan amount is the cash value of the Policy less one year's interest. Suppose Joe has a Policy with $10,000 cash value and a loan interest rate of 6%. If he requests a maximum loan, he will not receive $10,000. Instead he will receive $10,000 less $600 (6% x $10,000) or $9,400.

7 Should Joe choose to repay the $10,000, the full cash value of his Policy would be restored. If, however, he does not pay it back, but continues paying his premium, the company cannot cancel his Policy. The company can only cancel Joe's Policy if the loan plus accrued interest exceeds the cash value. This will not happen if Joe keeps paying his premium. Therefore, all the company can do in the event of nonpayment of a loan is to add the interest to the unpaid principal and charge interest on the total.

How will the loan ultimately be repaid?

1 Upon Joe's death, the company will **deduct the outstanding loan (including interest earned) from the death benefit** of the Policy and pay the remainder to Jolene. In the above example, if Joe died exactly one year after taking out the loan, the company would pay Jolene the face amount minus $10,000 ($9,400 that Joe got plus $600 that the company earned as one year's interest).

Face Amount
- Unpaid Loans
- Interest
_____

Proceeds

BORROWING CAN HURT

2 To protect against widespread financial panic, most states allow companies to defer Policy loans up to six months unless the loan is obtained to pay the premium on the Policy. This right would be exercised in only the most extreme economic situations.

3 As you are aware, cash values also build in an Annuity, and most Annuity contracts also provide for loans. However, the tax treatment is greatly different.If Joe has $15,000 in an Annuity, the $15,000 has come from two sources. Let's suppose that Joe has paid $10,000 into the account. He has already paid taxes on the $10,000 and he will never pay taxes again on that $10,000. However, the remaining $5,000, which comes from interest earned by the company, has not been taxed. The basic Annuity rules say that whenever Joe takes this money, he will pay the tax. Further, if he takes the money in a lump-sum distribution prior to age 59 1/2, he will be assessed a 10% penalty on top of his normal income taxes. (At any age, he can escape the penalty but not the tax if he takes his money in the form of a Life Annuity as opposed to the lump-sum distribution.)

4 These rules and one additional rule combine to really discourage people from borrowing against an Annuity. A loan is treated as a lump-sum distribution. Therefore, the tax and the penalty apply. But, you say, "the tax and the penalty only apply to the $5,000 of interest in the above example. The $10,000 is not subject to tax or penalty." Well, the IRS has an answer. The first dollars out in the event of a loan are the taxable dollars. If Joe borrowed $5,000, it is all taxable and all subject to the penalty. If he borrows $10,000, then only $5,000 is taxed and penalized. And, of course, he must pay interest to the insurance company to borrow any of it.

TIME LIMIT ON LAWSUITS

5 A Policyowner (or Beneficiary) must be given a reasonable period of time to file a lawsuit after the cause of legal action occurs. This period of time is usually one to three years, depending on state law.

Reasonable period of time to sue

METHODS OF SETTLEMENT

6 A company is forbidden from offering a settlement of less than the value provided by the Policy (minus any outstanding premiums, loans and interest). In addition, any death proceeds not paid to a Beneficiary within 30 days of submission begin to accrue interest at a specified rate.

THE PRACTICE OF BACK-DATING

1 In most states, an application may not be back-dated more than six months. If the Applicant had a birthday within the past six months, the application could be back-dated to that date to lower the Applicant's insurance age and, thus, the premium. However, the premium would be charged from the effective date of the Policy.

6 months

APPLICATION OF STATE LAW

2 The law of the state in which the Policy is delivered is the law under which the Policy will be enforced, regardless of the home state of the company or the Applicant.

-state sold-

3 The next three required provisions are among the most important. With each, the Policyowner has several options. For this reason, these provisions are normally referred to as options. Each will be discussed separately in the next chapter. For now it is enough to know that all of the following options must appear in the Policy, if appropriate.

I'd rather think about it tomorrow

DIVIDEND OPTIONS

4 If the company pays dividends, then it must say so. The alternative methods by which the Policyowner may receive the dividends must also be stated.

SETTLEMENT OPTIONS

5 The Policyowner (and under certain circumstances, the Beneficiary) may select the method by which the Policy proceeds will be paid.

Scarlett O'Policy

NONFORFEITURE OPTIONS

6 As you have learned, Whole Life and Endowment policies build cash value. If, as the Policyowner, Joe elects to cancel his insurance and recover the equity, he has several methods of recovery. These optional methods must be explained in the Policy provisions.

FREE LOOK PROVISION
(OR, RETURN/EXCHANGE PROVISION)

7 A Free Look (or Right to Examine the Policy) is a provision which gives the Policyowner **the right to return the Policy to the company within a specific number of days of its delivery for a full 100% refund**. If the Policy is returned, however, then coverage never existed and the company would not be liable for any claim under the Policy.

8 The Free Look provision is a consumer protection device which most states require by law, and which a number of life insurance companies include voluntarily even where not required by law. While the length of the Free Look varies somewhat from state to state, most commonly it is a Ten Day Free Look. In certain types of life insurance sales (such as replacement of an existing life Policy), a longer free look period may be required. The Free Look provision applies only to individual life policies, not group policies, and it usually appears on the Policy face.

Free Look

DISCRETIONARY PROVISIONS

1 The discretionary (or optional) provisions tend to protect the *company*. The opening chapter of this book stated that companies wish to exclude coverage on catastrophic and intentional losses. The discretionary provisions are the exclusions which are used to accomplish this objective.

SUICIDE CLAUSE

2 The Suicide clause states that if the Insured commits suicide during some specified period of time, generally within two years of the date of Policy issue, the company's liability will be limited to the **return of premium paid** (without interest and minus any indebtedness). As with the other provisions, companies could be more generous and write a Suicide clause of one year or they could pay interest on the return of premium, but they cannot be more restrictive than the statutory limit.

3 The next four exclusions or semi-exclusions are the:

- **Military Service Clause**
- **Aviation Clause**
- **Hazardous Occupation (or Hobby) Clause**
- **Foreign Travel or Residence Clause**

"HAMLET"
Act 3, Scene 1
"To be or not to be."
But if within the stated
time period then . . .
only return of premium

4 At one time, it was not uncommon to see any or all of these restrictions function as 100% exclusions. If you died in a plane crash, the Policy did not pay. Today, however, it would be unusual to find a Policy using any of these as a blanket exclusion. While all of these factors magnify the company's risk somewhat, it is now more commonplace to accept the risk and charge extra for it.

MILITARY SERVICE CLAUSE

5 This clause stated that if the Insured died while in the military or as a result of a declared war, the insurance company would not pay the death benefit but would only return the premiums paid. Today, most companies do not use a war clause per se. If an Applicant indicates that he or she is in or plans to enter the military service, some companies will limit the amount of coverage they will sell to that individual.

6 On the other hand, if the U.S. became involved in a prolonged conflict, and hundreds of thousands of our young people were being drafted, it is quite likely that companies would begin to insert a full-blown military service exclusion into newly-issued policies. You see, even in earlier days, the purpose of a war clause was not to limit the company's exposure for existing policies. The purpose was to control adverse selection by making the purchase of new insurance less attractive to a draftee with combat orders.

AVIATION CLAUSE

1 With aviation, there may be as many different ways of handling things as there are companies selling life insurance. The general trend, however, is quite clear. In the old days, aviation was a 100% exclusion with most companies. Today, most policies cover aviation activities to one degree or another.

2 Almost any life Policy will cover you as a **fare-paying passenger on a regularly scheduled airline**, and many are much more generous. About the only aviation risks treated by some companies as a blanket exclusion are a *student pilot, stunt pilot or military pilot*. However, even with these categories, other companies will sell coverage for additional premium. As a new Agent, you are more likely to encounter a student pilot than either of the other two. In all likelihood, you will find that your company, like many, will charge additional premium while your client is a student pilot and then drop the additional charge once he or she is a licensed pilot. It's the learning process that strikes fear in the underwriter's heart.

HAZARDOUS OCCUPATION (OR HOBBY) CLAUSE

3 For many years the Insured's occupation was a determining factor in life insurance underwriting. However, in the last 35 years, the importance of the type of employment as a risk factor has decreased substantially because automation and increased attention to safety have dramatically reduced the incidence of fatalities in most industries.

4 Today much of the attention has shifted from hazardous occupations to hazardous hobbies, like sky-diving and automobile racing. Currently, death due to hazardous occupations or hobbies is not normally excluded. The trend is towards charging extra premium and perhaps restricting the purchase of accidental death benefits. For instance, if Joe Insured became a steeplejack and then tried to purchase insurance, many companies would charge him an additional $7 to $10 per thousand and not allow him to purchase an Accidental Death rider on the Policy. If Joe's hobby were stock car racing, he probably would be charged an additional premium of $5 to $8 per thousand.

FOREIGN TRAVEL OR RESIDENCE CLAUSE

5 Once again, what used to be handled as an exclusion is now generally available for an extra premium. Today, Joe can live in or have plans to visit for an extended period of time (more than three months) most parts of the world — and the only requirement most companies would place upon him is additional premium. For instance, if Joe is a resident of Nigeria when he purchases his life Policy, he would be charged an additional $4 to $6 per thousand. On the other hand, there are many foreign countries in which Joe can live without even having to pay extra premium such as Western Europe, Canada, and Northern Mexico. It is the practice of many companies to not make the Accidental Death rider available to Insureds contemplating foreign residence or extensive foreign travel at the time of application for insurance.

1 It is important to re-emphasize that most policies issued today have no Aviation restriction, Military Service exclusion, Occupation restriction or Foreign Residence clause attached. Even if Joe Insured states on his application that he is involved in one of these areas (or contemplating involvement), most companies would simply charge him higher premium. Only in extremely high risk circumstances (e.g., Joe is a stunt pilot) would some companies resort to an exclusion. Even then, it is very likely that Joe can find another company willing to issue the Policy without an exclusion — just higher premium. The only exception to this rule is the **Suicide clause, which is generally attached to all life contracts**.

2 Therefore, if Joe were a normal 40-year-old male running a restaurant in Joeville, U.S.A. today, the only restrictive clause that probably would be attached to his newly-issued Policy would be the Suicide clause. If next year Joe suddenly decided to work as a steeplejack, take flying lessons and move to Mainland China, his Policy would remain in effect without restriction. **The company cannot add restrictions or increase premium after a Policy is issued.** As long as Joe answers the questions on the application honestly at the time of the application, he will have full coverage.

3 Although the company cannot *add* these restrictions, the Insured can have them *removed*. If Jolene purchased a life Policy while she was a student pilot, she would probably be paying additional premium or there would be a restriction attached to her Policy. But if she could provide adequate proof that today she's no longer a student pilot, she could have the premium reduced or the restriction removed.

Things can only get better, they can't get worse - John Lennon 1967

Beneficiary PROVISIONS

4 As you will remember, in the Insuring clause, the company promises to pay the benefits of the Policy to the Beneficiary upon proof of death of the Insured. Usually, the *owner* of the Policy selects the Beneficiary at the time of application and the Policy is issued with a designated Beneficiary. Sometimes, the Beneficiary designation is made after the Policy goes into effect. It is usually possible to change beneficiaries after the original designation is made either by **filing (or recording)** the change with the company by **endorsement** where the designation or change is actually made by the company on the Policy itself at the request of the Policyowner.

Succession of Beneficiaries

5 **Primary Beneficiary** — The word "primary" means first. Since Jolene probably would be Joe's first choice as Beneficiary, she would be his primary Beneficiary.

6 **Contingent Beneficiaries** — All beneficiaries after the primary are known as *contingent beneficiaries*. The highest ranking contingent Beneficiary is the **secondary Beneficiary**, who would receive the proceeds of the insurance Policy if the primary Beneficiary died prior to receiving the Policy benefits. In Joe's case, the children probably would be his secondary beneficiaries. If Jolene predeceased Joe, or if Joe and Jolene died at the same time, the children would receive the benefit payment. If the proceeds of Joe's Policy were being paid to Jolene in installments, and she died prior to full payment of benefits, the remaining installments would be paid to the secondary beneficiaries.

The Beneficiary Food Chain

CONTINGENT

PRIMARY   SECONDARY   TERTIARY

Contingent = if

1 Third in line for the benefits of Joe's Policy might be his parents, Grandpa Joe and Mama Jo, who would be called the **tertiary beneficiaries**.

The Estate As Beneficiary

2 There are several conditions under which the death benefit of Joe's Policy would be paid to his estate:

- **No Beneficiary Named** — It was pointed out in the beginning of this section that the Policyowner usually names the Beneficiary when applying for the Policy. Although this is the normal procedure, the naming of a Beneficiary is not required by statute. If Joe dies without naming a Beneficiary, the insurance proceeds automatically will be paid to his estate and distributed in accordance with his will. If Joe should die without a will (***intestate***), state laws determine the distribution of the estate.

- **The Estate Named as Beneficiary** — Joe also can *name* his estate as Beneficiary, although under most circumstances it is unwise to do so. Proceeds paid to an estate are generally disbursed in a lump-sum payment (which may not be desirable) and are not subject to the same favorable probate and inheritance tax status as are payments made to a named Beneficiary. Also, increasing the proceeds of an estate adds to the costs of settling the estate.

- **All Beneficiaries Have Predeceased the Insured** — Assume Joe named Jolene as primary Beneficiary and he named no contingent beneficiaries. Under these circumstances, Jolene would be the only recipient as primary Beneficiary. If she were to die before Joe, and no other Beneficiary were named, the proceeds would be paid to Joe's estate.

A Trust As Beneficiary

3 In the settlement options section of the next chapter, you will learn that all of the methods by which the company can pay Policy proceeds to a Beneficiary have one thing in common — they are established formulas which require no judgment on the part of the insurance company and permit no deviation from established procedures. The company will not allow itself to be placed in a position where it is forced to make value judgments.

4 If the Policyowner desires *flexibility and judgment* in disbursing the proceeds of a death benefit, then a trust could be the answer. For example, if the sole purpose of Joe's Policy were to provide money for his children's education, he might name a trust as Beneficiary. With the trust as Beneficiary, the Policy proceeds would be placed in trust (probably with the trust department of a bank) and the trust would pay for the children's education under the direction of a trustee in accordance with Joe's instructions. While this approach is most often used when the beneficiaries are minor children, it is useful under any set of circumstances where flexibility and judgment are desired.

inter-vivos trust - created during Insured's lifetime

testamentary trust - created after Insured's death

Right To Name Beneficiaries

1 As you learned in the ownership provision section of the Policy, the right to name beneficiaries belongs to the owner of the Policy. The most common exception to this rule occurs when the Policyowner names only a primary Beneficiary, and death benefits are being paid to that Beneficiary on an installment basis. For example, if Jolene were a 70-year-old Beneficiary receiving payments over the next 20 years, she might not want the balance of the installments to be paid to her estate upon her death. If she believed that she would die prior to age 90 and would be unable to personally collect the full benefits, she could choose a contingent Beneficiary. However, **the right to name and change beneficiaries usually rests with the Policyowner**.

Owner's right

Revocable and Irrevocable Beneficiaries

2 All beneficiaries are named as either *revocable* or *irrevocable*. The distinction between naming someone as a revocable or an irrevocable Beneficiary is made on the basis of whether Joe wishes to retain the right to freely exercise his Policy rights (such as his right to change beneficiaries) or not.

- **Revocable Beneficiary** — If Joe wishes to retain his rights, then he should name his beneficiaries as revocable (changeable) beneficiaries. He then has the power to revoke (take back) the original Beneficiary designation and name another person. The courts have ruled that a revocable Beneficiary has no vested interest in the Policy and cannot, therefore, interfere with a re-designation. A revocable Beneficiary essentially has no Policy rights while the Insured is still alive.

Owner in control

- **Irrevocable Beneficiary** — If Joe, as the Policyowner, chooses to give up his right to change the Beneficiary or freely exercise other Policyowner rights, he could name Jolene as his irrevocable Beneficiary. Most courts would agree that, in this situation, Jolene has a vested interest in the Policy and is entitled to certain rights by statute.

Beneficiary in control

3 With Jolene as irrevocable Beneficiary, Joe may not change beneficiaries, borrow against the Policy, assign the Policy or even allow it to lapse **without the irrevocable Beneficiary's permission**. If he does allow the Policy to lapse, he forfeits his cash value to the irrevocable Beneficiary.

> Essentially, Joe has given up all of his ownership rights, save one — he still has the right to pay the premiums. He is still technically the owner, but about all he truly retains is the name.

Earlier you learned that if Jolene, as sole Beneficiary, were to predecease Joe, the Policy benefits would be paid to *his* estate. This would not be the case if Jolene were named *irrevocably*. The proceeds would then be paid to *her* estate, which would necessitate re-opening and re-settling the estate. Such an expensive procedure could be avoided by naming Jolene as irrevocable Beneficiary **on a reversionary basis**. Then, if Jolene died before Joe, the Policy rights would automatically revert to Joe and he would again be free to name a Beneficiary.

mix of the two

Uniform Simultaneous Death Act

1   With the information given to this point, it is interesting to observe what would happen if Joe and Jolene were to die together or within a few days of each other. For this example let's assume that Joe and Jolene have no heirs, and that no contingent beneficiaries are named. Joe is the Insured as well as the owner of the Policy, Jolene is the sole Beneficiary and she's named on a revocable basis.

Assume Beneficiary dies first

2   If Jolene died on February 10 and Joe died on February 12, how would the benefits be paid? As this is one of the basic situations in which the insurance proceeds would be paid into the Insured's estate, you should have answered, "Joe's estate." Let's say instead that Joe died on the 10th and Jolene on the 12th. Where would the proceeds go now? Without provisions to the contrary, the payment would be made to Jolene's estate.

He who dies last wins

3   But, where would the benefits be paid if Joe and Jolene died at exactly the same time? This question has been resolved in most states by the **Uniform Simultaneous Death Act**. This statute directs that if the Insured and the sole Beneficiary die simultaneously, the benefits are payable as if **the Insured outlived the Beneficiary**. Therefore, payment would be made to the estate of the Insured, Joe's estate. But if Jolene clearly survived Joe (if only by minutes), the statute does not apply and the proceeds would be paid to Jolene's estate, *unless the Policy contained the Common Disaster Provision.*

4   The **Common Disaster Provision** states that if the Beneficiary dies within 30 (or 60) days of the Insured, then the insurance company will proceed as if **the Insured outlived the Beneficiary**. If such a provision had been included in Joe's Policy in this example, the benefits would have then been paid to Joe's estate — even if Jolene clearly outlived Joe by, say, 10 days.

5   So, the general rule is, *He who dies last wins* — unless there's a Common Disaster Provision in the Policy, in which case we pay as if the Insured outlived the Beneficiary when the Beneficiary dies within 30 (or 60) days of the Insured.

freezes time

Minor Beneficiaries

6   Minors are frequently named as contingent beneficiaries and are somewhat less often designated as primary beneficiaries. If the minor has not attained the age of majority (18 in most states) when the Insured dies, the settlement process is somewhat complicated by laws governing the legal actions of minors. Although the company could pay the proceeds to the minor, the child's signature on the receipt would not be legally binding. At majority, the minor could claim non-payment of benefits and request a new settlement.

Minors can be beneficiaries

7   Obviously, insurance companies do not allow themselves to be trapped by the complications associated with paying benefits to minors. Therefore, the companies insist that a guardian be appointed to receive payments on behalf of the minor. The Insured could appoint a guardian before death by designating a guardian in the will or in the Beneficiary clause of the Policy. After the Insured's death, however, it would be up to the court to appoint a legal guardian on the Insured's behalf if none had been designated during the Insured's lifetime.

... but cannot collect directly

Naming The Beneficiary

1   It is worth noting that, by law, **a Beneficiary need not have an insurable interest to be named as a Beneficiary**. (Remember, you need an insurable interest in someone else's life to *purchase a Policy on their life*.) However, insurance law permits you, as the Policyowner, to name whomever you wish as Beneficiary. Some companies restrict this right in order to avoid difficulties that can arise. For instance, this occurs when a person names a fiancée as Beneficiary, marries someone else and does not change the designation. These restrictions are not insurance law, but company Policy.

No insurable interest necessary for beneficiary

2   It is also possible for a Beneficiary to be named without being aware of the designation. For example, if Joe were a bachelor with no living relatives, he might have, at one time, decided to purchase an Endowment at Age 65 to cover his retirement. He is the owner, the Insured and the Beneficiary. However, since this Policy contains a death benefit until age 65, Joe might have named a contingent Beneficiary. Being without a family or relatives, Joe could have named a Beneficiary totally unaware of his existence, such as the Metropolitan Museum of Art, the American Heart Association or the Buddy Holly Memorial Foundation.

3   One of the more important responsibilities you assume as a professional insurance Agent is to assist your clients in naming their beneficiaries. It would be an unfortunate situation for Joe to pay throughout his life on a Policy that, upon his death, paid benefits to the wrong person. While it is beyond the scope of this text to detail recommended wording for Beneficiary designations in all conceivable situations, a few examples might help to demonstrate the magnitude of the problem.

4   If Joe wanted to designate his wife, Jolene, as Beneficiary, he should not simply designate "my wife." The designation should be "Jolene Smith Insured, wife of the Insured." Then there would be no possible question concerning which wife Joe intended as the Beneficiary. In the case of children, a class designation often is used, avoiding the possibility of Joe naming Joe College and Betty Joe as beneficiaries and later forgetting to add Little Joe after his birth. A **class designation** such as "children of the Insured" would insure that Little Joe was included as a Beneficiary.

5   Class designations, however, can be done in one of two ways - per capita or per stirpes. Suppose Joe names his children as a class **per capita**. Further suppose that Joe College predeceases Joe. The per capita (per *surviving* person) designation would dictate that Betty Jo and Little Joe split the proceeds equally. A **per stirpes** (or per *bloodline*) designation would direct the deceased Joe College's share to his two children, Curly Joe and Moe.

6   Even more complications exist with clients who have adopted children, children from previous marriages, children born out of wedlock or children that are to be compensated differently than others. To avoid the possibility of benefits being paid to the wrong person, you must find out specifically what the Policyowner wants and make those requirements clearly known to your company. Care with this original designation process, a regular review of a client's Beneficiary designations and making appropriate changes when the Policyowner desires are well within the professional Agent's scope of responsibility.

SPENDTHRIFT CLAUSE

1   Most states have enacted legislation that protects the rights of the Policyowner and the beneficiaries from the claims of creditors. During the lifetime of the Insured the cash value of the Policy is not vulnerable to the claims of creditors unless the Policyowner pledged the Policy as collateral in the first place.

2   Upon the death of the Insured, the company has the obligation to pay the death benefit to the beneficiaries whereupon it becomes an asset of the Beneficiary. Therefore, the death benefit cannot be attached by **creditors of the Policyowner.** The same assets, however, might be vulnerable to the **creditors of the Beneficiary.** Protection from the creditors of the Beneficiary would require an installment payout of benefits and a spendthrift trust established during the lifetime of the Insured.

CONCLUSION

3   In this chapter we have examined the provisions commonly found in life insurance policies. These provisions typically fall into two categories: Required Provisions and Discretionary Provisions. We also looked at Beneficiary provisions.

4   The Required Provisions must be found in the Policy and they tend to protect the Policyowner. They include the following:

5   **ENTIRE CONTRACT CLAUSE** — The entire agreement between the insurance company and the Policyowner is contained in the Policy and the application (if attached). The Applicant's statements on the application, in the absence of fraud, are considered to be representations, not warranties. Only an executive officer of the insurance company has the authority to make changes to the Policy, and then, only in writing.

6   **INSURING CLAUSE** — Contains the insurance company's promise to pay in the event of the Insured's death.

7   **PREMIUM PAYMENT CLAUSE** — Premiums are payable in advance.

8   **INCONTESTABLE CLAUSE** — This clause states that the insurance company may not contest any statements on the application after the Policy has been in force for a certain period of time (generally one or two years, depending on state law).

9   **MISSTATEMENT OF AGE AND GENDER (SEX) CLAUSE** — If the age or gender of the Insured is misstated, the insurance company will adjust the amount payable under the Policy according to what the premiums paid would have bought at the true age or gender of the Insured. This is true regardless of how long ago the misstatement occurred and whether the misstatement was intentional or unintentional.

10 **GRACE PERIOD CLAUSE** — A period of time (usually 30 or 31 days, depending on state law) after the premium due date during which coverage exists even if the Policyowner has not paid the premium. If death occurs during the grace period, the insurance company will pay the death benefit less the overdue premium and interest.

1 **REINSTATEMENT CLAUSE** — The Policyowner has the right to reinstate the Policy within the reinstatement period (generally three to five years, depending on state law) if he or she has not surrendered the Policy for its cash value, pays all past due premium with interest, repays any outstanding Policy loans and provides proof of insurability.

2 **OWNERSHIP CLAUSE** — The owner (who is not necessarily the Insured) is the one who has all the Policy rights.

3 **ASSIGNMENT CLAUSE** — The Policyowner may transfer the ownership of the Policy but the company has to be notified in writing. There are two types of assignment: absolute (permanent) and collateral (temporary).

4 **Policy CHANGE PROVISION** — Subject to the insurance company's approval, the owner may exchange the Policy for another plan of insurance. If the change is to a higher premium form, it generally only requires additional premium. If the change is to a lower premium form, the company will probably require proof of insurability.

5 **LOAN VALUES** — If the life insurance Policy has cash value, the Policyowner may borrow all or a portion of it. However, the insurance company is allowed to charge interest on the loan in advance. The interest rate must be stated in the Policy and is regulated by state law.

6 Borrowing the cash value of an Annuity has three substantial disadvantages: (1) as with a life insurance Policy loan, the insurance company charges you interest in advance; (2) you will pay income taxes on the growth of your cash value and the first dollars out are considered the growth; (3) unless you are over age 59 1/2, you will also pay the IRS a 10% penalty on the amount you borrow.

7 **TIME LIMIT ON LAWSUITS** — The insurance company must allow a certain period of time for a Policyowner or Beneficiary to sue.

8 **METHODS OF SETTLEMENT** — The insurance company cannot offer a settlement of less than what the Policy promises.

9 **BACK-DATING** — An application may be back-dated for only a certain number of months (determined by state law).

10 **APPLICATION OF STATE LAW** — The state law where the Policy was sold controls.

11 **DIVIDEND, NONFORFEITURE AND SETTLEMENT OPTIONS** — If the Policy has these, the company must state what they are. (See the next chapter for a complete discussion of these options.)

12 The Discretionary Provisions tend to protect the company and generally act like exclusions. The only one of these common today is the Suicide Clause.

13 **SUICIDE CLAUSE** — If the insurance company includes this clause in the Policy, they don't have to pay the death benefit if the Insured commits suicide within the first year or two of the Policy (depending on state law). All the company must do is return the premium paid.

1 The following four clauses were common at one time but it would be rare to find any of them as blanket exclusions in a Policy sold today. Nowadays, these risks are generally provided for by charging more premium or limiting the face amount and the purchase of an accidental death rider.

- **MILITARY SERVICE CLAUSE**

- **AVIATION CLAUSE**

- **HAZARDOUS OCCUPATION (OR HOBBY) CLAUSE**

- **FOREIGN TRAVEL OR RESIDENCE CLAUSE**

2 **Beneficiary PROVISIONS** — The insurance company will pay the death benefit to the primary Beneficiary. If the primary is not alive, then the death benefit goes to the secondary Beneficiary. If neither the primary nor the secondary is alive, then it goes to the tertiary. All beneficiaries after the primary are contingent beneficiaries. It is possible to name a trust as Beneficiary. A trust will use flexibility and judgment in administering the money according to the wishes of the Policyowner. If no beneficiaries are named or if all of the beneficiaries died before the Insured, then the insurance company pays the death benefit to the estate of the Insured (assuming the beneficiaries were all revocable). Beneficiaries are named on either a revocable or an irrevocable basis.

Revocable Beneficiary — A revocable Beneficiary will receive the death benefit unless the Policyowner names someone else as Beneficiary before the Insured's death. In other words, the Beneficiary has no vested interest in the Policy.

Irrevocable Beneficiary — An irrevocable Beneficiary (or his or her estate) has the right to receive the death benefit. The Policyowner may not change beneficiaries or exercise any other Policy right without the permission of the irrevocable Beneficiary. In other words, an irrevocable Beneficiary has a vested interest in the Policy.

3 The only way for the Policyowner to regain the Policy rights would be to have named the Beneficiary "irrevocable on a reversionary basis". In that situation, the Policyowner regains all Policy rights upon the irrevocable Beneficiary's death.

4 **COMMON DISASTER PROVISION** — This provision says that if the Beneficiary only survives the Insured by less than 30 (or 60) days, then the insurance company will pay the death benefit as if the Insured survived the Beneficiary. This matters because it determines into whose estate the death benefit is paid. *He who dies last wins.*

LIFE INSURANCE POLICY OPTIONS

Life insurance policies, like automobiles, have options.

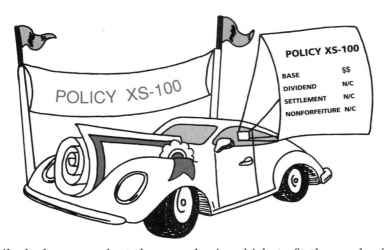

1   Automobile dealers can adapt the same basic vehicle to fit the needs of a variety of customers by using options (e.g., air conditioning, power steering and an automatic transmission). The same principle is used by insurance companies to make their standard life policies among the most flexible financial instruments available. The Agent can help the Policyowner *customize* the policy by using the three basic types of options available in the policy. These three categories of options — **dividend options, nonforfeiture options and settlement options** — are the subject matter of this chapter. After fully digesting the Policyowner benefits available through these three groups of options, we will look briefly at a recent innovation available from most life companies that addresses a huge consumer need - the Living Benefit Option or (as some refer to it) the Accelerated Death Benefit.

DIVIDENDS

2   As you observed in Chapter One, a policy which stipulates that the company will return any unneeded premiums to Policyowners is called a **participating policy** because the Policyowners are participating in the premium surplus. This return of premium is referred to as a **policy dividend** and is paid by **mutual companies**. Since the dividends paid Policyowners are a return of overcharge, **the dividends are not considered to be taxable income**. To understand why this overcharge occurs, let's review the factors a company uses to calculate the premium in the first place.

Dividends - return of unneeded premium

- **Risk Element** — In life and health insurance, companies are concerned with the probability that the Insured will suffer death, sickness or injury. This probability reflects the risk assumed by the company, and is a major factor in determining the premium. Companies use **mortality tables** when establishing life premium rates, and **morbidity tables** in setting accident and health premium rates.

- **Expense Element** — Insurance companies compute the total operating cost of the business for each $1,000 of insurance in force. This share of operating expense is then added, or *loaded*, to the premium when each new policy is sold.

- **Interest Element** — Companies do not simply collect and hold premiums. The money is invested to earn interest. The projected return on investment is also a part of the premium calculation.

- **Premium Mode Element** — Premiums are calculated on the supposition that the money will be paid annually in advance. Premiums that are paid semi-annually, quarterly or monthly are determined by adding the interest lost by the company as well as the additional costs of handling multiple payments.

1 The company's objective in setting premium rates is to generate the funds necessary to meet current obligations and assure the accumulation of capital to meet future obligations. The four factors just discussed are used to accomplish this objective. In particular, the **risk, interest and expense** factors require the company to predict the future. While the incidence of death or disability, the interest earned and the past operating expenses are well documented, they cannot be predicted with perfect accuracy. Therefore, participating companies take a conservative approach by over-estimating the premiums required. **The company then compares the *actual* experience to the *expected* experience and returns any excess to the Policyowners as dividends.**

2 In actual practice, most participating companies pay dividends annually. Although the statutes in the various states and provinces differ greatly, they normally require that participating companies compute dividends in frequencies varying from annually to every five years.

3 The process that companies follow in calculating dividends is fairly standard. First, the total dollar difference between expected experience and actual experience is determined. Money is then put aside to fulfill future policy guarantees. In addition to the increased reserves, other monies are put aside for unexpected setbacks in future years (e.g., severe investment losses in a recession or abnormally high mortality experience in a war). Whatever money remains is the dividend fund.

4 The next step is to make a distribution to the Policyowners *by class*. By paying to each dividend class in proportion to its contribution to the total dividend fund, equitable distribution is assured. In determining dividend classes, companies normally group Policyowners which share the following characteristics:

- Same type of coverage
- Same age at issue
- Same year of issue

5 The contribution of each dividend class is calculated using the factors of risk, interest, and expense. You can see that the more precision used in defining the dividend classes, the more equitable the distribution of dividends.

Gross And Net Premium

1 A company cannot guarantee that it will experience a savings in mortality, interest, or expense; thus, **dividends cannot be guaranteed**. However, by charging a slightly higher premium for participating policies, a company can be fairly certain that it can pay at least a small dividend each year. Since historically most American mutuals pay dividends annually, the ability to pay a dividend each year can be an important marketing consideration.

2 As an Agent, you must remember that a comparison between a participating and a non-participating policy based solely on cost per thousand is incomplete. If Joe Insured and his neighbor, Joe Kool, compare the policies each bought 10 years ago, there might be considerable differences in price. This difference might be attributable to the fact that Joe's policy is participating and Kool's policy is not.

3 For example, while the $300 Joe Kool pays is an accurate reflection of his annual premium and could be termed his *net premium*, such is not the case with Joe Insured. Joe's $400 premium is a gross premium, and his true annual premium is reflected only after deducting the $150 dividend he receives this year to indicate a *net premium* of $250.

4 The net premium for a participating policy is determined by subtracting the dividend paid from the gross premium. As it is unlikely that Joe's dividend will ever be the same dollar amount two years in a row, his net premium will vary each year. Joe

5 Kool's premium under his non-participating policy is unaffected by dividends, thus his net premium is constant.

Dividends cannot be guaranteed

6 Please recognize that this is a different use of the terms *gross premium* and *net premium* that you previously learned. In Chapter Three, you observed that the gross premium is calculated with the risk, interest and expense factors. The net premium included only the risk and interest factors. Since both uses of the words *gross* and *net premium* are common in the insurance industry, it is important for you to be fluent with either usage.

DIVIDEND OPTIONS

1 Now that you understand the source of policy dividends, it is important to learn the ways in which Joe can choose to receive his dividends.

2 The Policyowner selects the dividend option when he or she purchases the policy and it remains fixed until the Policyowner makes a change. Companies provide an automatic option if for some reason the Policyowner hasn't chosen one. For the most part, changes from one dividend option to another can be made easily.

3 The following dividend options are available for most policies issued in the United States or Canada:

- **Cash**

- **Reduction of Premium**

- **Accumulate at Interest**

- **Paid-Up Additions**

- **One Year Term**

- **Paid-Up Life**

- **Accelerated Endowment**

No tax on dividends

4 The first four are actually required by law in several states and are routinely offered by most companies in all states. The three subsequent options, although not required by law in any state, have been so well received by the insuring public that many companies offer them everywhere as well.

CASH

5 If Joe elects to receive his dividends in cash, he will simply receive a check from his company whenever dividends are declared. As you learned earlier, most American companies pay dividends annually, and traditionally, this payment is made on the anniversary date of the policy.

Get a check

REDUCTION OF PREMIUM

6 With this option, Joe directs the company to use the dividend to reduce the premium for the next policy year. In a previous example, Joe received a $150 dividend on a policy for which the annual premium was $400. Under the Reduction of Premium option, the company would send Joe a premium-due notice prior to the anniversary date. The notice would reflect the dividend that would be available on that date and that Joe would only need to send payment for the balance. In this example, the $150 dividend is deducted from the $400 gross premium, and Joe would then pay only the $250 net premium.

This year's dividend reduces next year's premium

ACCUMULATE AT INTEREST

1 With this option, Joe chooses to **leave his dividends with the company to accumulate at the rate of interest** stipulated in the policy. In a sense, a savings account has been created and, as with his bank savings account, Joe has the right to withdraw his money at any time.

like a savings account

2 Dividends, because they are a return of unneeded premium, are not taxable. But, unlike the dividend, **interest earned on dividends is taxable in the year that it is earned** — just like interest earned by a savings account.

TAX FACTS

PAID-UP ADDITIONS

3 In Chapter Four, you learned that Joe could purchase his policy with a single premium payment. With the Paid-Up Additions (or Paid-Up Adds) option, Joe uses his dividend as a single premium to purchase as much paid-up insurance of the same type as the original policy as the dividend will buy at his attained age. Paid-Up Adds are the **automatic option** if no other dividend option choice is made.

buy more insurance

ONE YEAR TERM

4 With the One Year Term option, the Policyowner uses the dividend as a single premium to purchase one year Term insurance. This option is used most frequently when a Policyowner has borrowed against the policy and has, therefore, reduced the amount of the death benefit. For instance, if Joe had a $50,000 life policy with a cash or loan value of $10,000, a $10,000 loan would reduce the death benefit to $40,000 until the loan was repaid. To keep the full face amount of the policy payable in case of death, Joe could instruct his company to use his dividend to purchase One Year Term insurance in the amount of $10,000 to cover the outstanding policy loan.

buy Term to fill the coverage gap

5 It is, of course, very unlikely that the amount of Joe's dividend is the precise amount needed to purchase the appropriate amount of One Year Term. If the dividend is not sufficient premium for the amount of term desired, most companies will allow Joe to pay the difference necessary to generate adequate premium dollars. On the other hand, should the amount of the dividend exceed the sum necessary to purchase the One Year Term, Joe could elect to receive the excess under any other dividend option.

PAID-UP LIFE

6 As you learned in Chapter Four, the two most common ways to purchase a Whole Life policy are Straight Life (Continuous Premium) or Limited-Pay Life. Regardless of which payment method Joe selects, he might find it desirable to complete his payments sooner than originally scheduled. If at age 40, Joe purchases a 20-Pay Whole Life policy, he is obligated to pay premiums until he reaches age 60. One way in which he can pay for his policy sooner is to select the Paid-Up Life option. Under this option, the company holds the dividends and the interest earned until the policy is paid up. With most participating policies, Joe's 20-Pay Life policy would be paid up in about 15 years. Had he originally selected the Continuous Premium payment method, he theoretically would pay premiums on his Whole Life policy for the rest of his life. By selecting the Paid-Up option, under most participating contracts, he would receive a paid-up endorsement at age 63 to 66.

shorten payment period

ACCELERATED ENDOWMENT

1   This dividend option was frequently available prior to 1984 for Endowment policies. Similar to the previous Whole Life example, if Joe had purchased a 20-Pay Endowment policy, he might wish to finish paying earlier than called for by the original payment timetable. This could have been accomplished by selecting the Accelerated Endowment option. As before, Joe's dividends and the interest earned were held by the company so that, with most participating companies, an Endowment originally designed to mature in 20 years could have reached maturity in 17 to 18 years.

shorten endowment period

NONFORFEITURE OPTIONS

2   The second major category of life policy options are the nonforfeiture options. In Chapter Four of this text, you learned how equity or **cash value** developed in Whole Life or Endowment policies. You will also recall that as a general rule, Term policies do not build cash value. The following section regarding nonforfeiture options therefore primarily pertains to Whole Life and Endowment policies.

only policies with cash value have nonforfeiture options

3   You will recall that life insurance policies that have cash value, such as Whole Life or Endowment, will either pay the face amount upon maturity or the cash value if the Policyowner surrenders the policy prior to maturity. We are going to see that **there are choices as to how the Policyowner recovers this cash value. These are called nonforfeiture (surrender) values.**

History Of Nonforfeiture Values

4   At one time in the life insurance business, if the Policyowner failed to pay the required premium by the end of the grace period, the policy would lapse and the Policyowner would *forfeit* (lose) any equity held in the policy. While this was financially beneficial to the insurance companies and to the Policyowners who kept paying premiums, it was less than equitable to the Policyowners who let their policies lapse or who could not afford to continue paying their premiums.

5   As a result, many companies voluntarily established procedures which allowed a Policyowner to stop paying premiums and not forfeit any of the equity in the policy. Although competition motivated insurance companies to be reasonable in determining these noncompulsory surrender values, it is generally accepted that truly fair surrender values were unavailable until mandated by legislation.

The Standard Nonforfeiture Law

6   The Standard Nonforfeiture Law was adopted by all of the states prior to January of 1948. Based on extensive studies by the Guertin Committee (and often referred to as Guertin legislation), these statutes define the minimum nonforfeiture value as the asset share of any policy at anytime during the policy life. While the calculation of asset shares is beyond the scope of this text, it is important to note that these values are basically determined by:

- The type of insurance

- The age of the Insured at issuance

- The length of time the policy has been in force

1   Today, minimum surrender values are required by law but many companies offer surrender values in excess of the legal requirements.

How Nonforfeiture Benefits Are Paid

2   Now that you understand that nonforfeiture benefits are required by law, you need to learn the options available to the Policyowner in receiving these benefits.

3   Remember that the nonforfeiture options are triggered by nonpayment of premium or surrender of the policy. Most policies provide the following nonforfeiture options:

- **Cash**

- **Reduced Paid-Up Insurance**

- **Extended Term Insurance**

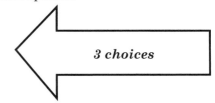

3 choices

4   Although the laws vary from state to state, Cash Value and thus Nonforfeiture Value must be available by the end of the third policy year.

Note to Student:

5   In order to illustrate the nonforfeiture options, we have used dollar figures typical of many companies. To compare these figures to the nonforfeiture value of another policy without considerably more information would be misleading. These figures are given as a learning aid, not as a standard for evaluation.

CASH

6   The simplest way in which the Policyowner can receive the **surrender value** of a policy is in cash. When the Cash option is selected, policy protection stops, and the company has no further responsibility under the policy.

7   If Joe Insured purchases a Straight Life policy today in the amount of $50,000, he can look in the Table of Guaranteed Values of his policy and see that in 10 years, the cash surrender value would be $147 per thousand (or $147 x 50 thousands = $7,350). Simply put, the policy could be surrendered for $7,350 at the end of ten years.

*SURRENDER
FOR
CASH*

*growth
guaranteed*

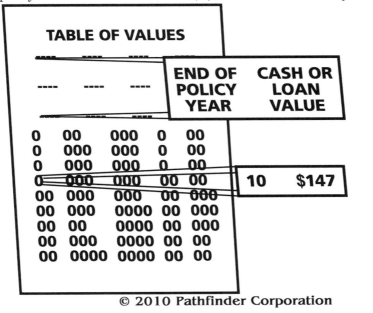

© 2010 Pathfinder Corporation

1 Although it is obvious that Joe would no longer have any insurance benefits from a policy that he has *cashed in*, there is another major disadvantage to the cash option that might not be so readily apparent. In Chapter 5, you learned that policies may be reinstated *if coverage has continued* and other requirements are met (e.g., the payment of back premium). Since no coverage continues under this option, **a policy surrendered for cash may not be reinstated**.

it's over if you take the cash

2 The policy's table of values indicate the cash available each year to the Policyowner upon surrender of the policy unless there is an outstanding loan. If there is a loan, the amount of the loan and interest would be deducted from the cash value to determine the surrender amount that would be paid.

May NOT be reinstated

3 While you can probably imagine circumstances in which Joe might want to surrender his policy for a lump sum of cash, you can probably also imagine situations in which he may surrender it because he no longer wishes or cannot afford to continue paying premium. He may still need insurance protection, however. The remaining two surrender options are methods by which Joe can recover his equity in the form of prepaid insurance.

REDUCED PAID-UP INSURANCE

4 Under this surrender option, Joe's cash value is used as a net single premium to purchase as much **paid-up insurance of the same type as the original policy** as is possible, given his attained age. If Joe at age 40 purchased a Straight Life policy in the amount of $50,000, he could surrender the policy in 10 years for a Reduced Paid-up Whole Life policy in the amount of $312 per thousand (or $312 x 50 thousands = $15,600).

LOWERS THE DEATH BENEFIT

1 Remember that Joe could have accepted $7,350 in cash for his $50,000 policy at the end of 10 years. Essentially, the company has determined that $7,350 can be used as a single premium to purchase $15,600 of Paid-Up Whole Life for a 50-year-old male at net premium rates. The calculation of net premium rates, as you recall, involves determining premium only on the basis of risk and anticipated earnings without loading for expenses. You should note that while the Reduced Paid-Up policy is the same type as the original policy, any riders and supplementary benefits attached to the original policy are not a part of the Paid-Up policy.

...no more premium

2 One important advantage with the Reduced Paid-Up insurance option is that normally, **the policy can be reinstated** to its original face value within three to five years of default. As you learned in the previous chapter, this requires payment of back premium with interest and submission of proof of insurability. The Reduced Paid-Up option is typically most attractive when the Policyowner reaches retirement age. Since most of life's financial responsibilities have been discharged, a smaller amount of insurance might be completely adequate, and the discontinuance of premium obligations is generally very desirable during the retirement years.

...bring back the

original **IF**

EXTENDED TERM INSURANCE

3 With Extended Term, the cash value of the policy is used to purchase **prepaid Term insurance of the same face amount as the original policy** for as long a period as the cash value will provide.

same face amount

4 For example, if Joe stops paying premiums at age 50 on his $50,000 Straight Life policy purchased at age 40, he will have enough equity to keep $50,000 of protection in force for 10 years 350 days. The company has determined that $7,350 of cash value is worth 10 years 350 days of $50,000 of protection for a 50-year-old male. So, Joe would have this amount of protection in force until age 60 and 350 days.

BUT SHORTER POLICY LENGTH

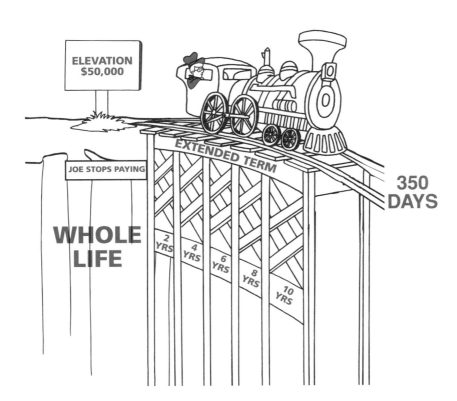

1 Interestingly, had Joe purchased a $25,000 Straight Life policy and stopped premium payments at the end of 10 years, the Extended Term option would have remained in effect for the same length of time — 10 years and 350 days. But, the amount of Term insurance would have been $25,000 rather than $50,000. Remember that **the Extended Term option provides protection in the same amount as the face value of the original policy**.

TERM LASTED A STATED PERIOD, BUT THAT'S ALL I NEEDED

2 In general, Extended Term is employed in cases where the need for the original amount of insurance protection continues, but the premium payments cannot be met. As with the Reduced Paid-Up option, under Extended Term, **the policy may be reinstated** (in accordance with the policy provisions).

3 If a Policyowner stops paying premiums and has not selected a nonforfeiture benefit, most companies provide in the contract that **Extended Term will be automatically implemented. However, it is quite uncommon for companies to make this option available to owners of rated policies** (i.e., policies under which the Insured's health, habits or occupation makes the Insured a higher than normal risk).

Automatic, but. . .

4 Under the Extended Term option, companies find that a certain amount of **adverse selection** will occur. For instance, if at age 50, Joe's doctor tells him that he will die in five years, Joe would be likely to stop paying premiums on his policy and recover his equity with Extended Term. That way, he would still have $50,000 worth of insurance in force but not have to pay premium. As a result, state laws allow companies to compute the Extended Term duration using a mortality incidence of 30% higher than normal.

RATED

---

5 You have now observed several events that take place if, after 10 years, Joe stops paying premium on his $50,000 Straight Life Policy. Under the nonforfeiture laws of each state, Joe does *not forfeit his equity* in the policy. The insurance company is obligated to make available the policy surrender values as described in the table of values section of the contract. When Joe discontinues premium payments, he must make a decision similar to the one illustrated below and decide in what form he would like to take his equity.

LET'S MAKE A DEAL

DOOR #1
CASH

$7,350

DOOR #2
REDUCED
PAID-UP

$15,600

DOOR #3
EXTENDED
TERM

$50,000

10 YEARS
350 DAYS

6 If he should take his surrender value in Cash, the company's obligation ends and the policy cannot be reinstated. Should Joe choose Reduced Paid-Up or Extended Term, the company retains some liability and the policy can be reinstated in accordance with the contract provisions.

SETTLEMENT OPTIONS

1 The final options to be discussed in this chapter are the settlement options. As a Policyowner, you are naturally concerned with the adequacy of the amount of insurance, but you should be equally concerned with how the proceeds of the policy will be paid when it matures. Remember that a Term policy matures upon the death of the Insured; a Whole Life policy matures upon the death of the Insured or upon the Insured's reaching age 100; and an Endowment policy matures upon the Insured's reaching the endowment age specified in the policy, or upon the Insured's death if prior to the endowment age. **The selected settlement option defines how payment will be made at maturity.** Additionally, these settlement options can be used to establish the method of payment if the Insured wishes to surrender a policy before maturity. For example, if after 10 years, Joe wishes to surrender his $50,000 Whole Life policy for cash, he will receive $7,350. He may take this amount as a lump-sum or he can receive it in installments determined by any of the settlement options described in this section.

2 The desired means of settlement may be selected by the Policyowner when the policy is initiated. This can be done on the application itself or on a separate memorandum or checklist furnished by the company. After this separate memorandum is certified and recorded, a copy is sent to the Insured to be attached to the policy. As you might expect, companies allow the Policyowner to change the settlement method at any time during the lifetime of the Insured. If the Policyowner has not chosen a settlement option prior to the death of the Insured, the Beneficiary may select an appropriate option.

3 The five settlement options we will discuss are:

- **CASH**

- **INTEREST**

- **ANNUITY CERTAIN:**

  A. **FIXED PERIOD**
  B. **FIXED AMOUNT**

- **LIFE INCOME (LIFE ANNUITY)**

4 To demonstrate the ramifications of each of these common settlement options, let's assume that Joe Insured dies at age 60 leaving his wife, 60-year-old Jolene, an insurance settlement of $100,000. The dollar amounts used are those Jolene would receive under each option from a typical company on a policy issued when Joe would have purchased the policy. It should go without saying that comparing these figures to a policy you own or that your company is currently marketing without knowledge of the other pertinent facts (e.g., the cost of the policy) would be an unfair and misleading comparison.

CASH

5 At one time, all life insurance policy proceeds were paid in a **lump sum cash payment**. Even today, if no selection is made, the proceeds are automatically paid to the Beneficiary in a single cash payment. Therefore, if cash were the selected option or if no choice were made, Jolene would receive a lump sum payment of $100,000 in our example.

1   If any **loans** are outstanding against the policy, the **amount of the loan, together with accrued interest, would be deducted from the proceeds before payment.** On the other hand, if dividends are left to accumulate, those accumulations would be paid in addition to the face amount.

2   Although the Cash option is not as appropriate for most Beneficiaries as some of the *income options* that will be discussed shortly, it does have some specific uses. Its best family application is in the situation where a large amount of money is involved and the Beneficiary has the financial acumen to manage the money. Many business uses of life policies (e.g., Key Employee policies) are also best served with the Cash option.

3   The drawbacks of the single payment option are also important to understand. One disadvantage that can have major repercussions on families in special circumstances is that the Cash option usually offers no protection against any creditors of the Beneficiary. As you may know, creditors cannot attach the cash value of the policy during the lifetime of the Insured (unless the policy is assigned to the creditor as collateral), but upon the Insured's death, creditors of the Beneficiary may attach the policy proceeds paid in a single payment. Under the subsequent options, spendthrift protection can be established to guard against such claims. Probably the most significant shortcoming of the Cash option is that it may not satisfy the most important need of most beneficiaries. As with most families that have just been deprived of the breadwinner, the most important need of Jolene and children is *income*.

4   This income need is what originally encouraged companies to begin offering the remaining four settlement options. They have in common the fact that the company pays out the death benefit over a period of time. During that time, the portion of the death benefit that remains with the company earns interest which is added to the Beneficiary's payout. Of course, **the interest portion is subject to the income tax**.

TAX FACTS

5   The rate of interest the company earns and pays in connection with any of these income-producing settlement options is, of course, of major importance to the Beneficiary. Generally, the insurance company *guarantees* a minimum interest rate which typically ranges from 3 1/2% to 4 1/2%. If the company can earn *more* than what is guaranteed, they will pay it; but they will not pay *less* than what they guaranteed.

6   Though most of us would look at the 3 1/2% to 4 1/2% guarantee with some disdain, we must remember that when the company guarantees this rate in the policy, they could be stuck with that promise for many, many years — perhaps for Joe's lifetime and the lifetime of his Beneficiary. Many financial institutions pay interest at rates exceeding 3 1/2%, but they do not guarantee those rates for 50 to 100 years.

INTEREST

1   With the Interest option, the proceeds remain with the company, and the interest earned is paid to the Beneficiary on a monthly, quarterly, semi-annual, or annual basis. The policy guarantees minimum rates, but interest earned above the guaranteed rate is normally paid in addition to the guaranteed interest. In most jurisdictions, there are legal limits to the time span that the company may retain the principal. Companies themselves normally limit this option to the lifetime of the Beneficiary or 30 years, whichever is greater.

2   If we assume that Joe's policy guarantees an annual rate of 4.25%, then Jolene would be paid at least $347 per month. If the company is currently paying 8% interest, then Jolene would get $643 per month for as long as the company could sustain that rate of interest earnings.

3   If the Interest option is implemented in its strictest form, the principal would remain constant while the interest is being paid. It ultimately would be paid out according to the directions placed in the Interest option. Common situations would be to pay Jolene just the interest until she reaches age 65 and then disburse the principal — or to pay Jolene just the interest and upon her death, pay the principal to the secondary beneficiaries.

4   **The Interest option is considered the most flexible** of the settlement options because of the additional rights a Beneficiary may be given:

- The right to withdraw part of the principal as desired, subject to the limitations stated in the wording of the option (e.g., withdrawal of principal limited to $500 per month).

- The unrestricted right to withdraw all or part of the principal at any time.

- The right to change to another settlement option as desired.

Eventually you must select another payout option

5   Under the Interest option in the example given, the $347 or $643 per month that Jolene receives is comprised solely of interest. If these amounts are inadequate, she might look at either of the next two options. Both are Annuities Certain options as we discussed in Chapter 4.

6   To refresh your memory, **an Annuity Certain pays installment payments of principal and interest for a fixed period of time.** Jolene can choose either the amount she wishes to receive each month or she can choose the length of time she wishes to receive benefits. If she selects the length of time for which she wants benefits, the company will then tell her how much she will be paid each month. If she selects the monthly amount, then the company will tell her how long that amount will be paid.

7   Depending upon what is important to Jolene — the length of time or the monthly amount — the two Annuity Certain options which follow travel under two different names.

ANNUITY CERTAIN

A. FIXED PERIOD

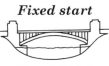

Fixed start

Fixed finish

1 If Jolene's most important concern is the length of time she will receive benefits, she should select the Fixed Period option. Under this option, Jolene will be paid a regular monthly (or quarterly, semiannual or annual) income comprised of principal and interest for the time period she specifies.

2 The size of the payment is determined by the following factors.

- The amount of the death benefit.

- The interest rate guaranteed in the policy or a higher rate currently being paid by the company.

- The length of time which Jolene selects to be paid the benefits.

- The frequency of payments (e.g. monthly, quarterly, annually).

*pay me for
10 years*

3 If Jolene wanted monthly payments for 10 years, the company would utilize the above factors and might tell her that currently they would pay her $1200 each month under such an arrangement. Further, the interest rate specified in the policy would guarantee at least $1000 each month for 10 years. Should Jolene want payments for 20 years, the monthly amount would fall to a guarantee of $600 a month with a current rate of, say, $800 a month.

4 Normally, the instructions contained in the Fixed Period option give Jolene the right to stop further payments and withdraw the balance in a lump sum, but she does not usually have the option to make partial withdrawals. Should Jolene die before the end of the payment period, payments would continue to any named contingent Beneficiary or be paid to Jolene's estate if none is designated.

5 The Fixed Period option is most valuable when the death of a principal breadwinner leaves a young Beneficiary with a difficult income readjustment period. Suppose Joe dies, leaving 40-year-old Jolene who thinks, "Eventually, I will be able to support myself, but can I survive the next 10 years with Little Joe and Betty Jo depending on me for income while I am making these adjustments?" Her need is obviously time (specifically, 10 years) and the Fixed Period option gives her that time.

B. FIXED AMOUNT

*pay me $1000
per month*

6 Like the Fixed Period option, the Fixed Amount option is a mathematical liquidation (paying out) of both principal and interest over a period of years. Under the Fixed Period option, the critical need of the Beneficiary was time. Under the Fixed Amount option, the need is for a specific amount of income each payment period. Assume Jolene said, "While I want the money to last as long as possible, I need at least $1,000 per month in income."

1 The Fixed Amount option would fulfill Jolene's need for a fixed monthly income. Under this option, the proceeds are payable in regular installments of a specified amount until principal and interest are exhausted. As Jolene has chosen the amount ($1,000) and the payment period (monthly), the company would use the factors below to determine the number of months she would receive payment.

- The amount of proceeds.

- The interest rate established in the policy or a higher rate currently being paid by the company.

2 Using these figures, Jolene would receive $1,000 per month for at least 123 months. If she had chosen to request $2,000 per month, she would be guaranteed the amount for only 55 months. Obviously, if the company is earning at a higher rate of interest and continues to do so, these periods could extend considerably longer. As the primary factor in this option is amount, excess interest earned by the company would not increase the $1,000 per month payment, but would increase the number of payments made to Jolene.

LIFE INCOME (LIFE ANNUITY)

3 As we learned in Chapter 4, the Life Income or Life Annuity options pay out a predetermined amount of principal and interest for as long as the Annuitant(s) live. This approach differs greatly from the previous settlement options. They were designed to pay until principal and interest were exhausted and to terminate at that point. If the Annuitant lives with a continued financial need beyond that time, the previous options are of no help.

pay me for life

4 On the other hand, the Life Annuity options are designed to provide payments for whatever length of time the Annuitant(s) live. The installments are normally paid monthly. For a thorough review, please see chapter 4.

You can NOT outlive a life annuity

5 And, as we saw before with the Life Annuity, **once the Annuitant(s) begin getting the payments, he or she cannot switch to another option**.

Straight Life (or Life Only) Annuity

6 The Straight Life Annuity will maximize the amount of each payment, but stops paying altogether upon the death of the Annuitant(s).

Win? Lose?

Life Annuity With Period Certain

1 For a reduction in monthly benefits, the Annuitant can be guaranteed income for a certain period of time - such as 5, 10 or 20 years. If the Beneficiary outlives the guaranteed time period, payments continue to be made. Remember, this is still a Life Annuity.

Life. . . but maybe longer

Refund Life Annuity

2 Again, for a reduction in monthly benefits, the company will pay the Annuitant a life income, AND gaurantee to pay back at least the annuitized value of the account.

Life. . . but get all V. A. back

Joint and Survivor Life Annuity

3 In contrast to the **single life** example we used above, the Joint and Survivor Life Annuity recognizes two or more Annuitants and pays as long as any Annuitant survives. Please remember that you cannot outlive a life income!

more than one life

4 The willingness of insurance companies to modify their traditional methods of paying life insurance benefits has never been more evident than in the early 1990's, when consumer need triggered the development of the benefit which will serve as our final subject of this chapter – Living Benefit Options and Agreements.

Living Benefit Options and Agreements

5 By the early 1990's, it became apparent that the traditional settlement options that we have just discussed were not serving several important needs of the public. Suppose that Joe has adequate life insurance, but he is terminally ill and anticipates huge medical bills over the next five months that the doctors expect him to live. Or, suppose Joe outlives Jolene, but at age 77 he has to move into a very expensive nursing home. In both cases, the money is needed **now**, but the traditional death benefits are not payable until later.

might have greater need when alive

6 With a little redesign, the *living benefits* Joe needs can be built into his life insurance policy. Many companies now offer a special benefit for life insurance policies called the **Accelerated Death Benefit**. **It is designed to pay a portion of the face amount of insurance to Joe rather than his Beneficiary**, to cover the incredible costs of getting old or dying in America.

7 The Accelerated Death Benefit has the following characteristics:

1. The **maximum benefit** is a percentage of the face amount of insurance, usually 50%. There may also be a dollar limit, such as $100,000.

   Limits

2. Specific conditions must exist before payment of the benefit may be made, such as suffering from a **specific disease**, having only a **very limited remaining lifetime** due to illness, or being **admitted to a nursing home** under doctor's orders.

   Triggers

3. The **face amount of insurance is reduced** after the payment, as well as reduced premium for the remaining policy and reduced cash value.

   Death benefit reduced

4. The benefit may be offered as a rider at a specific extra cost, or may be at no cost, or may be part of the policy itself.

   Forms

1   There are three forms of the **Accelerated Death Benefits**:

   1. **Dread disease benefit** – Only specified diseases trigger payment of the benefit, such as cancer, heart disease, liver malfunction, Parkinson's disease, etc. The expectation is that death will occur in the near future if the Insured has one of the specified illnesses.

   2. **Terminal illness benefit** – A doctor's certificate is required, stating that the Insured's health is so severely impaired that death is imminent within a short period, such as twelve months. The reason for the impairment is not important – just that a serious impairment exists.

   3. **Nursing home benefit** – The benefit payments are made if admission to a nursing home is required by the condition of the Insured's health. This may be measured by the inability to perform certain activities of daily living or simply by a doctor's certificate. Benefit payments are made monthly in amounts which are a small percentage of the face amount, such as 2%.

2   To show how this would work in practice, let's assume that Joe has a $200,000 Whole Life policy which has a current cash value of $100,000. Joe pays $3,000 each year for this policy. If Joe had a dread disease benefit, he could get as much as $100,000 as an advance death benefit if he has Parkinson's disease. If he takes that benefit, he would still have $100,000 of insurance remaining and his premium would drop to $1,500.

3   If Joe's policy included the terminal illness type of benefit, he could get the same $100,000, but his doctor would have to certify that Joe is so severely ill (regardless of cause) or injured that he is not expected to live more than twelve more months. Again, after the advance, Joe's policy would be reduced to $100,000 and the premium drops to $1,500.

4   If Joe had the nursing home benefit in his policy, and his doctor recommended that Joe be admitted to a nursing home due to ill health, or even because of deterioration of faculties, Joe could get a monthly income of up to $4,000 to cover his nursing home costs. The insurance amount and cash value would reduce proportionately each month as payments are made. Likewise, Joe's premium would gradually diminish. Monthly payments would continue so long as Joe remained in the nursing home, or until a total of $100,000 has been paid.

5   Each of these accelerated death benefits serves to help the Insured deal with the expense of final illness just before death or the costs of a nursing home. Without this benefit, many families would be hard-pressed to cover the costs. The insurance industry has moved to provide a helpful and socially desirable benefit at a nominal cost.

Viatical Settlement Companies

1   Viaticals are private companies that will **purchase your insurance policy at a discounted rate** if you are suffering from a terminal illness. They will pay 60% to 90% of the death benefit, **take over ownership of the policy** and assume responsibility for paying the premium and name themselves as the new purchase Beneficiary. At your death, the Viatical receives 100% of the death benefit which defines their profit.

2   Why would Joe sell his contract to a Viatical if he has a Living Benefit Option in his own policy? Suppose Joe's policy limits the living benefit to those deaths anticipated in less than 12 months and to the amount of 50% or less of the face value. If Joe becomes bedridden at a time thought by his physician to be 24 months before his death, a Viatical company's offer to pay 70% of the death benefit 24 months early might be desirable.

3   **Viatical Settlement Company** - A private company that will purchase your insurance policy at a discounted rate. In many states, they must be licensed by the Department of Insurance.

4   **Viator** - The Insured individual who is selling his policy to a Viatical.

5   **Viatical Producer** - Represents the Viatical.

6   **Viatical Broker** - Represents the Viators (Insureds).

CONCLUSION

1 In trying to remember the individual life policy options, you will find that it is helpful if you can recall the category to which each option belongs. For instance, if you are asked to explain the Reduced Paid-Up option, you must first be able to remember that it is a nonforfeiture option. Once you can identify the proper category, your task is relatively simple.

2 The summary table below can be useful in firmly establishing the contents of each of the three categories of options in your mind.

Dividend Options	**Nonforfeiture Options**	**Settlement Options**
Cash	Cash	Cash
Reduction of Premium	Reduced Paid-Up Insurance	Interest
Accumulate at Interest	Extended Term Insurance	Fixed Period
Paid-Up Additions		Fixed Amount
One Year term		Life Income (Life Annuity)
Paid-Up Life		• Straight Life Annuity
Accelerated Endowment		• Life Annuity with Period Certain
		• Refund Life Annuity
		• Joint and Survivor Life Annuity

DIVIDEND OPTIONS

3 A policy dividend, paid under a participating policy, generally from a mutual insurance company, is a return of unneeded premium. A policy dividend is not guaranteed!

4 **Cash** — Send me a check.

5 **Reduction of Premium** — Use my dividend to reduce next year's premium.

6 **Accumulate at Interest** — Hold onto my dividends, let them pile up and earn interest. Eventually, my Beneficiary will get them added onto the death benefit, or I'll get them added onto my cash value if I surrender my policy.

7 **Paid-Up Additions** — Take my dividend as a single premium and give me more insurance of the same kind as I have.

8 **One Year Term** — Take my dividend as a single premium to buy me some Term insurance. This will temporarily patch up a hole in the face amount I created when I took out a policy loan.

9 **Paid-Up Life** — Use my dividend to get my Whole Life policy paid-up sooner.

10 **Accelerated Endowment** — Use my dividend to get my policy to endow sooner.

NONFORFEITURE OPTIONS

11 These options come into play on policies which have cash value (like Whole Life or Endowment) if the Policyowner surrenders the policy or stops paying premium.

12 **Cash** — Give me my guaranteed cash value. If I take the cash, though, I can never reinstate my policy.

1 **Reduced Paid-Up Insurance** — Instead of giving me my cash, I'll take my equity in the form of insurance. The face amount will be greatly reduced, but it will be the same form of insurance as my surrendered policy. Later on, I can reinstate my original policy as long as I meet the Reinstatement provisions.

2 **Extended Term Insurance** — Instead of giving me my cash, I'll take my equity in the form of Term insurance. That way I can maintain the same face amount as my original policy. If I don't expire before the Term does, my Beneficiary will get nothing! However, I do have the right to reinstate my original policy as long as I meet the Reinstatement provisions. This nonforfeiture option is generally the automatic one unless I have a rated policy.

SETTLEMENT OPTIONS

3 These are the options available upon maturity of the policy. Maturity occurs when the Insured:

- dies during the covered period for a Term policy,
- dies or attains age 100 (whichever comes first) for Whole Life,
- dies during the endowment period or reaches the endowment date or age for an Endowment policy.

4 **Cash** — Send the Beneficiary the money.

5 **Interest** — The insurance company holds onto the death benefit, invests it, and sends the Beneficiary the interest it earns.

6 **Fixed Period** — The insurance company pays out the death benefit to the Beneficiary over a set period of time.

7 **Fixed Amount** — The insurance company pays out a set amount to the Beneficiary until the death benefit is used up.

8 **Life Income (Life Annuity)** — The company takes the death benefit as a single premium and agrees to pay the Beneficiary an income for life.

- **Straight Life (or Life Only) Annuity** — When the Beneficiary dies, the company stops paying.

- **Life Annuity With Period Certain** — The Beneficiary gets an income for life plus a guarantee that it will last for at least a certain number of years.

- **Refund Life Annuity** — The Beneficiary gets an income for life plus a guarantee that at least the whole death benefit will be paid out.

- **Joint and Survivor Life Annuity** — The Beneficiary and someone else get an income for as long as either one of them lives.

SPECIALIZED LIFE INSURANCE POLICIES AND RIDERS

7

1   In Chapter 4 you met the basic building blocks of insurance – Term, Whole Life, the antiquated Endowment Policy, and the Annuity. Most likely these contracts would satisfy the needs of the majority of your clients. However, some people have circumstances or specialized needs that these policies alone do not adequately address.

2   In this chapter we will find that policies can be combined, modified, and redesigned to fit a whole host of situations. In addition, we will also take a look at Policy Riders

3   We will examine in turn:

- **Combination Life Insurance Policies** – Policies which combine Term Insurance and Whole Life Insurance to address a specific situation.

- **Modified Life Insurance Policies** – Life insurance Policies in which there has been some modification in how the premium is paid, or in how the death benefit is paid.

- **Business Uses of Life Insurance** – Life insurance Policies used in connection with business needs.

- **Life Insurance Policy Riders** – Extra coverage that can be purchased to provide additional benefits in exchange for additional premium.

4   These new variables should not alarm you; we are simply seeing some new applications of a few of our building blocks.

COMBINATION LIFE INSURANCE POLICIES

5   Combination policies combine Term and Whole Life contracts to fill a wide variety of specialized insurance requirements. For the most part, these products are designed to serve the needs of a family.

6   In this section we will examine the following contracts:

- Family (Protection) Policy
- Family Income Policy
- Family Maintenance Policy
- Enhanced Ordinary Life
- Modified Life Policy

Special combos fit special needs

1 The first three policies all utilize the word *family* in the name, but as you learn about them, you will probably find that they would not fit the needs of your family today. These policies were all designed to suit the family of the 1950's and are much easier to understand if you remember the needs of the '50's family. I know, I know — some of you are thinking, "I wasn't even *born* in the '50's. How can I *remember?*" Well, I wasn't born yesterday and I know that if you are eligible for an insurance license, you've seen at least two episodes of *Leave It To Beaver* and are fully aware of all of the *"Rules of the Fifties"*.

2 For those of you who are culturally deprived, let's briefly review.

3 **Rules of the Fifties**

1. Everybody was married. (No living together.)
2. Every marriage produced at least two children who had to leave home by age 26.
3. Divorce was *illegal*.
4. Dad was the breadwinner.
5. Mom was not allowed to work outside the home.
6. Mom was Dad's age or younger.
7. Dad always died first.
8. Remarriage after Dad died was *almost illegal*.
9. Widows become the breadwinners (this being the only authorized exception to Rule #5 above).
10. This whole arrangement was slightly stupid, but we weren't allowed to think so at the time.

"Honey, I'm home. . ."

4 Now, if you have a modicum of intelligence, you are wondering why we bother to learn about the Family Plans at all. Certainly, if they adhere to the rules above, they don't fit you or anybody you know. Well, there are two good reasons. Some families think it still is the '50's, and many companies still market these products to the few remaining *Happy Days* die-hards. The second (and most important) reason is that you will surely have clients who originally were Insured (maybe as children) under one of these plans. As you try to update their insurance programs, you will find that a good understanding of what they already own will be vital to your performance as a professional Agent.

Family (Protection) Policy

5 **The Family Policy combines Convertible Term and Whole Life insurance** to provide a moderate amount of insurance on **all members of the family** in a single Policy. The Policy is normally marketed in *units*, and a family may buy as many units as it needs. Some companies even allow the purchase of a partial unit if requested.

Everyone under one umbrella

Convertible Term & Whole Life

6 Typically, a unit of coverage provides $5,000 of Whole Life coverage on the breadwinner, $1,250 of Convertible Term on the spouse and $1,000 of Convertible Term on each child. For example, assume that Joe's family purchased two units of coverage. That program would insure Joe with $10,000 of Whole Life, Jolene with $2,500 of Convertible Term and each of the three children with $2,000 of Convertible Term.

1   The Family Policy accomplishes a number of worthwhile objectives. Most of the premium dollars are spent on insuring the life of the breadwinner, so most of the coverage is on Joe. (Remember Rule #4: *Dad was the breadwinner.*) However, there is enough insurance on Jolene and the kids to cover death expenses should one of them die before Joe (thus violating Rule #7: *Dad always died first.*) If Dad dies first (Rule #7), there is enough death protection to either support Mom or to allow enough time for her to take over as breadwinner. (Rule #9: *Widows become the breadwinners.*)

2   Depending upon the company, the Convertible Term insurance on Joe College, Betty Jo, and Little Joe is designed to be converted between ages 21 and 25. (Rule #2: *Children had to leave home by age 25.*) Most companies allow children to convert to permanent insurance in an amount up to five times the face value of the Term insurance. Their new Whole Life policies are issued without proof of insurability but at the rate for the attained age at the time of conversion. If the conversion option is not exercised, the Term protection expires at the end of the conversion period (between ages 21 and 25).

3   One very important feature of the Policy is that **children born after the issuance of the Policy are covered automatically** (either at birth or two weeks after birth, depending on the company) **with no proof of insurability and with no increase in premium**. Adopted children are treated similarly and are covered from the date of the adoption with no increase in premium.

Nice feature

4   Despite the variations which exist, the basic provisions of the Family policies available today *do* follow the pattern of coverages described in this section by providing **a modest amount of insurance on all family members through a single Policy**.

Newborns
are free

Family Income Policy

1 As the breadwinner in the family (Rule #4: *Dad was the breadwinner.*), Joe has two insurance concerns:

- His financial responsibility for Jolene, which will never end. (Rules #3 and #8: *Divorce was illegal* and *Remarriage after Dad died was almost illegal.*)

- His financial responsibility to his children, which is enormous when they are newborns but diminishes (in total) and finally ends when they become self-sufficient. (Rule #2: *Every marriage produced at least two children who had to leave home by age 25.*)

2 The Family Income Policy addresses both of those concerns in a single package of coverage. If we think about it, we can almost guess how this Policy would be constructed. What better choice to insure Joe's *permanent obligation* to Jolene than Whole Life? And, Decreasing Term would be an excellent way to cover his obligation to the children as it starts out with a large number of dollars, diminishes (in total) as the children get closer to leaving home and finally goes to zero when they are independent of Mom and Dad. It is important to recognize that with the Family Income Policy (unlike the Family Policy), Joe is the only Insured. Specifically, we have constructed **a single Policy made up of Whole Life and Decreasing Term with the principal wage earner as the only Insured**. The Policy is constructed to pay an income to the family if the breadwinner dies while the children are still dependent and would provide a death benefit to the spouse no matter when death occurs.

only the breadwinner is covered

FAMILY INCOME POLICY

$75,000 DECREASING TERM

$50,000 WHOLE LIFE

1 The Policy stipulates that in the event of the Insured's death within a specified period of time (such as *20 Years*, or *To Age 65*), the company will pay the Beneficiary a monthly income amount usually equal to 1% of the Policy face from the date of death for the remainder of the specified period. The face amount of the Policy is then paid to the Beneficiary at the end of this income payment period. If the Insured dies after the specified income time period, only the face amount of the Policy is payable to the Beneficiary.

The long and the short of it

2 For example, at age 40, Joe might choose a $50,000 20-Year Family Income Policy because in twenty years, the youngest child will be self-supporting. If Joe dies at age 41, Jolene would receive $500 per month (1% x $50,000) for the next 19 years with a death benefit of $50,000 paid at the end of the 19 years. The $50,000 can be taken as a lump-sum or in the form of any of the other settlement options. If Joe dies at age 50, Jolene will receive $500 per month for 10 years and then receive the $50,000 death benefit. If Joe dies after age 60 (i.e., after the income period), Jolene would be paid only the $50,000 death benefit.

periodic payout followed by a lump sum

3 Perhaps the greatest drawback of the Family Income concept is that it is often misunderstood by the public. The greatest source of confusion is over the 20-year income period. Many Policyowners mistakenly believe that the income period will be 20 years from the date of *death* of the Insured, regardless of when the Insured dies. This is, of course, not true. The income period begins to tick away *on the Policy's effective date of coverage*, and monthly income checks will not be paid at all unless the Insured dies within the income period. Should the Insured die within this period, income will only be paid until the end of the remaining specified period. The number of payments could be many, few, or none — depending on when death occurs. With a Family Income Policy, **the family income period begins with the issue date of the Policy**.

"clock" starts ticking when the Policy is issued

Family Maintenance Policy

1 The Family Maintenance Policy, like the Family Income Policy, is designed to provide regular payments to the family during the child-rearing period in the event of the breadwinner's death and to provide a death benefit for the surviving spouse. It is a **single Policy with the breadwinner as the only Insured, and it is constructed with Whole Life and Level Term**. Conceptually and structurally, the Family Maintenance Policy closely resembles the Family Income Policy. The major difference is that with the Family Maintenance Policy, **the stipulated payment period begins at the date of the Insured's death** rather than upon the Policy issue date.

FAMILY MAINTENANCE

$75,000 LEVEL TERM

$50,000 WHOLE LIFE

SUMMARY CHART

	Who is Insured?	How is it built?
Family Policy	Entire family	Whole Life & Convertible Term
Family Income	Breadwinner	Whole Life & Decreasing Term
Family Maintenance	Breadwinner	Whole Life & Level Term

Enhanced Ordinary Life

1   Enhanced Ordinary life is also known as **Economatic or Extra Ordinary Life**. It is a variation of Whole life available on **participating policies only**, and its purpose is to provide the most economic purchase possible of a Whole Life contract.

2   Joe could purchase a Policy that initially is composed of $60,000 of Continuous Premium Whole Life and $40,000 of Renewable Term insurance. Dividends are used as single premiums to purchase Paid-Up Adds each year, and the amount of Term insurance is reduced by an amount equivalent to the Paid-Up Additions.

3   If in year one, Joe's company pays a dividend large enough to allow the purchase of a $1000 Paid-Up Add, the $100,000 death benefit would be comprised of three elements - $60,000 of Continuous Premium Whole Life, $39,000 of Renewable Term and the $1000 Paid-Up Addition which is, of course, Whole Life.

4   This process would continue until all of the Term is replaced by Paid Up Whole Life. At that point, Joe could select another dividend option or add to the $100,000 death benefit with more Paid Up Additions.

*Policy dividends
used to replace
the Term with
Whole Life*

Modified Life Policy

5   The Modified Life Policy is **designed to serve the individual who has a need for permanent protection, is without the current resources to pay regular premium rates, but expects income growth in the future**. The premium is unusually *low* in the early years of the Policy and then *higher* than normal in the later years. This type of contract is most popular with young insurance buyers (particularly those supporting a family) who expect their earning power to increase significantly within a few years.

*permanent
protection on
a budget*

6   One method by which this need can be met is to construct **a Modified Life Policy by combining Convertible Term and Whole Life**. For the first few years of the Policy life (let's assume five years) the protection is provided by Level Term insurance, and the cost is relatively low. At the end of the five years, the Policy is **automatically converted to Whole Life** and the premium rate is likewise increased to the Whole Life rate for the attained age of the Insured. This structure accomplishes several very important goals. It can provide the coverage you need at a price you can afford, and it protects your insurability against a decline in health. Remember that with Convertible Term, the cost will increase at conversion, but you do not have to submit proof of insurability at that time.

*convertible Term
to Whole Life*

7   The Modified Life Policy may be particularly desirable for a young person just getting started in life, like Joe's son, Joe College. Suppose that, at age 20, Joe College decides that he wants $50,000 of Whole Life insurance. If the premium is more than he can currently afford, Modified Life can solve his problem. For the first five years he would pay an annual premium of $170. He anticipates that by the sixth year, his income will increase to the point that he can well afford the $550 annual premium required by the Policy (now Whole Life) for that and all subsequent years.

8   **It is also possible to convert the Policy in stages.** For example, Joe College could start with $50,000 of Term insurance and no Whole Life. Each year, some portion of the Term coverage is converted to Whole Life insurance. With this approach, each year he would have less Term insurance and more Whole Life in force until finally, his Policy would be 100% Whole Life.

MODIFIED LIFE INSURANCE POLICIES

1 Another way to make the basic policies fit a specialized need is to simply modify one or more of the basic characteristics of the contract. For instance, we have dealt primarily with policies which pay a death benefit when one person dies. It requires but little imagination to construct a contract which will pay when either of two people die. This variation has a new name, but it is only a Term or Whole Life Policy in disguise.

2 In this section we will examine six such contracts:

- Graded Premium Whole Life

- Re-entry Term

- Joint Life

- Survivorship Life

- Juvenile Life

- Interest Sensitive Whole Life

GRADED PREMIUM WHOLE LIFE

3

LOWER PREMIUM WHEN YOU CAN LEAST AFFORD IT

As we've just seen, the objective of the Modified Life Policy is to **lessen the premium in the early years** of the Policy while, at the same time, offering the advantages of permanent protection, regardless of the Policyowner's insurability. **These same objectives can be met by** issuing a Whole Life Policy and initially charging lower than usual rates and then charging somewhat higher amounts in later years. When the contract is structured in this manner, it is often called **Graded Premium Whole Life**.

4 Since Joe College is just starting down his career path, a Graded Premium Whole Life Policy may fit his needs perfectly. Suppose he determines that he needs a $50,000 Whole Life Policy. His company would charge him $9 per thousand, or $450 a year, for a Straight Life Policy. Since this is beyond Joe College's current ability to pay, he discussed the idea of Graded Premium Whole Life with his Agent. The Agent may show him two of the more common premium redistribution or graded-premium plans. **Both start with an annual premium significantly below the usual premium of $450 per year.** The first one increases each year during the preliminary period of 5 years and remains level thereafter. The second alternative allows for a more gradual increase over a preliminary period of 15 years.

POLICY YEAR	TOTAL INSURANCE BEG. OF YEAR	GROSS ANNUAL PREMIUM		POLICY YEAR	TOTAL INSURANCE BEG. OF YEAR	GROSS ANNUAL PREMIUM
1	$50,000	$288		1	$50,000	$255
2	50,000	340		2	50,000	278
3	50,000	393		3	50,000	301
4	50,000	445		4	50,000	324
5	50,000	498		5	50,000	347
6	50,000	550		6	50,000	370
7	50,000	550		7	50,000	393
8	50,000	550	OR	8	50,000	416
9	50,000	550		9	50,000	439
10	50,000	550		10	50,000	462
11	50,000	550		11	50,000	485
12	50,000	550		12	50,000	508
13	50,000	550		13	50,000	531
14	50,000	550		14	50,000	554
15	50,000	550		15	50,000	577
16	50,000	550		16	50,000	600
17	50,000	550		17	50,000	600
18	50,000	550		18	50,000	600
19	50,000	550		19	50,000	600
20	50,000	550		20	50,000	600

RE-ENTRY TERM

1 Many companies modify their Annually Renewable Term contract to include a **price benefit** to their Policyowners, and rename the product Re-entry Term. Except for this feature, the Policy works like any Annually Renewable Term contract.

What we already know is that with an annually Renewable Term to 65, Joe can renew every year until 65 **without proof of insurability**. We also know that premium costs escalate rapidly as Joe gets older. What we do not know is that there is another reason besides advancing age for this price increase.

2 Four or five years after Joe purchases the Policy, his company will stop rating him using the *select* mortality table (the best for Joe) and start using the *ultimate* mortality table (which is the worst for Joe.) The theory is that the more time which passes since Joe qualified for the insurance, the less desirable he is as a risk. With the re-entry feature, Joe can choose to **re-enter** the select group every five years if he can establish insurability acceptable to the company. Therefore, his premiums would climb for five years, and then drop back somewhat. . . then they would begin to rise again.

3 If at any time Joe does not qualify to re-enter, he could simply continue to renew to age 65 as if his Policy were simply a standard ART to 65 contract.

Pass a physical- Get a price break

JOINT LIFE (MULTIPLE PROTECTION)

4 **Joint Life insurance is simply one Policy covering TWO OR MORE persons and pays on the death of the FIRST.** If Joe and Jolene earn nearly equivalent paychecks, each would need about the same death benefit to pay the mortgage and rear the children if the other should die prematurely. A Policy written on both of their lives would average the risk factors (like age and sex), and the resultant premium would be a bit less than two separate policies. Obviously, the same contract could be applied to a business situation involving two partners who would each have the need to replace the other in the event of death.

Pays when the first Insured dies.

5 Joint Life policies can be written with Term or Whole Life, though the Whole Life forms are used more frequently. Many variations of Joint Life are found in the marketplace; some even pay double in the event of the death of both Insureds. But the most common variation is an attempt to solve the biggest problem of Joint Life - after the first Insured dies, the Policy has matured, and the survivor is left with no insurance. Many companies now offer guaranteed insurability to the survivor with a specified eligibility period granted in which new insurance can be requested.

1st 2 GO

SURVIVORSHIP LIFE

A variation of Joint Life is **Survivorship Life. It also has TWO OR MORE Insureds, but pays the death benefit only upon the death of the LAST Insured.** It can be used for a variety of purposes, but today it is most commonly written to solve a major estate tax problem (death tax). Under current tax law, assets can be passed from a deceased person to the surviving spouse without triggering the payment of estate (death) taxes. When the surviving spouse dies and the estate is passed to the children, the tax is due. Suppose Joe's principle asset is a family farm upon which all the kids live and work. It could pass from Joe to Jolene without problem. However, when Jolene dies and the children inherit the farm, they might have to sell the farm to pay the taxes.

Pays when the last Insured dies.

Last 2 GO

JUVENILE LIFE

1 *Juvenile insurance in its broadest sense is not a **special Policy** like the others discussed in this Chapter. Rather, it is a family of products that are only modifications of the standard forms of insurance designed to meet the needs of young children. Juvenile insurance refers to insurance contracts written on the lives of children from birth (although with some companies this is 14 days or 30 days after birth) up to age 14 or 15. The Policy is issued on the application of the child's legal guardian, and the primary benefit is the opportunity to begin an insurance estate for the child at an early age.*

2 A specific form of juvenile insurance is the **Jumping Juvenile (Estate Builder) Policy.** Normally these policies are Limited-Pay Whole Life and are obtainable from birth to age 14 or 15. **By age 21, the face amount jumps to five times the original value with no increase in premium.** If Joe buys a $1000 Jumping Juvenile (Estate Builder) paid at 65 Policy on the life of his 14-year old daughter Betty Jo, the original death benefit will be $1000. At the time she turns 21, the face value of the Policy increases to $5000, but the premium does not increase. (Mathematically, Joe *overpays* so that Betty Jo can later *underpay*.)

JUMPING JUVENILE
(ESTATE BUILDER)

Age 14
$1,000

3 In all forms of juvenile insurance, provisions can be made for the insurance to continue despite the death or total disability of the person who applies for the insurance and assumes the responsibility for paying the premium. This is called the Payor (Applicant Waiver) Provision, and we will examine it in the next few pages as a Policy rider. Certainly, there is a charge for this benefit, and it is conditioned upon the insurability of the premium payor.

INTEREST SENSITIVE WHOLE LIFE

4 We pointed out earlier that the interest rate guarantees made by insurance companies regarding the growth of cash value are very conservative when compared to other investment vehicles. The reason for this, you will recall, is that insurance companies may have to honor their guarantees for as long as 100 years - too long a period to be anything but conservative in their forecast.

Share the risks, and the potential rewards

5 Several products have emerged which place a small risk on the Policyowner in exchange for the possibility of a nice reward. The most notable of these contracts is **Interest Sensitive Whole Life** (sometimes called Current Assumption Whole Life).

6 This Policy works a bit like an adjustable rate mortgage. The company sets the initial premium (which is typically guaranteed for two or three years) based upon their current assumptions concerning risk, interest and expense. Thereafter, at designated intervals, they may lower or raise costs (up to a specified maximum) if the actual experience differs from the expected experience. If the cost goes down, the Insured pays less premium. If the cost goes up, the Insured can choose to pay more or to reduce the death benefits.

7 The second feature of Interest Sensitive Whole Life is that the cash value of the contract **can earn interest at a rate higher than the guarantee**. For instance, a company might issue a Policy guaranteeing that cash value will grow at the rate of 4%. However, the company might earn at a higher rate in any given year and pay 5 3/4%.

1 Certainly, Interest Sensitive Whole Life takes a step toward Policyowners willing to trade a little risk for the potential of reward. You will find that the *flexible feature policies* in Chapter 9 take this basic idea much further.

BUSINESS USES OF LIFE INSURANCE

2 Key Employee life insurance is bought by a business on the life of an owner or employee whose **services are crucial to the success of the business**. Certainly, if an employee could be replaced easily at nominal cost, insurance would be unnecessary. However, if an employee has specialized knowledge or skills, contacts that are critical to the future of the business, or is the chief source of the firm's credit, a Key Employee Policy might be essential to the company. Life insurance bought only for Key Employee purposes is the simplest of all business insurance plans. No special contract is required; no agreement between the employee and the company is necessary. The employee simply gives consent to be the subject of the insurance. **The business is the Applicant, the Po;icy owner, the Beneficiary, and the party responsible for the payment of the Policy premiums.**

1   In most cases, the tax ramifications of a Key Employee Policy (and most other forms of business insurance) are relatively easy to understand. **The premiums paid by the company are NOT TAX DEDUCTIBLE, but the death benefit paid upon the key employee's death is not usually considered as taxable income.**

No tax deduction but tax free death benefit

Business Continuation Plans
Buy And Sell Agreements
or Cross Purchase Plans

2   The death of the owner or one of the principal owners of a relatively small business could jeopardize the continued existence of that company. This risk is practically non-existent in giant corporations because their very size precludes inordinate dependence on any one person. However, this risk is a substantial one for smaller companies.

I don't want my partner's kids as partners.

3   Before discussing insurance as a business continuation vehicle, we'll remind you of two basic business concepts.

- A business is worth far more in operation than it would be if its assets were simply liquidated. Suppose Joe owned one-third of a diner with his buddies Bo and Moe. In his will, he named Jolene to receive all of his earthly goods. If Joe dies and the corporation is forced into liquidation, everyone loses. The physical assets of a diner amount to very little — some furniture, a freezer and a grill. Jolene gets very little, and Moe and Bo see their company destroyed.

Must keep the business in business.

- An apparent solution to the problem facing Moe, Bo and Jolene in the above example can create an even more difficult problem and leads to the second business concept we wish to point out. Upon Joe's death, Moe and Bo are now in business with *Jolene*. You can probably list fifty reasons that might preclude the success of this arrangement. An inexperienced heir who appears on the scene as a new partner is likely to be greeted as warmly as a case of leprosy.

Buy/Sell

Joint Life

4   *Insurance* and *advance planning* can provide the means to keep the company operating without upsetting the delicate business balance that is so critical to the surviving owners and employees. Let's suppose that they are organized as a closely-held corporation with each owning one third of the company. While they are alive, they should formulate a **Buy and Sell Agreement** which says that if one of them dies, the corporation has the right to purchase the deceased partner's share at a specified price or in accordance with a specified formula.

5   **Great, but how are they going to pay for this?**

6   For simplicity's sake, let's assume that Joe dies and the agreement gives his partners the right to purchase Joe's share of the business for $50,000. Now, the problem is **funding**, and **insurance can solve that problem**. If, when the buy-sell agreement was formulated, a $50,000 Policy was purchased by the corporation on each of the men's lives, they have established a *Stock Redemption Plan*. If each had purchased a Policy on the lives of the other two, the arrangement would be known as a *Cross Purchase Plan*. With the Stock Redemption approach, it is possible that the corporation could utilize a **Joint Life Policy** on Joe, Moe and Bo. It would pay on the death of the first to die and buy his portion of the business from his heirs.

Cross Purchase 6 policies

Stock Redemption 1 Policy

What would happen if during his lifetime Joe sold his portion of the business to Doe?
1 Moe and Bo would want the Joint Life Policy rewritten to cover Doe, Moe and Bo. If the original contract contained a **Change of Insured Rider**, this could be done in a way that preserves Moe and Bo's insuring ages and their insurability.

2 As with Key Employee insurance, **the premiums paid to fund Buy and Sell Agreements are not tax deductible, but the proceeds are not subject to the federal income tax**. Again, like Key Employee insurance, either Term or Whole Life can be used as a funding mechanism.

Can't deduct premiums, but the death benefit is tax free

3 A buy-sell agreement should not be structured without the advice of both an attorney and an accountant. In truth, the mechanics of a buy-sell agreement vary with the organizational structure of the company. The buy-sell agreement is written differently if the business is organized as a corporation, partnership or a sole proprietorship. Likewise, the insurance policies used to fund the agreement could be structured differently. The industry even calls the insurance by different names. If the objective is to continue after a partnership, the Policy is called **Buy and Sell Life Insurance**. If we are continuing a closely-held corporation, the same policies are called **Stock Redemption Life Insurance**. However, despite the intricate differences in implementation, that you will learn as a practicing Agent, the basic concepts remain the same.

splits both the premium and benefits

SPLIT DOLLAR PLANS

4 Split Dollar life insurance plans take their name from the fact that **both the premiums paid for the insurance and the death benefits are split between two entities** — typically an employer and a highly-favored employee. The objective of the plan is to enable the employee to purchase insurance protection at very low cost and allow the employing company to recover its total contribution upon the employee's death or retirement, thereby limiting the company's cost to simply the loss of use of the money until the employee's death or retirement.

Cash Value
Life Insurance

1. Under a classic Split Dollar Plan, the Policy purchased is always one which develops cash value. The employing company pays a part of the premium equal to the yearly increase of cash value and the employee pays the balance of the premium. Let's suppose that our buddy, Joe, is a famous chef. His employer, the Four Seasonings Restaurant, values him highly as an employee. Further assume that they agree to a split-dollar purchase of a $100,000 Whole Life Policy. If the annual premium is $2,800 and the cash value developed in the first year were $1,200, then Four Seasonings would pay $1,200 and Joe would pay the balance of $1,600. If the second year the Policy developed an additional $2,000 in cash value, then Four Seasonings would pay $2,000 and Joe would pay $800. At some point, it is possible that Joe would have to pay nothing at all. That's how the premium is split.

2. Now let's see how the benefits would be split. Assume that Joe dies in 10 years after the employer has contributed $18,000 in premium to purchase this Policy which has a cash value of $18,000. Four Seasonings gets $18,000 of the $100,000 death benefit, and Joe's Beneficiary gets $82,000. If Joe does not die but retires in 10 years, he can simply borrow the $18,000 in cash value to repay the loan his employer has made to him and continue the coverage if he wishes.

3. As we said in the beginning, the employer loses only the use of the money, and the employee is greatly aided in the purchase of insurance. Is this *financial benefit* taxable to Joe? Absolutely! He is getting a valuable benefit as the result of his employment *and* this is not a benefit available to all of the employees of the restaurant — it is unique to Joe's compensation package. **And since it is compensation, it is taxable**. Since the title of this book is not *Section 28 of the Internal Revenue Code*, we will not melt your mind with the details of how the taxes are computed. At this stage, simply recognize that the employer's contribution to **a Split Dollar Plan is taxable to the employee**.

4. Further, we should note that there are umpteen variations of this concept frequently utilized, and if business insurance becomes an important part of your practice, considerably more study will be necessary.

LIFE INSURANCE Policy RIDERS

A **RIDER** is a special provision which provides benefits not found in the original contract but has been attached to and made part of the contract — generally for additional premium. Riders take their name from the fact that they have no independent existence and have force and effect only when they are attached to (i.e., *ride on*) a Policy.

Riders are useful in tailoring policies to the specific needs of individual Policyowners. They can be used in conjunction with any of the primary life Policy types, or with any of the special policies discussed in Chapter 9. We will examine some of the more common Policy riders.

Multiple Indemnity Rider (or AD&D)

This rider obligates the company to pay a multiple (two, three, or four times) of the face amount of the Policy **if the Insured dies as a result of an accident**. The most common of these riders is *Double Indemnity in Case of Accidental Death*. For example, if Joe owned a $100,000 Policy with a Double Indemnity rider and died as a result of an automobile accident, Jolene, as Beneficiary, would receive a $200,000 death benefit. Most policies stipulate that the **death must be accidental and not contributed to by any other cause and must occur within 90 days of the accident** to be classified as *accidental*. For example, if it could be proven that Joe's automobile accident was the result of his fainting because of a bleeding ulcer, Jolene would receive only the $100,000 face amount of the Policy. Joe's loss of consciousness (technically a sickness) would have contributed to the cause of the accident. Or, if Joe contracted pneumonia while in the hospital following the accident, and the illness *contributed* to his death, the company would pay only the face amount. Multiple indemnity coverage is normally **limited to age 60 or 65**.

2X
3X

accident only
- *sole cause*
- *90 days*

Some companies use an Accidental Death and Dismemberment Policy (AD&D) to provide this benefit. When done this way, the rider may also provide dismemberment benefits (see Chapter 14 for a complete discussion).

Guaranteed Insurability Rider

The Guaranteed Insurability rider allows the Insured to purchase additional insurance at specified dates or upon specified events in the future **without submitting new proof of insurability**. Normally, this option may only be added to policies issued to new Insureds under a maximum age, such as age 40. The Insured is permitted, at stated option dates or upon specific events (e.g. when he attains ages 25, 30, 35 and 40 or **upon marriage or birth of a child**), to purchase the additional amounts of insurance specified in the rider. The Insured will pay standard rates based on the attained age at the option dates, but will *not* have to take a physical or otherwise prove insurability.

As needs grow, coverage can grow with no proof

Cost of Living Rider

The Cost of Living Rider allows the Policyowner to increase the face amount of the Policy as the designated cost-of-living index increases. If the index increases by 3%, Joe could boost his $100,000 Policy to $103,000. No proof of insurability is required, but premium for the $3000 would be based upon Joe's current age - not his age at issue of the original Policy.

Keep up with inflation

Waiver Of Premium And Waiver Of Premium With Disability Income Riders

1 The **Waiver of Premium** rider provides that if the Insured becomes **permanently and totally disabled**, the company **will waive the right to receive premium** and the Policy will continue as if the premium were being paid. There is usually a **six-month waiting period** to determine if the disability is, in fact, permanent. It is then common practice to refund the premiums paid by the Insured during this six month period and waive future premiums for the length of the disability.

2 Under the *Waiver of Premium with Disability Income* rider, not only are the premiums waived, but a small monthly income is also paid to the Insured. Please note that with both of these riders, the disability typically must be **permanent and total** — a very strict definition of disability since most companies make no provision for partial disability.

Payor Benefit Rider

3 The Payor Benefit rider functions much like the Waiver of Premium rider and provides much the same benefit. The Payor Benefit rider, however, is issued only in connection with *juvenile insurance*. If the payor (parent) of the child Insured under the Policy dies or becomes totally disabled, the **premium is waived until the child reaches some predetermined age**, such as 18, 21, or 25. At that time, the young adult-Insured begins paying the premium without any penalty. In some versions, if the payor dies, the Policy becomes fully paid instead of premiums simply being waived.

Helps orphans

temporary waiver

Accelerated Death Benefit Rider

4 In Chapter Six of this text, you learned that in certain circumstances the insurance company could pay a portion of the death benefit to the Insured to cover the exorbitant costs of a terminal illness or the even more exorbitant costs of a nursing home. If built into the Policy, this benefit is normally described as a Living Benefit option. If added as a rider, it is normally called an Accelerated Death Benefit rider and, depending upon the company involved, may or may not require additional premium.

Pays portion of "Death Benefit" before you die.

Automatic Premium Loan Rider

5 This rider differs from most of the others in that you do not pay extra to get it. With this rider, **the Policyowner gives the company the right to borrow against the Policy's cash value to pay any past due premiums**. This process would be initiated at the expiration of a grace period. Additional unpaid premiums are then paid from the cash value. Except that the company makes the loan *on the Policyowner's behalf*, the Automatic Premium Loan is treated just like any Policy loan that the Policyowner might initiate. If Joe should take a 60-day vacation and forget to pay his premium, he would return home to find that his premium has been paid and that he now has a loan outstanding.

6 This example presupposes that Joe has selected the Automatic Premium Loan rider. His next steps are to either repay the loan plus interest or not repay and allow the loan to be deducted from the death benefit of the Policy. While this option does **prevent the unintentional lapse of the Policy**, it can also allow the Policyowner to become lax in paying the premiums and ultimately exhaust the cash value of the Policy. As a result, some companies limit the number of times this option can be used before one of the nonforfeiture options goes into effect.

Auto pay from your cash value.

1 The effect of the Automatic Premium Loan rider may be closely related in your mind to the nonforfeiture option of Extended Term. There are, however, some significant advantages given to the Policyowner who selects the Automatic Premium Loan approach.

- To reinstate a Policy that is on Extended Term requires *proof of insurability*. **Proof of insurability is not required to regain full benefit of a Policy that has been continued under Automatic Premium Loan.**

- As discussed earlier, Extended Term is frequently not available as a nonforfeiture option on rated or substandard policies. Since these Policyowners may utilize the benefits of the Automatic Premium Loan, it is particularly important to them.

No cost rider

TERM RIDERS

2 **Family (Spouse or Children's) Term Riders** - Earlier in this chapter, you learned that Family, Family Income or Family Maintenance policies can be sold as integrated, packaged policies, or they may be constructed by selling a **Whole Life Policy plus the appropriate rider**.

3 A **Family Policy** could be constructed by adding the appropriate number of Convertible Term riders to the Whole Life Policy written on the principle breadwinner. The riders would provide coverage for the spouse and children.

4 To build a **Family Income** Policy, the Agent would add a *Decreasing Term* rider; to provide a **Family Maintenance** Policy, the Agent would add a *Level Term* rider to the Whole Life contract. Since the use of the riders offers a more flexible approach than a packaged Policy, many companies today offer these products *only* in the form of riders attached to basic policies.

5 **Return Of Premium Rider** - If Joe Insured purchases a Return of Premium rider, his company's obligation, in the event of Joe's death, could be substantially increased. This option normally provides that if the Insured dies within the first 20 years of the Policy (though it could be 5, 10, 15, or 25 years), the company will pay the Beneficiary the **face amount of the Policy plus the gross premium paid**. Suppose that Joe buys a $100,000 Straight Life Policy for which he pays an annual premium of $2,500. If a Return of Premium rider is attached and Joe dies at the end of the first Policy year, then the company would pay $102,500 to Jolene — $100,000 from the face amount plus $2,500 from the premium paid. At the end of the second Policy year, the company's obligation would increase to $105,000. Because the company's obligation is steadily increasing, **this rider is constructed with Increasing Term** insurance. As previously stated, the duration of this promise is normally 20 years. Therefore, the company would use a 20-Year Increasing Term Policy to build the appropriate rider. The rate of increase would be designed to keep pace with the premiums paid. It is important to remember, however, that, as with all Term policies, when this Increasing Term period ends, it ends. If Joe dies in the 20th Policy year, Jolene would receive $100,000 plus $50,000 (20 times $2,500). However, if he dies in the 21st Policy year, she would receive only $100,000 because the Increasing Term period would have expired.

6 **Return Of Cash Value Rider** - The Return of Cash Value rider is structurally similar to the Return of Premium rider. With this rider, the company promises, upon Joe's death, to **pay the face amount plus the pre-death cash value of the Policy**. Because Joe's cash value would increase each year, this rider is also constructed with **Increasing Term** insurance. Normally, the rider is written to expire at age 65.

CONCLUSION

1 In this chapter, we have seen how the fundamental building blocks of Term, Whole Life, Endowment, and Annuities can be combined or modified to form products to fit the family. Although these combination policies were designed for the family of the 1950's, you may still run into them today because some life insurance companies still market these policies, and because you may have clients who are covered by one of these plans.

2 In addition to the combination policies and modified policies, we examined life insurance Policy riders which are additional Policy benefits that can be tacked onto any life insurance Policy for, generally, a small amount of additional premium.

Combination Life Insurance Policies

3 **FAMILY (PROTECTION) Policy** — A single Policy made up of Whole Life on Dad and smaller amounts of Convertible Term on Mom and the kids, i.e., *the entire family is covered*. Children born or adopted after the Policy is issued are automatically covered (generally two weeks after birth) with no proof of insurability and no increase in premium.

4 **FAMILY INCOME Policy** — This is one Policy, comprised of Whole Life and Decreasing Term. This Policy covers only one person — the breadwinner. The Decreasing Term period is the income period. If the breadwinner dies during the term (the income period), the company uses the death benefit of the Decreasing Term to pay the surviving spouse an income *for the balance of the years left in the income period*. For example, if it's a 20-Year Decreasing Term and the Insured dies 5 years into the term, then the company will pay the surviving spouse an income (primarily derived from the Decreasing Term's death benefit) for the 15 year balance of time left. The Whole Life death benefit will be paid upon the breadwinner's death, but generally not before the end of the income period.

5 **FAMILY MAINTENANCE Policy** — One Policy, on the breadwinner, made up of Whole Life and Level Term. If the breadwinner dies during the term, the death benefit of the Level Term will provide the surviving spouse with an income for a period of time equal to the entire length of the term. For example, if it's Whole Life plus 20-Year Level Term and the breadwinner dies during the 20 year term, the Policy would pay the Whole Life death benefit plus provide an income for 20 years. If the breadwinner dies after the 20 year term, only the Whole Life death benefit is paid.

6 **ENHANCED ORDINARY LIFE** - This Policy insures one person and originates as a combination of Term and participating Whole Life. Each year dividends are used to purchase Paid Up Additions which gradually replace the Term coverage with Whole Life but keep the total death benefit the same.

7 **MODIFIED LIFE** — Designed for the person who wants *permanent protection* but can't yet afford it, Modified Life is a combination of Convertible Term and Whole Life. It starts out as Term, but then, either all at once or in piecemeal fashion, it automatically converts to Whole Life.

Modified Life Insurance Policies

1   **GRADED PREMIUM WHOLE LIFE** - It's Whole Life, but the insurance company has redistributed the premium so its cheaper in the early years, but higher-priced in the later years.

2   **RE-ENTRY TERM** - A form of Renewable Term which allows the Policyowner to submit new proof of insurability at regular intervals to enjoy rates lower than if he simply continued to renew.

3   **JOINT LIFE** - It's normally Whole Life but with two (or more) Insureds. It pays on the death of the first.

4   **SURVIVORSHIP LIFE** - It also covers the lives of two or more, but it only pays upon the death of the last.

5   **JUVENILE LIFE** - Life insurance policies written on the lives of children within specified age limits (usually under the age of 15), generally with the parents or grandparents as the Policyowners.

6   **JUMPING JUVENILE Policy** - Juvenile insurance on which the face amount automatically increases by a multiple (usually 5) of the original face amount when the Insured child reaches a predetermined age (like 18, 21 or 25). No proof of insurability or additional premium is required when the face amount is increased. Sometimes called an Estate Builder Policy.

7   **INTEREST SENSITIVE WHOLE LIFE** - The premium is established for the first several years but then may be adjusted up or down (within specified limits). The cash value grows at a guaranteed minimum rate, but if the company can earn more, cash value will grow faster.

8   **EQUITY INDEXED LIFE INSURANCE** - Permanent insurance where the cash value grows at a guaranteed minimum rate, but is linked to an outside equity index (like the S&P 500 Index). If the positive returns of the index exceed the guaranteed rate of growth, the cash value return will equal that of the index.

Business Uses of Life Insurance

9   **KEY EMPLOYEE LIFE INSURANCE** — This is life insurance that a business buys to protect itself from the death of an employee who is crucial to the business. The business is the *owner* and the *Beneficiary* of the Policy, and the key employee is the *Insured*. In case of the employee's death, the business can use the death benefit to pay for the costs of replacing the deceased employee. As we have seen before, the premiums are not tax deductible, but the death benefit is free from income taxes.

10 **BUY AND SELL AGREEMENTS** — A Buy and Sell Agreement is simply a contract that establishes what will be done with a business in the event an owner dies. Life insurance normally provides the funds necessary to implement the Buy and Sell Agreement because it can provide the exact amount of money needed at exactly the time it is needed. With a closely-held corporation, the corporation is the Policyowner and the Beneficiary.

SPLIT DOLLAR PLANS — This is generally Whole Life insurance which an employer helps pay for as an employee benefit. It is usually only offered to a highly favored employee. It's a form of employee compensation and is therefore taxable as such. There are many variations of the plan, but essentially the employer and the employee split the premium payments and the benefits.

Policy Riders

MULTIPLE INDEMNITY (AD&D) — Doubles (triples, quadruples, etc.) the death benefit if it was an accidental death, not contributed to by any other cause, and occurred within 90 days of the accident. Double Indemnity is the most common.

GUARANTEED INSURABILITY — Buy more insurance at specified times in the future without having to provide proof of insurability — at standard rates, based on attained age.

COST OF LIVING RIDER — Allows the Policyowner to increase the face amount of the Policy as the designated cost-of-living index increases to keep pace with inflation.

WAIVER OF PREMIUM — If you become permanently and totally disabled, you don't have to keep on paying your life insurance premium. The company will waive the premium and keep your life insurance in force. After becoming disabled, you have to wait six months for the company to verify that your disability is permanent and total.

PAYOR BENEFIT — If the life insurance is on a child and the parent or guardian paying the premium dies, the company will waive the premium until the child reaches a predetermined age, such as 18 or 21, at which point the child (now an adult) continues paying the premium as if nothing had happened.

AUTOMATIC PREMIUM LOAN — This works kind of like overdraft protection on your checking account. If you forget to pay your life insurance premium, the insurance company will take out a Policy loan for you from your cash value to pay the overdue premium. Just like a Policy loan, all you do to regain full value of your Policy is repay the outstanding loan plus interest — no proof of insurability required.

ACCELERATED DEATH BENEFIT — Can pay a portion of the death benefit before the Insured's death in the event of a terminal illness, a dread disease or admission to a nursing home.

TERM — Term (Family) riders can be used to construct a number of additional benefits:

- To build the benefits of a **Family Policy** we use Convertible Term riders.
- To construct **Family Income**, Decreasing Term is used.
- A **Family Maintenance** contract can be built with a Level Term rider.
- **Return of Premium** along with the death benefit can be arranged by adding an Increasing Term rider.
- **Return of Cash Value** in addition to the death benefit can also be provided by an Increasing Term rider.

PLANNING FOR RETIREMENT

8

1 Our principal focus up to this point has been **LIFE** insurance. Although it is true that some Life insurance policies can be of assistance in accruing funds (cash value) to use at retirement, this is typically not the intent of most life insurance policies. In this chapter we will examine plans designed specifically for saving money for retirement. These retirement plans include an array of employer sponsored plans, individual plans, and the beleaguered federal government plan, Social Security. Our first step in the process is to learn what constitutes a **Qualified Retirement Plan,** as opposed to a **Non-Qualified Plan.**

*Saving $$
for retirement*

QUALIFIED VERSUS NON-QUALIFIED PLANS

Non-Qualified Plans

2 A Non-Qualified plan is one that is **not** formed in conjunction with IRS tax code requirements and therefore is **not** eligible for special IRS tax treatment. Said another way, **nonqualified plans receive no special tax treatment.**

*IRS doesn't
like it.
Therefore,
no tax breaks.*

3 If you put aside $50 every week, place it in a jar, and bury it in your back yard, you are saving for retirement, but this would be a Non-Qualified plan. In other words, you could not deduct your "contribution" from your taxes.

4 Non-Qualified plans have no specific rules for either the employer or the employee. Under a Non-Qualified plan, an employer could provide a retirement plan for only the executives and ignore the general workforce. **Discrimination is possible in a Non-Qualified plan.**

Qualified Plans

5 A **Qualified** Retirement Plan is a plan approved by the IRS. The Plan therefore is eligible for **special tax treatment under the IRS Code.** With the exception of Roth Plans, the Qualified Plan tax breaks include:

*IRS likes it.
Therefore,
tax breaks.*

1. Contributions to the Plan made by the **Employer** are tax deductible as a business expense (investing pre-tax dollars).
2. Contributions to the Plan made by the **Employees** are tax deductible (investing pre-tax dollars).
3. The money invested in the Plan grows **tax deferred** (grow faster).
4. Since none of the money in the Plan has yet to be taxed, **ALL** of the money withdrawn from the plan as income at retirement is taxed as **ordinary income.**

1   For a plan to be **"Qualified"** by the IRS, it must meet certain standards specified in the Tax Code. The plan must:

Not for the employer

- Be designed for the **exclusive benefit of the employees, or their beneficiaries**.

- It **must not discriminate** in favor of officers, stockholders or highly-paid employees.

No discrimi- nation

- It must be **in writing**

in writing

- It must define contributions, or benefits.

- It must be a permanent plan.

- It must meet minimum **vesting** (ownership) standards.

Qualified Retirement Plans

While there are a multitude of plans, there are some common elements of most Qualified Plans.

2

A.   There are **dollar and percentage limits** on the amount which can be contributed each year.

Limits on everything

B.   Whoever makes the contribution (employee or employer) **can normally deduct** the contribution from current taxable income (Roth excepted).

C.   Earnings (growth) **are tax deferred until the proceeds are paid out.**

Tax deferred growth

D.   Except Roth Plans, **everything coming out is taxed** because neither the principal nor the interest have been previously taxed.

E.   If the retiree dies before his retirement is fully paid, his heirs would continue to receive benefits and pay taxes just as the retiree would have had he lived.

But all taxed coming out.

F.   In most circumstances, **money cannot be taken out prior to age 59 1/2** without penalty.

59 1/2

G.   Proceeds must start paying out by **age 70 1/2** (5% or more).

70 1/2

H.   Except Roth, retirement monies can only be invested in specific products. While Annuities are commonly used, any **Life insurance** must be **purely incidental** to the plan.

I.   In general, employees who have reached age 21 and have completed one year's service must be allowed to participate in the plan.

Vesting = Ownership

1 One major requirement imposed by ERISA (Employee Retirement Income Security Act) on all qualified pension plans is that they must have an established vesting schedule. **Vesting** refers to the **amount of ownership** employees have in the employer's contributions to a pension plan. Employees are entitled to their vested shares of the plan even if they leave the company before retirement.

2 **The percentage of ownership increases as the employee's length of service increases** until, at some point, the employee owns 100% of the amount the employer contributed to his or her account, i.e., the employee is "100% vested". All employee contributions, mandatory or voluntary, vest 100% when made. They are nonforfeitable.

3 The IRS allows some flexibility in **vesting schedules**, but every plan must at least equal one of the following:

- If there is an employee pension eligibility requirement of two years of service, then contributions must be fully vested as soon as they are made.

- The "graded-vesting" schedule allows for a minimum of 20% vesting within two years and 100% within a maximum of six years.

- The "3-Year Cliff" schedule would allow no vesting for up to three years but calls for 100% vesting at three years of service.

4 We will begin our discussion of qualified retirement plans with those suitable to very large employers. We will then look at the deferred arrangement plans which put most of the responsibility on the employee rather than the employer. Our discussion will proceed to the individual plans which do not involve an employer at all. Finally, we will address the plans that best fit a small employer as these combine elements of all the previous plans. Then we will look at Social Security.

LARGE EMPLOYER PLANS

CORPORATE PENSION AND PROFIT SHARING PLANS

5 Almost all corporate pensions or profit sharing plans of any size are qualified plans. As such, they must be *funded*. That means that contributions to the plan must be set aside in a separate fund held by a third party and invested until needed for payments to the participants. The third party could be a trustee, an insurance company or a bank custodian. The funds can be invested in **stocks, bonds, mutual funds** or a variety of other investments. Obviously, the ultimate value of the investment plan is greatly dependent upon the earnings of the account. Some plans are *Insured* in whole or in part. This could allow payment of a death benefit to the family of an employee who dies prematurely as well as provide a retirement income for employees who live.

Corporate Pension Plans

1 A **Corporate Pension Plan** is defined by the IRS as one "established and maintained by the employer primarily to provide for the payment of *definitely determinable* benefits to employees over a period of years, usually for life, after retirement." The corporation must contribute to the plan, and there are normally provisions for the employees to contribute additional amounts.

more than a gold watch

2 In general, plans meet these requirements by following either a defined contribution formula or defined benefit formula.

DEFINED CONTRIBUTION PLANS — Sometimes called *Money Purchase Plans*, these pension plans require a **set rate of contribution** from the corporation. Employee benefits at retirement will depend directly upon the amount of contributions made, the plan's earnings, and the employee's length of service in the plan. Estimated benefits are derived from actuarial projections which obviously use age and sex as considerations, but federal law may prohibit the use of sex as a consideration in the future. Under a Defined Contribution Plan, you know exactly what will be put in, but you can only guess at what will come out.

Known amount of dollars put in

3 **DEFINED BENEFIT PLANS** — This plan is just the opposite of a Defined Contribution Plan. Here, **you know what will come out**, but it requires a constant process of estimating to determine what must go in. These **fixed benefit** plans, sometimes called *Annuity Purchase plans*, establish a set benefit formula for employees. The defined benefit may be a percentage of pay for each year of service in the plan, or a flat sum, or some combination of the two. The dollar amount of the benefit may vary, as with a variable annuity plan, but the formula must be fixed in the plan. While some plans call for the purchase of an individual annuity for each participant, most plans are established as Group Deferred Annuity or Group Deferred Variable Annuity purchases.

"Guaranteed" amount of dollars to come out

Corporate Profit Sharing Plans

4 Profit Sharing Plans can also be tax qualified. They share most of the features of qualified Corporate Pension Plans. A Profit Sharing Plan is defined by the IRS as "a plan established and maintained by an employer to provide for the participation in his profits by his employees or their beneficiaries".

5 Rather than committing the employer to either a fixed benefit or to a fixed contribution plan, which must be paid regardless of the company's financial condition, **the Profit Sharing Plan allows the employer to vary the contribution** to the plan at the discretion of the board of directors.

... to a degree

6 To be qualified, the plan **must not discriminate** among employees. The employer may contribute any amount of profits to the plan; but in general, only an amount equal to 25% of all the compensation paid to plan participants is tax deductible. While contributions only need be made when there is a profit, **contributions must be regular and substantial** to keep the plan qualified. The employer's contribution must be allocated to all participants of the plan on an equal basis according to a predetermined formula. The benefits will depend upon the value of the participant's account at retirement.

No discrimination

1 The employer's contribution must be paid into a profit sharing trust. The trust invests the funds until they are needed. **As with all qualified plans, neither the contributions to an employee's account nor the earnings of the trust are taxed until withdrawn.**

2 For many years, the right to accumulate retirement benefits with pre-tax dollars was limited to employees of very large companies with qualified pension or profit sharing plans. Those of us who were self-employed, employed by a small company or otherwise had to fund our own retirement had to do so with after-tax dollars.

3 Beginning in the 1960's, Congress has slowly remedied this inequity by creating a number of qualified plans for those of us who do not work for Fortune 500 companies.

CASH OR DEFERRED ARRANGEMENT PLANS

4 These popular plans allow employees to balance their need for current income with their desire to build retirement funds. While the details vary from plan to plan, all allow the **employee to reduce their salaries by deferring a chosen amount into a retirement account.** In some plans the employer will *match* the employees deferral up to a specific percentage ceiling. The matching could be on a dollar for dollar basis or, perhaps, 50 cents on the dollar as called for by the plan. The following plans allow employees to save for retirement under Qualified CODA Plans.

CODA

Tax Sheltered (Deferred) Annuities (TSA's) (TDA) (403-B)

5 Employees of **not-for-profit organizations (501C-3 organizations) such as churches, hospitals and schools** are eligible for this specialized retirement plan with the misleading name. It is not *tax sheltered* but *tax deferred*. Further, it can be funded with a variety of products — not just an Annuity.

501's get 403

6 Qualified employees can have their employer set aside up to a specified percentage of their annual salary and pay income taxes just as if they had taken a pay-cut. This is not a deduction from your taxable income, but an actual *reduction* in your paycheck. For example, a teacher making $44,000 could have the school system reduce her salary by, say, $8,000. She will pay income taxes as if she made $36,000 this year. There is a maximum an individual can defer in any one year, such as $16,000, or 25% of the gross compensation, whichever is less.

401(k) Plans

7 A plan with some similarities to the TSA is the 401(k) plan. In fact, 501C-3 organizations may, today, establish a 401(k) for their employees in lieu of a TSA. It is a **company-sponsored jointly-funded defined contribution plan**. It does not have the *not-for-profit* restrictions of the TSA and is very popular with small employers. Under the 401(k), **each individual employee chooses a percentage** (not to exceed a percentage specified in the plan) to be withheld from his/her paycheck. The employer then *matches* the employee's contribution in some manner. The match could be dollar for dollar, dollar for dollar up to a certain level or, perhaps, the employer could match the employee on a percentage basis.

Employees save for retirement...

Employers help.

1. In most other respects, the 401(k) parallels the other qualified plans we have discussed with respect to taxation, non-discrimination and the like, except for one notable exception. Unlike most of the other retirement plans, it is possible for employees to borrow against their 401(k) plans under certain circumstances as long as they conform with some rather strict requirements concerning repayment.

The Roth 401(k)

2. Begining in 2006, 401(k) plans may permit participants to designate some or all of their employee contributions as "Roth contributions." Unlike salary deferrals made to a 401(k) plan, **Roth contributions are after-tax dollars** that are included in the participant's taxable wages at the time they are deducted from pay. The earnings on the Roth account are **tax free** as long as they are paid after the participant reaches age 59 1/2, dies or becomes disabled and at least 5 years have passed since the first Roth contribution was made to the account. If a payment occurs before the requirements are satisfied, the employee is subject to tax on the earnings along with a 10% penalty on the entire distribution.

Tax FREE income at retirement

3. In other words, Roth contributions are treated very much like 401(k) contributions under the 401(k) plan. For example, Roth contributions and 401(k) contributions together are subject to the maximum contribution for the tax year. They are reviewed annually in the non-discrimination testing. They are 100% vested and have the same withdrawal restrictions as the 401(k) contributions.

Section 457 Deferred Comp ‡

4. Section 457 of the IRS code makes non-qualified Deferred Compensation arrangements possible for employees of state and local government and for employees of not-for-profit organizations.

Non-Qualified But Deferred Arrangement for government employees

5. In most cases, this plan can be viewed as a salary reduction retirement plan for state and local government employees. The maximum deferral is 25% of the gross compensation or 33 1/3% of the remaining compensation up to the maximum such as $15,000 - whichever is lowest. An employee making $40,000 a year could set aside $10,000. That is 25% of $40,000. As always, deferred amounts remain the sole property of the employer until the participant *separates from service* or attains age 70 1/2. Separation from service is defined as termination, disability, death or retirement.

INDIVIDUAL PLANS

Individual Retirement Account (IRA)

6. In 1974, the Pension Reform Act created the **IRA (Individual Retirement Account).** It was originally intended to give persons with no other way of funding their retirement, with pre-tax dollars, a way to do so. The original IRA program worked for individuals in much the same way as the other plans worked for employer/employee. The **contribution was tax-deductible,** the **proceeds grew on a tax-deferred basis** and taxes were paid only as the money was withdrawn for retirement.

Individual Retirement Account

7. After several modifications, we find that today, **anyone with an earned income can establish an IRA.** However, if you have another tax-advantaged retirement plan, you may or may not be able to deduct your contribution from your taxes.

Individual Retirement Account (IRA)
IRA Characteristics

1. **CONTRIBUTION LIMITS** — There are legal limits of contribution which vary from year to year; a married couple may each contribute the maximum individual amount each year.

2. **TAX DEDUCTIBILITY OF CONTRIBUTIONS** — Anyone who is not an *active participant* in an employer-sponsored retirement plan can take a full deduction of their IRA contribution up to the legal limits. In simple terms, *active participant* means anyone eligible to make a contribution or receive a benefit in the past year.

3. **TAX DEFERRED GROWTH** — Although it is obvious why a person would establish an IRA if their contributions are tax deductible, it might not be so easy to understand why someone would contribute to an IRA if they could not deduct their contributions.

    Tax Deferred Growth

    The answer to this question points out the second major advantage that an IRA shares with other tax-advantaged retirement plans. **No taxes are paid on the earnings of the account until funds are withdrawn.**

4. **SOURCE OF FUNDS** — You invest your own money for your own retirement in your IRA. Therefore, you are **vested** (the money is yours) from the start.

    100% vested

5. **AUTHORIZED FUNDING VEHICLES** — IRA monies must be set aside in one or more of the following:

    *   Flexible Premium **Annuity** contracts — fixed or variable.

    *   A **trust or custodial** account of a financial institution, stock Brokerage or mutual fund.

    *   Government Retirement **Bonds** or Zero Coupon Bonds.

6. **FUND PAYOUT** — There are several events which could trigger the payout of benefits of an IRA.

    *   **Death** — Distribution can be made to the Beneficiary immediately.

    *   **Disability** — Distribution is available immediately without penalty, or the funds can be left to accumulate until a future date.

    *   **Retirement** — Distribution of funds must begin no earlier than age **59 1/2** nor later than age **70 1/2.** The withdrawal of funds prior to age 59 1/2 would subject those funds to a **10% tax penalty** in addition to normal income taxes. Payments into an IRA may be discontinued at any time and the accrued funds left to accumulate.

        50% tax on inadequate distributions

    *   Early withdrawals can be made without penalty (but **with** taxes) if used for a **first-time home purchase** or for **educational purposes** (no maximum). Withdrawals for catastrophic medical bills have been allowed since 1996 - again with tax, but without penalty.

7. **TAX CONSEQUENCES AT RETIREMENT** — Funds paid to you at retirement that were not taxed going into your IRA will be taxed at your normal income tax rate as they come out of your IRA. These funds can be paid to you in a lump sum or in installments.

8. **ROLL-OVER TO AN IRA** — One of the major uses of an IRA is in a roll-over capacity. Under most circumstances, it can allow the continued sheltering of pension funds that have been distributed to you before age 70 1/2. For example, suppose you've worked for XYZ Corporation for 20 years and have participated in their corporate pension plan. Now, at age 50, you quit to start your own business. In the 20 years you've worked at XYZ, you've accumulated $575,000 in your fully vested pension account. When you leave XYZ, they give you the money. You now have a major tax liability. But, if you can roll the money over into another tax-qualified account within **60 days**, you can defer taxes until you begin taking out the money. A Roll-Over IRA can serve this purpose. The *portable pension* has become a reality with the IRA.

Roll-Over

60 Days

9. **IRA Transfers** - We should distinguish between an IRA Rollover and an **IRA transfer**. A Roll-Over is from a different type of Qualified plan to an IRA. A transfer is just moving an IRA. If Joe does not like the way First Bank is managing his IRA funds, he can request a transfer to Third Bank. The money simply moves from one custodian to another.

YES!
NO withholding

ROTH IRAs

3
The Roth IRA differs from the traditional IRA in several ways. Most notably, **contributions are not tax-advantaged going into the account, but benefits paid out of the account (including interest and dividends) are TAX FREE**.

CONTRIBUTIONS – Roth IRA contributions are never tax deductible. However, when money is withdrawn, it is **tax free.**

ROTH:

ROTH CONVERSIONS - A traditional IRA may be converted to a Roth IRA. This conversion is treated as a *Rollover*. If properly done, there will be no assessment of the 10% early withdrawal penalty. Conversion methods:

1. No tax deduction, but

- **Rollover**: The taxpayer receives the distribution from a traditional IRA and puts the funds in a Roth IRA within 60 days of distribution. Earnings must be converted with the principal.

2. TAX FREE income at retirement

- **Trustee to Trustee Transfer**: The taxpayer directs the present Trustee to transfer the funds directly to the Trustee of a Roth IRA.

- **Same Trustee Transfer**: The taxpayer merely directs that their present Trustee place the funds being held in a traditional IRA into a Roth IRA.

DISTRIBUTIONS - Qualified distributions (of both contributions and interest) from a Roth IRA are not included in your gross income, and are therefore not taxed.

Unlike traditional IRAs, there is no rule which requires Roth IRAs to begin payout at age 70 1/2. In fact, under a Roth IRA, contributions can continue after age 70 1/2.

SMALL EMPLOYER PLANS

1 Rather obviously, a pension or profit sharing plan that fits a company like IBM or General Motors would not be appropriate for a small restaurant with five employees. A small business is dangerously vulnerable to the ups and downs of the marketplace, and the small business owner is normally fearful of being *locked in* to any highly regimented plan.

2 Additionally, small employers do not have the resources to administer and manage some of the more complex plans we've discussed. Certainly the small employer does not want to take on the responsibility of managing to retirement accounts of his employees. Therefore, several retirement plans have evolved which are more closely suited to the needs of the small employer.

KEOGH PLANS

3 The great-granddaddy of small employer retirement plans is the Keogh or HR-10 plan which became available in 1962. It allowed **self-employed individuals** to establish tax favored retirement plans for themselves with the requirement that their employees (if any) must also be covered.

Self-employed persons can include sole proprietors, partners in a business, farmers or professionals such as doctors or lawyers.

4 A Keogh may be established as a defined contribution plan or a defined benefit plan.

- If the Keogh is a **defined contribution plan**, the self-employed persons may annually set aside up to the legal limits. This contribution is tax deductible.

- This fund, including dividends and interest, **accumulates tax deferred** until it is withdrawn.

5 Individuals who work for self-employed people with Keogh plans and who are **at least 21 years of age** *must* be included in the plan if they have been **employed for one year or more** and **work for more than 1000 hours per year**.

6 For example, let's say Joe is a self-employed restaurant owner. His chef, Julia Child, is a full-time employee, 55 years old, and has worked for Joe for five years. Joe has a Keogh plan into which he contributes 15% of his annual salary. Because Julia must also be included in the Keogh plan, Joe must contribute an amount equal to 15% of her salary into the Keogh plan for her. This contribution on Julia's behalf is taken from the restaurant's income — not from Julia's paycheck.

SIMPLIFIED EMPLOYEE PENSIONS (SEPs)

1 A SEP is much like a **cross between a profit sharing plan and an IRA**. In years of profitability the employer makes a contribution to each employee's IRA. Since an IRA is a qualified plan already, the SEP is easy for the employer to establish and administer.

"IRAs" for employees

2 The employer's contribution is not considered taxable income to the employee and is capped at 25% of compensation.

3 As always, this Qualified Plan must be nondiscriminatory. All employees who are at least 21 and have earned at least $450 from the employer during three of the previous five years must be included.

SEPs / IRAs

SIMPLE PLANS

4 The *Savings Incentive Match Plan for Employees*, or SIMPLE plan, is another alternative for businesses with less than 100 employees. As the name implies, it allows employers to establish a tax-favored retirement savings plan without addressing many of the usual burdensome requirements.

SIMPLE plans aren't

5 SIMPLE plans can be structured as an IRA or 401(k). Participating employees can defer income up to a specific dollar ceiling ($16,000 currently) and the employer matches dollar for dollar any contribution up to 3% of the employee's annual compensation. If employees choose not to contribute, the employer can make a contribution of an amount up to 2% of the employee's compensation.

6 All contributions are 100% vested immediately and the normal rules concerning taxation and withdrawal apply.

SOCIAL SECURITY

7 What is commonly called Social Security is officially titled **Old Age, Survivors, and Disability Insurance (OASDI)**. It was created by the Social Security Act of 1935 and has been amended by Congress many times since then. It is funded through payment by employers, employees, and self-employed persons.

OASDI

most are covered

8 There are a number of Social Security benefit programs, but the three most commonly thought of as Social Security benefits are:

- **Social Security Retirement Income** – which pays covered individuals and their eligible dependents lifetime monthly retirement benefits.

Retirement

- **Social Security Disability Income** – which pays qualified individuals a monthly disability income if the worker is totally disabled.

SSDI

- **Survivor Benefits** – which pays survivors of covered workers lifetime or temporary monthly payments and/or a lump-sum death benefit.

Life Insurance

1 Social Security covers most employed persons. Since nearly 90% of all employed persons are covered by Social Security, it is considerably easier to learn who is not covered rather than to remember who is. **Persons not covered** by Social Security include individuals covered by the **Railroad Retirement Act, policemen** with their own retirement system, very low income self-employed people, and members of religious orders who have taken a vow of poverty.

2 A person becomes qualified for Social Security benefits by becoming *"Insured."* Most types of benefits are only payable if you are **Fully Insured**. Some Social Security benefits are available if you are either fully or **Currently Insured**. As the words indicate, fully Insured is better than currently Insured. Your classification status does not dictate the amount of benefit you receive; it simply determines if you are eligible for a benefit at all. For example, a person who is only currently Insured is not eligible for retirement benefits, but a worker who is fully Insured is. You become Insured by acquiring a certain number of quarters of coverage. To be **fully Insured**, a worker must have **40 quarters of coverage, or one quarter of coverage for each year since age 21** or 1950 (whichever is later), with a **minimum of six quarters**. To be currently Insured, a worker must have at least six quarters of coverage out of the last 13 quarter period ending with the quarter of death, disability, or retirement.

Fully is better

Fully/Forty

40 Quarters

3 If you are *fully Insured,* you are eligible for all three areas of benefits. If you are only *currently Insured,* you are eligible *only* for some of the survivors' benefits.

Fully v. Currently

4 Now let's turn to the questions pertaining to *how much* you will receive if you are qualified. Social Security benefits are based on ***the amount of the monthly payment*** you would be eligible for upon retirement. This amount is called the **Primary Insurance Amount (PIA)**. Your PIA in turn is based upon your **"average monthly wage"** or "average indexed monthly earnings" from the year you reached age 22.

PIA

5 Calculating your monthly Social Security income is unbelievably complex. However, it is important for you to know that while the basic concepts of the Social Security programs are fairly static, the benefit minimums and maximums are subject to annual change. If you are to stay current with your knowledge of this program, a regular review of the changes will be absolutely necessary.

6 Since you now understand (1) the three broad areas of benefits, (2) how eligibility is determined, (3) that all benefits are stated in terms of the PIA, and (4) the basis for computing the PIA, let's look at the details.

Social Security Retirement Benefits

1   As you recall, only **Fully Insured** individuals are eligible for retirement benefits. A worker retiring at the designated retirement age, which varies depending upon when one was born, is entitled to a **lifetime monthly benefit** equal to their **Primary Insurance Amount**. An individual may also choose to retire early as age 62+ with an offsetting reduction of benefits. (A early retiree would be eligible for 80% of the PIA throughout retirement.) The reverse occurs when an individual elects to work beyond age 65, the normal retirement age. The broad heading of retirement benefits also includes these two additional benefits:

early - 80%

- **Wives' or Husbands' Benefits** – The spouse (65+) of a fully Insured retired individual is eligible for a monthly payment of one-half of the worker's PIA. The spouse who is also fully Insured and entitled to retirement benefits of their own will be paid whichever amount is higher – their own PIA, or one-half the principal breadwinner's. If the spouse is under 65 at the wage earner's retirement, the spouse's benefits are reduced accordingly.

Spousal Benefits

- **Dependent Children** – Any unmarried children of a fully Insured individual who retires at 65 are entitled to one-half the worker's PIA if they are under 18.

Blackout Period

2   The period of time following the expiration of the Dependent Children's benefit and the beginning of the Wife's or Husband's benefit is known as the **blackout period**. In simple terms, suppose Joe dies today with minor children in the home. Jolene would receive a check for the children until the youngest reaches 18, and she is 50. She would not start getting her Wife's benefit until retirement age - thus creating an insurance need for the **blackout period**.

Social Security Disability Benefits - SSDI

3   The SSDI benefit is also only available to **fully Insured** workers. It provides monthly disability benefits after a **five month waiting period** during periods of disability prior to age 65. Disability under Social Security is defined as *the inability to engage in any substantially gainful activity by reason of medically determinable physical or mental impairment that can be expected to* ***result in death*** *or that has continued or can be expected to continue for at least **12 full months***. After the **5 month waiting period**, the disabled worker will begin to receive the Primary Insurance Amount as a monthly benefit. Spouses and dependent children of disabled workers may receive the same monthly benefits as though the breadwinner had retired.

12
12
5

PIA

4   After the five month waiting period and two years of benefit payments (total of 29 months), the disabled worker is entitled to full **Medicare benefits** even if he or she is not yet age 65.

Survivor Benefits

There are six important categories of benefits available when a covered worker dies. Survivors of an individual who is *either* Fully Insured or Currently Insured are entitled to benefits in the first three areas.

1. **Mothers or Fathers of Dependent Children** – Widows or widowers of any age who have dependent children in their care are entitled to a monthly benefit of 75% of the PIA until the youngest child reaches age 16.

2. **Children** – Children under age 18 who remain unmarried are eligible for a monthly payment equal to 75% of the deceased parent's PIA.

3. **Lump-Sum Death Benefit** – The death of a fully or currently Insured worker will authorize a single payment of **$255** to the surviving spouse and dependent children.

WOW!
$255

Only the death of a *fully Insured* worker will trigger the availability of the last three categories.

4. **Widows** – A widow of age 65 is qualified for a monthly payment equal to her deceased husband's PIA. She may elect to take a reduced benefit as early as age 60 (50 if disabled).

5. **Widowers** – A dependent widower is entitled to the same benefits as a widow.

6. **Parents** – A monthly payment equal to 82 1/2% of the PIA will be made to a 62-year-old parent of a deceased fully Insured worker *if* the parent was receiving one-half of his or her support from the worker. If two parents are eligible, each receives 75% of the PIA for a total of 150% of the PIA.

CONCLUSION

1 We have seen in this chapter that businesses can use life insurance and annuity products for several purposes.

- To protect itself from the risk of a valuable employee's death (Key Employee Life Insurance) or a businessowner's death (life insurance used to fund a Buy and Sell Agreement).

- To retain a valuable employee by enhancing his or her compensation package (Split Dollar Plans, Deferred Compensation and Executive Bonus Plans).

- To provide retirement benefits (Corporate Pension and Profit Sharing Plans, Keogh Plans, 401(k) Plans, SEPs and SIMPLE Plans).

2 We've also seen that employees of not-for-profit organizations can provide for their own retirement through a Tax Sheltered Annuity (TSA), and that anyone with earned income may establish an Individual Retirement Account (IRA).

3 **QUALIFIED RETIREMENT PLANS** — In order for a retirement savings plan to be qualified (i.e., for special tax treatment), it must meet certain requirements such as it must be for the benefit of the employees or their beneficiaries, it must not discriminate, it must be in writing, it must define the contributions or the benefits, and it must be a permanent plan. A retirement plan does not *have to be* qualified; but if it isn't, then it doesn't get the special tax treatment. Examples of *non-qualified* plans are Deferred Compensation Plans and Split Dollar Plans.

4 Both the employer and the employee benefit under a qualified plan. While each plan has its idiosyncrasies, the pattern is almost universal. Whoever contributes the money can do so in a tax-advantaged manner. An employer can treat his contribution as a business expense. If an employee pays into his own retirement account he can deduct his contribution (IRA) or offset his income (401(k)).

5 The retirement account is invested and grows on a tax-deferred basis until retirement. At retirement, any untaxed contributions and all interest is taxable. Typically, retirement can start as early as 59 1/2 and must start by 70 1/2. Any early withdrawals are, of course, taxed, and in most cases are subject to a 10% penalty.

6 **LARGE EMPLOYER PLANS** – Large Employer Plans include **Pension Plans** and **Profit Sharing Plans**. Pension Plans are written on a **defined contribution** or **defined benefit** basis. Profit Sharing Plans call for contributions only in years in which the employer makes a profit.

7 **CASH OR DEFERRED ARRANGEMENT PLANS** – The CODA plans all allow the employee to take a **salary reduction** today in order to fund retirement tomorrow. In some cases the employer will *match* the employee's contribution up to certain limits. These plans include the **TSA or 403-B** plan which is for employees of 501C-3 (not for profit) organizations, the **401(k) plan**, and the **Section 457** plan for employees of state and local governments as well as employees of not-for-profit entities.

1 **INDIVIDUAL PLANS** – Though originally intended for people with no other retirement plan, today anyone with an earned income can have an **IRA** and most of us qualify for the somewhat newer **Roth IRA**. The traditional IRA follows the normal pattern of retirement plans. Workers who have no other plan or earn below a specified annual salary can fully deduct their contributions, watch the account grow on a tax-deferred basis, and then pay taxes at retirement. The **Roth IRA** contributions are **not tax deductible**, grow on a tax-free basis and distributions at retirement are **not considered taxable income**.

2 **SMALL EMPLOYER PLANS** – These plans include the **Keogh** for sole proprietorships and partnerships. Remember that employees of these organizations must be included in the plan if it is to be considered a qualified plan. **SEPs** and **SIMPLE** plans simply provide a way for a small employer to contribute to the employee's *IRA or 401(k)-like* account and eliminate the responsibility for managing the retirement investments of his employees. The SEP is much like an employer-sponsored IRA (with higher limits), and the SIMPLE plan functions much like a 401(k). The employee takes a salary reduction and the employer matches (within limits) the employee's contribution.

SOCIAL SECURITY

3 What are usually referred to as **Social Security (OASDI)** benefits include:

- **Social Security Retirement Income** – which pays covered individuals and their eligible dependents lifetime monthly retirement benefits.

- **Social Security Disability Income** – which pays qualified individuals a monthly disability income if the worker is totally disabled.

- **Survivor Benefits** – which pays survivors of covered workers lifetime or temporary monthly payments and/or a lump-sum death benefit.

4 Most employed persons are covered by Social Security, although there are exceptions – such as **government employees**. To become qualified for *most* types of benefits, you must be **fully Insured**. If eligible, the benefits in most of the programs are based on the amount of the monthly payment you would be eligible for upon retirement, called the **primary insurance amount (PIA)**. Under the Social Security Disability Income program, in addition to being fully Insured, the worker must be deemed "disabled" which means *unable to engage in any substantially gainful activity by reason of medically determinable physical or mental impairment that can be expected to **result in death** or that has continued or can be expected to continue for at least **12 full months***. Then, there is a **5 month waiting period** before the disabled worker will begin to receive the monthly benefit.

FLEXIBLE FEATURE POLICIES

1   Up to this point, we have studied the mechanics of the three traditional life insurance products – Term, Whole Life, and Annuities – as well as many of the combinations, modifications and variations possible with these three basic building blocks.

2   The distinguishing characteristics of traditional policies are that, in most respects, their values are **guaranteed, predictable, and unchanging** – traits which have been described as their greatest strengths. However, these same traits have also been described as their greatest weaknesses; Whole Life especially is often criticized as being **rigid, unresponsive and unchangeable**.

3   In this chapter, you will enter some new terrain. In short, we will explore products that contain features and benefits which may be significantly different from traditional, ordinary life insurance policies. These *nontraditional* or *flexible feature* policies have not only changed the way many people think of life insurance, but also how and why they buy it.

4   In this chapter, we will focus on the key flexible feature products:

- Adjustable Life
- Variable Life
- Universal Life
- Variable Universal Life

Historical Background

5   Prior to the early 1970's, Whole Life insurance was the workhorse of the life insurance industry. It would be safe to say that people who could afford the higher premium purchased Whole Life; others purchased Term, often with the intent of converting it to a Whole Life plan at a later date.

6   However, for the last 40 years or so, Whole Life has become the object of a great deal of criticism. To better understand why, let's review the key characteristics of Whole Life.

7   **LOCKED-IN GUARANTEED PREMIUM** – If, at age 20, Joe Insured purchases a Whole Life Policy with an annual premium of $1,000, that premium will remain the same for as long as the Policy is in force.

8   **LOCKED-IN GUARANTEED DEATH BENEFIT** – With a traditional Policy, the death benefit is fixed and it does not change.

© 2010 Pathfinder Corporation

1 **LOCKED-IN GUARANTEED GROWTH OF CASH VALUE** – The Policy contains a cash value per thousand growth schedule which is the same for all Insureds of a given age and sex. This rate of return is generally between 3% and 4.5%. The Policy is designed so that the cash value will grow steadily and predictably until, at age 100, the cash value will equal the death benefit and the Policy will endow/mature for the full face amount.

low rate of return

2 Other features of Whole Life you should remain aware of during our discussion of flexible feature products include:

- **The insurance company assumes all the risk.** Once Joe's Policy has been issued, all he has to do is keep paying the premiums. The benefits and values are guaranteed.

Risk

- **Costs are "bundled".** There are really only three figures Joe needs to know about – premium, death benefit and cash value. Matters involving interest earnings, premium taxes, administration costs and other expenses are not disclosed, nor do they need to be. These costs are all bundled together and cannot be separated.

Bundled

- **The Policyowner does not control** how the cash value is invested, or any other aspect of Policy administration.

No control

The Changing Marketplace and Environment

3 These locked-in, guaranteed features of Whole Life have long been considered its greatest strength. They provide unshakable stability. But they were unable to take into account several sociological factors – specifically:

- New lifestyle patterns.

- New attitudes about risk versus reward.

4 In our grandparents' day, life was reasonably predictable. In your twenties, you married once and stayed that way. By age 25, you had the job you would still hold at 65. You had one litter of children who left the nest by the time you were 40, and who had finished college by the time you were 45. This left you 20 years to prepare for retirement at 65, and you were dead by 75.

Life insurance needs have changed.

5 Today, nobody lives that way. Divorce is commonplace. Children under one roof may be yours, mine and ours. Some people don't marry for the first time until well into their thirties or forties, and some couples don't start having children until they are into their forties and fifties. People frequently change jobs, mates and economic levels. Some families even have *tag team* breadwinners – "You work while I go to school and then I'll work while you go to school unless I join a cult, marry my receptionist and leave you with the children."

Flexibility required

6 Even without going through all of the soap opera possibilities, the odds today of making one life insurance purchasing decision that would last a lifetime are infinitesimally small. The message to the insurance industry was simple: **Design policies flexible enough to adjust to the changes we go through in life.**

1 A second major factor which forced the insurance industry to design this new family of products has to do with our Policyowner's willingness or unwillingness to take **investment risk**. Many of our grandparents were children of the Great Depression. As such, a *guarantee* of 3% or 4% cash value growth in a traditional Policy was very attractive to them. And, this very conservative approach to life insurance worked reasonably well for people whose primary earning years were the decades of the 50's and 60's. But those of us who reached adulthood later in the twentieth cenruty live in a different world. We're not children of the Depression. We grew up as the inflation generation. We learned that buying a product which earns 4% when inflation is 10% is a sure road to poverty.

No Risk
Low Return

2 Two major factors also accelerated the evolution of Whole Life policies: the advent of inexpensive computers, and the public's growing interest in the stock market as a way to increase their rate of return on investments.

The Computerization of Whole Life

3 The original creation of Whole Life many hundreds of years ago was considered to be a mathematical Wonder of the World. It is estimated that the math alone required 25 man-years to complete without the assistance of computers. The same work can now be done in 25 seconds! The capacity to provide change and flexibility was greatly facilitated by the advent of inexpensive computers, beginning in the 1960's and 1970's.

Adjustable

Universal

4 The first computerization of Whole Life was called **Adjustable Life**. Ten years later an even more flexible version of Adjustable Life was created called **Universal Life**.

The Securitization of Whole Life

5 Prior to the 1970's, a great majority of Americans were not familiar with investing in securoties. However, as inflation raged in the 1970's, investors sought alternative investments that could beat inflation, which securities (investing in stocks and bonds) frequently accomplished. The insurance companies responded, first with a securities version of Whole Life, called **Variable** Whole Life, followed by a securities version of Universal Life, called Variable Universal Life.

6 We will start with a look at Adjustable (Whole) Life.

Adjustable Life Insurance

1   Introduced in 1971, Adjustable Life was the first successful attempt to computerize Whole Life to dramatically enhance its flexibility. Its primary advantage was that Insureds could periodically adjust (hence the name) the amount of death benefit, the amount of premium, or even the type of coverage (Term versus Whole Life as their needs changed over their lifetimes.

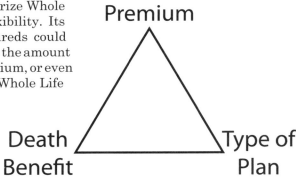

2   In most respects, Adjustable Life was simply a traditional Policy with flexibility. For instance, if Joe College decided to buy an Adjustable Life Policy, he would be presented with three choices. He would make decisions on two, which would then automatically determine the third.

- **The amount of life insurance protection / death benefit.**

- **The amount of premium** / Within certain limits, Joe can actually set the amount of premium he wants to pay.

- **The type of plan** / Term versus Whole Life as we studied in Chapter 4.

1 What we actually have are a number of possible Policy types within one Policy –called Adjustable Life. Suppose Joe College initially wants $100,000 of protection and can afford to pay annual premiums of $400. These two choices (along with his age and other underwriting factors) might dictate that the contract will initially be a Term to Age 65 Policy. Or, interested in building up cash values, he may decide he wants a Whole Life plan and is able to afford an annual premium of $600. Based on these two factors, the company will determine the amount of death protection the plan can provide.

2 The appeal of Adjustable Life is that its flexibility isn't limited to the plan at issue. **At any time** after the Policy is in force, Joe can contact the insurance company and **request a change**. Specifically, the Policy can be adjusted to:

Instant Changes

- Increase or decrease the face amount

- Increase or decrease the premium or the payment period

- Extend or reduce the protection period

Pick 2, and the computer solves for the third

3 Adjustable Life was nothing short of revolutionary in the flexibility and control it provided Insureds. For example, what happens if in five years Joe's needs change (as in all likelihood they will)? No problem. All he has to do is contact the company and adjust his Policy. **At any time**, Joe's Policy can be adjusted to reflect his changing life insurance needs and/or financial objectives. In this way, Joe always has the exact amount of coverage he needs, for the premium he is most able to comfortably afford.

4 Of course, there may be some restrictions. Some companies limit the number of adjustments that can be made per year or charge a fee to cover at least part of the cost of making the change. Also, some adjustments (such as significant increases in face amount) are contingent upon proof of insurability.

Strengths and Weaknesses of Adjustable Life

5 Adjustable Life was a big first step in meeting the public's need for flexibility in their life insurance programs. For the first time, consumers could meet a lifetime of insurance needs with a single life insurance Policy which could be adjusted and streamlined periodically, as needed.

6 However, Adjustable Life has several drawbacks. First, it is a **fairly complicated** product to understand. Policyowners are not always aware of how their decisions will affect Policy values. Also, Adjustable Life has proven to be somewhat cumbersome and costly from an administrative point of view. All changes require formal requests from the Policyholder and create time-consuming adjustments at the home office. As a result, the **relative cost per thousand** of coverage under the various plan options tends to be somewhat **higher** than with traditional policies, dulling an otherwise highly competitive edge. Finally, when the Adjustable Life Policy is in a cash value mode, **it earns a fixed rate of return**. In other words, Adjustable Life does not specifically address the question of competitive rates of return on the Policy's cash value.

7 In this respect, Adjustable Life essentially is a traditional ordinary life insurance Policy which, thanks to the computer, can be converted to other forms of ordinary life policies. As a result, most companies' Adjustable Life policies have evolved into either Variable or Universal Life policies, which have proven to be even more effective in meeting a broader range of consumer needs.

Variable Whole Life

1 Adjustable Life pioneered the concept of flexibility in life insurance plans. However, it was Variable Whole Life, introduced in the high-inflation days of the 1970's, which effectively addressed the demand on the part of consumers for a **competitive rate of return** on cash value. It did this by separating (unbundling) the cash value from the rest of the Policy and **allowing the Policyholder** (rather than the insurance company) **to choose how his cash value will be invested** from a series of separate investment sub-accounts or mutual funds. These sub-accounts (Mutual Funds) are invested in securities like stocks and bonds, are managed separately, with the net gain (or loss) credited directly to the Insured's cash value. As a result**, the cash value in a Variable Whole Life Policy is not guaranteed**. *The Insured, not the insurance company, assumes the risk* of cash value investment decisions. At the same time, since the Insured directly participates in all gains, there is also virtually unlimited potential for cash value growth – and in turn, death benefit growth.

2 Because of the way the cash value is invested and credited, Variable Whole Life has been described as **Whole Life insurance with the Policyowner choosing the investment portfolio for the cash value**.

Key Features

3 Like traditional Whole Life policies, Variable Whole Life:

- Offers permanent, lifelong insurance protection.

- Provides a guaranteed **minimum death benefit**.

- Provides for the payment of **fixed, level premiums**.

4 However, *unlike* traditional Whole Life policies:

- The cash value in a Variable life Policy is *not* invested in the company's **General Account**, which is principally invested in bonds and mortgages. Though quite safe, the investment return is not very attractive. The cash value in a Variable Life Policy, on the other hand, **is *not* guaranteed**. Instead, it floats freely, increasing or decreasing in direct response to investment performance of the **separate cash value** investment portfolio selected by the Insured.

- The death benefit can increase or decrease – although indirectly, not dollar for dollar – with corresponding increases or decreases in the cash value; however, the death benefit can *never* drop below the guaranteed minimum, as long as scheduled premiums are paid and the Policy remains in force.

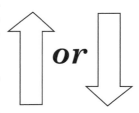

- You must possess a special **securities license from the SEC or NASD / FINRA**, in addition to your regular state life insurance license, if you are to sell Variable Life because it is considered to be a security.

The Separate Investment Account

1 The key to the value of Variable Life is in the way cash value is allocated, controlled and managed. Throughout our earlier discussions of traditional Whole Life insurance, we purposely avoided any reference to *investments*. With Variable Life, however, we must address investments, since specific securities investment vehicles are part of the Policy itself. In fact, Variable Life has been designed specifically to take advantage of the benefits of tax-advantaged investment growth potential, effectively combining elements of traditional life insurance protection with contemporary investment concepts.

2 The uniqueness of Variable Life is that it gives Insureds enhanced investment control – a choice in how their cash value is invested. Most companies offer dozens of cash value investment options. Each account functions as a totally separate investment pool and is managed by separate folks.

3 Typical investment portfolio choices include, but are not limited to, a Common Stock fund, a Bond fund, a Money Market fund and perhaps a Managed (or Balanced) fund. Each fund has its own investment objective. Generally, one or two will be aggressive by design (with above average risk, accompanied by above average potential for gain), while others will be more conservative. Generally, one will even offer a fixed, guaranteed rate of return. In this way, Insureds can select investment accounts which reflect their personal financial objectives and investment philosophies.

Mutual Funds

4 Joe can also change his premium allocation and switch his cash value from one account to another at any time to reflect the changes in market performance of the funds, as well as his own changing attitude about risk.

5 This combination of investment options and the ability to switch investment vehicles affords the Policyholder a high degree of investment control.

Flexibility

Changes in the Death Benefit

Variable Whole Life has a minimum death benefit, often referred to as the "selected amount". As long as the Policy remains in force, the death benefit cannot fall below this amount. However, the death benefit can be increased in several ways:

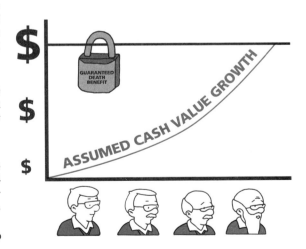

- The death benefit can increase or decrease with corresponding increases or decreases in the cash value, but it will not decrease below the guaranteed minimum death benefit

- The Policyholder can pay additional premium, within limits, thereby building up the cash value which, after a certain point, will automatically lead to increases in the death benefit.

- Above average cash value growth may lead to mandatory increases in the death benefit.

Perhaps you're wondering why the death benefit *must* increase with increases in the cash value. The answer lies in the legal definition of life insurance. Under current law, life insurance enjoys some rather important tax benefits. However, in order to retain that special status as life insurance (rather than a Modified Endowment Contract) a certain minimum ratio must be maintained between the death benefit and the cash value in a Policy. This is never a problem in traditional cash value policies, since the cash value growth is carefully controlled. However, it can become a problem in Variable Policies. This is why, to maintain that ratio, when the cash value in a Variable Life Policy reaches a certain level, the death benefit must be increased automatically.

What actually happens is fairly simple. When the Policy is issued, the company does not *guarantee* a rate of return on cash value, but it does *assume* a rather conservative investment return called the **Assumed Interest Rate (AIR)**. If the rate of return *exceeds* the AIR, then the cash value could equal the face value long before the Insured reaches age 95, or it could grow at a rate faster than would be generated under a Seven-Pay Whole Life Policy. To avoid the tax problems which would be created by this occurrence, the face value is increased to create a "**corridor**" between the face value and the cash value. If the rate of return should then decrease below the AIR, the face value would drop, **but never below the minimum guaranteed death benefit of the Policy**.

How to avoid a Modofied Endowment Contract

Loan Values

The Variable Whole Life rules and procedures governing the withdrawal of cash value or obtaining Policy loans are somewhat different from those of traditional Whole Life. Since cash value in Variable Life policies is created as soon as the first premium is paid, Policy loans are theoretically available immediately (although most policies require that loans not be taken for the first year). After the first Policy year, the Insured can borrow up to a certain percentage of the cash value (between 75% and 90%, depending on the company).

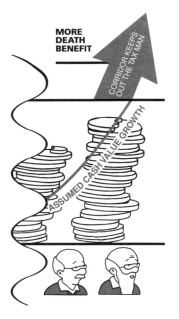

Regulations and Agent Responsibilities

1 Variable Life is unique in that it has **characteristics of both life insurance and securities**. Because of its dual personality, Variable Life is **dually regulated** under the appropriate state insurance and securities laws, as well as under the federal Securities and Exchange Commission (SEC).

2 Since Variable Life is also regulated as a security, **you cannot market a Variable product until you meet the necessary licensing requirements**. These include:

FINRA: Financial Industry Regulatory Authority

- A life insurance license.

- **A securities license from the SEC or NASD / FINRA.**

- And, in some states, a separate Variable Contracts license.

3 Also, while you cannot misrepresent any life product to a member of the public, you must take additional care when discussing Variable Life and other variable products. Specifically, be sure to comply with the following **Disclosure Rules**:

A. **A current prospectus** *must* be provided to the Prospect at the time of your presentation.

B. **Only approved sales literature and illustrations** should be shown or given to a Prospect.

C. **No verbal guarantees or statements** of any kind not expressly contained in the prospectus or Policy should be given to a Prospect.

D. **Your recommendation of a variable product must be suitable** for your client's needs and situation.

E. The 12% rule says that Agents may not use a rate in excess of 12% to illustrate projections. Even if a remarkable return of 15% was enjoyed one year, projecting it into the future would create unrealistic expectations on the part of the client.

Universal Life - UL

1 Universal Life is conceptually the natural next step beyond Adjustable Life. Universal Life, created in the 1980s, is essentially Adjustable Life on steroids. The computer has rendered the concept of Whole Life totally flexible!

2 Before we tear the Policy down and examine its components and even before we analyze the unique structure of Universal Life, let's briefly mention a few of the benefits its structure allows:

1. UL can imitate either of the two traditional insurance products – Term or Whole Life.

   Term

2. UL is **permanent insurance**. Even though the protection element of the Policy is **always expressed Term insurance**, the contract can provide coverage through age 100.

3. As with Adjustable Life, **death benefits can be raised** (with evidence of insurability) **or lowered** according to the needs of the Policyowner.

   How much DB do you need today?

4. As with Variable Whole Life, the **cash value can grow at a much higher rate of interest**, but

   Interest Sensitive

5. Unlike Variable Whole Life, there is a **minimum guaranteed rate of interest**.

   Min. Interest Rate

6. Though Policy loans can work just as they do with other cash value policies, it is also possible to make a **cash withdrawal (partial surrender)** from a UL Policy that neither has to be repaid, nor requires the payment of interest. Principle comes out first. Therefore, the tax ramifications are minimal.

   Partial Surrenders

7. **Premiums are even more flexible** than with Adjustable Life as they can be raised, lowered or even skipped entirely ("Stop and Go" feature).

   Flex Premiums

8. It is possible to structure UL so that the **cash value is paid *in addition to* the death benefit**.

   D.B. & C.V.

3 About the only benefit we have seen in any Policy that is *not found* in a typical UL Policy is the provision for the Policyowner to decide how the cash value will be invested.

   =Variable VL

The Structure of Universal Life

1   The premium Joe Insured pays into a Universal Life Policy is first credited to a fund which is called the **cash value** of the Policy. Soon, the amount of cash value not only reflects what Joe has paid, but also what the company has earned with Joe's money. First, there is **a guaranteed minimum rate** of interest – typically in the range of 4%. Next, there is also a **current rate** which reflects what the company is currently paying on the cash value of the money. These rates will vary with market conditions but have ranged from 5% to 8%. As with all other life insurance policies we've studied, the **cash value of a UL Policy grows on a tax deferred basis**. From the cash value, money is taken to:

Minimum Rate

Current Rate

- **Pay company expenses** – commissions, premium taxes, and administrative costs.

Expenses

- Purchase Term insurance – which is **always** the protection element of a UL Policy.

Term

2   It is interesting to note that none of these components are new to you. You know what cash value is. Term insurance as pure protection is not a new concept, and company expenses as an element of pricing is hardly a foreign concept. However, it is the unique arrangement of these familiar components that allows the UL Policy to function as it does.

CASH VALUE NOT CARVED-IN-STONE

3   – Unlike the traditional policies, UL policies do not attempt to *force* a particular cash value that the Policy should have at any given time. Yes, at the time of purchase, the company can tell Joe that if he pays a specific premium, he will have at least a cash value of a specific amount after a specific time. And yes, the rate of growth is subject to a minimum guarantee. But, Joe's cash value under a UL Policy can be whatever he wants it to be. The more he pays in premium, the greater his cash value and vice versa.

Save as Much as You Want

4   By not guaranteeing the cash value in the traditional sense, the company essentially allows Joe to decide how he wants his Policy to function. When Joe purchases the Policy, he is typically quoted two numbers – a **minimum premium** and a **target premium**. If he pays the *minimum premium*, the Policy will closely resemble Term insurance. There will be no build-up of cash value, as nearly all the dollars will be drained to buy the Term and pay the expenses. If he pays the *target premium*, the Policy will function much like a Whole Life Policy. Based upon interest rates guaranteed in the Policy, the cash value would equal the face value by age 100. If he pays more than the target premium, the Policy can begin to work similarly to an Endowment, but of course, the federal guidelines dictate that the cash value cannot build at a rate faster than a Seven-Pay Whole Life contract. If it should, the contract becomes *a Modified Endowment Contract* (in the jargon of the federal tax code) and loses many of its tax advantages.

Minimum Premium
Target Premium

COMPANY TAKES OUT FEES, CHARGES AND EXPENSES

1 Most importantly, if the needs of a client change, the Policy can change to accommodate. Joe could start out paying minimum premium and use his UL coverage much like a Term Policy. If later, his ability to pay premiums increases and he wants the Policy to function more like Whole Life, all he has to do is pay more premium. He does not have to make a formal request for a change in his plan, as changes are computed automatically based upon the amount of premium paid (or, for that matter, not paid).

Flexible Premium

2 **PREMIUMS CAN BE SKIPPED** – It's also possible for the process to work in reverse. Suppose Joe paid the target premium for several years and suddenly took a severe salary cut. If he wanted to start paying only the minimum premium, it would be no problem. In fact, it's possible that if Joe lost his job completely and wanted to discontinue paying premiums altogether for awhile, he could do so. The company doesn't care how much cash value Joe has as long as there's enough to buy the insurance and pay the expenses. Depending upon the amount of cash value Joe has when he stops paying and the interest rate at which that money is earning, it is possible for Joe to avoid paying premiums for quite a long time.

can even skip premiums

3 **PREMIUMS WILL VARY** – Let's suppose that at age 40, Joe buys a UL Policy in the amount of $100,000, and he tells the company that he plans to pay the target premium of $1450 on an annual basis. After he's paid his initial premium, the company will not send him a *premium due notice* per se. Since (within limits) he can pay whatever he wants, the company will actually send him a *reminder notice*. However, it might not always indicate $1450 as the target premium. It could be $1350, or it could be $1500 – depending upon the current interest earnings the company is experiencing on the Policy's cash value.

4 **DEATH BENEFIT POSSIBILITIES** – With a UL Policy, **Joe can make his death benefit whatever he wants it to be**. If he starts with a $100,000 death benefit and later in life finds that his needs for insurance have decreased, he can decrease the death benefit. If, on the other hand, his need goes up, he can increase his death benefit if he can show proof of insurability.

two options

5 But that's no big deal – we've seen that before. With a UL Policy, the death benefit is greatly dependent upon how the Policyowner wants the Policy to function. For instance, if Joe wants the Policy to work in a manner similar to a traditional Term Policy, he can choose a death benefit of, say, $100,000 and pay the minimum premium. Under these circumstances, the death benefit would always be $100,000. The positive aspect is that it costs Joe the fewest dollars today. The negative, of course, is that it will cost him more dollars tomorrow.

Option #1

OPTION #1

6 If Joe chooses to have his Universal Life Policy function similarly to a traditional Whole Life Policy, he has two options. **Option #1** works very much like Whole Life insurance, and the standard rules apply – the death benefit is level, and **the Policy can pay either the death benefit or the cash value, but not both**.

Death Benefit Only

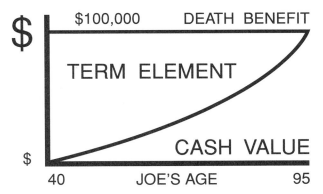

As you can see in the illustration above, the death benefit is a constant – in Joe's
1   case, $100,000. However, the source of the $100,000 changes gradually. In year
one, most of the death benefit comes from the Term insurance element. As the years
pass, the Term decreases as the cash value increases to become a larger and larger
part of the death benefit. One real advantage of this option is that Joe is purchasing less and less Term insurance each year to fund his desired death benefit. And,
this need for less Term insurance comes exactly at the time when the cost of Term
begins to get expensive.

One potential tax problem can be created by this arrangement. As you recall, the
2   Tax Reform Act of 1988 said that cash value could grow no faster than it would under a Seven-Pay Whole Life Policy. If the company set the target premium a little
high, or if the Policyowner was paying additional premium, or if the interest earned
on the cash value was more than anticipated – the contract would be considered an
investment contract / MEC and we would have tax ramifications galore. The usual
solution to this predicament would be as shown in the illustration below.

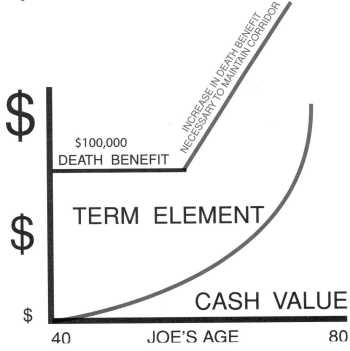

As you can see, the death benefit automatically increases to create a cash value cor-
3   ridor which maintains the contract's status and tax treatment as a life insurance
Policy. Another approach would be to withdraw some of the cash value.

1   Regardless of how it's handled, it should be obvious that the death benefit of a UL Policy is not the absolute carved-in-granite number it tends to be with the traditional products. Even with the relatively straightforward Option #1, there are several ways in which the death benefit could be different than the $100,000 that Joe originally selected.

- Any **cash withdrawals** (partial surrenders) which are not paid back would reduce the death benefit.

- When the cash value gets too close to the face value, the cash value corridor approach would raise the death benefit to exceed $100,000.

Option #2

2   Option #2 completely violates a fundamental rule we learned with traditional policies. Under this approach, the death benefit is composed of **LEVEL TERM INSURANCE PLUS THE CASH VALUE**.

the Death Benefit

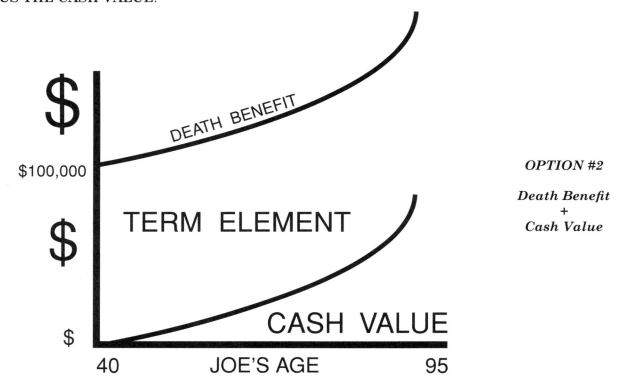

OPTION #2

*Death Benefit
+
Cash Value*

3   With this option, Joe has absolutely no idea what the death benefit will be. Even if he does nothing to foul the works (like skipping premium payments or withdrawing cash), he does not know when he will die, and therefore, he can't know what the cash value will be. All he can know is that its death benefit will be $100,000 plus whatever the cash value happens to be when he dies.

4   The obvious disadvantage to this approach is that the cost of Level Term insurance at advanced ages becomes very expensive. Many Policyowners who start with Option #2 ultimately switch to Option #1 when the cost of the Term simply becomes too great.

1   **SIMPLICITY** – Probably as important as any of the mechanical benefits of UL is its basic simplicity. The **death benefit and the cash value are completely separated (unbundled)** which makes it quite simple for the Policyowner to **see how much he is paying for the Term protection portion and exactly what he is earning with his cash value**. In many respects, the UL Policy is a response to the consumer who wants to "buy Term and invest the rest". The UL Policy allows the insurance industry to respond with, **"Okay, buy our Term and invest the rest with us – on a tax deferred basis."**

2   **Waiver of Cost of Insurance** - Since premiums vary with Universal Life, the traditional Waiver of Premium rider can work in either of two ways. If it is called a **Waiver of Premium** rider it pays, in the event of the Policyowner's disability, what has been the average premium paid during, for instance, the last 36 months. A less expensive version is called the **Waiver of Cost of Insurance** rider. It pays only enough to keep the cost of the Term insurance paid.

Variable Universal Life

3   Following Universal Life is a little like following a Beatles reunion – you can perhaps find a better drummer, but you can only go so far. Variable Universal Life is simply the next logical evolution of product development as it combines all of the features of Universal Life with the investment control benefit of Variable Life.

securities version of U.L.

4   Specifically, VUL contains the features we found in Universal Life, which include:

- The ability to increase, decrease or even skip premiums altogether (within limits).

- Dump large amounts of money into the plan.

- Increase (with evidence of insurability) or decrease the amount of life insurance.

- Take money out of the plan as a cash withdrawal or as a Policy loan.

Investment Vehicle

Partial Surrender

In addition, VUL gives the Policyowner the **right to select the investment vehicle** for the Policy's cash value from a number of different options. Furthermore, the opportunity to change from one investment fund to another without charge is typically offered four to five times a year.

However, unlike Universal Life, most of the investment vehicles **have no guaranteed return**. Like Variable Life, Variable Universal Life is considered **a security**. It is dually regulated and the Agent must be dually licensed.

1

SECURITIES REGULATION

There are three primary federal laws that regulate the sale of securities in this country:

- The Securities Act of 1933 – This law regulates the sale of new security issues. Example: Coca-Cola is going to sell another one million shares to fund its expansion into China.

- The Securities Exchange Act of 1934 – This law regulates the trading of existing shares and the markets (exchanges) through which the shares are traded.

- The Investment Company Act of 1940 – This law regulates companies who take your money (and a lot of other people's) and invest it on their behalf. Example: Mutual Funds and Variable Annuities.

No Churning - the buying and selling of securities within a client account for the purpose of generating commission income is forbidden

CONCLUSION

2
Though the chart on the previous two pages is an excellent reference concerning the many differences that exist between the policies you have just learned about, it would be a bit much to memorize. Therefore, we have condensed and modified it somewhat to reflect only the information you absolutely, positively need to know. It is easy to memorize and can easily (and legally) be recreated on scratch paper at a test center.

Distinguishing the Four Policies

	PREMIUM	DEATH BENEFIT	CASH VALUE	TYPE OF INSURANCE
ADJUSTABLE	FLEX.	FLEX.	GUAR.	TERM/WL
VARIABLE WHOLE LIFE	FIXED	MIN. GUAR.	NOT GUAR.	WL
UNIVERSAL	FLEX.	FLEX.	MIN. GUAR INT. SENS	TERM
VAR. UNIVERSAL	FLEX	FLEX.	NOT GUAR.	TERM

Here's a key to the terms used in the chart above:
FLEX=FLEXIBLE
GUAR=GUARANTEED
MIN. GUAR=MINIMUM GUARANTEED
NOT GUAR=NOT GUARANTEED
WL=WHOLE LIFE
INT SENS=INTEREST SENSITIVE

1   A quick glance at the chart answers most of the questions that could be raised about these contracts. *Is the cash value of a Variable Whole Life Policy guaranteed?* No. *The insuring element of a Universal Life Policy is what kind of insurance?* Term.

2   Although Chapter 9 introduced some contracts that have flexibility and features well beyond the traditional life policies, these flexible feature contracts are not difficult to understand when broken down to their key components. Learn the chart and use it!

DON'T GO ON UNTIL YOU KNOW THESE

LIFE INSURANCE

TERM INSURANCE	Provides the most insurance for the least dollars. Death protection only. Matures only at death. . . during the term.
LEVEL PREMIUM TERM	Premium remains level.
DECREASING TERM	Death Benefit decreases with time.
INCREASING TERM	Death Benefit increases with time.
LEVEL TERM	Death Benefit always remains level.
RENEWABLE TERM	Term that can be renewed without proof of insurability. . . but at a higher premium.
RE-ENTRY TERM	Renewable Term which allows the Insured to reestablish insurability. . .to earn a lower premium.
CONVERTIBLE TERM	Term that can be converted to Whole Life (at attained age) without proof of insurability. . . but at a much higher premium.
WHOLE LIFE	Death Protection to age 100 with guaranteed cash value growth and premiums remain level.
FAMILY Policy	Whole Life and Convertible Term for the entire family.
FAMILY INCOME	Covers only the breadwinner with Whole Life and Decreasing Term.
MODIFIED LIFE	Term that automatically converts to Whole Life.
GRADED PREMIUM	Whole Life that starts out cheap and becomes more expensive.

INTEREST SENSITIVE WHOLE LIFE	A Whole Life Policy written using current assumptions concerning mortality, interest and expenses. Cash value can grow at rates higher than the guaranteed minimum.
ADJUSTABLE LIFE	Policyowner can choose two of the three: death benefit, premium or type of insurance (Whole Life/Term).
VARIABLE LIFE	AKA Variable Whole Life. Cash value not guaranteed. A minimum Death Benefit is guaranteed. Owner can control where cash value is invested.
UNIVERSAL LIFE	Death protection is always Term. Owner can make Policy function like Term or Whole Life by pumping in more or less cash. Owner can take money from cash value without paying it back.
VARIABLE UNIVERSAL LIFE	Same as Universal plus owner can also control where cash value is invested. No guaranteed cash value.
MODIFIED ENDOWMENT CONTRACT	Occurs when your cash value grows too fast. When it happens you lose all the tax benefits of a life insurance Policy.
JOINT LIFE	Two or more Insureds. Pays upon death of the first.
SURVIVORSHIP LIFE	Two or more Insureds. Pays upon death of the last.

ANNUITIES

(STRAIGHT) LIFE ANNUITY	Provides retirement income for the rest of your life.
LIFE ANNUITY WITH PERIOD CERTAIN	Guarantees retirement income for the rest of your life. Even if you die, the company will continue paying your income until the end of the period certain (i.e. 5 years, 10 years, etc.).
REFUND LIFE ANNUITY	Guarantees you an income for life, but if you die before collecting the total face amount of your annuity, the company will refund the remainder to your heirs. NOT A DEATH BENEFIT!!
JOINT AND SURVIVOR LIFE ANNUITY	Provides retirement income so long as either you or your spouse is alive.
DOUBLE JOINTED ANNUITY	Provides income for anyone who can reach an arm over their head and pull their wallet out of their back pocket. Primarily for **circus people.**
IMMEDIATE ANNUITY	Begin receiving income now.
DEFERRED ANNUITY	Wait to start collecting income.
VARIABLE ANNUITY	The value of your account is in units, not dollars. Company guarantees a certain number of units for the rest of your life. Value in dollars can go up... or down.
ANNUITY CERTAIN	Not guaranteed for life. You put money in. Company pays it out. Definite start, definite stop - like a bridge.

Life Insurance Tax Facts

The Prime Directives:

Part I...   The Fed's don't tax wealth. They tax the transfer of wealth...ownership of the money must change hands for there to be a tax impact.

Part II...   If the money is earned, the receiver is taxed. If the money is a gift, the giver pays the tax.

Part III...   *The coming or going rule*: if you were not taxed on the way in, you'll be taxed on the way out. If you were taxed on the way in, the principle will not be taxed on the way out.

Some Specifics:

Life Insurance Proceeds:

One, No income tax impact... *Two*, to the Beneficiary... *Three*, on a death benefit. **However,** interest earned on the proceeds will be subject to tax.

Cash Value:

Taxes on the growth are sheltered as long as the money is left with the company. **Should** the Policyowner take the cash value, the **growth** will be taxed as **ordinary income** for the **year** in which the money was **received.**

Cash Value:

Dividends, paid by a mutual to a Policyowner are not subject to tax (after all it was always their money...no real change in ownership). **However,** interest earned on dividends will be subject to tax.

Loans:

No tax...again no change in the ownership,

Whoosh   Cash value that grows **too quickly** will lose tax advantages...Tax Reform Act of 1984 virtually eliminates the Endowment Policy... under **TAMRA**, any Policy whose cash value grows faster than a 7 Pay Whole Life...Shazam! becomes a **Modified Endowment Contract.**

Whoa, Nellie! Flexible and variable policies have corridors which keep the death benefit ahead of the cash value to avoid negative tax impacts.

1035, Good Buddy:

A Section 1035 Exchange is when one Policy is exchanged for another...**No Tax!**

Business Uses of Life Insurance:

The Place to Start...Who is the Beneficiary?...If the business is the Beneficiary, no tax on proceeds, but the premiums are not tax deductible. *Examples:* Key Employee and policies funding Stock Redemption Agreements. Policies in which the business is not the Beneficiary the premium will be deductible as an expense. Example: The employer's portion of a Group Life Policy.

Part III
HEALTH INSURANCE

FUNDAMENTALS OF HEALTH INSURANCE

10

1   We are aware that with the passage of the Health Care Reform Law of 2010, some of what we know about health insurance will change in the future. It is important to realize that some of those changes will be gradually introduced, and others will become effective much sooner.

2   Some changes will be reflective of a fundamental difference in how the health insurance business is conducted, while others are more subtle and will have less of an impact. Whatever the case, there is still a need for you to understand the language of the business. So, for example, while coverage for *preexisting conditions* will change, the definition of the term is still important.

Change is in the air

3   Please trust that Pathfinder is monitoring relevant changes as they are implemented and will publish addenda as required. For now, the depiction of health insurance in our text is still accurate for the exam that you will be taking.

4   The next six chapters of this text address the subject of health insurance. As we did in life insurance, we will first identify the consumer needs served by the health products we will study, and then take an overview of the subject in this chapter. We will find that health insurance focuses on two problems with two products which can be purchased in two ways from two suppliers which may address one or both of two perils. As we recover from our overdose of "two's", we will look at the elements common to almost all health policies regardless of which problem we're solving or which Policy we use or which kind of supplier we choose to buy from. Finally, since tax ramifications so often guide consumers with any purchase, we will examine the tax consequences of buying health insurance.

2s

WHAT'S WORSE THAN DEATH?

5   In the first chapter of this text, we created an example in which Joe and Jolene were each earning $25,000 a year for life. If this continued for 40 years, family income would total $2 million, and with careful planning, they should be able to enjoy a comfortable lifestyle. We pointed out that the *economic death* of either could shatter this blissful picture in any one of three forms – physical death, retirement death or living death (disability). In the first portion of this text, you studied contracts designed to offset the financial loss which follows death or retirement.

1 As we turn our attention to living death (disability), we should note from the beginning that we are now focusing on a problem that is much more likely to occur than death, and one which could prove to be even more financially devastating. At age 40, Joe and Jolene each have about a 50% chance of becoming disabled for three months or longer before age 65. This is about 300% greater than the probability of death at the same age. Even more important than probabilities are the financial ramifications of a prolonged disability. A disability can eliminate income just as surely as death or retirement. But with death or retirement, the consumption of dollars stops or slows down. With disability, the normal expenses of living continue, and on top of everything else, we find a layer of new expenses – the medical costs of treating the disability. Although it is somewhat cruel to say, it is probably true that Joe's family could better withstand the economic impact of his death than his prolonged disability.

Living Death

Our Fastest Growing Problem

2 As we enter the second decade of a new century, we find that in the United States, we are spending more than $2 trillion a year on health care; that's more than $7,000 per person every year, and an increase of more than 900% in the last two decades. Doctor's fees, hospital bills and other medical expenses account for nearly 23% of our total expenditures as a society.

$ $!

3 As you might guess, the price of health insurance is growing just as rapidly. Health insurance premiums have been increasing at the rate of more than 25% each year. Unfortunately, this cost increase comes at a time when the average American (or average American family) simply cannot do without health insurance. We live in a world where the cost of treatment in a community hospital averages $1,500 per day. Having a baby without complications can cost upwards of $20,000. Even something so minor as a child with an earache can easily cost $1,000.

4 All things considered, we might give some consideration to adopting the ancient Chinese custom of purchasing health care – they paid the doctor when they were well and stopped paying when they were ill.

Mental Shift

5 As you move from the study of life insurance to health insurance, you will find that the basic insurance principles will remain intact. However, there are some additional complications in health insurance that will require more attention to detail on your part. For one thing, commonly used terms can have very different meanings. In this area of insurance, even the title of the subject is not consistent. You will hear health insurance called *accident and health* insurance, *sickness and accident* insurance, and in the laws of about a dozen states, *disability* insurance. In this text, we will use the term health insurance as the all-inclusive heading for the various categories of policies generally sold and regulated as health insurance.

However, some of the inconsistencies simply cannot be handled this easily. You will
1 encounter policies that would consider a surgeon to be disabled if he so much as cut a finger on his operating hand. You will find others which would not consider the same surgeon disabled if he had two broken arms and two broken legs! This was not a possibility in life insurance as there are but few ways to define *death*, but there are at least a half a dozen commonly accepted definitions of *disability*. These variations are beneficial to the consuming public because they represent consumer choices in both price and coverage. However, this spectrum of meanings only complicates the task of learning about health insurance. In order for you to get the most from our discussion, you must be willing to accept diversity and you must be attentive to the nuances of difference that exist from one Policy to another. In fact, you must be willing to accept from the start that there is no such thing as a "standard" health insurance Policy.

Health: Shades of grey

Though no one set out to make health insurance complicated, it's somewhat the na-
2 ture of the beast. The promise of life insurance was relatively straightforward – if you die, we will pay. Death was the only peril, there was but one claim per customer, proof of loss was hard to falsify, and the exclusions were few.

an evolution- ary mess

Things are not as simple in health insurance. In this arena, almost every Policy is
3 complicated by each company's attempts to contain costs. Exclusions, restrictions and limitations are numerous and differ from Policy to Policy and from company to company. Numerous types of deductibles and a variety of cost-sharing devices are used to discourage the over-utilization of the Policy, to eliminate small claims and to keep the price affordable.

complicated policies

Although the idea of a dead person trying to acquire life insurance is almost laugh-
4 able, the reality of someone who is already ill trying to purchase health insurance is a real problem, and it's not a problem that stops with adverse selection. Out and out fraud is a much bigger concern in health than in life insurance. Despite what some of our spouses might say, most of us are not too adept at playing dead, but most of us have been accomplished at playing sick since about the third grade. Therefore, health policies contain multiple devices to screen out preexisting conditions, and proof of loss can be *purposely* quite complicated. Even intentional losses are a concern on this side of the business. No matter how much life insurance we might have, most of us are unwilling to die in order to collect. However, if you make $6,000 a month working and own three policies which would each pay you $5,000 a month if you were disabled, you could probably find a way to get disabled and stay disabled.

fraud rampant

Suffice it to say, the only way you can determine if a specific loss is covered under a
5 health Policy is to read that specific Policy. Since this text is designed for the entry level Agent, our objective is to simplify rather than complicate. We will outline how the commonly used policies function most of the time for most companies in most states. If you are aware of a difference between a Policy you own or plan to sell and a similar Policy addressed in this text, please do not let that alarm you. Most companies will differentiate their products to some degree. Your job at the present is to learn the basics of health insurance. You will spend the rest of your career learning the exceptions.

Health care is complicated

Two Problems

1 As we have already suggested, an American wage earner who suffers a severe **sickness** or **accidental injury** faces two problems – not one. The cost of medical care is a biggie. Since most of us operate on budgets that are barely out of the red, even a trip to the doctor's office and the pharmacy places a minor hardship upon us. A couple of weeks in the hospital, a serious operation or an extensive series of treatments could easily wreck most family budgets. It's wonderful that we live in an age where medical science can routinely do miracles, but the cost of these miracles is staggering. A coronary by-pass is rather commonplace in the 2000's, but the average cost for the surgeon alone was $10,000 at the beginning of the decade and approached $30,000 in the year 2010. Despite the obvious financial impact of the costs of medical care, the second problem may be of even greater consequence than the first.

income down

2 A simple fact of life for most of us is that if we don't work, we don't get paid. How soon you have to deal with an empty pay envelope will vary somewhat with the benefits package your employer offers (or fails to offer), but at some point, even the most generous employer cannot continue to pay you to stay home.

expenses up

3 When these two problems are super-imposed over each other, the financial stability of most families could be shattered beyond repair in a rather short period of time.

bankruptcy

TWO POLICIES

4 To deal with the two problems we've outlined, we find that two broad and very distinct categories of insurance exist under the heading of health insurance.

Disability Income Policies – These policies are designed to replace your paycheck if you become disabled and cannot work. Though you may encounter these policies under names like Loss of Time, **Loss of Income** or Income Protection policies, these names are nothing more than another way to say Disability Income. All of them simply provide a **substitute paycheck** if you become disabled and cannot continue to work.

lost income

Medical Expense Policies – The purpose of these policies is to **offset the costs of health care** (doctors, hospitals, etc.). Policies in this category can be rather limited in scope and benefits like the Basic plans we will meet shortly, or they can be all encompassing arrangements like Major Medical or Comprehensive Medical Expense.

medical bills

5 Beyond this rather significant difference in purpose, there are at least a half-dozen more ways in which Medical Expense and Disability Income policies differ from one another.

1 **Who Gets Paid?** – **Disability Income** policies are generally designed to **pay the Insureds** – Joe and Jolene. **Medical Expense** policies are designed to **pay their health care providers** – doctors and hospitals.

2 **For What Purpose?** – The dollars paid to Joe and Jolene from a **Disability Income** Policy function as a **substitute paycheck**. If Joe was bringing home a paycheck of $500 a week, his Policy might pay $400 each week while he is disabled. (Companies will typically sell policies which only cover 60% to 80% of your regular salary in order to provide an incentive to return to work.) The important point to understand is that this money *is not designed to pay Joe's medical bills* – **it is to cover his normal expenses** like rent, food, utilities, clothing and daycare. The **Medical Expense** policies, on the other hand, are designed to **cover the medical costs** Joe incurs during his disability.

DI

Face Amount

3 **How Are Benefits Promised?** – **Disability Income policies** are **valued (or stated amount) contracts**. These policies resemble life insurance contracts in that they have a *face amount*. They will pay $600 per week or $2,000 every two weeks or $3,000 a month, depending upon the income of the Insured, the frequency of payments called for by the contract and the size of the dollar benefits purchased.

4 **Medical Expense** policies, however, are designed to **pay on a reimbursement or a service basis**. You can pay for the treatment you need and we'll reimburse you, or we will provide the services you need when you need them. Either way if the medical procedures and the charges for the procedures are *reasonable, necessary and customary*, the Medical Expense contracts will cover them. For instance, if you break your leg in Lansing, Michigan, your medical bill might be $2,000. If I suffer an identical injury in Chicago, Illinois, my bill could be $3,000. Disregarding deductibles and coinsurance for now, your Medical Expense Policy would pay $2,000, and mine would pay $3,000. (Yes, people who live in areas where medical costs are higher pay more in premium.) However, the critical concept to note is that Medical Expense policies do not have a specific dollar amount established for broken legs. These policies simply **reimburse** for reasonable, necessary and customary charges.

Med Expense

Make Whole

5 It is worth noting that until recently, Medical Expense policies sold by regular stock or mutual companies were even more obviously **reimbursement** contracts. They were written with the idea that if you needed medical care, you paid the bill and submitted a claim. The company would then *reimburse* you for what you had paid. Nowadays, that process doesn't work very well. Most people could not cover a 10 day hospital stay out of their checking account while they were waiting to be reimbursed. Most of us simply **assign** benefits to the hospital and then negotiate installments to pay for anything the Policy did not cover. Despite this, Medical Expense policies are still reimbursement contracts – even if they are not as obvious about it as they once were.

reimbursement or service contracts

6 **When Are Benefits Paid?** – Since **Disability Income** policies are designed to function as *substitute paychecks*, they normally are written to **pay at the same interval that you receive your paycheck**. Though most state laws prohibit contracts that pay less frequently than monthly, almost any other timetable is possible. Most commonly, DI policies pay monthly.

periodically

Notes

once

1 **Medical Expense** policies are written to pay *lump sum benefits*. If Jolene is admitted to St. Joe's Hospital and the bill is $2,200, then the Policy pays $2,200. (Again, we are disregarding deductibles and coinsurance at this point.)

2 **Who Is Insured?** – Because **Disability Income** policies replace income, these contracts insure the **breadwinner(s)** of the family. Since Joe and Jolene are dual breadwinners, each should have Disability Income coverage. It would not make sense to insure their children under a Disability Income Policy as the kids don't contribute to the household income. Only if your little darling happens to be the Gerber baby or a TV celebrity or a pinball wizard would a Disability Income Policy be appropriate.

breadwinner

3 Alternatively, *Medical Expense policies cover the entire family* – mom, dad and the kids. In fact, given the level of germ warfare going on in most schools, kindergartens, and daycare centers across the country, it may even be more important to have the children covered than the parents.

whole family
kids to
age 26

4 **Is The Cost Predictable?** – This question is critically important to both the insurance company and the Policyowner. Insurance companies naturally feel more comfortable issuing a Policy that has an actuarially predictable cost of claims. For the Policyowner, this means that long-term price guarantees are possible, and this is the case with a Disability Income Policy. If Joe is promised $900 a week during a period of disability, the company is simply predicting the likelihood of a disability and the *cost* of dollars in the future. The company can easily quantify its risk and put a price tag on it. Joe could, therefore, purchase a **Disability Income Policy at age 25 that would guarantee price until age 65**.

DI - yes

5 Such is **not the case with Medical Expense policies**. The company has agreed to reimburse for all reasonable, necessary and customary medical costs. We said earlier that today you could repair a broken leg for $2,000 to $3,000. What will a broken leg cost in the year 2025? Nobody really knows. We might base a guess on the 900% increase we've seen in the last 20 years, but it would still be only a guess. You see, in addition to the things that we normally blame for the increase in the cost of health care – physician's salaries, unnecessary procedures, waste, inefficiency, malpractice claims and the like – there are also some miraculous medical breakthroughs that, unfortunately, carry a fairly high price tag. What if, in the year 2025, someone invents an Atomic Bone Healer? After two hours of therapy, your broken leg is completely healed. That would be fantastic, but the price of a broken leg just jumped to a reasonable, necessary and customary $20,000. As you might have guessed, insurance companies are not inclined to make long term price guarantees with Medical Expense policies. If Joe buys a Medical Expense Policy at age 25 that he plans to keep until 65, his company will, in all likelihood, reserve the right to *adjust* the premium over time. Of course, the word *adjust* is insurance lingo meaning *raise*.

Med Expense - no

costs out of
control

6 **How Are Deductibles Expressed?** – In health insurance, as in many areas of insurance, companies utilize *deductibles*. In simplest terms, a deductible tells the Insured, "First you pay and then we'll pay." Deductibles can be of great value to both the insurance company and the Policyowner. They tend to **discourage the over-utilization of the benefits** as well as to eliminate the most expensive of claims – the small claim. Consequently, the premiums are more affordable for the Policyowner. In fact, it is generally a good rule of thumb in the purchase of health insurance to establish a deductible at as high a level as you can withstand in order to obtain a better product at an affordable price.

D-Duck

"Skin in the
Gane"

Time deductible

$

1   Disability Income policies make use of a device known as an **Elimination Period** which is simply a **deductible expressed in terms of time**. For example, if Joe owns a Disability Income Policy with a 30-day Elimination Period, **he has to be disabled for 30 days before he is eligible for benefits**. If he recovers and becomes disabled again 10 years later, he will again have to go through the 30-day Elimination Period before he is eligible for benefits. The length of the Elimination Period could range from zero days to 365 days or more. Obviously, the longer Joe can meet his obligations without earning a paycheck and the longer deductible he can withstand, the lower his premium will be.

2   Medical Expense policies express deductibles in a form familiar to us all – dollars. As we will discover in our discussion of Medical Expense policies, dollar deductibles can come in many shapes, sizes, flavors and colors. But, at this point, only the most basic understanding is required. *You pay first, then we pay.*

Note to Student:

3   At this point, Medical Expense policies and Disability Income policies should be completely separate entities in your mind. If there is still some confusion, the following chart summarizes the differences that we have outlined and should help crystallize the characteristics of each.

Disability Income	Medical Expense
Covers a wage earner	Covers the entire family
Designed to replace income (Pay rent, food, utilities, etc.)	Designed to pay medical bills (Pay doctors, hospitals, etc.)
Valued(Stated Amount) Contract	Reimbursement Contract
Regular, periodic benefits	Lump sum benefits
Predictable claim cost	Unpredictable claim cost
Time Deductible (Elimination Period)	Dollar Deductible

Two Ways to Buy

1   In addition to the two Policy types that we have just examined, we find that with health insurance, as with life insurance, policies may be purchased on a **group** basis or on an **individual** basis. The odd thing about health insurance is that 90% of the Medical Expense coverage provided by insurance companies is delivered through the *group* mechanism, and 70% of Disability Income contracts are written as *individual* policies. However, both are available on either a group or an individual basis.

Individual
v.
Group

2   In this text, we will first discuss how both Policy types function as individual contracts. Then, we will note the differences that arise when either is sold as a group contract. In truth, the policies themselves vary only slightly – the major differences have to do with marketing, pricing, administration and underwriting. Since group insurance most frequently provides coverage for individuals and families through a master contract issued to an employer, there is much less likelihood of adverse selection. Marketing and administration costs are greatly reduced; hence, group insurance generally costs less than an individual plan with comparable coverages. Frequently, members of larger groups can obtain coverage without having to produce evidence of insurability. And, if anything, group policies tend to be slightly more generous with their benefits and less restrictive with exclusions and limitations.

"all of us. . ."

3   About the only place in our discussions where you will really need to be careful is in Chapter 12 – *Individual* Medical Expense policies. You may have to remind yourself several times that in all likelihood, you are not covered by an *individual* plan, but by a *group* plan. The differences are not big ones, but they can cause confusion if you try to fit your personal knowledge about your own group coverage into our discussion of individual plans.

Two Perils - Accident - Sickness

4   There are two major *causes of loss* (perils) under a health insurance Policy: **accidental injury** and **sickness**. A Policy can be written to cover both accident and sickness, or just **accident only**. While "accident only" policies serve some specific needs (i.e., flight policies, school policies or camp policies), anyone who purchases an "accident only" Policy thinking that he has full health coverage would be sadly mistaken. **About 90% of the health Policy claims in this country stem from sickness** – only about 10% of the claims are the result of an accident. For this reason, most states require "accident only" policies to be announced as "limited policies" on the first page of the contract.

Accident Only coverage. . . more holes than five pounds of Swiss cheese

5   For the most part, it is not difficult to classify an event as an accident or as a sickness. Tuberculosis is a sickness and a broken arm is an accident. About the only situation that confuses some of us is **pregnancy**. Despite what our parents told us, pregnancy is *not* an accident – it's a sickness.

MAJOR HEALTH INSURANCE PROVIDERS

Stock and Mutual Companies

*Stock
&
Mutual*

1 There are about 700 Life, Health, and (in some states) Casualty insurance companies writing health insurance contracts across the United States. They provide almost 100% of the commercially available Disability Income coverage sold and about 30% of the Medical Expense contracts in force. Both types of coverage are available to groups and to individuals, but, as we've noted, Disability Income policies tend to be sold to individuals and Medical Expense policies tend to be sold through the group mechanism.

2 For many years, the most obvious distinction between the commercial companies and the Blues was that the commercial companies paid benefits to the Policyowner while the Blues paid the medical vendor. Today, that distinction is practically gone. Most of us *assign our benefits* to the hospital and simply pay the deductible and any other costs not covered by the Policy. However, even though it is not as obvious, the commercial insurers still sell reimbursement contracts; they have no relationship with the providers of medical services.

Blue Cross and Blue Shield

service providers

the Blues Brothers

3 As we have pointed out, prior to the Great Depression, individuals and families were expected to pay medical costs out of their savings. But with the onslaught of the Depression, that noble concept became about as practical as the Oklahoma Department of Agriculture. Oh, yes, people still needed and received health care – they just couldn't pay for it. As hospitals saw their incomes evaporating, they looked with interest at the Baylor Hospital Experiment where a group of Dallas, Texas, schoolteachers essentially prepaid their hospital costs. From this idea came the Blue Cross plan. At first, **members or subscribers** to a Blue Cross contract only had coverage at a single hospital. But, due to the promotional efforts of the American Hospital Association, by the mid-1930's most plans had become statewide plans.

4 Obviously, the same Depression that made it difficult for hospitals to get paid for their services affected individual physicians as well. Local medical associations emulated Blue Cross by forming prepaid plans for doctors known as Blue Shield plans. This time, the American Medical Association began to promote these plans and eventually established a national coordinating body.

*501(c)
not for profit*

1. By the mid 1940's, the Blues owned the Health insurance marketplace. Consumers liked buying a **service contract**. Since the Blues simply treated Joe's broken arm rather than paying him for it, he avoided the need to pay up front, fill out the claim for us and wait to be reimbursed.

2. Of all the misinformation held by the average consumer about the Blues, two major misconceptions stand above all the others.

   - Blue Cross-Blue Shield is **not** a national organization.
   - Blue Cross is **not** the same as Blue Shield.

3. Today, there are about 39 organizations from which you can purchase Blue Cross and Blue Shield coverage. While they are normally set up to operate within a single state, some densely populated states have more than one organization with each working within a defined geographical area of that state. Likewise, in some sparsely populated areas, one organization may cross state boundaries. While there is a national organization designed to set broad standards and coordinate efforts, each local plan is operated by its own governing board. Therefore, the coverages, costs, benefits and contracts issued by these state organizations may differ substantially from one to the other. Since showing the benefits of one plan is easier than showing the benefits of 39 plans, it is generally accepted that the stock and mutual companies have at least one advantage over the Blues in marketing group insurance to organizations that have employees all over the country.

local or regional providers

4. As we've already said, Blue Cross was a plan designed to pay hospitals, and Blue Shield was designed to pay doctors. For many years, the subscribers to one plan tended to be subscribers to the other, and therefore, it has been only natural for the two plans to merge.

General Characteristics

5. Since the Blues operate independently throughout the country, there may be important differences between anything we say is generally true of the Blues and how the Blue Cross - Blue Shield plan operates in your particular state. Certainly, if you are employed by Blue Cross-Blue Shield or if you plan to compete with them, finding out how they operate in your own backyard will be important.

   - **Organization** – In most states, the Blues are organized as nonprofit organizations and regulated by the State Insurance Department under special legislation.

   501(c) s

   - **Taxes** – Their nonprofit status has historically exempted the Blues from state and federal taxation. While the Tax Reform Act of 1986 partially eliminated the federal tax advantage, the Blues generally enjoy some tax advantage over their competitors.

   - **Type of Contracts** – Though many states have relaxed their laws and today allow the Blues to sell other life and health products, the Blues mainly sell Medical Expense contracts.

- **Level of Benefits** – As the Blues are a product of the Great Depression, their contracts were originally rather basic in nature – low benefit levels, few limitations and very small (if any) deductibles. But in the early 1950's, when the stocks and mutuals became serious competition, the Blues began to broaden their scope and sell Major Medical and other *catastrophic* type coverages. Within the Medical Expense field, the contracts offered by the Blues today do not differ substantially from those sold by the traditional companies.

- **Individual vs. Group** – While Medical Expense coverage is dominated by Group coverage, the Blues will sell both individual and group plans.

  Group

- **National Coverage** – Though you typically purchase coverage from the Blues on a state-wide basis, your Policy is honored nationwide. Due to the differences in contracts from one state to the other, your benefits might not be precisely the same if you need health care out of state, but the essential services will be provided.

- **Two Contracts** – Probably the most significant difference between a traditional insurance company and the Blues is that the Blues have a contract with *both the subscriber and the health care provider*. This duality has created three important results. First of all, contracts issued by the Blues are generally viewed as less flexible than those sold by commercial insurance companies. A change in one contract could, obviously, affect the other contract.

  no bricks & mortar

  Even more importantly, the Blues actually negotiated as part of their contract with the doctors and hospitals the price to be paid for various health care services. This often resulted in Blue Cross-Blue Shield subscribers being charged lower rates than other patients. When hospitals began raising their rates for everyone else in order to discount the Blues subscriber, several states passed laws prohibiting such discounts.

  Finally, it is because of the two-contract approach that we have the basic distinction between the Blues and the commercial companies. Despite all the moves each type of organization has made to emulate the other, the original distinction remains the same: **the Blues provide medical services while the stocks and mutuals provide reimbursement for those services**.

Know This

Health Maintenance Organizations
(or, in some states, Health Insuring Corporations)

1 Like the Blues, Health Maintenance Organizations (HMO's) are **service** providers. However, with some exceptions, the HMO's take the service concept one step beyond the Blues. Where the Blues contract with the provider hospitals and physicians to provide medical care, the **HMO's actually provide the medical care themselves**. The simplest example of an HMO is the so called **Staff Model**. The **HMO employs the doctors, owns the clinic and maybe even the hospital** in which the subscribers receive treatment. Another approach is the **Group Practice Model** in which the HMO, in effect, *leases* the clinic and its doctors. If it is an exclusive arrangement, it is known as a **closed panel** medical group. If the medical group reserves the right to treat patients not belonging to the HMO, it is an **open panel group practice**. An **Independent Practice Association Model** works just like the Group Practice Model except that the providers are located throughout the coverage territory and operate on an open panel basis. While provisions are made for the member subscriber who needs specialized care beyond the capacity of the HMO or the subscriber who needs care while traveling outside the geographic limits of the HMO, **most HMO's are designed to function within the boundaries of a specific community**.

HMO = HIC

We do the work ourselves

2 Through the HMO Act of 1973, Congress greatly encouraged the growth of HMO's. If federally qualified, an HMO could receive start-up funding from the federal government, grants to solicit subscribers, loan guarantees to cover initial deficits and, through the Act, force employers with more than 25 employees to offer the HMO as an alternative to their regular health plan. This is known as the **dual choice provision**. The federal government's decidedly pro-HMO posture was based on one important characteristic that seems to differentiate the HMO from the plans offered by traditional companies or the Blues. **There seemed to be every incentive to keep the lid on the cost of health care.** Most of the characteristics which differentiate HMO's from insurance companies and from the Blues can be linked to the idea of cost containment.

Own-a-Doc

- **Identify Problems Early** – Even in the most comprehensive Medical Expense policies, the Blues and the traditional companies tend to exclude coverage for routine physicals, well-baby care, immunizations and other **preventive** maintenance. HMO's emphasize preventive care in the hope that small problems identified immediately can be treated as small problems rather than large ones.

- **Encourage Early Treatment** – The insurance companies and the Blues generally write contracts that require a deductible and further require that the Insured share in the cost of the treatment beyond the deductible to the tune of 20%. The HMO philosophy is that people are more likely to seek early treatment if there is no deductible and the Insured is covered 100%.

- **Encourage Out-Patient Treatment** – The HMO's were the first to recognize that costs begin to skyrocket as soon as the Insured is hospitalized. Therefore, unlike the Blues and the insurance companies, HMO contracts provide benefits for out-patient care at the same level as they do for in-patient treatment.

- **Minimize Unnecessary Tests and Procedures** – Since the physicians working within a Staff Model HMO environment are employees, they have no financial incentive to prescribe additional and, perhaps, unnecessary treatment. Also, because the HMO covers their malpractice insurance, they are also less inclined to order additional tests simply to substantiate their original diagnosis if a question arises in the future.

- **Gatekeeper concept** – Within the HMO, the Primary Care physician (PCP) functions as a *gatekeeper*. While part of his function is to refer subscribers to the Referral (Specialty) physician for necessary treatment, it is also part of his job to disapprove any requests for treatment that are not medically necessary or advantageous.

1   All in all, the HMO concept has worked fairly well. Statistics indicate that HMO subscribers are hospitalized less frequently than the individuals covered by the Blues or the insurance companies. Whether this is due to the emphasis on preventive care or whether it is due to the fact that younger people given a choice are more likely to choose an HMO is still a subject of much debate. However, the fact remains that medical expense insurance is provided by HMO's for about 25% of all Insured Americans (as compared to a 37% market share for the Blues). Certainly, numbers would indicate that the HMO has become a permanent fixture as a supplier in the medical expense arena.

Federally Qualified HMO Requirements ‡

2   To become federally qualified, an HMO must offer the following **basic** health care services:

- Physician's Services
- Hospital Inpatient
- Outpatient Medical Services
- Radiology Services
- Emergency Services
- Preventive Services
- Laboratory Services

3   Federally qualified HMO's *may* offer any or all of the following **supplemental** services:

- Prescription Drugs
- Vision Care
- Dental Care
- Home Health Care
- Nursing Services
- Long Term Care
- Mental Health Care
- Substance Abuse Services

New Trends

1. Most of the newly formed HMO's are for-profit corporations which, strangely enough, do not seek to be federally-qualified (and, therefore, are not eligible for the federal grants, loan guarantees, start-up funding, etc.). The reason that these newer HMO's choose to forego federal funding is that a federally-qualified HMO can only use **community rating** to price its products. Since HMO's typically write only group medical expense coverage, they can be much more competitive by skipping the federal aid and utilizing the **experience rating** mechanism to price their products.

Community Rating v Experience Rating

2. While a great many HMO's were started by consumer groups, an increasing number are sponsored by insurance companies or the Blues. Sponsorship may also come from physicians, hospitals or labor unions.

Community rating may become the law

HMO Objections

3. Probably the two biggest shortcomings of the traditional HMO from the consumer's viewpoint are:

- Limited ability to select a physician
- Limited geographic selection

4. With an HMO, you must go to their clinic (even if it's across town) and see their doctor (even if you've never seen him before or cannot stand him). As a result, some of the newer HMO's are set up as **individual practice association plans**. Instead of employing (or contracting with) doctors in one place (the **group practice plan**), these HMO's contract with doctors all over town and the individual subscriber may choose a location and a physician (the independent practice plan). However, except in emergency situations, subscribers must only utilize physicians from the HMO list.

5. Probably the most important reaction to consumer objections about HMO's is the development of a third type of service provider – the Preferred Provider Organization.

Preferred Provider Organization (PPO)

6. The Preferred Provider Organization (PPO) is essentially a hybrid between the insurance company/Blues system (where the Insureds had practically complete freedom to choose their medical provider) and the HMO system (which locked them into a specific group of providers). **The PPO contracts with a large number of medical providers across a community**. The PPO typically enjoys lower rates because it is anticipated that they will channel a large volume of business to their **preferred** doctor or hospital. The providers can service only the PPO (closed panel), or they can serve non-members as well (open panel). If the claimant utilizes a physician or hospital on the preferred list, benefits are structured somewhat as they would be with an HMO – small (if any) deductible, low cost sharing and some coverage for preventive care. **However, the Insured may choose medical providers not found on the preferred list and still have coverage.** With this alternative, benefits are paid similarly to what the insurance companies or the Blues would pay on a Major Medical type contract – the claimant would be responsible for a deductible and about 20%-50% of the costs after the deductible – a big penalty for choosing an outside provider.

Rent-a-Doc

"Use ours and it will cost you less. . ."

smaller d-duct

less coinsurance

The fact that you may, under a PPO, use any health care provider you choose is the major difference between an HMO and a PPO. A second distinction is also true – **HMO's provide service on a prepaid per person per year basis (or capitation)** whereas **a PPO pays the health care provider on a fee-for-service basis** (or, perhaps, a **negotiated** fee-for-service basis).

Actually, there are two types of PPO's. The majority are the **comprehensive** PPO's as we have described. However, there are more than a few **limited range of service** PPO's that only include hospitals, or doctors or dental care or prescription services. Sometimes, using several limited range PPO's can create a better, more cost efficient plan than if you bought just one comprehensive plan.

Managed Care

Managed Care is a buzzword which refers to any program designed to contain health care (medical expense) costs by **controlling the behavior of the participants in** the plan. Insurance companies and employers have developed a number of approaches which have been incorporated into health care benefit plans. Managed care plans contain features which range from the requirements of second opinions and hospital pre-certification to plans which limit one's choice of medical providers, negotiate provider fees, and use case management. Managed care plans should have the following characteristics:

cost containment

A. **Controlled Access of Providers** - In order to control costs, managed care plans encourage or force participants to use predetermined physicians and hospitals. Primary care physicians act as **gatekeepers** to determine the necessity of seeing a physician.

B. **Large Claim Management** - This is used for patients with long-term or catastrophic illnesses such as head and spinal cord injuries, AIDS, severe strokes, and premature births. When a potentially large claim is identified, a case manager is assigned to work with the patient, the patient's family, and the patient's physician to develop a course of treatment which is then implemented and periodically monitored for appropriateness and cost effectiveness. **Utilization review**, a method of assuring that a patient is not given a level of medical care that exceeds medical necessity, is performed at all levels, such as preadmission reviews (or **prospective reviews**), **concurrent reviews** (while confined in the hospital), and discharge planning.

C. **Preventive care** - Managed care plans encourage preventive care and living a healthier lifestyle.

D. **Hospitalization alternatives** - Any course of treatment which can avoid or minimize hospitalization is generally a plus for cost containment. If treatment can be done on an **outpatient (or ambulatory)** basis, or at a **surgical center, birthing center** or in a **skilled nursing facility** it is better management of benefit dollars. A **hospice** is a facility designed for the comfort of the terminally ill. It can provide pain control for the patient and counseling for the family more economically than a hospital.

E. **Second Surgical Opinions** - A second, confirming opinion before an operation can be mandatory or optional. Either way, the cost of obtaining the second opinion is typically covered 100%.

F. **Preadmission Testing** - Frequently, the first day or two of a hospital confinement prior to a surgery is devoted to tests and x-rays. These tests can usually be performed on an outpatient basis to avoid unnecessary hospitalization.

G. **Catastrophic Case Management** - Good management of resources at the initial stages of a serious illness or accident can greatly influence the final outcome in terms of patient recovery and dollars spent. If sending a stroke victim to a specialized out-of-state facility can save time, money and increase the patient's likelihood of healing, this step should be earlier rather than later.

H. **Risk Sharing** - Physicians and hospitals share in the financial consequences of medical decisions in order to eliminate unnecessary medical care. For example, a doctor who minimizes diagnostic tests may receive a bonus under an HMO or PPO arrangement.

I. **High Quality Care** - Providers are carefully selected and the quality of care is monitored so that participants are pleased with their care and recover quickly and fully.

1   Most employers have benefit plans that use some aspect of managed care. Studies have shown that the higher the degree of managed care, the lower the annual benefit costs. Examples of managed care include HMO's and PPO's.

HEALTH BENEFIT PROVIDERS OF TODAY

2   In this text, we have managed to place the major health care providers into one of two categories – the traditional insurance companies who work on a *reimbursement basis,* and the *service organizations* which generally include the Blues and HMO's. While all of these systems continue to evolve, copy each other and begin to overlap, there are three new concepts that are beginning to play an important part in the health care arena.

Self-Funded Plans

3   The Employee Retirement Income Security Act of 1974 (ERISA) gave employers the right to establish either Insured (through an insurance company) or self-Insured employee benefit plans. Many larger groups with healthy employees believe that they can save a fair amount of money, avoid state-mandated benefits as well as state premium taxes, and improve their cash flow by not sending money to any health benefits provider. Instead, they put the dollars aside and pay the claims themselves. This typically works best in the following situations:

regulated by the FEDS

- **Fairly Predictable Claims** – A history of a large number of small claims is probably the best environment.

- **Noncontributory Plans** – In a *noncontributory* plan, the employee does not chip in to pay for the coverage. In a *contributory* plan, the employee is paying something for the coverage, so bad feelings can erupt if a claim is denied. In a self-funded plan, it's not the insurance company saying "no" – it's the employer.

- **Non-Union Situation** – If a union notices a savings, you can bet they'll have some ideas about how to spend the savings.

1 The two key issues of a self-funded plan are **claims administration** and **stop-loss coverage**. Most employers are better off to subcontract the claims work to an insurance company under an Administrative Services Only (ASO) contract or to a **Third Party Administrator (TPA)**. The stop-loss coverage can be handled by one, or both, of two methods. Aggregate stop-loss coverage establishes an agreement where an insurance company or a Lloyd's syndicate picks up the tab beyond a predetermined level of loss such as, say, 120% or 140% of what was anticipated. The second stop-loss approach is written on a per employee basis. If one employee goes over, say, $25,000 in benefits, all benefits over that amount are paid by the insurance company for the remainder of the Policy period. Either of these arrangements can be considered **reinsurance** and are treated as such by regulatory officials in many states.

Bosses don't like saying "no" to their employees

Health Savings Accounts (HSAs)

2 A **Health Savings Account** can be thought of as a cross between a Self-Funded Plan and a traditional Medical Expense Contract with a very high deductible. It can be sold on an individual (or family) basis or to groups.

HSAs

3 The Medical Expense coverage is written to cover **catastrophic medical costs**. The **deductible is quite high** – ranging from around $2,000 for a single person to around $3,000 for a family. If in any year the deductible is exceeded, then the Medical Expense coverage pays. With some companies, the Medical Expense coverage pays without a coinsurance requirement, while other companies retain the coinsurance requirement.

like an IRA for health care

4 The individual Insured (or family) contributes money each year to the account. This money is treated as a reduction in income, thus **reducing current taxes**. Under a group plan, the **employer can make part of the contribution** and treats this as a business expense.

5 Standard medical costs (non-catastrophic) can be paid out of the Health Savings Account. These expenditures would count towards satisfying the deductible. The HSA can also be used for other *medically related* expenses such as dental or vision, but these expenditures cannot be counted to meet the deductible. If used for standard medical costs or medically-related expenses, withdrawals from the HSA are not taxable.

Employee's Bucks

6 Even though deposits in the HSA vest immediately, they cannot be withdrawn for non-medical purposes without a 10% penalty prior to age 65 (not 59 1/2). Of course, even after age 65, taxes must be paid upon the principal and the interest earned over the years if the withdrawal is for a non-medical purpose.

Health Reimbursement Arrangement (HRA)

7 Much like the HSA, the HRA establishes an account in conjunction with high deductible plan which employees can access to pay for medical expenses which are their responsibility (i.e. deductibles, prescription drugs, etc.). And, just as with an HSA, dollars that are not used roll over to the next year.

8 However, there is a major difference between the HSA and the HRA concerning ownership. In an HSA that exists with group insurance, **the employee owns the money in the HSA** and if the employee leaves a company, the HSA money can be moved to an Individual Health Savings Account.

Boss's Bucks

9 In an **HRA, the money in the account belongs to the employer**. In fact, HRAs cannot be funded by employee contributions. Thus, if the employee were to leave the company the HRA money would be forfeited.

Multiple-Option or Point of Service (POS) Plan

1 The Point of Service Plan (POS) is not really new at all – it is merely a combination of nearly everything we've addressed. Suppose an employer covers his employees with Blue Cross - Blue Shield. He also has an HMO alternative and Blue Cross - Blue Shield owns the HMO. They also own a PPO and, of course, can administer all three programs. With the Point of Service Plan, the employees do not have to make a decision between the three plans that locks the employee and his family into one plan. Literally a different choice can be made every time a need arises for medical services. If Joe has a long history of ulcers, he may select to use the Blue Cross - Blue Shield approach so that he can stay with his own doctor. If we assume Jolene is very healthy and only needs regular physical exams, she might utilize the PPO. If Little Joe and Betty Jo need camp physicals, they might go the HMO route. And, if next week they all have a different need, they can make another choice. Obviously, the same arrangement could be constructed with a traditional company that owns (or contracts with) an HMO and a PPO.

the Combo Plan

...capitation and fee-for-service

2 **Recently, the Point of Service plan has taken on a rather specific look. You join the HMO. If for some reason you wish to use a doctor who is not part of the HMO, you may do so but you will pay a higher coinsurance percentage for the privilege.**

COMMON ELEMENTS

3 While many aspects of a Disability Income Policy are not applicable to Medical Expense policies and vice versa, there are several elements that are common to both.

- Insuring Clause
- Consideration Clause
- Renewal Provisions
- General Provisions
- Benefit Provisions
- Free Look Provision
- Exclusions and Exclusion Riders
- Definitions Section
- Probationary Period

4 Although companies are traditionally free to arrange their policies in any order they wish, there are several elements that, by law or tradition, appear on the first page (or Policy face) of the contract. All states require that the renewal provision appear on the first page of the Policy. Nearly all states require that any Policy which covers accidents but not sickness be clearly identified as an accident-only contract on the Policy face. Most states further require a *Free Look* provision to appear on the first page of the contract. As we will see, this provision functions much like a trial subscription to a magazine in that it allows you as the buyer to cancel the coverage and get all your money back within a specific time period. Although not required by law in most states, it is customary for companies to print the Insuring Clause on the first page of the Policy.

Insuring Clause

1   The Insuring Clause of a life insurance Policy is a fairly clear statement which summarizes the essence of the contract; the Insuring Clause of a health Policy is much less informative. For example, notice what you learn and fail to learn from the following Insuring Clause of one company's Disability Income Policy.

the company's consideration

The Promises

> *We will pay for disability of the Insured commencing while this Policy is in force and resulting from accidental bodily injury sustained while this Policy is in force and not contributed to by any other cause, or sickness, the cause of which is contracted while this Policy is in force, subject to all the conditions and provisions hereof.*

2   A careful reading tells you that: (1) the Policy is a Disability Income contract, (2) it covers both sickness and accident, and (3) it is not going to cover any preexisting conditions. However, we do not have any idea how generously or restrictively *disability* is defined. We know neither when payments will start nor how long they will continue. The Insuring Clauses of other companies are even less illuminating:

> *We will pay benefits for a loss as set forth in this Policy.*

3   Suffice it to say that all health policies contain Insuring Clauses, but they are not terribly informative.

Consideration Clause

4   As was true in life insurance, the statements made on the application for a health Policy cannot be used to contest a claim unless the application itself is made a part of the contract. In life insurance, this was accomplished in the *Entire Contract Clause.* In health policies, we get the same result, but the enabling language is found in either the Insuring Clause:

The Exchange of Value

> *In consideration of the application, a copy of which is attached hereto and made a part hereof, the company will pay for disability of the Insured commencing while this Policy is in force . . .*

5   or set out separately in the Consideration Clause:

> *We have issued this Policy in consideration of the representations in your application and payment of the first term premium. A copy of your application is attached and is a part of this Policy.*

6   In either form, the Consideration Clause simply summarizes the factors that led the company to issue the Policy in the first place – the Insured has completed an application and paid some premium in exchange for the company's promise to provide insurance. Viewed in tandem with the Insuring Clause, the Consideration Clause ties back to the fundamental idea of contract formation – there is a "meeting of the minds" and an exchange of consideration.

it's all on the table

Renewal Provisions

1   In order to select the appropriate health insurance policies, Joe and Jolene have to consider a huge number of factors. However, none may be so important as the degree to which they preserve their right to keep the Policy in force. The most generous health insurance contract ever written sold at bargain-basement prices would be virtually worthless if the company could cancel the contract at the first sign of illness. As you would guess, the contracts with more favorable terms of renewal are more expensive than those with less favorable terms. There are at least six forms of renewability found in the marketplace today. We will examine each in turn, beginning with the most generous promise of renewability.

2   In our examples, we will typically use 65 as the coverage age limit. We should point out that there is nothing magic about age 65 - it is simply the most common retirement age today. As the Medicare eligibility age advances, we will sell policies written to age 66 and then to age 67. In fact, today, we use the same renewal provisions for policies sold to senior citizens and the cutoff is not an age but an event - death.

1. **Noncancellable** – A Noncancellable Policy gives Joe **the right to keep it in force** up to a specified age (which is almost always age 65) at a **guaranteed price**. All Joe must do is pay the premiums at the agreed rate. Notice that we did not say the premium is level. It could be stepped. Joe could pay $200 a month until age 50, $300 a month from age 50 to 60 and $400 a month from age 60 to 65. However, he would know exactly what he must pay at age 55, for example, when he buys the Policy at age 40. During the 25 years the Policy is in force, the company may not cancel the contract, change the benefits or raise the stated price.

Guarantees both

Cost overage

Since the Noncancellable form of renewability not only preserves Joe's right to maintain coverage but also the price he pays, this form of renewability is normally found only in Disability Income policies. Given the inflationary spiral affecting medical costs, companies almost always want to reserve their right to modify the premium charged for Medical Expense policies.

2. **Guaranteed Renewable** – Both Medical Expense policies and Disability Income policies can be sold as Guaranteed Renewable contracts. With this approach, Joe has the **right to keep the Policy** until age 65, but the **rates are not guaranteed**. Although the company cannot single out Joe individually and triple his rates, the company does reserve the right to *adjust the rates over time by class* – which is a polite way of saying "raise the rates for all Insureds sharing certain characteristics" (e.g. men aged 45-50 of a certain occupational category).

Guarantees

Coverage only

poof

3. **Conditionally Renewable** – A Conditionally Renewable Policy gives Joe the right to maintain coverage until age 65 **if** important changes listed in the Policy do not occur. Since this form of renewability can be used with both Medical Expense and Disability Income policies, the stated reasons for nonrenewal may vary based upon the type of coverage. However, the company cannot refuse to renew Joe simply because of a change in his health. The kinds of changes which might be listed to trigger nonrenewal include:

- The Insured changes to a more dangerous occupation.
- The Insured retires.

Although the rationale behind the *more dangerous occupation* trigger is obvious, perhaps the *retirement* trigger merits some discussion. If Joe bought a Conditionally Renewable health Policy at age 40 and retired at age 55, the company would love to have the opportunity to dump him at renewal. The reason for this is that most people who take early retirement do so because of ill health. If Joe took early retirement for some other reason (say, for example, he won the lottery), then the company could, at its option, choose to continue his medical expense coverage if he wanted it. Any disability income coverage would, in all likelihood, not be renewed because there would be no further need for the insurance.

Guaranteed. . .

...IF...

Conditional

Possibly the most common usage for the Conditionally Renewable concept is to provide coverage after age 65 for individuals Insured under a Noncancellable or Guaranteed Renewable Policy. Many modern contracts are written to be Noncancellable or Guaranteed Renewable until age 65, and then they shift to Conditionally Renewable if the Insured is still employed and still wants coverage. When the Insured does stop working, the retirement trigger eliminates future renewals.

4. **Optionally Renewable** – Optionally Renewable policies are renewable up to age 65 **at the company's option**. Said another way, the company can choose not to renew Joe at any premium due date or Policy anniversary date. Although this form of renewability gives Joe almost no rights of renewal, several states have laws which prohibit nonrenewal solely on the basis of a deterioration of health. Furthermore, many companies voluntarily limit nonrenewal to situations involving:

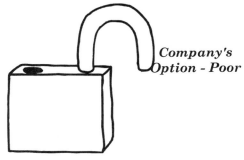

Company's Option - Poor

it's the company's option

- fraud.
- moral hazards.
- overinsurance.
- discontinuance of a class of business.
- submission of false claims.
- malingering.

5. **Cancellable** – Although illegal in most states, a Cancellable Policy is cancellable **at the option of the company** at any time, as long as the company gives the Insured a 5-day written notice and returns any unearned premium.

Very Bad

6. **Term (or Stated Period of Time or Nonrenewable Term)** – A Term health Policy (unlike a Term life Policy) gives Joe **no rights of renewal** whatsoever. As harsh as this may seem, it is appropriate with certain Policy types. For example, if Joe buys a Policy to cover him on Flight #402 from Seattle to Chicago, a Policy which expires when the plane safely touches down is appropriate. If Joe wants coverage on his return flight, he simply buys another Policy. Typically, Term health policies are also accident only policies. The policies purchased on children attending school are Term health policies (which expire at the end of the school year), as are summer camp policies (which expire when the children return home).

until the airplane lands

Note to Student:

1. Although somewhat outdated, the term *Commercial* or *Commercially Renewable* has been used to describe policies that are Conditionally Renewable, Optionally Renewable or Cancellable. Though still in use by some companies, this is a term that probably should be dropped from our insurance vocabulary. Given the large differences in meaning amongst these three forms of renewability, using one term to describe any or all only adds to the confusion.

General Provisions

2. For the most part, the general provisions of any health insurance Policy are made up of the appropriate mandatory and optional provisions of the National Association of Insurance Commissioners (NAIC) Model Uniform Accident and Sickness Policy Provisions Law. This law is notable for two things. First, no normal human being has ever remembered the name of it, and secondly, all fifty states have adopted some version of it to encourage uniformity from one health Policy to the next and from one state to another. The 12 required and 11 optional provisions included in this law will be the subject of Chapter 15 of this text.

3. About the only other item typically found in the general provisions is the **Military Suspension** provision. This provision gives the Insured the right to suspend health coverage (and premiums) while on active duty in the military service of any country or international authority. The same provision gives the Insured the right to place the Policy back in force **without evidence of insurability or back premiums** when active duty ends.

Benefit Provisions

4. In both Disability Income and Medical Expense policies, the benefit provisions tend to flesh out the bare bones promise made by the Insuring Clause. In a Disability Income contract, the benefit provisions do the following:

- Define the length of the elimination period.
- Define the maximum length of the benefit period.
- State the amount and frequency of the periodic benefit.

5. The benefits section of a Medical Expense Policy cannot be addressed so easily. As you will see in Chapter 12 of this text, there are several distinctly different medical expense plans available, and the benefits section of each can differ greatly from the benefits section of another plan. We can oversimplify at this point by dividing medical expense policies into two groups – the Basic plans and the more comprehensive Major Medical plans.

6. The Basic plans tend to offer first dollar coverage (little or no deductible), but the dollar limits are not very high and the coverages are not very broad. For the most part, the benefits sections of these plans are concerned with establishing the parameters of the coverage. Does it cover you only while you are in the hospital, or is there outpatient coverage as well? Does it only cover hospital charges or does it also cover physician services? Would a surgery be covered and, if so, to what limits?

1 On the other hand, the Major Medical type plans tend to state that the Policy will cover all medical expenses that are reasonable, necessary and customary. Then, the limitations on this very broad and seemingly unlimited promise begin. There is often a maximum lifetime benefit, as well as deductibles and coinsurance requirements. There are flat-out exclusions as well as limitations. For instance, Joe's $1 million lifetime benefit contract may pay no more than $200 a day for a hospital room; charges exceeding $200 would be Joe's to pay.

2 As we examine Disability Income contracts in Chapter 11 and Medical Expense policies in Chapter 12, you will gain greater insight into what each covers. At this point, it is enough to know that the benefits section of each Policy will give you a more precise understanding of what the Policy is designed to do and not do than you gain by reading the Insuring Clause.

Free Look Provision

3 As we observed at the beginning of this chapter, the only way you can know what is covered and not covered by a particular Policy is to read that Policy. The regulatory authorities and the legislatures across the country apparently agree with this conclusion because individual health policies in most states require what is called a **Free Look** provision. It gives the purchaser a **limited period of time to examine the Policy** and the **right to return it for a 100% refund** if dissatisfied with it in any way. With health policies, coverage usually starts on the Policy date, but the **Free Look doesn't start until the Policy is actually delivered to the Insured**. The length of time given the Policyowner varies from state to state and from contract to contract, but 10 days, 20 days, and 30 days are the most commonly found time periods.

10 days to read your Policy

4 Suppose Joe purchases a Major Medical Policy with **a 10 Day Right to Examine** (Free Look) provision. Let's assume the Policy is dated April 1 and the Policy is delivered to him on April 5. Although he has coverage beginning on April 1, he has until April 15 to return the Policy for a full refund. If he surrenders the Policy and takes the refund, the company will treat the situation as if coverage never existed. Obviously, if Joe had a heart attack on April 13, he would have coverage and would be an idiot to ask for a refund. Even unsatisfactory coverage is better than no coverage at all.

Note to Student:

5 As we look at the remaining elements commonly found in all health policies, we will be examining several different methods that companies use to accomplish the same basic objectives – to minimize claims. Health insurance companies must very carefully limit what they pay out if they are to remain solvent and profitable. We will note that there are losses for which companies absolutely exclude coverage for all Policyowners; other circumstances where the exclusion is temporary or applies to only one Policyowner; and, yet other times where companies simply raise the rates. Although each of these approaches is different, they are all intended to:

controlling cost of claims

- Eliminate adverse selection.
- Not cover preexisting conditions.
- Assure that the premium charged is commensurate with the risk.

1 When Joe applies for health insurance, his company can (1) accept him, (2) reject him, (3) accept him but exclude specific ailments or body parts or activities, or (4) accept him "as is" if he is willing to pay an upcharge, i.e., issue a rated Policy. The circumstances which would typically result in a *rated* Policy being issued are risks that are *generalized* in nature (i.e., more likely to result in claims to the company, but difficult to predict the exact type of claim which may occur and minor enough to merit writing the coverage despite the condition). As an example, a company might rate Joe's health Policy if he has a history of hypertension, alcoholism, sinus problems or diabetes.

may not be possible in the future

2 Once his Policy is issued – at normal or substandard rates – Joe will find some exclusions. Most exclusions apply to *all* Insureds of that particular Policy. An exclusion that applies *only to Joe* is known as an Exclusion (Impairment) Rider.

Exclusions and Exclusion Riders

3 Both Disability Income and Medical Expense policies contain some exclusions. A number are common to both Policy types, and some are found only in Medical Expense policies.

4 Throughout this text, we have seen that **exclusions are an underwriting device designed to keep the Policy affordable**. They can protect against adverse selection by screening out pre-existing conditions. They can eliminate coverage for situations better covered elsewhere which avoids duplicate coverage. It is also quite common for exclusions to preclude coverage for catastrophic events which would cause losses for many Policyowners simultaneously.

5 However, as we examine the health insurance exclusions, it is important to remind ourselves of two other basic tenets of insurance. Insurance is designed to cover (1) losses beyond the *control* of the Insured, and (2) losses which would cause the Insured *severe* economic hardship. Many of the losses excluded in health insurance are exclusions because they simply do not fit within the purpose of insurance. For example, cosmetic surgery is within your *control*, and routine dental care will not cause *severe* economic hardship.

6 Disability Income and Medical Expense policies typically exclude losses due to the following:

- War
- Active military duty - normally a suspension that ends when the Insured is released from duty
- Intentionally self-inflicted injury
- Participation in a felony
- Preexisting conditions (may be changed under new laws)
- Uncomplicated **pregnancy** and childbirth (This exclusion is found in individual and small group policies. A 1978 amendment to the Civil Rights Act requires that groups over 15 members treat pregnancy like any other illness.)
- Alcoholism or drug addiction*
- Mental illness*

1   Medical Expense policies also typically exclude the following:

- Occupational injuries or diseases to the extent that benefits are provided by **workers' compensation** laws or similar legislation.
- Services furnished by or on behalf of government agencies, unless there is a requirement that the patient or the patient's medical expense plan pay.
- **Cosmetic surgery**, unless such surgery is to correct a condition resulting from either an accidental injury or a birth defect if the parent has dependent coverage when the child is born.
- Routine physical examinations, such as *well baby care*.
- **Convalescent, custodial or rest care.**
- Medical treatment provided or sickness incurred **outside the U.S. or Canada**.
- **Dental** care except for (1) treatment required because of injury to natural teeth, and (2) hospital and surgical charges associated with hospital confinement for dental surgery.
- Expenses either paid or eligible for payment under Medicare or other federal, state, or local medical expense programs.
- Eyeglasses and hearing aids.

Things not covered

Federal Law may modify dental coverage

2   In addition to the exclusions which apply to *anybody* covered by the Policy (like Joe and all his dependents), Joe's coverage may be restricted by an exclusion that applies *only to Joe*. As we've seen, companies prefer to increase premium to offset negative, *generalized* health conditions, but if a condition is *specific* to one area or system of the body, most companies prefer to exclude coverage for that specific body part by issuing an Exclusion (Impairment) rider.

3   **Exclusion (Impairment) Rider** The great New England Patriots quarterback, Tom Brady, is as well-known for his bad knees as he is for his great throwing arm. A Medical Expense or Disability Income Policy issued to Tom Brady might very well exclude claims resulting from his knee injuries. If our buddy, Joe Insured, has a history of kidney stones, his policies might exclude disability or treatment due to all diseases of the kidneys or genitourinary tract. The rider can be written in such a way that there will never be coverage, or it may be written so that if the Insured can reasonably go without treatment for a specified period of time, the company will drop the rider and the ailment will be covered. It is also possible to use an Exclusion Rider to eliminate coverage for an Insured participating in certain high risk activities. For example, if Joe Insured's hobby is flying airplanes, he could have an Exclusion Rider attached to either his Medical Expense or Disability Income Policy to eliminate claims for accidents he incurs while flying.

no extra cost

Your very own exclusion

Note to the Student:
4   Again, the differences between life and health insurance are apparent. In life insurance, riders are normally *extra goodies* that you purchase willingly. Although this *may* be true in health insurance, the most common health rider is the Exclusion Rider, which subtracts rather than adds coverage. However, it *is* free. Since it is a change to the Policy applied for, the applicant's signature would be required on an amendment form upon Policy delivery.

5   Two of the exclusions we examined which apply to both Disability Income and Medical Expense are *intentional injuries* and *preexisting conditions*. These terms can be interpreted in many ways. To avoid confusion, Joe should carefully read the Definitions section of his Policy in order to understand exactly what the terms mean in his contract.

Definitions Section

1   The two perils covered in most health policies – sickness and accident – are defined in the Policy. With each term, the company is less interested in supplying a dictionary definition than it is with stating that there is no coverage for an ailment suffered by the Insured prior to the effective date of the Policy. For example, most policies define a covered **sickness** as an illness or disease that **first manifests itself** while the Policy is in force. Some companies modify the language to say *first diagnosed and treated* while the Policy is in force, but in either case, the intent is to screen out preexisting conditions.

"it happens on our watch..."

2   For the peril of **accident**, most companies use the phrase **accidental bodily injury which occurs while the Policy is in force**. Obviously, the company will not cover the broken leg Joe suffered three days before he bought the Policy. The term **accidental bodily injury** is further defined as an **unforeseen and unintended event that happens at a known place at a known time**. This language would deny coverage if Joe intentionally broke his leg in order to enjoy a lengthy summer vacation courtesy of his Disability Income insurance carrier.

...by chance...

...here and now...

3   At one time, companies used the phrase **accidental means** instead of accidental bodily injury. This very restrictive language said, in essence, that both the injury and the cause of the injury had to be accidental. The classic illustration was that if Joe jumped from a ladder three rungs from the bottom and broke his leg, there was no coverage. Although we could presume that Joe did not intentionally break his leg, *he did intentionally jump*. Only if Joe unintentionally fell from the ladder would there be coverage. Today, the accidental means definition is illegal for most policies in most states.

accidental means is ..."meaner"...

Pre Existing Conditions

4   Another important term which is typically explained in the Policy definitions is **Preexisting conditions**. Suppose that Joe injured his neck playing football in high school, received treatment for 60 days and has been free of discomfort ever since. Today, at age 40, he begins to experience neck pain. Is this a preexisting condition? "No," say the laws of all 50 states, "too much time has passed." The length of time a company can go back into a person's health history varies from state to state and from contract to contract, but most policies will define preexisting conditions somewhat like the following:

Eliminating Pre-existing Conditions may be outlawed.

5   *Preexisting condition* means a medical condition which exists on the effective date and during the past two years (for example) either:

- Caused you to receive medical advice or treatment; or

- Caused symptoms for which an ordinarily prudent person would seek medical advice or treatment.

Note: Individual policies only

6   For example, a company could deny a neck pain claim from Joe if he had received treatment for his condition in January, bought a new Policy in February, and filed a claim in April simply by using the first prong of the above preexisting conditions clause. We should note that several states do not allow the *prudent person* prong to be included in the definition, and therefore, only allow medical conditions for which the Insured actually received medical advice or treatment to be considered as preexisting.

1 Under most contracts, Joe's neck would ultimately be covered, assuming he didn't have an exclusion rider on it. The preexisting conditions definitions typically will allow for coverage in the future (again, with many variations) under one of two circumstances:

- After the passage of a specific period of time (one year, for example), there is automatically coverage for the preexisting condition,

or

- If the Insured goes without treatment for a specific period of time (such as six months), there is coverage.

Time marches on

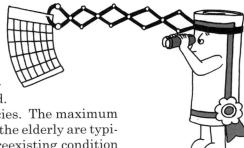

2 As we've pointed out, how far back into a person's health history a company can go in defining a preexisting condition and how far into the future a company can deny claims on the basis of a preexisting condition is a function of state law and the particular Policy being sold. For instance, in some states, a company can go back 5 years in defining a preexisting condition, and then be allowed to exclude that condition for 2 years after the Policy is issued. That same state might have different time periods for other policies. The maximum time periods allowed for preexisting conditions on policies sold to the elderly are typically much shorter. For example, in that very same state, a preexisting condition in a Medicare Supplement Policy may be restricted to no more than 6 months prior to the Policy date, and then may exclude coverage on that condition for only up to 6 months after the Policy date. In other states, any of these time periods could be significantly different.

Probationary (Waiting) Period

3 The final device that companies use to screen out preexisting conditions is the probationary period. Simply put, a probationary period is a specified time immediately following the issuance of the Policy for which coverage is not provided. Probationary periods may be general in nature, thereby eliminating any kind of a claim for a certain time, or they may only eliminate coverage for specific conditions for that time period.

we don't buy claims

4 Although somewhat uncommon with individual disability income policies, group disability income contracts typically require that the Insured employee be at work for a specified period without illness or injury before coverage will apply. A typical time period might be 3 months or 6 months.

5 Group medical expense policies sponsored by an employer frequently use the *blanket* probationary period to eliminate any kind of claim for a short time period. Typical time periods are 10 days or 30 days. Some even differentiate between accident and sickness. For instance, there could be a 5 day probationary period for accidents and a 10 day probationary period for sickness. In industries that are very competitive for skilled employees, employer-sponsored group medical expense policies might have no probationary period.

NOTE: Probationary Period excludes preexisting illness

6 The individual medical expense Policy is probably the best illustration of the probationary period screening out specific health conditions. For example, most individual major medical policies exclude pregnancy but if you want pregnancy coverage, you can purchase it for additional premium. When pregnancy coverage is purchased, there is typically a probationary period of, say, nine months, which effectively precludes pregnancy coverage for anyone who was already pregnant when the Policy was purchased. Although it is not common, some companies still use a 90 day probationary period to screen out semi-elective surgery for hernias, tonsils, hemorrhoids and gall bladder disease.

Insuring clause excludes preexisting accident

TAX TREATMENT OF HEALTH INSURANCE BENEFITS

1 **Individual Disability Income** – The **premiums are not deductible** and the **benefits received are not subject to federal income tax**.

2 **Individual Medical Expense** – In most cases, the **premiums are not deductible and the benefits are not taxable**. If, however, you itemize deductions on your tax form and if your total unreimbursed medical expenses including the premium you paid exceed a specific percentage of your adjusted gross income, then you may deduct the portion exceeding that percentage. The benefits are still not subject to federal income tax.

TAX FACTS

ownership is

3 **Group Disability Income** – **Premiums paid by the employer are deductible** to the employer, and the premiums are not considered to be part of the employee's income. **Benefits paid to the employee** as the result of employer contributions **are fully taxable** to the employee. In a shared contribution arrangement, the employer's contribution and benefits attributable to the employer's contribution are handled in the same way as far as the employer is concerned; any contribution made by the employee, however, is not deductible to the employee, but **any benefits attributable to the employee's contribution would not be taxable**.

4 **Group Medical Expense** – As with group disability income, group medical expense **premiums paid by the employer are tax deductible to the employer**. Any premiums paid by the employee are not tax deductible to the employee except to whatever degree the premiums paid and all other unreimbursed medical expenses exceed a specified percentage of the employee's adjusted gross income. In any event, **medical expense benefits received by the employee are not taxable income**.

OWNERSHIP	DISABILITY INCOME	MEDICAL EXPENSE
Individual • Premium • Benefits	Not Deductible Not Taxed	Not Deductible Not Taxed
Group • Premium • Benefits	Deductible **Taxed**	Deductible Not Taxed

OCCUPATIONAL vs. NONOCCUPATIONAL COVERAGE

1 Earlier in this chapter, we listed exclusions typically found in Disability Income and Medical Expense policies. Our list implies that Disability Income policies cover occupational (on-the-job) accidents and illness, and that Medical Expense policies always exclude these losses. That implication is probably 99% true. The other 1% of the truth is that *group* Disability Income contracts may also exclude occupational losses if the group Policyowner (generally the employer) requests. Therefore, a thumbnail sketch of the whole truth would look like the following:

on the job

2 **Individual Disability Income** – Covers occupational **and** nonoccupational losses.

3 **Individual Medical Expense** – Covers nonoccupational losses. Excludes occupational losses.

4 **Group Disability Income** – *Normally* covers occupational and nonoccupational losses.

5 **Group Medical Expense** – Covers nonoccupational losses. **Excludes occupational losses.**

WORKERS COMPENSATION

6 The reason that occupational coverage is a question at all has to do with a contract that is not even a Life and Health Policy. **Workers Compensation** is normally an employers liability Policy and is sold by Property and Casualty Agents.

Worker's Comp is KING!

7 While the benefit levels and coverage details vary from state to state, the concept of Workers Comp is fairly uniform nationwide. In essence, the Workers Comp laws say that if Joe's employee, Flo, suffers an occupational accident or sickness, then Joe as the employer is legally responsible. Only in the most extreme circumstances (Flo being intoxicated, in some states) would Joe **not** be considered legally liable. 99.9% of the time, Flo's *sole remedy* for her injuries is Workers Compensation. A customer in Joe's restaurant could conceivably sue Joe for millions following a *trip and fall* accident which results in a broken leg. Flo, however, would be limited to the benefits provided by the Workers Comp laws in that particular state.

8 Generally, Workers Comp provides the following benefits:

- Medical care
- Disability income (normally at very low levels)
- Death benefits
- Rehabilitation benefits

9 Since these benefits overlap into health insurance, it is easy to see occupational coverage can become a question. As we have seen, Medical Expense policies tend to exclude occupational injuries because they are already covered by Workers Comp. However, Disability Income policies tend to cover occupational losses because the Workers Comp benefit levels are so low. The contracts which do take Workers Comp into account normally just treat it as an offset to the Disability Income benefit. For example, if Flo had a $1000 a month Disability benefit, she would receive only $800 a month if she were getting $200 a month from Workers Comp.

CONCLUSION

1   The focus of this chapter has been on the fundamentals of those policies designed to offset the risk of *living death*, or disability. A disability can be financially devastating because on top of losing your ability to earn income, there are often substantial medical costs incurred for hospital and doctor bills. Unfortunately, statistics from the past 20 years have shown a rapid upward spiral in medical costs, forcing health insurance companies to raise their premiums and devise methods to contain those costs. Unlike life insurance, there is no "standard" health insurance Policy format and therefore, the only way you can determine if a specific loss is covered under a health Policy is to read that specific Policy.

There are two primary health insurance policies designed to handle the risk of *living death* – Disability Income and Medical Expense. These coverages may be sold on either an individual or a group basis, and they may be written to cover both accident and sickness, or accident only. Accident and sickness are **perils**, or causes of loss.

2   **Disability Income** policies are generally designed to replace a **wage earner's income** in the event of disability so that the normal living expenses (like housing, food, and utilities) can be paid. Disability Income policies are **valued** (or **stated amount**) contracts, which means that if Joe is disabled, he will receive a stated amount of money on a **periodic basis** from his insurance company, such as $1600 a month, or $400 a week. From the insurance company's point of view, this means that the cost is fairly predictable and so a *long term price guarantee* to the Policyowner is possible. Disability Income policies, like most insurance policies, have a deductible, but it is "paid" in terms of time, not dollars, and it is called an **Elimination Period**. For example, if Joe has a 30 day Elimination Period and is disabled for six months, he will only receive five months of benefits because he must "pay" by not receiving benefits for the first 30 days.

3   Modern **Medical Expense** policies are designed to pay for reasonable, necessary, and customary **medical costs**, such as doctor and hospital bills, and often cover the **entire family**. Medical Expense policies are usually written as **reimbursement** contracts so they pay **lump sum benefits**, generally to the medical care provider since most Policyowners *assign* their benefits to their hospital, doctor, etc. The Policyowner must pay any charges not covered by the Policy, the **deductible** (which is a usually a set dollar amount), and, perhaps, a percentage of the covered expenses (called coinsurance). Because nobody really knows what medical costs will be in the future, the claim costs are unpredictable. Therefore, the insurance company is unwilling to make a long term price guarantee on Medical Expense policies, and normally reserves the right to *adjust* (raise) the premium over time.

4   Besides the reimbursement contract approach, another common method of selling Medical Expense is on a *service* contract basis. **A service organization**, like the traditional **Blue Cross - Blue Shield** plan, promises services to the **subscriber** (Insured) rather than a reimbursement of dollars. The Blues contract with the provider hospitals and physicians as well as with the subscriber. Traditionally, Blue Cross was designed to pay hospitals, and Blue Shield was designed to pay doctors. Both are generally not-for-profit organizations which usually operate on a state-wide basis. However, there is substantial variation among the Blues plans.

1 Other service providers include **Health Maintenance Organizations (HMO's)** or Health Insuring Corporations (HIC's) and Preferred Provider Organizations (PPO's). The classic HMO is usually a program that operates by hiring its own doctors to staff its own local clinics. The HMO approach emphasizes **preventive care**, so routine physicals, immunizations, and office visits are covered and there are usually no deductibles or coinsurance. With a **Preferred Provider Organization (PPO)**, benefits are structured like an HMO if the subscriber chooses a physician or hospital from an approved list. If the medical provider the subscriber wants is not on the preferred list, then the PPO plan works much like the typical Medical Expense reimbursement Policy. You should note that there are many variations on these basic models, and there are sure to be even more in the future.

2 You will find that Disability Income and Medical Expense policies have several common elements, such as the following:

- **Insuring Clause** – states the bare bones promise.

- **Consideration Clause** – says that the insurance company relied on the statements you made on the application in issuing the Policy, so if you lied, the insurance company has a possible way out of paying the claim. It also states that the Policy and the application comprise the entire contract between the insurance company and the Policyowner.

- **Renewal Provision** – describes the Policyowner's right to keep the Policy in force.

  - **Noncancellable** – guarantees both the price and the right to keep the Policy in force until a stated age. This form of renewal is generally only found in Disability Income policies.

  - **Guaranteed Renewable** – guarantees the right to keep the Policy in force until a stated age, but no price guarantee. The company has the right to *adjust* the premium over time by class.

  - **Conditionally Renewable** – guarantees the Policyowner's right to keep it until a stated age IF certain events don't occur, such as early retirement.

  - **Optionally Renewable** – the *company's* option, that is. The company has the choice whether to renew on the Policy's anniversary date or, perhaps, on the next premium due date.

  - **Cancellable** – the company can cancel the Policy *anytime* as long as there is a five-day written notice and refund of unearned premium.

  - **Term** – lasts a stated period of time and cannot be renewed.

- **General Provisions** – consist mainly of the mandatory and optional provisions of the NAIC Model Uniform Accident and Sickness Policy Provisions Law adopted by the state. (See Chapter 15 of this text.)

- **Benefit Provisions** – tell you exactly how much the company will pay, for how long, with what frequency, for what things, and the limits. In other words, if the Insuring Clause is the bare bones promise, the benefit provisions are the "meat" of the promise.

- **Free Look Provision** – gives the Policyowner a limited period of time to examine the Policy and the right to return it for a 100% refund if dissatisfied with it in any way. The Free Look period does not start until the **delivery date** of the Policy.

- **Exclusions** – a list of what is not covered. **An Exclusion (Impairment) Rider** is an exclusion which applies to one specific individual covered by the Policy for usually one specific ailment or body part. For example, if Joe has had two operations and frequent periods of treatment on the elbow he injured in college athletics, his Medical Expense Policy may be issued with an Impairment Rider on his elbow.

- **Definitions Section** – lists all the important words of the Policy and their meanings as far as the Policy is concerned, such as *accident, sickness, preexisting condition, disability*, etc. If Joe wants to know, for example, whether he can collect a disability income benefit, his disability must fit the definition of "disability" stated in his Policy's Definitions Section.

- **Probationary Period** – a specified period of time beginning on the Policy's effective date (start date) during which there is no coverage. The main purpose is to screen out preexisting illness.

1   The tax treatment of health insurance depends on who paid the premium. As a general rule, if you bought the Policy, then you won't be taxed on any benefits. Also, your premiums are usually not tax-deductible. If, on the other hand, your employer bought the Policy, then you will be taxed on your benefits if it is disability income, but not if it is medical expense. The premiums your employer pays are tax-deductible for the employer.

11

DISABILITY INCOME

1 At age 40, Joe Insured has the world by the tail. He and Jolene both work and earn enough to pay all their bills, save for retirement, and help their oldest son through college. Joe is comfortable with his insurance program. He has Homeowners and Automobile insurance, Life insurance on both himself and Jolene, and a small amount of Convertible Term life insurance on each of the children. He also has a 401(k) for his retirement, and Jolene has an employer-sponsored pension plan. Through Jolene's employee benefits, they also have Medical Expense and dental coverage on the entire family. Joe relays this information to his Agent, confident that he and Jolene have provided for everything.

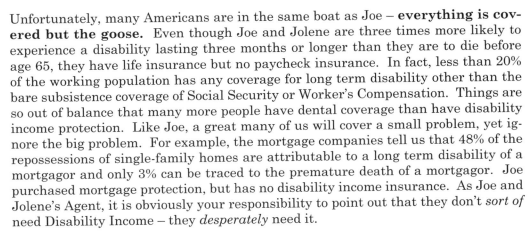

Need to insure the Golden Goose

2 His confidence is severely rattled, however, when his Agent says, "Haven't you forgotten to insure the goose?" (Or, perhaps, "geese" in this instance.) His Agent points out that all of what their family has is dependent upon Joe and Jolene's continued ability to bring home a paycheck. After some discussion, Joe realizes that if either he or Jolene became disabled, they could withstand it for a short period of time, but not for more than a couple of months.

3 Unfortunately, many Americans are in the same boat as Joe – **everything is covered but the goose.** Even though Joe and Jolene are three times more likely to experience a disability lasting three months or longer than they are to die before age 65, they have life insurance but no paycheck insurance. In fact, less than 20% of the working population has any coverage for long term disability other than the bare subsistence coverage of Social Security or Worker's Compensation. Things are so out of balance that many more people have dental coverage than have disability income protection. Like Joe, a great many of us will cover a small problem, yet ignore the big problem. For example, the mortgage companies tell us that 48% of the repossessions of single-family homes are attributable to a long term disability of a mortgagor and only 3% can be traced to the premature death of a mortgagor. Joe purchased mortgage protection, but has no disability income insurance. As Joe and Jolene's Agent, it is obviously your responsibility to point out that they don't *sort of* need Disability Income – they *desperately* need it.

Who's gonna bring home the bacon

4 In this chapter, we will examine the various definitions of "disability" available in the marketplace; we'll discuss several methods of handling the problem of partial disability; we will look at some of the riders typically sold with this Policy; and we will explore the business uses of the Disability Income contract. To begin, let's quickly review the important points we have already made about Disability Income policies.

Characteristics of Disability Income

1. Disability Income policies function like **substitute paychecks**.

...a short review...

2. They **pay you** and are designed to cover your continuing living expenses during a period of disability.

3. They are **valued** (or stated amount) contracts and benefits are paid on a periodic basis.

The ATM machine is broken

4. In the context of a family, only the **breadwinner(s)** would be covered.

5. Disability Income policies are most frequently written as noncancellable (price guaranteed) or guaranteed renewable (price not guaranteed) to age 65 and are conditionally renewable thereafter.

"if you are hurt and miss work... it won't hurt to miss work." *Yogi Berra, 2001*

6. The deductible is expressed as **time without benefits** as opposed to dollars and is known as an **elimination period**.

7. These policies can be purchased on a group basis, but 70% are sold on an individual basis.

8. If **you purchase** Disability Income yourself, benefits are **not taxable**; if your **employer pays** the premium, benefits are **taxable**.

9. While some states allow the Blues to sell Disability Income policies, most are purchased through commercial carriers.

Disability Income Alternatives

When helping a client plan their Disability Income needs, there are several common sense factors that should be considered.

- How much income is really needed to replace Joe if he becomes disabled? If he currently makes $5000 a month, that might seem to be the answer. But, if he is disabled, he may be able to drop some expenses. The second car may no longer be a necessity. Downtown parking, a closet full of suits and power lunches may no longer show up as expense items.

needs...

...if...

and how much...

- Other sources of income - **Social Security, Workers Compensation**, retirement funds and Jolene's paycheck could be considerations. Does Joe have 90 days worth of sick leave accumulated at work? Does his employer have a group Disability Income Policy? At what level of benefits? Long term or short term?

- How long will the current obligations continue? Is the house nearly paid for? Are the children in college or kindergarten? When will Joe retire?

- Is Joe's Major Medical coverage adequate? Will he need to use any of his Disability Income benefits for medical care?

Occupation As An Underwriting Factor

1 Although the Insured's occupation is a rating factor in most policies, it is a relatively minor consideration in life insurance and medical expense insurance. With a life insurance Policy, the company simply raises the rates to accommodate kamikaze occupations like rodeo rider, astronaut, and deep sea diver. With most occupations, there is no pricing difference at all. For instance, a healthy 30-year-old doctor and a healthy 30-year-old truck driver would pay identical premiums for identical coverage from most life companies. With group Medical Expense policies, the insurance company is relatively unconcerned about the Insured's occupation because these contracts exclude injuries suffered on the job anyway — at least those covered by Workers Compensation.

*Occupation
is #1*

2 **With Disability Income policies, however, the Insured's occupation becomes *the* critical underwriting and rating consideration.** It dictates the kind of Policy you can offer the proposed Insured and the benefits available, as well as the premiums which will be charged.

*it's not just a job. . .
it's an
underwriting tool*

Occupational Classifications

3 Most companies have established four to six occupational classes into which they categorize their Insureds and proposed Insureds. The following is an example of one company's approach.

*Lowest
Risk*

Class 1:   Professional occupations such as CPA's, architects, bankers, engineers, etc.

Class 2:   Executives, managers, technical workers, skilled office workers, good-looking insurance instructors, etc.

Class 3:   Supervisors of employees performing manual operations, salespersons and retail workers, assemblers of small parts.

Class 4:   Skilled manual laborers, such as plumbers, contractors, light machine operators, and carpenters.

*Highest
Risk*

Class 5:   General laborers, heavy machine operators, bricklayers, welders, farmers, commercial fishermen, and lumberjacks.

4 In determining which classification you best fit, insurance companies ask four specific questions:

- What is your job?
- How dangerous is it?
- Could a minor injury prevent you from doing it?
- How stable is your job and your industry?

5 **What Is Your Job?** – The insurance company is primarily interested in what you *do* – not what your job title is. Joe may be a restaurant owner, but that alone does not dictate his occupational class. The real question is what he does each day. Does he only supervise his cooks and waiters, or is he the one who's doing the cooking? That will determine his classification. Even if he only cooks when his regular chef is on vacation or takes a day off, that will affect his classification because normally, the most hazardous duty will determine his occupational classification.

*What do you
actually do?*

© 2010 Pathfinder Corporation

How Dangerous Is It? – Some occupations are easily recognizable as hazardous. If
1 Joe makes his living as a human cannonball, a window washer at the Sears Tower, or
as a professional bull rider, it is unlikely that any company will sell him a Disability
Income Policy. But some occupations cannot be pigeon-holed as easily, and we have
to examine the **claims history of that occupation**. Most of us would put a court
reporter in the same category as a stenographer or secretary, but the claims history
of court reporters is so high that most companies drop them a notch in rating, and
some refuse to write them at all.

Could A Minor Injury Prevent You From Doing Your Job? – Although some
2 occupations are perceived to be perfectly safe, there may be a *hidden risk* involved.
For instance, a relatively minor injury, such as a fractured wrist, could prevent a
surgeon or a dentist from doing her job, but probably not a bank president. As you
might guess, a minor injury creates a real double bind for an occupation like carpen-
ter where a broken wrist is both likely to occur and likely to result in a disability.

How Stable Is Your Job And Your Industry? – It is an indisputable fact that
3 when layoffs occur, disability claims increase. Even occupations which are seasonal
in nature show a higher incidence of claims in the off season. Therefore, some occupations may be rated at a lower classification only because of the seasonality or
instability of the industry.

Benefit Limits

*Insure you for
a % of your
earned income*

In addition to a proposed Insured's job classification, there is a second factor which is
4 critical in structuring disability income benefits – **earned income**. Since the whole
purpose of a Disability Income Policy is to replace income you could have earned during
a period of disability, the maximum benefit you can buy is based on what you earn.
Generally, how much you can buy is determined by **what you earned last year**.

The insurance company will not allow an Insured to purchase enough disability income
5 coverage to completely replace his or her income. If Joe could earn the same income
by becoming disabled that he can earn by working full time, he may be inclined to
get disabled and stay that way. ***To avoid adverse selection, there has to be a
financial incentive for Joe to return to work.*** Companies tend to limit benefits so
that he will receive no more than about 90% of his after tax income from all sources
– including Social Security and Worker's Compensation. As a percentage
of *before-tax* income, this would amount to around 85% for Insureds with
lower annual incomes (and lower taxes) to around 65% for Insureds with
higher incomes (and higher taxes).

Figuring the correct percentage can get rather complicated when we
6 are dealing with a two income household. To keep things simple,
let's structure our examples with Joe's income only. If we assume that Joe is earning $25,000 a year, paying $5,000 in taxes
and taking home $20,000, the insurance company might choose to
limit his total annual benefits to, say, $18,000, or $1,500 per month.
Assuming Joe's company calculates that he could collect as much as
$800 per month from Social Security, then they would be willing to
sell Joe a $700 monthly benefit. If Joe makes $50,000 a year ($40,000
after taxes), the company might limit him to a total benefit of $3,000 per month with
$1,000 coming from Social Security and $2,000 from his Policy benefits. Given the low
ceiling of maximum Social Security benefits, the potential impact of Social Security
greatly diminishes in the higher income brackets.

1   While this approach appears reasonable, there is one major problem. Due to the extremely strict Social Security definition of disability (about 75% of the claims are denied), it is quite possible for Joe to be disabled and qualified under his Policy for benefits, but *not be* qualified for benefits under Social Security. In the previous example, Joe was earning $40,000 a year after taxes, but would only receive $24,000 a year in Policy benefits without Social Security. Insurance companies have solved this dilemma by offering a **Social Security or Social Insurance Supplement (SIS) Rider** which says that the company will pay what Social Security refuses to pay. In our example, Social Security denied Joe $1,000 per month. With this rider, the company will pick up the amount Social Security won't pay ($1,000 per month), so Joe would receive a total of $3,000 per month ($2,000 under the regular Policy benefits, and $1,000 under the rider) for a total of $36,000 per year.

Note to Student:

2   Although company practices in this area vary enormously, all subscribe to these basic concepts:

- The Insured should be able to purchase a benefit large enough to allow for the maintenance of a lifestyle similar to that enjoyed before the disability.

- The total benefits available should never exceed what the disabled person earns when not disabled.

3   But the methods by which companies apply these concepts are all over the map. Some companies are only concerned about the potential impact of Social Security in the lower income brackets while others apply the reduction across the board; others are concerned not only with Social Security, but also Workers Compensation and any other *social insurance* to which the disabled person is eligible; some will pay the amount covered by the Social Security Rider during the process of applying to Social Security with an **Additional Monthly Benefits** (AMB) rider which pays an extra benefit for up to one year and others will not; if Social Security pays a partial benefit, some of the riders will pick up the difference and others pay nothing if Social Security pays anything. As is so often the case in health insurance, all you can do is be familiar with the basic concept and read the Policy in question to fully understand how it will be implemented.

4   You might also note that all of our examples were based upon the assumption that Joe's benefits are not taxed. Since the majority of Disability Income policies are individually purchased, an untaxed benefit is the most likely situation. If, however, Joe's employer pays the premium, benefits are taxable. In that event, the insurance company will allow the purchase of a higher benefit limit in order to cover both Joe and Uncle Sam.

Defining Total Disability

1   Once the insurance company has determined Joe's occupational class and calculated the maximum benefit limit he can purchase, Joe must choose a definition of disability from those offered by his company. Obviously, the more generous the definition, the more expensive the Policy.

2   There are four definitions of "disability" offered by most companies in most states. All share the following requirements:

- **The disability must result from a sickness or accident not excluded under the terms of the contract.**

- **During a period of disability, the Insured must be under the care of a physician.**

3   While the first is easily understandable, the second requirement merits a little elaboration. The need for a doctor's care is obviously necessary at the onset of a disability and will probably remain necessary throughout a disability from which Joe could recover. However, if Joe is disabled because he lost both legs in an auto accident at age 40, there would be no reason for him to remain under a doctor's care for the next 25 years. While his Policy may say that he must be *under the care of a physician*, no company would interpret that phrase literally. Common sense dictates and numerous courts have held that Joe cannot be denied benefits because of this provision if medical care is not necessary to his well-being or potential recovery.

Better for Insured...

4   **"Your Occ" or "Own Occ"** – The most generous definition of total disability offered today is the **regular occupation** definition which is usually referred to as *Your Occ*. Since most companies make this definition available only to those in its top occupational class, Joe may or may not be eligible to select this one.

...more expensive

5   Under this definition, you are disabled if you are unable to perform the important duties of your own occupation – the work in which you were engaged when the disability began. Whether you are able or willing to do another job has no bearing on the determination of your disability. **If you can't do *your job*, you are disabled.** For instance, suppose Joe is a brain surgeon with a $500,000 annual income. If, at age 40, he is stricken with arthritis and can no longer do brain surgery, he is disabled. Even if he later goes to work as something else . . . say, a medical school professor earning $200,000 a year, he would still be eligible for the total disability benefit in his Policy. Even if he goes back to school to change his career, gets a law degree, and ends up earning more as a lawyer than he earned as a brain surgeon, he will still continue to receive his total disability benefits, since he still cannot do his *own* job (the one he was doing when the disability started).

Can you do your job?

6   **"Any Occ"** – The most restrictive definition of disability commonly available today is the **gainful occupation** or **reasonable occupation** definition which is commonly (if somewhat inaccurately) referred to as *Any Occ*. At one time, there were policies sold which literally meant that if you could do *any* job you were not disabled. This exceedingly narrow definition is now prohibited in almost every state.

Best bet for the company...

7   As the Any Occ is applied today, it means that you are disabled if you cannot do your job or **any other job for which you are reasonably suited by education, training or experience**. Obviously, the intent is to assure that any new career will keep the Insured at approximately the same **economic status** as he was before. If Joe, the surgeon-turned-professor-turned-lawyer in the previous example had owned a Policy with this definition, he would probably have never been considered disabled. Even with arthritis, there are many medical occupations for which he could qualify and in which he could find work.

Reasonably suited ...less expensive

1 Although the Any Occ definition is more restrictive than the Own Occ definition, it is also less expensive. Joe might save as much as 10% on his annual premium if he decides that he can live with this lesser definition.

2 **"Your Occ, Then Any Occ"** – Essentially, this definition is something of a hybrid of the two previous definitions. Under this approach, you are considered disabled if, initially, you cannot perform the important duties of your regular occupation. Even if you work at some other occupation, you will still continue to receive benefits for as long as this definition is in force. After a period of time (such as two years, five years, ten years, depending upon what you bought from the choice of time periods that your company makes available to your occupational class), the contract switches to the Any Occ definition. The switch from Your Occ to Any Occ can be handled in either of two ways, depending upon the Policy language.

sliding scale

3 **Presumptive Total Disability** – Most Disability Income contracts will utilize one of the three previous definitions and include with it **a presumptive total disability benefit**. With this benefit, you are automatically considered to be totally disabled (even if you can and are doing your job or any job) if sickness or injury results in the loss of:

we assume you are disabled . . . even if you aren't

- sight in both eyes.
- hearing in both ears.
- power of speech.
- use of any two limbs.

"The Rush Limbaugh Clause"

4 For example, let's assume that Joe's cousin, Go Go Joe, works as a disc jockey and loses his sight in both eyes at a ZZ Top light show. Even if he continues his career as a disc jockey, he is considered to be totally disabled and receives full benefits.

The Length of the Benefit Period

5 Another important decision that Joe must make is the length of his benefit period. In other words, if he is disabled at age 40, how long does he want benefits to continue? He can select a benefit period of two years, five years, to age 65, or for life. Obviously, the longer the benefit period, the higher Joe's premium will be.

Short

6 While it would appear that everyone would select the long term benefits, such is not always the case. Approximately 98% of all disabled persons recover in less than one year. Therefore, Joe could cover 98% of the problem and save 50% to 60% of his premium dollars if he views it this way. But, most people buy insurance to cover them if the worst possible situation occurs. From this perspective, we should point out that if Joe suffers a disability which lasts longer than one year, it is unlikely that he will ever return to gainful employment. This fact certainly lends much credibility to the longer benefit periods.

Long

7 The way in which insurance companies use the words *short term disability* (STD) and *long term disability* (LTD) can make the choice even more difficult than it needs to be. To be 100% accurate, the distinction between long and short term disability is as follows:

With **group** Disability Income, a benefit period **of less than two years is considered short term** and anything paying benefits for two years or more is long term.

With **individual** Disability Income, a benefit period **of less than five years is short term** and anything paying for five years or longer is long term.

Good Stuff

1 Given the discrepancy between the group and the individual plans, you are probably only safe in describing any benefit period of less than two years as short term and any period of five years or longer as long term.

Elimination Period

2 Probably the most difficult and certainly one of the most important decisions Joe must make in purchasing a Disability Income Policy is the length of the elimination period. As you recall from Chapter 10, the elimination period is a **deductible expressed in time**. *It is the period of time that Joe must be totally disabled before he is eligible for total disability benefits.* Most companies make available elimination periods of 30 days, 60 days, 90 days, 180 days and 365 days. As we have pointed out, the longer the elimination period Joe can withstand, the lower his premium will be. At age 40, Joe could save about 30% by selecting a 60-day elimination period over a 30 day period. By going to 90 days, he could save 40%, and if he chose a 180-day elimination period rather than a 30-day period, he could cut his premium in half.

TIME DEDUCTIBLE

3 In determining the length of the elimination period, Joe must keep at least three things in mind. The first is obvious – how long can his family meet their obligations without a paycheck? It would certainly be unusual to find an American family that could manage more than 60 or 90 days without a paycheck, but if you consider the impact on premium, most families need to extend the period as far as they possibly can. Since Joe and Jolene are dual breadwinners, Joe might be tempted to assume that if he is disabled, Jolene's paychecks will continue. However, it is certainly a possibility that one automobile accident could render both of them disabled.

4 The second thing Joe must consider in selecting an elimination period is that **benefits are paid in arrears**. In other words, if he selects a 60 day elimination period, he is *eligible* for benefits on the 61st day, but he will not receive a check until about the 91st day. In helping Joe design his program, you might start by asking how long they can live without income, but you must remember to subtract 30 days from that period and then set the elimination period to match the remainder.

Remember when choosing

5 Finally, Joe should verify that his contract follows the example of most companies and utilizes the same elimination period for both sickness and accident.

The Partial Disability Problem

1   To this point, our discussion of Disability Income coverage has focused entirely upon *total* disability. But what if Joe's disability leaves him with the ability to do *part* of his job but not all of it? He is not "totally" disabled, but his forced reduction in hours (or duties) results in a loss of income. For many years, Disability Income policies contained a **partial disability provision** which essentially provided a short-term transitional benefit as a disabled person went from totally disabled back to totally employed. In recent years, another approach, called the **residual disability benefit**, has all but replaced the partial disability provision. It can provide the same kind of transitional benefit as the partial disability provision, but it can also provide income for the Insured who becomes **permanently partially disabled**.

fight malingering

2   As we explore each of these approaches to the partial disability problem, there are a couple of things you should notice. With both partial and residual benefits, there is only coverage if the Insured suffers a **loss of time** (e.g., Joe can only work half-time) or a **loss of duties** (e.g., Joe can only do some of the tasks he did before) which then results in a loss of income. Also, you will discover that with one exception, these coverages only apply if the Insured is first totally disabled. Since we can all imagine circumstances under which a person can go from fully employed to partially disabled without ever being fully disabled, why does the company insist upon a period of *total disability* before paying partial disability benefits? One of the company's biggest fears about disability income is that Joe might attempt to fabricate a claim as a way to semi-retire. If he must first meet the Policy's more stringent definition of *total disability* for a period of time, it is more likely that his partial disability claim is legitimate.

Partial Disability Benefit

3   Although at one time the partial disability benefit was the only way of handling the partial disability problem, its use today is generally on the decline. The companies who make use of it generally do so for their less favorable occupational risks. As we pointed out, this benefit serves primarily as a transitional benefit for an Insured who has been totally disabled and can now return to work, but cannot resume all of his or her duties or cannot yet work full-time.

4   Typically, this benefit will pay **50% of the total disability** indemnity for a **period not to exceed six months**. As an example, suppose Joe had a heart attack and was totally disabled for five months. At the expiration of his elimination period, he became eligible for a total disability benefit of $2000 per month. If, after several months of total disability, Joe's doctor allows him to return to work, but limits his hours to 25 - 30 per week, under a partial disability benefit, Joe will receive a benefit of $1000 a month (50% of his total disability benefit) for up to six months. After six months, his partial benefits will stop – even if Joe still cannot work-full time. At that point, he is not *totally disabled* (since he is back at work), and his six months of *partial disability* benefits have been consumed.

"1/2"

Residual Disability Benefit

1 The major limitation of the partial disability benefit is that it ends too quickly. Suppose that Joe has been earning $4000 a month, but at age 40, he becomes **permanently partially disabled** to age 65. He now can earn only $1600 a month, and the six month benefit of partial disability will play out twenty-four and a half years too early. How will Joe replace his loss of $2400 a month?

ONCE . . . NOW

2 The **residual disability benefit** solves the problem. It pays a portion of the difference between what Joe can now earn ($1600) as compared to what he earned before the disability ($4000), and the benefit will continue for the same period as total disability benefits would have been paid under the same Policy. If Joe's Disability Income Policy was written with a benefit period to age 65, his residual disability benefits pay to age 65.

*permanent
partial
impairment*

3 Since the company always wants to provide Joe an incentive to return to full employment, the contract is never written to restore 100% of his income loss. Therefore, Joe must lose a specified amount of income – normally 20 - 25% – to be entitled to any benefit at all. On the other hand, if his income loss exceeds a certain percentage – like 75 - 80% – most companies consider him to be totally disabled and pay total disability benefits.

*Make up
the lost income*

The residual disability benefit is offered as a rider by some companies, and built into the Policy automatically by others.

Other Disability Income Policy Provisions

4 In addition to the coverage provisions of the Disability Income Policy which we have discussed to this point, there are numerous additional provisions built into the basic Policy. Many of these, like the Grace Period or the Free Look, are common to all health insurance and were discussed in Chapter 10. Only those provisions *unique* to Disability Income will be examined here.

Recurrent Disability

5 Suppose that Joe is totally disabled for a year, returns to work for a month, suffers a relapse, and is totally disabled again for another year. Will he have to wait through another elimination period to be paid for his second year of disability? The answer is "no" because of the **recurrent disability provision**.

Sick again

1 The recurrent disability provision states that **a later, separate period of disability will be considered a continuation of a prior period of disability if it starts within six months after the end of the prior period of disability and is the result in whole or in part of the same or related injury or sickness.** Loosely translated, "If it happens again, no deductible." This is an important provision to both Joe and his company. Without it, Joe would never return to work following a disability unless completely certain that his recovery was complete. With the recurrent disability provision, Joe is not penalized for trying to go back to work; in fact, there is a very strong incentive for him to do so.

Waiver of Premium

2 A waiver of premium provision is often added to Life insurance and Medical Expense policies as a rider, but with Disability Income it is normally built right into the Policy. It certainly would not make sense for the company to be paying you because you cannot work and then ask you to turn right around and hand money back in the form of premium.

Don't pay us when we're paying you

3 With most companies, the Insured must be totally disabled for a stated period of time – like 90 days – and then the company will waive all future premiums during the period of disability. Some companies even allow for the return of any premiums paid during this waiting period.

Rehabilitation Benefit

4 Although a company cannot force a disabled Insured to enroll in a retraining or rehabilitation program, it is often in the interest of both parties for this to occur. With a rehabilitation benefit provision in the Policy, the company can cover any costs not covered by other insurance or public funding if the disabled person participates in a rehabilitation program designed to help him return to work.

5 Some policies have a stated limit (like 12 times the monthly indemnity) for this benefit, and others are open-ended. Certainly, all have a presumed limit of good sense on the part of the company. If Joe is a disabled chef, the company will not likely cover the costs of retraining Joe to be a poet. Unless Joe finds work as a poet, benefits continue and the rehabilitation dollars have been wasted.

Transplant Benefit

6 If the Insured becomes disabled as the result of donating an organ for transplant, the company will treat the disability as if it were the result of a sickness.

Non Disabling Injury Benefit

7 If the Insured suffers an accident that requires medical treatment, but does not require time away from work, this benefit will pay for the cost of the treatment. (It is like a mini-Medical Expense Policy, and is sometimes known as a **medical reimbursement benefit**.)

Optional Disability Income Policy Benefits

1. In addition to the basic coverages we have described, there are a number of optional benefits that can be added by rider to the basic Policy for additional cost. Of the five most commonly offered riders, we have already addressed two of them:

   - Residual Disability Rider
   - Social Security (or Social Insurance) Rider

2. These two can be sold as either part of the basic Policy (as we have already discussed) or as riders. They function similarly in either configuration.

3. The three remaining are:

   - Future Income Option (FIO)
   - Cost of Living Adjustment (COLA) Option
   - Lifetime Extension Option

Future Income or Guaranteed Insurability Option (FIO)

4. Just as our benefit amounts cannot stay in fixed dollars if we are unlucky enough to become disabled, our level of insurance probably should not remain constant if we are lucky enough to stay healthy. It is generally true that over our working lives, our income increases and our health deteriorates. If at age 40 Joe purchases a Disability Income Policy with a $3000 a month maximum benefit level, he may qualify financially for a $5000 a month limit by age 50. However, he may not qualify physically for any additional benefits. This rider would enable him to buy additional amounts of coverage in the future regardless of his health.

Remember

Insurability. . . buy more

renewability. . . keep what you've got

5. The specific benefits available for future purchase and the frequency of option dates varies so greatly from one company to the next that it is pointless to outline the specifics of how this rider is implemented in even the vaguest of terms. All you can do is study your company's contracts (as well as your competition's) to see how it would work for your clients.

Cost of Living Adjustment (COLA) Option

6. Earlier in this text we addressed the problem that inflation causes for people who are retired on a fixed income. Obviously, the same problem exists for a person who is totally disabled for a long period of time. Joe's total disability benefit may be adequate for him in year #1, but if in 10 years the cost of living has doubled and his benefit remains the same, then his benefit in year #10 will only provide him with about half of the purchasing power that he had in year #1.

COLA

7. With a **Cost of Living rider**, Joe's disability benefit will **be automatically increased** at a given rate after he starts receiving benefits. Depending upon the company, this can be done by stating a guaranteed percentage (typically between 5 - 10%) or tying the benefits to an inflation index like the Consumer Price Index (CPI). Some companies compute the increase as simple interest and others use the more generous compound interest approach. Some contracts put a cap or ceiling on how high the indexed benefits may climb, and others do not.

Lifetime Extension

1 If Joe owns a Policy which would pay benefits until he is 65, the purchase of this rider will extend benefits for total disability until his death. The most common rationale for purchasing this rider is the supposition that a disabled person cannot prepare financially for retirement as easily as that same person could if he or she were able-bodied. With that idea in mind, these riders often state that the disability must occur before some limiting age, like 50, 55 or 60. Obviously, a person who becomes disabled at 64 1/2 has had the same opportunity to provide for retirement as anyone else. Despite this, a few companies offer this rider in a form which says that benefits will be paid for life as long as the disability begins before age 65. While the language is obviously more generous, the cost is considerably higher.

Other Benefits ‡

2 Given the number of companies marketing Disability Income policies, it should come as no shock that there are at least a half-dozen other riders offered by some companies which are occasionally sold to somebody. Two options that were popular for a while made it possible for people who had no disability claims to recover much of what they had spent on Disability Income premiums. While neither is being actively sold today, many people still own one or the other.

- **Return of Premium** - This rider allows a refund of a percentage of your premium at specified intervals. One company, for example, will, at 10 year intervals, refund 80% of premiums paid minus any claims. This amount can be taken in cash or used to prepay a portion of the next 10 years premium.

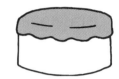

Frosting on the cake

- **Cash Surrender Value** - This rider creates a cash value of 60% to 80% of the premium minus any claims paid. Typically, the cash value is only available to the Policyowner when he chooses to no longer renew the contract - like at age 65.

INCOME REPLACEMENT CONTRACTS . . . A NEW ALTERNATIVE

3 Before Joe decides to purchase a Disability Income Policy with residual benefits, he might want to consider an alternative which has only become available in the last few years. An Income Replacement contract is designed to do the same job as Disability Income with residual benefits, but its design is radically different.

4 With traditional disability income contracts, benefits depend greatly upon your ability or inability to go to work. The Policy's promise may hinge on whether you work in your own occupation, a different occupation, or an occupation for which you are reasonable suited. The Income Replacement Policy is not about occupations. In an oddball sense, it's not even about disability. The Policy doesn't even define the word "disabled." **The Income Replacement contract is only about income,** and its promise is inherently simple. If Joe makes $50,000 a year today, and, due to a covered accident or sickness, suffers a loss of income, the company will replace the income up to a stated percentage, like 70% or 80%. Suppose Joe's contract promises 70% of his $50,000 salary, or $35,000 a year. If Joe's earnings drop to $30,000, the contract will pay him $5000. If his earnings drop to zero, he will be paid $35,000. Under this concept, **partial** (residual) disability is not an extra consideration – it is part of the same basic promise.

1 Most of the standard features of disability income – like the elimination period, the benefit period, recurrent disability, waiver of premium, rehabilitation benefits, indexing and the future income option – are easily applied to the income replacement concept. The essential differences between the two contracts boil down to four important ideas.

Indemnificate

not

No definition of total or partial disability. With an Income Replacement contract, if you lose income because of a covered accident or sickness, you are covered.

No need for loss of time or duties. With traditional Disability Income contracts, there had to be a loss of time or duties to trigger coverage. With Income Replacement policies, this is unnecessary. If you can work as many hours as ever, if you can do everything you could do before, but you lose 50% of your income because you cannot do it as well, you still receive benefits.

Face Amount

No need for total disability to gain residual disability benefits. Generally, there has to be some period of total disability before residual benefits can be paid under a Disability Income Policy. Since Income Replacement policies don't even define total or residual disability, this step is obviously unnecessary.

Partial benefits are computed differently. With the Income Replacement contract, we simply subtract anything Joe can now earn from his benefit limit and pay the difference.

2 Beyond its simplicity, another major attribute of an Income Replacement contract is *price*. Generally, they are a little less expensive than their Disability Income equivalent. This price differential is mainly due to the fact that you really cannot *win* under this approach; you can only stay even. With standard Disability Income contracts, you can – at least in a financial sense – *win*. If you have a traditional Policy with an Own Occ definition, you can receive full benefits for life even if you change occupations and do something else that pays more. Or, say you write romance novels for a living. If you lose both legs in an accident, a standard Disability Income Policy will classify you as totally disabled (presumptive disability) and pay benefits even though you can continue to churn out tear-jerkers at your regular pace. In neither of these situations would an Income Replacement contract pay any benefit whatsoever.

3 It will be interesting to watch the future to see if Disability Income and Income Replacement remain as two distinct and competitive products, or if they begin to blend together into one homogenized product.

BUSINESS APPLICATIONS OF DISABILITY INCOME POLICIES

4 A business, like a family, can grow accustomed to a specific level of income and be financially devastated if that stream of income is disrupted. With a small business in particular, the disability of an owner or other key person could be enough to severely impair the company's profitability . Joe's Restaurant is a small business, and, depending upon the nature and structure of that business, Joe may have a tremendous need for one of these products. In each case, we are simply modifying the traditional Disability Income Policy to serve a specific purpose. Therefore, we are not truly looking at a new product, but simply a new application of a product with which we are already familiar.

Business Overhead Expense

1 **Situation #1:** *Let's assume that Joe owns a small restaurant with a staff of five employees. Joe cooks behind the counter and is more popular than his food. He sings, dances, tells jokes, and is the clearinghouse for all local gossip. Yes, people buy his food, but for all intents and purposes, Joe is the product.*

2 If Joe should become disabled, he will have two worries – his home and his business. His home and family will be fine if he has purchased adequate Disability Income coverage, but what about the business? Joe has a favorable lease at a fantastic location and must continue paying rent in order to keep it. He cannot afford to lose three of the five employees; therefore, some salary continuation is necessary. Since Joe has a locker full of meat and a highly advertised phone number, he needs to keep his utility and phone bills paid.

3 All of this adds up to be a rather large amount of money – money for which Joe has no readily available source. The business has only enough cash assets to cover these expenses for 30 days. Joe's personal Disability Income Policy benefits would be totally consumed at home. The solution to Joe's problem is a contract known as the **Business Overhead Expense** Policy. A Business Overhead Expense (BOE) Policy is nothing more than a modified Disability Income Policy written to cover *business expenses* rather than personal or family expenses.

Keeps the doors open

4 **Benefits Not Based On Salary** – Maximum benefit amounts from Joe's Business Overhead Expense Policy have nothing to do with Joe's salary – they are established based on allowable overhead items which Joe chooses to cover. The contract spells out specifically what is covered and what is not.

5 Items Which Can Be Covered:

Pays ordinary business expenses

- Employee salaries
- Rent
- Utility bills
- Accounting, billing, and collecting fees
- Janitorial and telephone answering service
- Other fixed expenses normally incurred in managing and operating the business

6 Items Which Cannot Be Covered:

- **Salary for the owner**
- Payment on principal of indebtedness
- Cost of equipment, furniture, or merchandise

no dough for Joe

Reimbursement – Not Stated Amount – Another characteristic of Disability Income to this point has been a stated or fixed amount benefit. With Business Overhead Expense, **the Policy will only pay the expenses Joe's business actually incurs up to a stated dollar limit, for a stated number of months.**

© 2010 Pathfinder Corporation

Key Employee (or Partner) Disability Income Policy

Situation #2: *Assume that Joe's restaurant is thriving, and that for the last two years, he has planned the opening of a second "Eat at Joe's" in another small town 100 miles away. Throughout the two year period, Joe has invested hundreds of hours of his time to train his assistant manager, Schmoe, to operate the new restaurant. At the grand opening, Schmoe slips on an ice cube, fractures his skull and cannot return to work for six months. Since Joe's entire savings is invested in his new restaurant, Joe decides to split his time between the two businesses to assure that each functions properly, but for the six months that his assistant manager is disabled, Joe will need an assistant manager at each location. Where will the money to pay the assistant managers' salaries come from?*

1

People you can't do without

A Key Employee Disability plan could provide the funds necessary to replace his assistant manager throughout his absence. The way this works is Joe's restaurant purchases a Policy with his assistant manager as the Insured and the business as the **"Beneficiary"**. If his assistant manager is disabled, the business receives a stated amount benefit which can be used to offset the extra cost of doing business for this period. This is a short term plan to give the company a period of time to regroup during the disability of a key employee. The maximum period of indemnity is typically six to twelve months, and any elimination period called for in the contract would also be extremely short.

2

breaks the basic rule

Benefits are not paid to the employee but to the employer. We should also point out that Key Employee Disability Income is not a coverage that you will commonly see used. Although it is beginning to gain some notice in the small business community, many are still unaware of its existence or its applications.

3

Employer = Beneficiary

Oftentimes, the company receives the benefit and uses some or all of the money as a **salary continuation plan** for the disabled employee.

4

Disability Buy-Sell (Business Disability Buyout)

Situation #3: *Let's assume that Joe has formed a corporation with two other small restaurant owners in his area – Bo and Moe. To compete with the chain restaurants, they do collective advertising, purchasing, accounting, warehousing and have even centralized their payroll and personnel functions. Each owns one-third of the corporation which in turn owns the three restaurants. They have a Buy-Sell agreement which will be activated in the event any of the three of them die, but they also need a similar agreement in the event any of the three should suffer a lengthy disability.*

5

As was the case with life insurance, the first step has nothing to do with insurance. The three businessowners must agree to a plan that, when written in contract form, becomes the Buy-Sell Agreement. Suppose they agree that if one of the three becomes disabled, the other two can carry on without him for a year. If, at year's end, the disability continues, the corporation will buy the disabled person's share for a stated amount needed for the buyout.

6

Periodic followed by a lump sum

1 Since the corporation often does not have the cash needed, the need for insurance is obvious. "But," you might say, "Disability Income policies pay in installments – they don't pay in lump sums of $500,000 or any other amount." Well, this one does. The need for funding of disability buy-out agreements has resulted in the development of a whole new line of products for just this purpose.

2 Although they are considered to be Disability Income policies, they differ radically from the basic concepts of disability income we've established up to this point.

- They pay the business not the Insured.
- The benefit amount is not related to a paycheck – it is based upon the amount necessary to purchase your stock in the corporation.
- The benefit is paid primarily in a lump sum rather than in installments.

Tax Notes on Business DI Policies

3 Two of the business uses of Disability Income contracts that we have explored mirror their Life insurance counterparts in concept and in tax consequences. Just like Key Employee Life and Life used to fund a Buy-Sell Agreement, the **premiums paid for Key Employee Disability Income and Disability Buy-Sell are not tax deductible** as a business expense. However, **benefits paid by either of these policies is not considered to be taxable income**.

TAX FACTS

4 The oddball is Business Overhead Expense. With this contract the **premiums are treated as a business expense**, but the **benefits are** considered to be **taxable income**.

Conclusion

5 One of your greatest assets is your ability to earn an income. This asset can be Insured with a Disability Income Policy. Unfortunately, however, a large percentage of the American work force has not recognized the need to protect this asset. People insure their home, their car, and their life, but often overlook the need to insure their income.

6 Disability Income policies are generally designed to pay a stated amount benefit on a periodic basis in the event of the Insured's disability. In underwriting Disability Income, **the Insured's occupation is the single most important rating factor**. Insurance companies writing Disability Income generally have an occupational classification system based on considerations such as job duties, claims history of the occupation, and stability of the industry. When applying for coverage, the proposed Insured will first be categorized according to what he or she does for a living which, in turn, will dictate the type of Policy he or she can buy, the benefits available, and the premium that will be charged.

7 Another important factor used in determining Disability Income benefit limits is the Insured's **earned income**. The insurance company will allow a wage earner to purchase *only up to a certain percentage* of his or her income. By limiting how much Disability Income coverage an Insured can buy, the insurance company creates a financial incentive for the Insured to return to work. In addition to earned income, the insurance company will also take into account the Insured's tax bracket, and other potential sources of income during a period of disability, such as Social Security Disability Income and Worker's Compensation.

1 There are various definitions of "disability," but all of them share the following requirements:

- The disability must result from a sickness or accident not excluded under the terms of the contract.

- During a period of disability, the Insured must be under the care of a physician.

2 The most generous definition of total disability is the **Own Occ (Your Occ)** definition. Under this definition, you, as the Insured, are eligible to receive benefits if you are **unable to do the important duties of your own occupation**. For example, if Joe were a dentist and he broke his fingers, he would be probably be considered disabled under an Own Occ definition. However, if he were an attorney, he probably would not be considered disabled because he could continue to do his own job even with broken fingers. The Own Occ definition is generally only available to people in the insurance company's top occupational class (like doctors, lawyers, certified public accountants, etc.) and it is the most expensive definition available.

3 The most restrictive definition of total disability is the **Any Occ** definition under which you are considered disabled only if you are unable to **do any gainful occupation for which you are reasonably suited** by training, education, or experience. Returning to our previous example in which Joe, the dentist, broke his fingers, if he had a Policy with an Any Occ definition, he might *not* be considered disabled. Although he could not do his own job with broken fingers, he would probably be reasonably suited by training, education, or experience to do many *other gainful occupations*. If he could find work as a dental supplies salesman, for example, then he would not be considered disabled. The Any Occ definition of disability is stricter than the Own Occ definition, but it is also less expensive and available to Insureds of all occupational classifications.

4 A **presumptive total disability** benefit can be included in a Disability Income Policy. If Joe loses sight in both eyes, hearing in both ears, use of any two limbs, or the power of speech, he is automatically considered to be totally disabled, even if he continues to work at his own or any other job.

5 The problem of **partial disability** used to be handled with a provision which, after a period of total disability, the Policy would pay **50% of the total benefit** for up to **six months** if the Insured returned to work but was still suffering a loss of income due to loss of time or loss of duties. Nowadays, a **residual disability** benefit is usually the method used to handle the partial disability problem. If you, as the Insured, suffer a loss of income due to loss of time or loss of duties of your *own occupation* (if you have an Own Occ definition) or of *any suitable occupation* (if you have an Any Occ definition), then your Policy will pay a partial benefit. With a residual disability benefit, there is not a six month limit on the benefit period.

6 Before becoming eligible to receive Disability Income benefits, the Insured must be *totally disabled* for a specified period of time, known as the elimination period. **The elimination period is a deductible of time** – not dollars. For example, if Joe is totally disabled for 90 days and he has a 30 day elimination period, then he will be entitled to 60 days of disability income benefits. Keep in mind though that the insurance company **pays benefits in arrears,** so although he is *eligible* for benefits beginning on day 31, he won't actually receive his first check until about day 61.

1 Disability Income benefits will continue for either as long as the Insured is disabled or as long as the Policy benefit period lasts, whichever is shorter. A Policy whose benefit period lasts only up to two years is generally considered to be **short term**. If the benefits last for up to five years or longer, it is considered to be **long term**. Benefit periods of two to five years may be considered as either short term or long term, depending on whether the Policy is written on a group or an individual basis.

2 Other provisions sometimes included with Disability Income policies include:

- **Social Security Rider** – If the government won't pay you, we will.
- **Recurrent Disability** – If you go back to work and suffer a relapse, we will waive your elimination period.
- **Waiver of Premium** – If you're disabled for very long, you can stop paying your premium and we will keep your Policy in force.
- **Rehabilitation Benefit** – We will pay for your retraining to help you get off disability.
- **Transplant Benefit** – If you become disabled from donating an organ, you're covered.
- **Non Disability Injury Benefit** – A Medical Expense coverage for an injury not serious enough for a disability.
- **Cost of Living Adjustment (COLA) Option** – We will increase your benefit check so you can keep pace with inflation.
- **Future Income Option (FIO)** – You can buy more coverage at specified times in the future without having to provide proof of insurability.
- **Lifetime Extension Option** – If your disability lasts after age 65, we will keep on paying you until you die.

3 A relatively new alternative to traditional Disability Income is the **Income Replacement** Policy under which you will receive benefits if you lose income due to a covered accident or sickness, regardless of whether you consider yourself or the insurance company considers you to be *disabled*. Even if you are working full-time doing all the same duties you did before, if you suffer a loss of income because of a covered accident or sickness, you get paid.

4 Disability Income can be utilized not only to meet an individual's needs, but also to meet various needs of a business. A **Business Overhead Expense** (BOE) Policy is a modified disability income Policy designed to pay for the monthly expenses of a business, generally of a self-employed professional or a sole proprietor. The Business Overhead Expense Policy is written on the businessowner, but **it pays the business** so that the office rent, the employees' salaries, and other business expenses can be paid. However, BOE never covers the salary of the businessowner, and benefits are paid on a **reimbursement** basis for the business expenses actually incurred.

5 A **Key Employee Disability Income** Policy is essentially a Disability Income Policy purchased by an employer on a key employee. If the employee becomes disabled, rather than paying the Insured, **the benefit is paid to the employer**. The employer may use the benefit to replace the key employee or to continue the key employee's salary during his or her disability.

6 **Disability Buy-Sell** coverage is designed to **provide benefits to a corporation** to buy out a disabled stockholder/director's share of the business. If one of the primary stockholder/directors becomes disabled, the Policy will generally pay an installment benefit to the corporation for up to a year and then finally pay out a **lump sum benefit** to the corporation so it can **buy out** the disabled partner.

MEDICAL EXPENSE

12

1 Unlike Disability Income, the average American family is only too well aware of the need for medical expense insurance. It's a little hard to ignore in a society which spends $22 of every $100 on health care. In this area of health insurance, almost everyone (85% of the American public) has some type of coverage. Oddly enough, those without medical expense coverage are not the homeless or the jobless — they are covered under federal or state welfare plans like Medicaid. The 15% who are uninsured are mostly the self-employed or people who work for the self-employed. With medical expense insurance, the problem is not convincing people that they need it – the problem is "Can anyone afford it?" With the costs of medical care skyrocketing as they have over the last 40 years, medical expense premiums are increasing at the rate of 25% each year. Since the average family cannot keep up with these kinds of increases, it's not surprising that 90% of the covered population gets coverage through group insurance, normally provided by the employer.

Major changes under way at the national level

2 While shifting the burden to the employer has been an interesting way of camouflaging the problem, the costs have escalated so rapidly and consistently that the problem is beginning to reach the stage where it can no longer be disguised. Although obtaining our medical expense insurance through a group plan at work may temporarily sugar-coat the problem for you and me as consumers, ultimately, we get the bill. We may not directly pay an insurance company, but we still pay. You see, when Joe Insured finds that the cost of group health insurance on his restaurant employees just went up 25%, he doesn't fund the increase out of his pocket. He raises his prices and funds the increase out of the pockets of his customers – you and me and the others who eat at Joe's. The increased cost of health insurance for Joe's employees may be invisible to them, but it is still a cost that must be paid. It is now a fact that General Motors spends more on health care than it does on steel, which goes a long way in explaining the price of a new car.

Group Health

Cost of employee benefits

3 It is unlikely that any insurance industry problem in history will reach the magnitude of the health care crisis that began to gain national attention in the early 1990's and it came to a head in 2010. As we view the various medical expense policies currently in use, the backdrop of skyrocketing costs must always be kept in mind. The downturn in popularity of older products, the emergence of new products, the exclusions, reductions and limitations found in most products are invariably explained by one thing – **cost**.

4 While there are some big differences between individual and group health insurance in the areas of underwriting and distribution, the structure of the products available through either mechanism varies only slightly. In this chapter, we will explore the structure of medical expense. Later, in the chapter devoted to group insurance, we will spotlight the differences which do exist in the products sold through the group delivery system.

Lest We Forget . . .

In Chapter 10 of this text, we previewed the subject of health insurance in general. In so doing, we established a few fundamentals of **medical expense** contracts that we should keep in mind as we begin to examine the contracts in detail.

1. Medical expense policies are designed to **pay your medical bills** – the doctors, hospitals and surgeons.

   Doc

2. Since health care providers generally require immediate full payment, **benefits are paid in a lump sum**.

   Claims

3. Because medical costs are so unpredictable, health insurance companies reserve the right to *adjust premium* over time. Therefore, most medical expense contracts are written on a **Guaranteed Renewable** basis (guarantees your right to renew but not the price) until some limiting age, like 65, and then may be **Conditionally Renewable** (conditioned upon not retiring) thereafter.

   Renewability

4. In the context of a family, we typically cover **every family member**.

5. These contracts may cover accidents only, but most cover **sickness and accident**.

   2 perils

6. Even for covered accidents and sickness, you generally don't get "full" reimbursement. There are normally dollar **deductibles** up front and a sharing of the cost (**coinsurance**) thereafter.

   Cost sharing

7. Preexisting conditions are normally excluded from coverage (at least temporarily). **Probationary periods** can be used to screen out a specific preexisting sickness, such as a nine month probationary period for pregnancy. **Exclusion riders** can be used to eliminate coverage for a particular part of the body (like Joe Namath's knees) for as long a period as the company wants.

   Exclusions

8. Premiums paid by you individually are not normally tax deductible, but premiums paid by your employer for group coverage are deductible (for the employer). Regardless of who pays the premium, **medical expense benefits are not taxed**.

   Benefits not taxed

In this chapter we will see how these concepts apply (or don't apply) to the various medical expense contracts on the market: the rather limited **Base Plans**, the catastrophic coverages of **Major Medical**, and a policy which is essentially a marriage of the Base Plans and Major Medical, **Comprehensive (Supplementary) Major Medical**. In the next chapter, we will also apply these ideas to the newest entries in the medical expense field – those designed for the elderly – **Medicare Supplements** and **Long Term Care** policies.

The Base Plans

1   At the onset of the Great Depression, the stock and mutual companies began to withdraw from the health insurance field altogether. While the Blues did little with disability income, their development and implementation of the contracts known as **Base Plans (or Basic Plans)** was the major factor in their phenomenal growth through the 1930's and 1940's. In their original form, the Base Plans met the needs of society almost perfectly. In the midst of a national depression, most families simply did not have the cash available to pay medical costs. The Base Plans provided a way in which benefits could be pre-paid with a small amount of premium so that health care was available when needed. Just as importantly, these plans met the needs of the doctors and hospitals in that full payment was assured.

Base plans are coming back

2   In an effort to make health care affordable, all the medical services a person might need were divided into three separate areas, each covered by a different Base Plan. For "full" coverage, you needed all three; if you could not afford all three, you could buy one or two of the plans and cross your fingers.

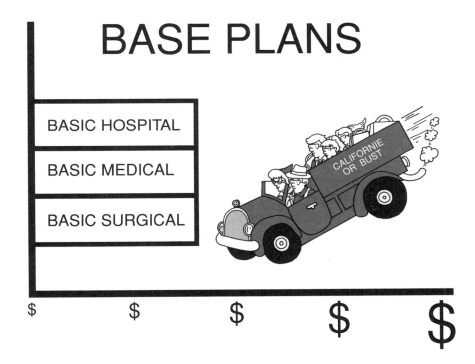

3   To cover the costs of going to the hospital, you could purchase a Basic Hospital plan. To pay for your doctor, you purchased Basic Medical, and to cover any surgery, you could buy Basic Surgical. While this division may seem a bit arbitrary at first, we must remember that Blue Cross and Blue Shield were not always one organization. Your Basic Hospital policy was purchased from Blue Cross, whereas the Basic Medical and Surgical were supplied by Blue Shield.

4   If you think of the **Basic Hospital** plan as a way to cover (at least partially) the numerous expenses of being in the hospital except for the costs of any doctors or surgeries, you are close to a full understanding. If you think of the **Basic Medical** as a contract to reimburse the doctor who visits you once or twice a day in the hospital, you are on the right track. Finally, the **Basic Surgical** plan should be considered the policy which pays the surgical team which removes your appendix.

a little coverage

1 As we examine each Base Plan to see exactly what coverages are offered and exactly how each works, we will find many differences among them. However, there are two characteristics shared by all three plans.

Low Dollar Limits – These plans were not designed to cover catastrophic losses. Obviously, the Base Plans designed in the 1930's have limits that would be laughable by today's standards, but even the modern versions are woefully inadequate in covering major surgeries and extended hospital stays.

small bucks

No Deductible, First Dollar Coverage – As you would expect of a plan designed during the Depression, the Basic Plans typically had no deductible whatsoever. The modern versions of the Base Plans have low, if any, deductibles.

no D-ducks

Basic Hospital

2 Basic Hospital Expense contracts provide benefits for expenses incurred while confined to a hospital, such as: room and board, general nursing care, laboratory and x-ray services, medicine, the use of operating or treatment rooms, oxygen, blood, surgical dressings, anesthetics, and ambulance service to the hospital. The more up-to-date contracts also cover some out-patient services like emergency treatment for accident or sickness, pre-admission testing prior to hospitalization and any hospital charges relating to out-patient surgery. As you can see, our previous rule of thumb was not far off – everything you would find on your hospital bill except charges for doctors and surgeries.

DBR

3 The contract divides the benefits of Basic Hospital into two parts:

- Room and board charges (Daily Board and Room or DBR), and
- Everything else.

4 To establish coverage limits for each part, the policy will specify a reimbursable limit for the hospital **room and board** charges. This limit is normally a specified dollar amount ranging from $50 to $250 per day of continuous confinement, up to a maximum number of days. (Some companies have dropped the dollar limits and now pay the hospital's daily semiprivate room rate.) The maximum number of days can range from 30 to 365. For example, Joe's Basic Hospital policy might provide a room and board limit of up to $200 per day for a maximum of 90 days for each period of continuous confinement. Therefore, the maximum room and board charges that Joe's policy would pay for any one hospital confinement would be $18,000 ($200 x 90 days).

Limits on R&B (room and board) $/day days/stay

5 Hospital costs *other than room and board* are grouped together as **miscellaneous** (or **ancillary**) expenses. The limit in this area is expressed by taking a number designated in the policy (normally between 10 to 20) multiplied by the daily room and board limit (DBR). In our example, let's assume the multiple in Joe's policy is 20. To calculate the maximum miscellaneous charges that Joe's policy would pay for any one hospital confinement, you would multiply 20 by his maximum daily room and board limit ($200). Therefore, Joe's miscellaneous limit for each period of continuous confinement would be $4,000 (20 x $200).

other stuff

The **total benefit** available under the Basic Hospital policy is the sum of the maximum room and board per stay plus the maximum miscellaneous expenses per stay. Therefore, the maximum total benefit under Joe's policy per hospital stay would be:

1

> $18,000 maximum **room and board**
> + 4,000 maximum **miscellaneous (ancillary)**
> $22,000 maximum **total benefit** per hospital stay

Please recognize that we have generated numbers which reflect the *maximum* the policy would pay. If, in the above example, the hospital charged only $12,000 for room and board for a 90 day stay and $2,000 for miscellaneous expenses, then the contract would only reimburse the $14,000 actually charged. On the other hand, if Joe's total bill were $30,000, his policy would pay only to its limit of $22,000.

2

Basic Medical

The Basic Medical contract provides for the non-surgical services of **doctors** for treatment of injury or sickness in or out of the hospital. There is normally a dollar limit per visit or treatment with a maximum number of visits. Typically, the benefit ranges between $20 and $50 per visit for up to 60 visits per year.

3

Doc's $

Basic Surgical

Basic Surgical contracts provide benefits for **surgical services** performed in or out of the hospital. The policy pays in accordance with a **schedule of indemnities**, which is an exhaustive list of surgical procedures with a dollar limit assigned to each. The normal approach is to take the most severe and complex operation scheduled and assign the highest reimbursable amount to that procedure. For all other surgeries on the list, the company simply scales down from the top. The maximum on policy schedules issued today will range from $500 to $4,000. Therefore, if you had one of the most generous schedules available and the most expensive surgery on your schedule was a triple bypass, then your policy would pay up to $4,000 for that procedure (which is obviously not enough). If a hysterectomy were considered to cost one-fifth of what a bypass does, then the schedule would show that the contract would pay up to $800 for a hysterectomy. The scheduled amount for an operation is intended to apply to the total professional fees involved for that procedure, including the surgeon, any assistant surgeon involved, the anesthesiologist, and post-operative care.

4

"menu" of benefits

If you look at one of these schedules, you'll get the feeling that anything that could possibly be done to your body appears somewhere on the list. Of course, this is not true. Any surgical procedure not on the list is simply equated to one that is on the list. Let's make use of our previous example, and further assume that the removal of a gall bladder does not appear on the list. If it would normally cost about the same for a gall bladder removal as a hysterectomy, then again the contract would pay up to $800.

5

1 If two or more surgical procedures are performed on a patient through the same incision for the same or related conditions, the maximum payment is limited to the amount payable for the most expensive procedure performed. However, if it is a separate incision or for an unrelated condition, then the benefit is the amount payable for the more expensive procedure plus 50% of the scheduled amount for the second operation.

2 Two fairly recent developments with the Basic Surgical policy involve the use of a non-scheduled benefit plan and encouraging insureds who have been advised to have elective non-emergency surgery to get a second opinion.

3 The **non-scheduled benefit** approach eliminates the traditional schedule of indemnities and structures the policy to pay **reasonable and customary** charges for the procedure involved. *Reasonable and customary* is defined as the amount typically charged for the same procedure by surgeons in the same geographic area.

4 Obtaining a **second opinion for non-emergency surgery** is encouraged by many modern contracts in two ways – a reward if you do seek a second opinion and a penalty if you don't. The *reward* is that the company will pay for a second opinion. All that is required is that another opinion be obtained before surgery – it does not require that the doctors agree. If the insured proceeds with surgery despite a negative second opinion, full benefits are paid. The *penalty* is if the insured does not secure a second opinion; in that case, the surgery benefit payable can be reduced by 40-50%. (Some companies that have used the second opinion approach have already dropped it. Their thought is that since the second opinion almost always concurs with the first, it is simply a waste of money.)

The Major Medical Policy

5 As we have pointed out, the stock and mutual companies almost completely withdrew from the health insurance field at the onset of the Great Depression. The Base Plans we have just discussed were products developed by the Blues which perfectly suited the needs of the average American in the 1930's. The Blues further solidified their stranglehold on the medical expense market with the Group Base plans that they introduced in the 1940's. By the late 1940's or early 1950's, the traditional stock and mutual companies were more than ready to re-enter the marketplace, but they found that it was literally owned by the Blues. Rather than simply repackaging products designed for the average American of the 1930's, they began to take notice of how things had changed since the thirties to see if they could discover new needs and new markets.

6 Their approach could not have been sounder. The differences between 1932 and 1952 in this country could hardly have been more dramatic. The Great Depression had ended and so had World War II. The Korean Conflict was concluding, and our economy was on a roll. Jobs were available at every level; the returning veterans were building houses through the VA while going to school on the GI Bill and starting the baby boom in their spare time. Most Americans "liked Ike," and those who didn't could tolerate him. We were on the verge of technological and sociological changes (like television and rock and roll music) that would alter our country forever. As we all know from watching our own TV's, the 1950's were truly "Happy Days" for most of us.

1 The changes in medical care were no less dramatic. Antibiotics were curing diseases that would have meant certain death only two decades earlier. Surgical procedures had advanced to the level of miraculous. Our doctors and nurses were veterans of at least one war and had accumulated more than enough practice with the latest in medical technology and procedures. However, these modern miracle workers were no longer willing to view themselves as human servers. They wanted to be paid real money and lots of it. They wanted Wednesday afternoons off to explore the mysteries of newly-discovered golf courses and to enjoy their ongoing romance with the luxury automobile. Put simply, the demand for medical care, the level of medical care, and the price of medical care in this country had risen dramatically.

Why Major Medical?

2 As the stock and mutual companies surveyed the situation in the 1950's, they noticed two factors that led to the development of the Major Medical contract:

- The advances in medical services had evolved to the point that many common-place procedures could cost far more than the Base Plans were designed to pay. There was a need for **catastrophic coverage** in the minds of many Americans that the Base Plans simply did not fulfill.

big stuff

- Not all, but some Americans were concerned *only* with their need for catastrophic coverage. This group could easily afford basic medical services out of their pocketbooks.

3 The Major Medical policy that hit the marketplace in the early 1950's could be used to serve either of the needs we've just outlined. For the segment of the population that still needed the coverages of the Base Plans but were concerned about catastrophic coverage, the Major Medical could be sold as a *supplement* to an existing Base Plan. The Base Plan paid first, in the sense that it paid the small claims entirely, and it functioned much like a huge deductible. The Major Medical benefits were triggered only for catastrophic losses. For the smaller segment of the population who could afford to pay for basic medical services themselves, the Major Medical contract could be purchased without underlying coverage but with a large dollar deductible . . . any where from $500 to $5,000. Results showed that the stocks and mutuals had done their homework properly; by 1956, they had more medical expense coverage in place than the Blues.

Characteristics of Major Medical

4 To help you gain an understanding of how Major Medical contracts function, we will examine the policy from two different perspectives. We will first address it as an individual contract to enable you to understand how it would operate for a policy-owner with no other coverages. We will then turn to group insurance. In the group environment, Major Medical policies exist primarily for the purpose of building a superpolicy – the **Comprehensive (Supplementary) Major Medical**. With both, the essential promises and limitations of the Major Medical benefits are the same – **after a sizable deductible, the company will pay the lion's share of all eligible medical expenses up to a specified maximum**.
Contained in that rather simplistic statement are four important variables:

- Deductible
- Eligible Expenses
- Cost Sharing (Coinsurance)
- Maximum Benefit

5 We will address each in turn.

Deductible

1 The deductible is simply the part of the claim paid by the policyowner. The deductible is also the key to the affordability of the Major Medical contract. With medical expense insurance (and most other kinds of insurance as well), the most frequent claims and the most expensive to administer are small claims. By having the policyowner cover the small losses entirely and at least the initial costs of a large claim with the deductible, the company relieves itself of the most expensive part of the process. The benefit dollars are, therefore, reserved for the truly major losses, which is precisely what the policy was designed to do.

2 As you will discover, deductibles come in many flavors. Although all Major Medical deductibles are expressed in dollars, that is about the only common element. Probably the least generous approach to deductibles is the **flat dollar deductible** which calls for a deductible every time you seek medical service. There is also a **per cause deductible** which must be satisfied for each cause that requires you to get medical care. For example, if you suffered a heart attack, the first, say, $2,000 would be on you. But, if you were released from the hospital, saw your doctor six times and were then re-admitted for a triple bypass, no further deductible would be levied. Most common today are **maximum annual deductibles** written on a per person or per family basis. For instance, the contract might specify that after your family has spent $2,500 on medical care, the deductible is satisfied for the remainder of the policy year or calendar year.

all kinds

3 Suffice it to say that there are numerous deductible plans available with which you will need to become acquainted. Several of them would be impossible for you to understand until you gain a greater knowledge of the Major Medical variations we are examining. Therefore, we will keep our full discussion of deductibles on the back burner for awhile. In our claims settlement examples which will enable you to see who pays how much for what, we will use the flat dollar deductible. Although it is not as common as it once was, it does allow us to keep our examples simple and avoid burying you in math.

Eligible Expenses

4 Major Medical plans cover **usual and customary** charges for medical services, supplies, and treatments prescribed as **necessary** by a physician. For example:

"All Risk" Coverage

The cornucopia of coverages

- Professional services of doctors of medicine and osteopathy, and other recognized medical practitioners,
- Hospital charges for semi-private room and board, and other necessary services and supplies,
- Services of registered nurses and, in some cases, licensed practical nurses,
- Physical therapy,
- Anesthetics and their administration,
- Diagnostic x-rays and laboratory procedures,
- X-ray or radium treatments,
- Oxygen and other medicinal or therapeutic gases and their administration,
- Blood transfusions, including the cost of blood (when not replaced by blood donations),
- Local ambulance services,
- Rental of durable mechanical equipment required for therapeutic use,
- Artificial limbs or other prosthetic appliances, except replacement of such appliances,
- Casts, splints, trusses, braces, and crutches, and
- Rental of a wheelchair or hospital-type bed.

1 In addition, plans may provide limited coverage for confinements in **skilled nursing facilities** (recovery) as well as coverage **for home health care expenses** and **hospice care** (dying) expenses. Some plans even cover the costs of drugs and medicines which require a physician's prescription.

2 The major limitations placed on the very generous Major Medical coverages were discussed in Chapter 10 of this text. These include the common exclusions, ailments subject to an Impairment Rider, preexisting conditions, and any sickness or accident subject to a probationary period.

3 One limitation on Major Medical benefits that you have not yet encountered in this text is an inside limit. An **inside limit** is simply a limit on a specific category of medical expenses. For example, the policy might limit hospital room and board expenses to $200 a day or the semiprivate room rate, whichever is lower. There could be a $500 limit on x-rays for each claim, a $20 limit on doctor visits, and a $2,500 lifetime limit on psychiatric care. Some contracts even contain dollar limits on surgical procedures, similar to the old Basic Surgical schedules except that the amounts are much higher. In reality, these inside limits are nothing more than a formalized expression of the **usual and customary** parameters placed on the benefits from the outset. What is *usual and customary* is somewhat subjective – these inside limits simply aid in more precisely defining the promises of the policy. As you would guess, any charges above these stated limits are borne 100% by the policyowner.

Limits within limits

Coinsurance
(or Cost Sharing, or Percentage Participation)

4 **Coinsurance** is used to control costs, to retain the insured's financial awareness of the cost of services, and to curtail unnecessary utilization of services. **The coinsurance clause defines the company's and the insured's percentage share of the costs remaining after the deductible has been satisfied.** The most typical arrangement calls for the company to pay 80% and the policyowner to pay 20% and is expressed as an 80/20 plan. It is not unusual to find 75/25, or even 50/50 cost sharing arrangements in today's cost conscious marketplace.

Joe's share "after" the deductible

80% / 20%

5 Although not at all common, it is certainly possible to find policies with different coinsurance percentages for different categories of expenses. For example, some companies which place inside limits on the costs of hospital room and board will pay 100% of the room and board costs up to the stated inside limit, which in coinsurance lingo would be expressed as 100/0. All other expenses might be shared 80/20 or 75/25. Other companies might utilize a 50/50 coinsurance arrangement for outpatient psychiatric care. Any number of possibilities exists.

6 While the purpose of coinsurance is **to control the over-utilization of the policy benefits**, a truly catastrophic loss could cause the policyowner's 20% share to appear more as a punitive measure than as a gentle reminder to keep the costs down. For this reason, most companies have what is known as a **two-step coinsurance** requirement, or **Stop Loss** feature. With either name, the results are the same. Once the total costs have exceeded a specific amount (often $5,000 or $10,000), the **company pays 100% of the *eligible* expenses** above that amount. Thus, step one of this plan calls for 80/20 cost sharing, and step two calls for 100/0. Or, said another way, the policyowner's *losses* are *stopped* after the claim has reached a specified dollar level.

7 A common mistake made by agents in explaining the Stop Loss is that they say, "Once the total claim reaches $10,000, the company pays 100%." WRONG!! The company, in fact, only pays 100% of the *covered losses*. The usual, customary and reasonable restriction still applies as do all of the exclusions.

Note to Student:

1 Companies can express the Stop Loss feature in any number of ways. Most commonly, it is on the basis of total dollars spent as we just discussed. However, some contracts will say that after so many dollars, say $5,000, have been subjected to coinsurance, the company will pay 100%. Others state that after the insured has spent a specified amount from his or her own pocket *in a given year*, say $5,500, the company will pay 100% of the eligible expenses.

Maximum Benefit

2 One additional limitation of the company's liability in a Major Medical policy is the maximum benefit limit. It simply establishes a ceiling for how much the company will pay to any insured under the policy. Today, it is commonplace to find **lifetime limits** of $1-5 million. (Throughout the 1980's, many companies eliminated dollar limits and sold policies with *unlimited coverage*. By the early 1990's, however, most who had experimented with this stopped doing it.) Less commonly, you may find policies where the limit is not expressed as a lifetime maximum but as a **per cause maximum**. Here, the company might state that it will pay no more than, say, $250,000 for any one covered accident or sickness. Under either approach, the reinstatement of the dollar limits is possible after the passage of a prescribed period of time without claims.

New Federal Law will eliminate Lifetime Limits

Summary of Major Medical Characteristics

3 As you have seen, there exists a wide variety of individual medical expense plans with the name "Major Medical." It therefore might be helpful to summarize the most common elements.

4 A Major Medical policy normally pays 80% of covered medical costs after a sizable deductible ($500 to $5,000) has been paid. When total losses reach a stated figure (like $10,000), the company pays 100% of the covered losses thereafter. The following chart is a good visual summary of Major Medical as we've studied it.

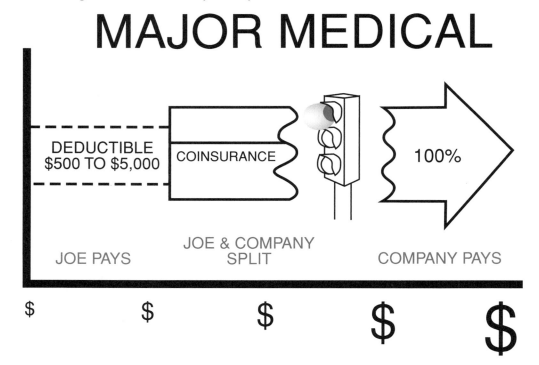

MAJOR MEDICAL

DEDUCTIBLE $500 TO $5,000

COINSURANCE

100%

JOE PAYS

JOE & COMPANY SPLIT

COMPANY PAYS

$ $ $ $ $

Major Medical Claims – A Practical Exercise

1   It should be obvious by now that settling a Major Medical claim could be exceedingly complicated. If you have to consider maximum annual deductibles, inside limits, a variety of coinsurance limits and a Stop Loss limit, the calculations get very complicated very quickly. However, as an agent, you should be able to handle a straightforward claim without too much difficulty. For instance, assume Joe Insured owns a Major Medical policy with a flat $2,000 deductible, a coinsurance clause of 80/20 and a Stop Loss feature of $10,000. If he suffers covered losses of $8,000, how will the claim be settled?

Exercise

	Joe Pays		Company Pays	
Total Claim	$8,000		$8,000	
Minus Deductible	- 2,000	$2,000	- 2,000	
Net	$6,000		$6,000	
Apply Coinsurance	x .20			x .80
	$1,200	$1,200	$4,800	$4,800
Totals		$3,200		$4,800

2   While the math is not overwhelming, it is helpful for many people to sketch out the problem as shown below.

MAJOR MEDICAL
TOTAL CLAIM $8,000

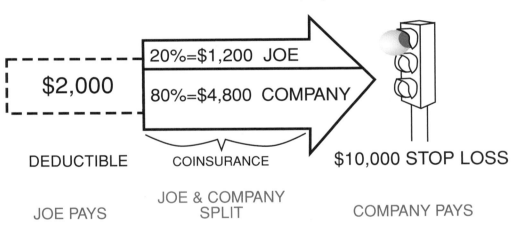

3   Once you have taken the time to diagram the problem, you can easily answer any question. For example:

- How much did Joe pay in all? $3,200
- How much did the company pay? $4,800

The Comprehensive (Supplementary) Major Medical Policy . . .
The Union of Base Plans & Major Medical

1. The biggest drawback to the stand-alone Major Medical plan for most individuals and families was the huge up front deductible. Therefore, its value as an employee benefit in the group market was questionable. As we will see, the Comprehensive (Supplementary) Major Medical contract still retains a deductible, but it is much smaller. A Base Plan provides most of the initial dollars, thus relieving the policy-owner of bearing the total burden of the initial costs of medical care but still allowing the Major Medical portion to function as catastrophic coverage.

Characteristics of Comprehensive (Supplementary) Major Medical

2. A Comprehensive (Supplementary)Major Medical policy is nothing new at all. It is simply a **Major Medical policy superimposed over a Base Plan** (the Base Plan in this case includes all three coverage areas: hospital, medical, and surgical). The Major Medical and the Base Plan could both be products of the same company, or they could be products of different companies. Initially, most Base Plans were provided by the Blues and the Major Med portion was the product of a stock or mutual company.

3. The most important thing to remember is that each of the two policies retains all of its fundamental characteristics. The **Base Plan pays first dollar** coverage up to a rather low maximum, say $4,000. After Base Plan benefits are exhausted, the **Major Medical policy takes over.** But what comes first with Major Medical? That's right . . . a deductible. Even though most companies greatly reduced the amount of the Major Medical deductible when it was sold as a supplement – assume a $250 deductible for example – it still precedes the Major Medical benefits.

Wed the Base Plan to Major Med

4. Therefore, we have the rather odd situation of having a deductible in the middle of the coverage rather than in the beginning. Because of its unusual placement, the deductible in a Comprehensive (Supplementary) Major Medical plan is often referred to as a **corridor deductible**. A typical structure for a Supplementary Major Medical policy is shown on the next page.

COMPREHENSIVE MAJOR MEDICAL

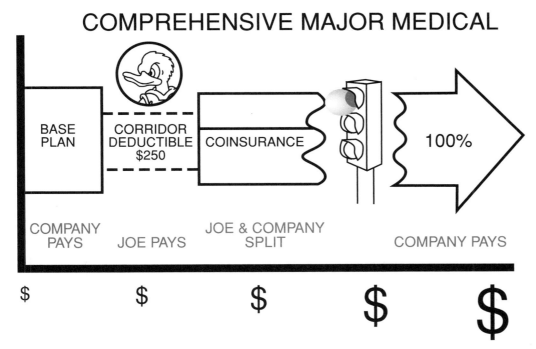

It would be logical to ask why it is necessary to bother with a deductible at all if it's going to be placed in the oddball position of a corridor deductible. There are at least two good reasons.

- Because of the limitations in the scope of the Base Plans, there are often procedures covered by Major Medical that are not covered by the Base Plans. But, requiring a deductible only on Major Med items not covered by the Base Plans would be an administrative nightmare; it is simpler to levy a lower deductible across the board.

- Any time coverage exists with no deductible, the possibility of over-utilization of the policy benefits exists. A deductible, even if not felt until the middle of the claim, will help raise the cost-consciousness of the policyowner.

Comprehensive (Supplementary) Major Medical Claims – A Practical Exercise

Since the Comprehensive (Supplementary) Major Medical policy is nothing more than the marriage of the two policies we have already studied in depth, there is not a great deal more to learn. As we've expressed, the biggest differences for the policyowner revolve around the deductible.

- The Comprehensive (Supplementary) Major Medical policy has a lower deductible ($100 - $500) than the traditional Major Medical contract ($500 - $5,000).

- The deductible appears in the middle of the coverage as the Base Plan benefits are exhausted and the Major Medical benefits are engaged.

1 Even a simplified claims settlement problem can be a bit of a challenge with this policy.

2 Suppose Joe owns a Comprehensive (Supplementary) Major Medical policy with Base Plan limits of $3,000, a corridor deductible of $500, a coinsurance of 80/20, and a Stop Loss of $10,000. He incurs a covered loss of $9,500. How would the claim be settled?

	Joe Pays		Company Pays	
Total Claim	$9,500		$9,500	
Minus Base Plan	- 3,000		- 3,000	$3,000
	$6,500		$6,500	
Minus Deductible	- 500	500	- 500	
	6,000		6,000	
Apply Coinsurance	x .20		x .80	
	$1,200	$1,200	$4,800	$4,800
Totals		$1,700		$7,800

More exercise

3 Again, a simple block diagram such as the following can be helpful.

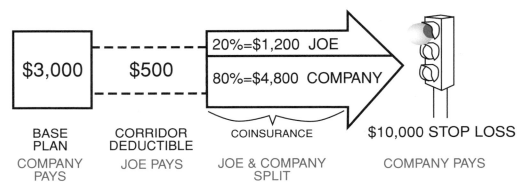

COMPREHENSIVE MAJOR MEDICAL
TOTAL CLAIM $9,500

$3,000 $500   20%=$1,200 JOE   80%=$4,800 COMPANY $10,000 STOP LOSS

BASE PLAN   CORRIDOR DEDUCTIBLE   COINSURANCE

COMPANY PAYS   JOE PAYS   JOE & COMPANY SPLIT   COMPANY PAYS

4 Once you have blocked it out on your diagram, you could answer any question about the claim.

5 How much did the company pay under the Major Medical portion of the coverage? *Enough exercise...*
$4,800

...rest

6 How much did the company pay in all? $7,800

7 How much did Joe pay in all? $1,700

Medical Expense Deductibles

Earlier in this chapter, we examined the important variables that surround most medical expense contracts. At that point we lightly touched upon one of the more important variables – the deductible. As you recall, we chose to hold our complete discussion of deductibles until after you had a greater understanding of the workings of the Major Medical-type contract. Some of the deductible approaches with which you should be familiar only make sense in the context of one of these policies.

- **Flat Deductible** – This is the deductible approach we have used in all of our examples and claims problems because it is so simple. Under this idea, **every time there is a claim, the deductible must be satisfied**. Although it is understandably not too popular, the flat deductible's similarity to Auto Collision and Homeowners policies deductibles makes it instantly understandable to the policyowner.

    Flat

- **Corridor Deductible** – This is the deductible approach we discussed in connection with the Comprehensive (Supplementary) Major Medical policy. When the Base Plan benefits are exhausted, a specific dollar deductible precedes the payment of any benefits from the Major Medical portion of the policy.

    Corridor

- **Integrated (or Variable) Deductible** – The integrated deductible is a less common alternative to the corridor deductible in a Supplementary Major Medical plan. Again, it is positioned (integrated) between the Base Plan and Major Medical benefits. Under this arrangement, the deductible applied is the *higher* of (1) a substantial stated amount, like $1,000, or (2) whatever the Base Plan pays. For instance, if we use $1,000 as the stated amount, and the Base Plan pays $1,200, then no further deductible is charged. If, however, the Base Plan paid only $800, then the chargeable deductible would be $200 ($1,000 – $800). With this plan, it obviously pays to have a good Base Plan.

    Integrated

- **All Cause (or Calendar Year) Deductible** – This deductible establishes a calendar year total (like $200 for an individual and $500 for a family) for which the policyowner is responsible. After the stated amount has been paid, either as the result of one claim or several, the policyowner has fully satisfied the deductible for that calendar year. For the remainder of the calendar year, the policy will pay benefits in accordance with the coinsurance percentage stated in the policy up to the Stop Loss. This approach is most commonly used with the Major Medical policy or the Comprehensive Major Medical policy and is by far the most popular deductible arrangement in today's marketplace.

    Annual

Medical Expense Policy Provisions

In addition to the coverage provisions of the medical expense policies that we have discussed, there are numerous additional provisions built into the basic policy. Many of these, like the Grace Period and the Free Look, are common to all health insurance policies and were discussed in Chapter 10. Only those provisions *unique* to medical expense policies will be examined here.

Assignment

1 Unlike life insurance, with medical expense policies, the word *assignment* as it is commonly used has nothing to do with ownership. Generally, assignment in medical expense policies indicates a **re-direction of the flow of benefits from the policyowner to the health care provider.** Remember that medical expense policies are written as reimbursement contracts. The idea (at least originally) was for you to pay the health care provider, submit the claim to the insurance company, and then wait to be reimbursed by the company for its portion of the claim. With health care costs at the level they are today though, almost no one can afford to do things that way. Most of us need a second mortgage just to cover the deductible and our part of the coinsurance. Covering the insurance company's portion, even for a few days, is impossible.

Health. . . benefit

Life. . . ownership

2 Therefore, built into most contracts is a provision allowing us **to assign the benefits** of our policy to the health care provider. This enables the company to pay the doctors or hospitals directly; the providers are assured they will be paid; all we have to be concerned with is our own portion of the bill.

3 Although it is certainly possible to *change ownership* of a medical expense policy, it seldom makes any sense to do so because medical expense policies do not have inherent value like cash value life insurance policies. About the only time that a change of ownership is needed with medical expense is if the policyowner becomes incapable of managing his or her own affairs and a spouse or guardian has to step in. Of course, any change of ownership of a medical expense policy requires the permission of the insurance company.

Newborns and Adopted Children

4 As we have pointed out, medical expense policies tend to cover every member of your family, including children. But this raises the question of how we deal with newborn and adopted children. It has been a requirement in most states for many years that **newborns** be covered under the parents' policy from the **moment of birth without requiring proof of insurability**. It does not matter whether the parents are covered under a group or an individual plan. Nor does it matter whether the policy has maternity benefits. For the first 31 days (in most states), coverage exists on the newborn even though the insurance company has not been notified. However, the **policyowner must notify the company of the newborn within 31 days of birth** and pay any required upcharge.

Coverage NOW

No preexisting conditions

31 day notice

5 By the early 1990's, most states had enacted laws which require that a **newly adopted child** be treated exactly like a newborn with **the date of placement** substituting for the date of birth. Since proof of insurability is not a requirement for the newborn, neither is it a requirement for the adopted child. Again, a 31 day requirement for notification exists in most states.

adoption = birth

Rights of Conversion

6 While it is generally accepted that Joe and Jolene's medical expense policy will cover their children as well, this is not intended to go on forever. In most states, the company can drop coverage on dependents at age 19 (or age 23 if the child is a full-time student); this is called the **limiting age**. Whether the child actually leaves home is irrelevant to the insurance company, even though it may be very relevant to the parents.

Federal law now says age 26

1 To ease this transition, many companies provide for **conversion rights** in their medical expense policies. Normally, this gives dependent children 31 days after reaching the limiting age to convert to their own individual medical expense policy without having to show proof of insurability. If a loss occurs within that period of time, it is covered regardless of the dependent's decision to convert or not. In some states, conversion is mandated by law and in others it is totally at the option of the insurance company.

children's rights

Rights of Dependent Children

2 Unfortunately, in some cases a child will never truly be capable of leaving home and supporting himself or herself. The laws in almost every state **prohibit the insurance company from terminating coverage on a dependent** who is and who continues to be *both* of the following:

must keep covered. . .

- Incapable of self-sustaining employment because of a physical or mental handicap, and

- Chiefly dependent upon the policyowner for support and maintenance.

3 Under these circumstances, coverage on your handicapped child can never be terminated as long as the premiums are paid. Even your death should not interrupt the flow of premiums. If you die wealthy, your estate can pay the premiums. If you die broke, Medicaid (as we will see in Chapter 17) can pay the premiums.

but. . .

4 Obviously, when a child reaches the limiting age of 19 or 23, proof must be given to the insurance company that the child meets the two requirements outlined above in order to remain covered under the family policy. Most states allow the company to ask for proof of continued disability and dependency at *reasonable intervals* over the first two years that coverage is continued under these circumstances. After the first two years, companies are generally limited to requesting proof no more frequently than annually.

does not force acceptance

Common Situations for Errors and Omissions ‡

5 Like most professions, insurance agents and their companies can be sued for mistakes in professional judgment or lapses in executing the important steps of putting a policy into effect. In the insurance industry, this type of professional liability is known as **errors and omissions**. Strict adherence to the law and specific attention to detail at the points of sale and delivery can greatly minimize the likelihood that you will end up on the wrong side of an errors and omissions suit.

6 **At Point of Sale** - As we have noted, most states' laws treat any communication with the public as **advertising** - down to and including your presentation. The laws then require that all advertising be 100% truthful. You cannot elaborate the coverages of your policy without pointing out the exclusions. You cannot talk in glaring generalities. If you say that a Major Medical policy pays 100% of the cost after the stop loss, you have blundered. The policy **pays 100% of the eligible or covered costs** following the stop loss.

1 You have in Health insurance essentially the same responsibilities in taking the application and collecting the initial premium that you do in life insurance. You must be certain that the application is completely and accurately filled out. Any changes must be made in the applicant's presence with his or her initials attesting to their knowledge of the corrections. In accordance with any **Information and Privacy Protection laws** you must disclose what information will be collected on a proposed insured, how it will be used, and with whom it will be shared. In most cases, you will collect premium along with the application using either a conditional receipt or an approval form of receipt. Explaining carefully when the policy takes effect is, of course, critically important.

2 **At Policy Delivery** - While mailing a policy that is already in effect is technically possible, personal delivery is always preferable. If the policy does not take effect until delivery (premium did not accompany the application or a rated policy is issued requiring additional premium), personal delivery is not a choice but a necessity.

3 At delivery, you should:

- Explain the Free Look provision
- Explain the coverages
- Explain any nonstandard premium charges
- Obtain a statement of continued good health when appropriate
- Begin to build a personal relationship with your policyowner

4 **Policy Replacement** - As with Life insurance, replacement is not illegal, but it is strictly regulated. It is also a place where agents should be acutely aware of their errors and omissions exposure. As an agent, you should be particularly conscious of the **underwriting requirements** of the replacing company. Will the proposed insured be rated on the new policy? You should compare the **exclusions, limitations** and **benefits** of the new policy to the existing coverage. Will the insured be covered as favorably under the new policy as under the old?

5 You should be extra careful of new **probationary periods** and of **preexisting conditions exclusions**. Some states have **no loss-no gain** laws which require replacement policies to cover ongoing claims from former policies. With Group Health insurance, there is normally a **transfer of benefits statement** attached to a new policy as assurance that the new policy will continue all of the benefits of the old.

6 Most importantly, you must make full disclosure to the policyowner. Some states require a **Notice Regarding Replacement of Health Insurance** just as they require with Life insurance replacement. And, as you will see in the next chapter, all of these concerns are magnified greatly if you are selling to the senior citizen market.

Conclusion

1 In this chapter, we have seen various types of medical expense policies and their structures. We started with the rather limited **Base Plans** which are characterized by low dollar limits, no deductible, and (at least originally) in-hospital coverage only. The **Basic Hospital** contract provides benefits for expenses incurred while confined to a hospital and is divided into two coverage parts: room and board, and miscellaneous (or ancillary) expenses. The **Basic Medical** contract pays for the non-surgical services of doctors in or out of the hospital. The **Basic Surgical** plan provides benefits for surgical services in accordance with a schedule of indemnities, or in more modern policies, in accordance with reasonable and customary charges incurred in or out of the hospital. Some modern Basic Surgical policies also may require that the insured obtain a second opinion for non-emergency surgery.

2 **Major Medical** was designed to pay for catastrophic medical expense losses, and typically has a Brobdingnagian deductible (like $500 to $5,000). **Comprehensive (Supplementary) Major Medical**, like Major Med, is capable of covering catastrophic losses, and is essentially Major Medical with a base plan as point man. All of the varieties of Major Medical have the following in common:

- **Deductibles** – A deductible is a dollar amount stated in the policy and is the part of the claim paid by the policyowner. It may be a **flat deductible**, which requires that you pay every time you get medical services; it may be a **per cause** deductible, which requires that you pay, not every time, but for each cause that requires medical services (kind of like a *two-for-one* sale); or, most likely nowadays, it may be a **maximum annual** (all cause, or calendar year) deductible written on a per person or per family basis.

- **Eligible Expenses** – These are the **usual and customary** charges for medical services, supplies, and treatments prescribed as **necessary** by a doctor. Some medical expenses are covered only up to an **inside limit** which is a limit on a specific category of medical expenses. Expenses which are *not eligible* include policy exclusions, impairment rider ailments, preexisting conditions, and probationary period losses.

- **Coinsurance** – This is a provision which requires you and the insurance company to share the covered expenses which exceed the deductible. The proportion is stated in the policy and the company generally pays the larger share, such as 80% in an 80/20 coinsurance arrangement. Normally, a **Stop Loss** feature will be included in the policy which will stop the cost-sharing at a stated amount, such as $10,000. Once the stated amount has been reached, the company picks up 100% of the eligible expenses.

- **Benefit Maximums** – Major Medical policies usually have a **lifetime limit** which is simply a ceiling on how much the company will pay out under the policy. The limits tend to be high – $250,000 to $1,000,000. A less common alternative is a **per cause maximum** which is a ceiling on how much the company will pay out for any one accident or illness.

May be outlawed

Comprehensive (Supplementary) Major Medical is structured exactly like Major
Medical, but it is intended to be a *supplement to a Base Plan*, and its deductible is
low (in the $100 to $500 range). The Base Plan, which could be from the same or
another company, provides most of the initial dollars. After the Base Plan benefits
are exhausted, then the Major Med takes over, beginning with the deductible. Because the deductible is placed between the Base and the Major Medical benefits, it's
called a **corridor deductible**. An integrated (variable) deductible is another, but
much less common, approach under which the policyowner pays the difference (if
any) between a substantial stated amount and his or her Base Plan.

Medical expense policies are made up of a variety of provisions, such as the Grace
Period, a Free Look, etc. (discussed in Chapter 10). Other provisions *unique* to medical expense policies include:

- **Assignment** – This provision allows the policyowner to transfer the benefits
  of the policy to the health care provider (doctor, hospital, etc.). This avoids the
  problem of having to pay big bucks to the hospital, go home and file a claim with
  the insurance company, and wait for a check.

- **Adding Newborns & Adopted Children** – Newborns are covered under the
  parents' medical expense policy at the moment of birth, and no proof of insurability is required. Adopted children are also covered under the parents' policy
  without proof of insurability beginning on the date of placement. The parents
  must notify the insurance company of the new insured within 31 days of birth
  or placement.

- **Conversion Right** – Since children are only covered under their parents' policy
  until the limiting age (19, or 23 if a full-time student), this provision gives the
  dependent the right to convert to an individual policy without having to show
  proof of insurability. If a loss occurs during the conversion period, it's covered
  whether or not the dependent intended to convert.

- **Rights of Dependent Children** – As long as the premiums are paid, an insurance company is prohibited from terminating coverage on a dependent who
  is and who continues to be incapable of self-sustaining employment because of
  physical or mental handicap and chiefly dependent upon the policyowner for
  support and maintenance.

Health Insurance Tax Facts

Always begin your analysis with:
Are we talking about a disability income or a medical expense policy?

Disability Income:

Are the premiums deductible?

No, if you pay for it yourself.

Yes, for your boss, if he buys the policy for you.

Are the benefits subject to tax?

No, if you paid for the policy.

Yes, if the boss bought the policy for you.

Business Uses of DI Insurance

Prime consideration: Who is the beneficiary? Same rule as life insurance, if the business is the beneficiary, then the premiums are not deductible, but the proceeds are not subject to tax.

Exception to this Rule

Business Overhead Expense policies, the premiums are deductible, but the proceeds are taxed as income.

Medical Expense:

Are the premiums deductible?

Same as D.I.; No, if you buy the coverage. Yes, your boss again gets the deduction if he pays.

Are the benefits subject to tax?

No and No

© 2010 Pathfinder Corporation

13

SENIOR CITIZENS POLICIES

As a group, senior citizens have a special set of needs that can be addressed in a number of ways. There are government programs, such as **Medicaid and Medicare** that act as a crucial safety net. Certainly, not everyone receiving Medicaid or Medicare is elderly, but Senior Citizens will be our focus as we discuss how the insurance industry has created products that supplement and work hand-in-hand these programs.

In the case of Medicare Supplement Policies (MSPs), we will discuss policies created to pay for things that would normally be the Insured's responsibility under Medicare. With Long Term Care (LTC) Insurance, we will examine a Policy designed to pay for custodial type care that can be provided by Medicaid, if the Insured doesn't mind becoming poverty stricken first, so they meet Medicaid's stringent eligibility requirements.

In this Chapter we will look at:

1. **Long Term Care Insurance (LTC) / Residential Care** – Policies sold by insurance companies to pay for custodial / nursing home care.   *LTC*

2. **Medicaid** – A government **welfare** medical expense program for the poor that can, among other benefits, pay for nursing home care.   *Medicaid*

3. **Medicare** – A government program designed to provide medical expense benefits for people primarily over age 65.   *Medicare*

4. **Medicare Supplement Plans (MSP)** – Medicare pays about 2/3 of medical costs. MSPs fill in the rest.   *MSP*

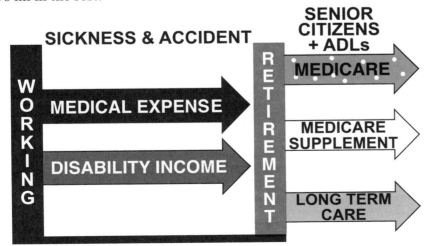

© 2010 Pathfinder Corporation

1 Long-Term Care (LTC) policies are designed to pay for the costs of at-home or nursing home care when senior citizens can no longer take care of themselves. **Medicare Supplement Policies (MSP)** are written to plug many of the coverage holes that exist in the Federal Medicare Program. While not 100% true, think of the **MSP** (and **Medicare**) as providing medical expense coverage when an elderly person is sick or injured, or is **convalescing** in a hospital or nursing home. Think of **Long-Term Care** as providing nursing home benefits to elderly persons requiring medically necessary **custodial services** (like help with eating, dressing, bathing, or taking medicine) either at home or in a nursing home. Medicare and MSPs are triggered by sickness or accident. LTCs can be triggered simply by advanced age.

LTCs
MSPs

2 Perhaps the most embarrassing chapter in the history of our insurance business addresses some of the shabby products designed as LTCs or MSPs and the dishonorable methods used to sell them. By the early 1990's, the National Association of Insurance Commissioners (NAIC) had drafted model legislation outlining minimum standards to be followed in both the product design and the marketing approach for these two contracts. Almost every state has adopted the NAIC models which we will examine momentarily. While there are some differences from state to state, the intent of the law remains unchanged.

Fears in the Golden Years

3 As you study the medical policies, you should be thinking constantly of consumer protection. Almost every sentence in both laws was written to correct a previous abuse. For example, both specifically limit what can be excluded as a preexisting condition. Since we are insuring the elderly, it would be easy enough to write a preexisting conditions clause so broadly that it would exclude practically any claim ever made. By defining precisely what can be considered a preexisting condition, this legislation slams the door on that possibility. This legislation also specifically prohibits cancellation of a Policy solely on the basis of the Insured's age or deterioration of health. Obviously, it would be grossly unfair to take an old person's premium and then cancel the coverage they have purchased at the point they need it.

Long-Term Care

4 The need for Long-Term Care coverage is often overlooked. This is probably because many senior citizens mistakenly believe that Medicare will cover the costs of a nursing home. Nothing could be farther from the truth. In reality, Medicare only covers about 2% of the cost of a nursing home, as most Medicare coverage is triggered only by sickness or accident.

Coverage for "care", not "cure"

5 In most respects, Medicare is Medical Expense insurance for people over age 65. Like the Medical Expense policies we've studied, it is designed to cover two perils - sickness and accident. **Eighty percent of the people going into a nursing home are neither sick nor hurt. They are simply old.** They can no longer carry out the activities of daily living (ADLs) without assistance. They need help bathing, dressing, getting in or out of bed, eating and getting around. A Medical Expense Policy will not help them. **They need a Policy that covers a different peril - ADLs or, simply, old age.**

ADLs

1   The chain of events for many seniors today is:

- As they get older, they need someone to help them in their own home, or they need to go to a nursing home. Medicare is of little or no help.
- They pay $4000 - $8000 a month for the help they need until they are impoverished.
- As bankrupt wards of the state, they become eligible for Medicaid.
- If they are aware of what is happening, they are tempted to cheat by hiding or disposing of assets so they can get on Medicaid sooner.

2   The objective of the LTC is to break this rather depressing cycle.

3   Long-Term Care policies provide coverage for necessary services which a person receives in a setting other than a hospital, such as a nursing home, adult day care center, or, perhaps, even one's own home. Long-Term Care policies are generally considered to be health insurance, but a life insurance Policy can also provide Long-Term Care-style benefits through the Living Benefits provision. Long-Term Care policies are not the same as Medicare Supplement Policies.

4   The NAIC model legislation used in most states defines **Long-Term Care** insurance as any insurance Policy (group or individual) or rider designed to provide coverage for not less than **12 consecutive months** for each covered person for *necessary diagnostic, preventive, therapeutic, rehabilitative, maintenance or personal care services provided in a setting other than an acute care unit of a hospital.* If Grandpa Joe is in the acute care unit of a hospital, his Medicare and MSP will provide coverage. Grandpa's need for Long Term Care is not always triggered by hospitalization. It is generally triggered by old age.

Nursing home coverage for at least 12 months

"consecutive" "12"

Renewability and Inflation Protection

5   Individual LTC policies must clearly state their renewability provision on the Policy face, and the form of renewal must be either **guaranteed renewable** or **noncancellable**. If you will remember, these are the two highest forms of renewal available. They both guarantee the Policyowner the right to continue coverage until a stated date or age by simply paying premiums, and the insurance company cannot unilaterally change any provisions. Noncancellable policies also guarantee price.

Highest degrees of renewability

6   Another factor to be considered is whether the LTC benefit will remain adequate if long-term care is needed over a period of years. The NAIC took this inflation problem into account. Insurance companies *must* give LTC Policyowners the option to purchase an **inflation protection** feature which at least:

- Increases benefit levels annually at a rate of not less than 5%, or
- Guarantees the right to periodically purchase additional coverage (5% of the current benefit) without proof of insurability.

Benefits must keep pace

7   A third alternative is a Policy which covers a specified percentage of reasonable charges and does not include a maximum periodic limit.

8   Furthermore, the insurance company is required to make a graphic comparison of a Policy's benefit levels over at least a 20 year period with inflation protection versus a Policy without inflation protection, and an estimate of what the premium increase would be to exercise the option.

Group Conversion Rights

1   Group LTC policies must provide their Insureds who would otherwise lose their coverage with the **right to continue or convert** their LTC coverage into an individual Policy **without proof of insurability**. For example, let's say Joe works for Acme and he is covered by his employer's group LTC Policy. If Joe leaves Acme (perhaps he retires, or simply quits), he has the right to convert his group LTC coverage into an individual Policy – without proof of insurability. This conversion privilege extends not only to the covered group member, but also to individuals who are covered by means of a qualifying relationship to the group member, such as a covered spouse. To continue with our example, let's say Acme's group health plan covered both Joe and Jolene, and before leaving Acme, Joe died. Jolene would have the right to convert her coverage to an individual plan because of her qualifying relationship to Joe.

Right to convert

no proof needed

2   The individual coverage must be as good as or better in terms of benefits than the original group Policy. The individual must make application and pay the premium for the converted Policy within **31 days** of termination of coverage under the group Policy. Since most LTCs are sold on a level premium basis, the Insured (essentially) converts at age of Policy inception not his age at conversion. This is becoming more and more important because companies are beginning to drop the minimum age to which an LTC can be sold from the 50-60 range to much younger people. Some companies will go as low as 18 years of age.

31 days

3   This continuation or conversion privilege is mandatory except where the termination of coverage is due to non-payment of premium, or when the group LTC coverage is immediately (within 31 days) replaced by another group Policy. In the situation where one group LTC is replaced with another group Policy, the new contract must cover everyone who was covered under the original Policy on the date of termination, and the new LTC may not add exclusions for preexisting conditions that would have been covered under the original Policy. In other words, the new Policy picks up as if the original were still in place.

Prohibition Against Post-Claims Underwriting

4   One transgression committed by some of the early LTC underwriters was to allow *anyone* to buy the contract, and then deny claims for reasons that should have precluded issuing a Policy in the first place. Obviously, this is unfair, and the NAIC model specifically prohibits this practice.

5   Underwriting LTC policies does incorporate a factor not important to other health insurance contracts. How well (or how poorly) the proposed Insured can perform the activities of daily living (ADLs) is key to Grandpa Joe's insurability under an LTC. A great heart, healthy lungs and good circulation will not guarantee a senior citizen to be a good LTC risk. If Grandpa Joe cannot get out of bed, bathe and dress without help, he is a poor LTC risk even though he is in *good health*.

Can't shut the barn door after the horse is gone

6   The standard health questions are also important and all applications for LTC insurance must contain clear and unambiguous questions to determine the physical condition of the Applicant. If the application asks whether the Applicant has had any medication prescribed by a doctor, it must also ask the Applicant to list those medications. After the Policy is issued, the company cannot deny coverage for medical conditions known to be associated with those listed medications.

1 The application must also contain the following warning which must be conspicuous and close to where the Applicant signs:

Caution: If your answers on this application are incorrect or untrue, the company has the right to deny benefits or rescind your Policy.

2 For an Applicant who is age 80 or older, the insurance company must obtain prior to issuing the Policy one of the following:

- A report of a physical examination,
- An assessment of functional capacity,
- An attending physician's statement, or
- Copies of medical records.

3 No matter whether it is a group or an individual LTC Policy, the Applicant must be given a copy of the application no later than upon delivery of the Policy. Also, the Policy, once issued, must contain a conspicuous statement such as the following:

Caution: The issuance of this LTC insurance Policy is based upon your responses to the questions on your application. A copy of your application is attached. If your answers are incorrect or untrue, the company has the right to deny benefits or rescind your Policy. The best time to clear up any questions is now, before a claim arises! If, for any reason, any of your answers are incorrect, contact the company at [insert address].

4 In the rare circumstances where an LTC Policy is sold on a guaranteed issue basis, this section does not apply. In all likelihood, the guaranteed issue approach would only arise in a group situation (such as an employee group or a *Golden Oldies* association group).

— Levels of Care Definitions

5 Problematic with some of the early LTC policies was that they only paid for *skilled nursing care*. If Grandpa Joe's only problems are the activities of daily living, he does not need skilled nursing care. Obviously, if the Policy will pay for lower levels of care, everybody wins. Grandpa gets the coverage he needs at a greatly reduced cost which helps keep the coverage affordable. The trend today is to cover Grandpa Joe at whatever level is necessary and at whatever location is appropriate for his needs - be that a nursing home, his own home or an adult day care facility.

6 Obviously, the levels of care available under an LTC Policy must be defined in the contract. The NAIC model LTC bill requires a Policy to offer the same dollar coverage **for at least the first three levels of care.**

1. **Skilled Nursing Care** - Nursing and rehabilitative care which is required **daily** and can only be performed by a **skilled nurse** under doctor's orders.

2. **Intermediate Care** - Nursing and rehabilitative care which is required **occasionally,** and can only be performed by a **skilled nurse** under doctor's orders.

3. **Custodial or Residential Care** - Help in performing the ADLs, and can be performed by someone without medical skills or training, but still based on doctor's orders.

© 2010 **PATHFINDER CORPORATION**

4. **Home Health Care** - In most policies, intermediate or custodial care performed at the patient's own home.

At Home

5. **Adult Day Care** - Allows a family member to serve as the primary care giver and still go to work. Most policies provide coverage in both a true Adult Day Care facility or in the home.

Drop Pop off

6. **Respite Care** - Many LTC policies provide the cost of temporarily replacing a family member as primary care giver for a day or a weekend.

Time off for the Caregiver

Long-Term Care Disclosure and Performance Standards

In marketing Long-Term Care policies, companies must provide full and fair disclosure and the policies they market must meet certain requirements. For example:

Uncle Sam looks over your shoulder Don't need

1. No Long-Term Care Policy may be **cancelled or nonrenewed** on the basis of the Insured's age or a deterioration of health.

2. Long-Term Care policies may not contain any provision which establishes a **new waiting (probationary) period** or new preexisting conditions if the Insured converts or replaces the Policy with another Policy from the same company.

3. A Long-Term Care insurance Policy may not provide coverage solely for *skilled* nursing care (or much more coverage for skilled care than for lower levels of nursing care).

Level #2 & #3 Care mandatory

4. **Preexisting condition** cannot be defined more restrictively than a condition for which medical advice or treatment was recommended by, or received from, a provider of health care services **within 6 months** preceding the effective date of coverage. Losses due to a preexisting condition **may not be excluded after 6 months** of the effective date of coverage.

-6 +6

5. Long-Term Care policies may **not** condition eligibility for benefits on the Insured's being **hospitalized** prior to receiving Long-Term Care benefits. There is an exception to this, however, *for post-confinement, post-acute care or recuperative benefits*. For those types of benefits, the Policy may require up to 30 days of prior institutional care.

to be in hospital first

6. A **30-Day Free Look** is required for Long-Term Care policies.

Big Look = 30 Days

7. During the initial solicitation and before the time of application, the Applicant for a Long-Term Care Policy must be given an Outline of Coverage (also called a **Shopper's Guide**). An **Outline of Coverage** is a summary of the benefits and coverages of the Policy. It explains important facts such as the form of renewability, the company's right to change premium, continuation or conversion provisions, Policy exclusions, etc.

Benefits Outline

8. In addition to an Outline of Coverage explained above, along with any Long-Term Care coverage sold through a *life insurance* Policy, insurance companies must also deliver a **Policy Summary**. This document explains how the Long-Term Care benefits affect the life insurance Policy benefits (e.g., reduced death benefit) and what the limitations on the Long-Term Care coverage are.

9. If the Long-Term Care coverage is funded through life insurance by the acceleration of the death benefit, the insurance company must send the Policyowner **monthly reports** when the Policy is in benefit payment status. The monthly report summarizes how much was paid out that month, the effect on the death benefit and cash values, and the amount of Long-Term Care benefits left in the Policy.

10. Pricing of the LTC coverage must not be unconscionable. In other words, the insurance company cannot gouge the customers by charging exorbitant premiums and then pay hardly any claims. The model regulations specify **loss ratios**, which are the total dollars paid out in benefits compared to the total dollars taken in in premium. The purpose of the loss ratio is **to place a ceiling on the profitability** of LTC insurance. For example, if Joe's insurance company has collected $1,000,000 in premium on its LTC insurance policies this year, it should expect to return at least a certain percentage of that money to its Policyholders in the form of claims payments. For individual LTC policies, the insurance company must expect to pay out at least 60% or $600,000 (in our example).

Exclusions

The following exclusions are allowable under Long-Term Care policies.

- Preexisting conditions or diseases
- Mental or nervous disorders (**Alzheimer's, however, is covered**)
- Alcoholism and drug addiction
- Illness or treatment due to war, participation in a felony, attempted suicide, aviation, etc. (the typical exclusions in health insurance)
- Treatment covered by Workers' Compensation, Medicare, etc.

(TAX) QUALIFIED LTCs ‡

A (Tax) **Qualified LTC** is specifically noted as such on the first page of the Policy. It essentially gives the LTC the same tax status as a regular medical expense Policy. In other words, the premiums for a Qualified LTC can be treated as a business expense under an employer-sponsored plan and the premiums are not considered as income to the employee. If you purchase an individual Qualified plan, itemize your deductions and qualify for medical deductions; then you may deduct the premium for your LTC based upon a sliding scale based upon age.

Federal law specifically describes how a *Qualified* LTC must be written. For instance, to be *qualified* an LTC must coordinate with Medicare, the coverage triggers are set by federal statute and **the contract must not develop cash value**.

MEDICAID – TITLE 19

In 1965, Congress also added Title 19, Medicaid, to the Social Security Act. Medicaid is a very different type of medical expense program than Medicare. It is a system of federal grants to the states to cover medical bills incurred by "needy" persons. **Medicaid is a medical assistance (welfare) program – not an insurance program.** The federal government sets the minimum requirements, and each state designs its own program within the federal guidelines. Medicaid, therefore, is a *federal-state partnership* designed to provide complete medical services to the needy *at no expense to the recipients*. Usually, a state's Medicaid program provides much broader coverage than the Medicare program.

Medical expense assistance = Welfare

Eligibility

The first requirement is for an individual to be **financially needy**. Need is determined by each state regarding the income and the net worth of Medicaid Applicants. Once **NEED** has been established, eligible persons must be one of the following:

Poor +

1. Over age 65

2. Blind (any age)

3. Permanently and totally disabled (any age)

4. Children receiving welfare benefits

New Federal Laws may greatly expand Medicaid eligibility

Benefits

Title 19 mandates that the states provide at least the following services:

- Physician's services

- Inpatient hospital care

- Outpatient hospital care

- Skilled nursing home services

- Laboratory and x-ray services

- Home health care services

- Rural health clinic services

- Periodic screening, diagnosis and treatment

- Family planning services

In addition, the states can voluntarily expand Medicaid to provide a broader range of medical services and care, such as: prescription drugs, dental services, private duty nursing services, eyeglasses, check-ups, and medical supplies and equipment. For people eligible for both Medicare and Medicaid, Medicaid may pay for what Medicare does not.

Funding

1 Medicaid funds come from federal, state and local taxes. In New York City, for example, the federal government pays 50% of the expenses, and the state and city governments each pay 25%. (Remember, Medicare is 100% federally funded. Medicaid is a federal-state-local partnership.)

tax, tax, tax

Administration

2 Typically, each state's **Department of Public Welfare** administers the Medicaid program within established federal guidelines.

DPW

MEDICARE – TITLE 18

3 To somewhat oversimplify, Medicare is a federal medical expense insurance program for people age 65 or older.

Eligibility

4 Medicare benefits become available when an individual reaches **age 65**. This is true even if the individual continues to work beyond age 65. Medicare benefits are also available to **anyone, regardless of age, who has** :

Age 65 +

No income threshold

- received **Social Security disability income benefits for two years,** or
- **chronic kidney disease** (renal impairment).

Every Medicare patient must be under the care of a physician.

Two Parts

5 Traditional Medicare benefits are divided into two piles - **Hospital Insurance (Part A)** and **Supplementary Medical insurance (Part B)**. For now, Part A pays the hospital; Part B pays the doctor.

A is Automatic

B is Optimal

Enrollment

6 Enrollment in Part A is *automatic* for individuals eligible for Social Security. They become eligible for Part A benefits on the first day of the month in which they turn 65. Part B coverage is *optional* because it requires payment of a premium (really, just a deduction from your Social Security check). When you become eligible for Part A, you are told that you will get (and pay for) Part B unless you decline it. If you later decide you want Part B after initially declining it, you must wait until the next **open enrollment period** (Jan 1 through March 31) to enroll.

Part A

Part A Benefits - 'Hospital'

1   Part A of Medicare provides for four different types of benefits:

- Inpatient hospital care
- Skilled nursing facility care (limited)
- Home health care
- Hospice care

2   While each of these benefits has its limitations, the first two in particular are loaded with deductibles, coinsurance and other limitations and reductions.

Inpatient Hospital Care

3   Medicare's **inpatient hospital care** benefit helps pay the reasonable charges that result from hospitalization in a semi-private room for medically necessary care. This includes room and board, regular nursing services, drugs taken in the hospital, medical tests (X-rays, lab, etc.), and the **use of oxygen**, wheelchairs, crutches, operating rooms and other supplies and services.

In the hospital

4   After an annual deductible, Part A pays the full cost of hospitalization for the **first 60 days** during any benefit period. For the 61st through the 90th day a daily coinsurance charge is levied against the patient. If the benefit period extends beyond 90 days, the patient may draw upon their **60 lifetime reserve** days which can be utilized only once. The patient's daily coinsurance charge increases significantly with the use of lifetime reserve days.

5   A *benefit period* is "Medicarese" for **"hospital stay" (or occurrence)**. As long as your hospital stays - benefit periods - are 60 days apart, you could have an unlimited number, and your first 90 days of benefits would start over each time. However, if you are discharged from the hospital, suffer a relapse and are readmitted within 60 days, your readmission is treated as part of the original benefit period and the countdown continues.

Covers Oxygen

Skilled Nursing Facility Care

6   If after being discharged from the hospital, and you must go to a skilled nursing facility, Medicare will help pay for up to 100 days in any one stay = *benefit period*. Inherent in this benefit description are several requirements / limitations:

Skilled

- You must have been hospitalized for at least 3 days in a row (not counting the day of discharge) before admission to the nursing facility.

- You must be admitted to the nursing facility within 30 days of your discharge from the hospital.

- You must need **skilled** nursing care (which is rare!)

7   Notice that the hospitalization requirement and the emphasis on **skilled** nursing care greatly differentiate this coverage from Long Term Care coverage where the emphasis is on assistance with the **activities of daily living (ADLs).**

ADLs

8   Part A will pay the full cost of covered services for the first 20 days. A daily coinsurance amount is charged during the next 80 days. Again, a relapse within 60 days is treated as part of the same benefit period. Benefits start all over after 60 days, but you must again be hospitalized for at least 3 days to qualify.

1 **Blood** might be necessary for a patient in a hospital or skilled nursing facility. Blood is a benefit of both Part A and B of Medicare - but there is an **annual deductible of 3 pints.** You must either pay for or replace (by donation) the first 3 pints of blood you use. If you satisfy the deductible in Part A, you need **not** do so again for Part B.

Now we have a blood deductible!

Home Health Care

2 If you are confined to your home and require skilled care for an injury or illness, Medicare can pay for care in your home by a home health Agency. **There is no hospitalization requirement, and there is no deductible charged for home health care.**

3 Medicare Part A will pay the entire cost of medically reasonable and necessary services provided by nurses, aides, medical social workers and therapists. The number of covered visits is **unlimited** as long as they are medically necessary and performed on an **intermittent** rather than constant or full-time basis. Again, this is **not** Long Term Care coverage.

4 Beyond the personnel costs, the home health care benefit will cover the full costs of supplies used by the caregivers and will pay 80% of the cost of specified durable equipment such as hospital beds or wheelchairs.

Hospice Care

5 For the terminally ill, hospice care is an alternative to regular Medicare benefits in managing a final illness. The coverage is provided for up to 210 days with the emphasis on relief from pain as opposed to curing the illness. The benefits are almost 100% - maybe $5 a day in coinsurance and another $5 coinsurance charge for each prescription.

Care for the dying

6 A second benefit of hospice care is not necessarily for the dying. If Grandpa Joe requires home health care in Joe's home, Joe and Jolene are the primary caregivers. They may need an occasional vacation (respite) from their responsibilities. This **respite care** can be provided under the hospice care benefit for periods not exceeding 5 days.

Part B Benefits = Medical (Doctor Care)

7 Medicare Part B picks up where Part A leaves off. It pays the **approved costs** for a wide variety of medical services but most importantly, **doctor bills.**

B   Ambulance

8 The other Part B benefits generally fit into the category of outpatient services - X-rays, lab tests, mammograms, pap smears, breast prostheses, artificial limbs, some durable medical equipment and ambulance transportation.

9 The patient's cost in Part B is fairly straightforward - there is a $100 annual deductible and a 20% coinsurance requirement.

Medicare Advantage (Part C)

1. Medicare Advantage (also known as Medicare + Choice) expands health care options for Medicare beneficiaries in many areas of the country. Medicare Advantage Plans include:

- Medicare Managed Care Plans (HMO)
- Medicare PPOs
- Medicare Private Fee-for-Service Plans
- Medicare Specialty Plans

New Federal Laws will greatly reduce the advantages of the Medicare Advantage Programs

2. Instead of receiving benefits through the traditional Medicare program, **recipients can choose an HMO, PPO, Health Savings Account or one of several other managed care plan types.** In some states, only the HMO option is available, and in others, the full range of choices is open.

3. To join a Medicare Advantage plan, a senior must have both Medicare Part A and Part B. A separate premium is paid to the Medicaare Advantage plan, but **there is no need for a Medicare Supplement.** These plans cover much of what is provided by a traditional MSP.

Prescription Drug Coverage (Part D)

4. Starting in 2006, prescription drug coverage became available to people enrolled in Medicare A or B. Those enrolled in a Medicare Advantage plan generally find that their plan also offers drug coverage.

5. Insurance companies and other private companies will offer these plans within the guidelines established by Medicare. There is a **monthly premium**, an **annual deductible** and **copayments** on the drugs as the prescriptions are filled. Seniors who do not enrollll when first eligible for this coverage will pay a higher premium if they enroll at a later date (think adverse selection).

"D" for "Drugs"

Medicare Exclusions

6. Medicare does not pay for personal convenience items (like a TV or telephone), private duty nurses, the extra cost of a private room (unless medically necessary), routine physicals, eyeglasses (except after cataract surgery), hearing aids, treatment received outside of the United States or custodial care.

Funding

7. The Hospital Insurance (Part A) is financed by the federal government through the Social Security compulsory payroll tax collected by the IRS. For the Supplementary Medical Insurance (Part B), 80% is funded by federal tax revenues and 20% by the voluntary participants in the plan. The participants pay their 20% on a monthly basis through a deduction in their Social Security retirement income.

A = Federal Funding

B = Optional & pay extra premium

Administration

Medicare is administered by the **Centers for Medicare and Medicaid Services** within the United States Department of Health and Human Services. Social Security Administration offices across the country process applications and claims for Medi care and provide general information about the program. The Centers for Medicare and Medicaid Services is a federal Agency, and it sets the standards which hospitals, skilled nursing facilities, home health agencies, and hospices must meet in order to be certified as qualified providers of services.

Medicare Supplement Policies

MSPs

To summarize Medicare:

1. Medicare is a medical expense insurance program that covers you after age 65.

2. Part A of Medicare covers hospital expenses.

3. Part B of Medicare covers doctors and surgeons.

4. Medicare pays about 2/3 of the actual medical costs. The *holes* or *gaps* in Medicare can be filled by any of several supplemental programs:

    A. For the elderly who are **broke, Medicaid** will pay for whatever Medicare does not cover. In other words, impoverished people do not buy a supplement; the government will give them one.

    B. Some employers allow retiring employees to continue their group insurance, or convert it to Medicare Supplement coverage.

    C. **Persons who continue to work after 65 may keep their group health coverage, and Medicare becomes a secondary payer to the group plan. No need for a supplement.**

    Big groups (1st employees)

    D. Some groups and associations offer supplemental Medicare coverage to their membership age 65 and over.

    E. Some HMO's offer a Medicare Replacement plan.

    F. Most often, a **Medicare Supplement Plan (MSP)** is purchased to fill the holes in Medicare. This Policy is also known as a **Medigap** Policy.

    MSP / "Medigap"

NAIC

1 A Medicare Supplement Policy (MSP) is an individual or group health Policy which is **designed primarily as a supplement to the hospital, medical or surgical expense reimbursements available under Medicare**. The Model Act and Regulations, developed by the National Association of Insurance Commissioners (NAIC), were designed to protect the public and to provide for the standardization and simplification of coverage of Medicare Supplement Policies.

2 The Act prohibits a company from issuing an MSP which merely duplicates the benefits provided by Medicare. The Act also gives the state insurance commissioner a wide range of powers. One of these is the power to adopt regulations to establish specific standards for Policy provisions, such as:

- Terms of renewability
- Conditions of eligibility
- Nonduplication of coverage
- Probationary periods
- Benefit limitations
- Requirements for replacement
- Definitions of terms

Same definitions

3 The Medicare Supplement Policy regulations require that MSP terms not be defined more restrictively than as defined in the Medicare program. Without this requirement, we could end up in a claims situation where Medicare pays, but the MSP does not, thus defeating the purpose of the MSP from the outset. For example, commonplace words such *as accident, hospital, physician*, and *sickness* are all defined under the Medicare program, and therefore must be defined at least as generously under the MSP.

-6
+6

4 One term that is not left for the insurance commissioner to define, but rather is defined by the Act is **preexisting condition**. Like the Long-Term Care definition, a preexisting condition cannot be defined more restrictively than *a condition for which medical advice or treatment was recommended by, or received from a provider of health care services **within 6 months** preceding the effective date of coverage*, and losses due to a preexisting condition may not be excluded **after 6 months** of the effective date of coverage.

Auto Adjust

5 The regulations also require that MSPs contain a provision that allows for an automatic change in Policy benefits which are designed to cover cost sharing amounts, such as deductibles and coinsurance, under Medicare. For example, if Joe's MSP, when originally issued, covered the Medicare Part B deductible which at that time was $75, but then the Medicare program raised the Part B deductible to $100, then Joe's MSP would have to automatically increase the benefit to cover the new deductible amount of $100.

Continuation of Coverage

1 The loss of Medicare Supplement coverage could entail serious financial consequences for an Insured. Remember that MSPs are sold not only to individuals, but also to groups. For example, imagine what could happen to a covered member who is uninsurable if the group Policyholder decided not to renew the group Policy or to change insurance companies; or imagine Grandma Joe's predicament if Grandpa Joe, who was the Policyowner of an MSP covering both of them, died. The MSP regulations protect Insureds in these types of situations.

Guaranteed Renewable

2 In the case of Grandma Jo, for example, *if* the MSPs renewability provision is ***noncancellable or guaranteed renewable***, the insurance company cannot terminate her coverage solely because Grandpa Joe died, or because either of them suffers a deterioration of health. The regulations require that all MSPs issued nowadays be **guaranteed renewable**. The company can, however, cancel or refuse to renew a Policy for nonpayment of premium or material misrepresentation.

Conversion Privilege

3 In the case of group MSPs, the Insureds have a **conversion privilege**. If a group Policyholder terminates and does not replace its MSP, the insurance company must offer the members who were covered a choice of *individual* MSPs: one which has comparable benefits to those of the terminated group Policy, and another which just meets the basic *core* package of benefits required of all MSPs (a *bottom-of-the-line* Policy, which would, naturally, be less expensive). The company may offer more than those two choices, but no fewer. If a group Policyholder does not completely terminate coverage, but just *replaces* the coverage with another MSP, then the new insurance company must take on all of the members that were previously covered under the old Policy as if there had been no change (i.e., no new exclusions for preexisting conditions that were covered under the old Policy). Note: The conversion and continuation privileges just described *do not* guarantee that premiums will remain the same.

4 What happens if Joe becomes eligible for Medicaid while covered by an MSP? First, Joe should promptly (within 90 days) notify his insurance company. The insurance company will then be required to refund premium for the time that Joe was eligible for Medicaid. If later on Joe loses his eligibility for Medicaid, then his insurance company has to take him back as if nothing had happened, provided he notifies the company promptly and pays the premium.

Open Enrollment Guaranteed Issue MSPs

5 Recently, the model regulations were revised to prohibit a company from rejecting (or even rating) someone for an MSP who is 65 or older and who for the first time has enrolled in Medicare Part B within the last 6 months. The Policy may, however, be issued with a preexisting condition clause as long as it complies with the definition and time limits (6 months) set forth above.

MSP Benefit Plans

1 The Act gives the Commissioner the power to regulate minimum standards for MSP benefits. Under the accompanying regulations, MSPs can be sold in only 12 standard plans, designated "A" through "L." The chart below shows the benefits included in each plan. The basic **core package** of benefits is **Plan A**. **Every company that sells MSPs must offer Plan A.** Companies may make any of the other benefit plans available in addition to Plan A, but at least Plan A must be available. Also, with one minor exception, no plans other than the ones below may be offered.

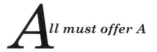

All must offer A

	A	B	C	D	E	F	G	H	I	J	K**	L**
Basic Benefits	✔	✔	✔	✔	✔	✔	✔	✔	✔	✔	*	*
Skilled Nursing Coinsurance			✔	✔	✔	✔	✔	✔	✔	✔	50%	50%
Part A Deductible		✔	✔	✔	✔	✔	✔	✔	✔	✔	75%	75%
Part B Deductible			✔			✔				✔		
Part B Excess (100%)						✔	✔		✔	✔		
Foreign Travel Emergency			✔	✔	✔	✔	✔	✔	✔	✔		
At-Home Recovery				✔			✔		✔	✔		
Preventive Care					✔					✔	***	***

* See Page 13-17 for details

** Plans K and L provide for different cost-sharing for items and services from Plans A-J. Once you reach the annual limit, the plan pays 100% of the Medicare copayments, coinsurance and deductibles for the rest of the calendar year.

*** The out-of-pocket annual limit is different for Plans K and L and will increase each year for inflation.

2 The benefit plans must be uniform in structure, language, and format. Therefore, Plan J will have the same style, arrangement, and overall content of benefits whether purchased from XYZ Insurance Company in Indiana or ABC Insurance Company in Arizona. Also, each state will mandate which plans may be sold in that state.

Basic Benefits - MSP plans A-J must pay the following:

1. Part A coinsurance (co-payments) for the 61st through 90th day of hospitalization.
2. Part A coinsurance for the 60 lifetime reserve days.
3. All charges for 365 days of hospitalization once Part A inpatient and lifetime reserve days are used up.
4. Blood deductible for the first 3 pints.
5. Part B coinsurance on Medicare-approved charges for doctors and medical services.

Basic Benefits for MSP Plans K and L - These two plans pay only a percentage of the Basic Benefits. Generally, this is 50% for Plan K and 75% for Plan L.

Optional Benefits - An MSP (B-J) may pay the following:

1. **Skilled Nursing Facility Care** covers Part A coinsurance for the 21st through 100th day of skilled nursing facility care.
2. **Part A Deductible** pays the inpatient hospital deductible for each benefit period.
3. **Part B Deductible** pays the calendar year deductible for doctors and medical services.
4. **Part B (Excess Charges)** pays for doctors charges which exceed the Medicare limit at 80% or 100%.
5. **Foreign Travel** pays for emergency treatment in a foreign facility at a rate equal to 80% of what Medicare would have paid in a US facility.
6. **At Home Recovery** pays for some assistance with activities of daily living while an Insured tries to qualify for Medicare home health visits. Also, the same coverage for up to 8 weeks following the last Medicare-approved home health care visit.
7. **Preventive Care** pays for an annual physical, doctor-ordered tests or other preventive measures and for an annual flu shot.

Note to the Student:

You may have noticed that there are nursing home and at-home care benefits in some of the MSP plans. However, we should point out that **these coverages are very limited**. They don't come close to the benefits typically provided under a Long-Term Care (LTC) Policy as we have previously discussed. The **Skilled Nursing Coinsurance** (Plans C-J) pays for the charges Medicare does not pay for *up through the 100th day* in a *post-hospital* skilled nursing facility. If you were not in the hospital for at least three days just prior to going into the skilled nursing facility, this benefit pays nothing. Or if you have to be there for more than 100 days, the additional days would be completely out of your own pocket. The **At-Home Recovery Benefit** (Plans D, G, I, and J) provides *short-term, at-home* assistance (from someone such as a nurse's aide) with activities of daily living (bathing, dressing, eating, changing bandages, etc.) for those recovering from an illness, injury, or surgery. The at-home visits must be recommended by a doctor and are only reimbursable up to $40 per visit, $1,600 per calendar year, and no more than 7 visits in any one week. In other words, if you want LTC benefits, don't look to a Medicare Supplement Policy for them!

One exception to the 12 standard plans outlined in the chart is that a company, *with prior approval of the Commissioner*, may add new or innovative benefits to a plan. These new or innovative benefits would have to be appropriate for an MSP, not otherwise available, cost effective, and consistent with the general goal of simplification of MSPs.

Other Odds and Ends on MSPs

1   The commissioner also has the power to regulate minimum standards for MSP:

- loss ratios
- marketing practices
- compensation arrangements
- advertising
- claims payment

2   Remember that a **loss ratio** is the amount an insurance company pays out to Policy-holders in benefits in relation to the amount of premium dollars it charges for those policies, and the purpose is to place a ceiling on the profitability of the insurance. For MSPs, the company must expect a loss ratio of at least 75% for its group policies, and at least 65% for its individual policies. If the company's loss ratio is substantially lower than the mandated percentage, then a refund or credit (plus interest) is required. The refund is done on a statewide basis according to the type of MSP benefit plan.

$'s out

$ s in

3   Medicare Supplement Policy sales, like Long-Term Care policies, require that the Applicant be given an **Outline of Coverage** which describes the principal benefits and coverages, the renewal provisions, and premium increase provisions. In addition to the Outline of Coverage, the commissioner may require that the Applicant be given an informational brochure about Medicare to improve the buyer's understanding of the Medicare program and to help him or her in choosing an appropriate Medicare Supplement Policy.

4   Medicare Supplement Policies, like Long-Term Care, require **a 30 Day Free Look**. If the buyer is dissatisfied with the Policy for any reason, he or she may return the Policy to the company within 30 days of its delivery for a refund of premium.

Another Big Look

5   In order to put some teeth into the Act, the Commissioner also has the power to penalize any company that violates any provision of the Act.

LTC and MSP Marketing Requirements

6   As you have probably gathered by now, Long-Term Care and Medicare Supplement policies are heavily regulated, but up to this point, we have only seen how these laws control your company in terms of Policy design and contract benefits. These laws also control your activities as an Agent selling these products in terms of marketing and sales practices.

Application Forms and Replacement Coverage

1 Application forms for LTCs and MSPs must include questions designed to elicit information as to whether, as of the date of application, the Applicant has another LTC, MSP, or any other health insurance Policy in force, and whether the Applicant plans to replace an existing Policy with the new coverage. The application form, to be signed by the Applicant and the Agent, must contain the following types of questions:

1. *Do you have **another** LTC/MSP Policy in force? If so, with which company?*

2. ***Did** you have another LTC Policy in force during the last 12 months?*
   (a) If so, with which company?
   (b) If that Policy lapsed, when did it lapse?

3. *Do you have **any other** health insurance policies that provide benefits which this Policy would duplicate? If so, with which company?*

4. *Do you **intend to replace** any of your medical or health insurance coverage with this Policy?*

5. *Are you covered by **Medicaid**?*

Mandatory Questions

2 As an Agent, you must also list any other health insurance policies you have sold to the Applicant. This includes policies you sold which are still in force, and policies sold in the past 5 years which are no longer in force. The bottom line is, as an Agent, **you must make reasonable efforts to determine the appropriateness of a recommended purchase or replacement.** In fact, it is **illegal to sell an individual more than one MSP.**

 *Know This*

3 If the sale involves replacement, then you must give your client and your company, prior to issuance or delivery of the Policy, a **Notice to Applicant Regarding Replacement** signed by both you and your client. This Notice tells the Applicant to review the new coverage carefully, compare it with any existing coverage, and to terminate the existing Policy only if, after due consideration, he or she finds that the purchase of the new Policy is a wise decision. The Notice also states that there is a **30 Day Free Look** on the new Policy. In addition, you, as the Agent, certify on the Notice that you have reviewed your client's insurance coverage and that you believe the replacement materially improves his or her position. In the case of an MSP, you must certify that the replacement **does not duplicate coverage**, and state the reason for the replacement. Your company, once having received the Notice from you, also has an obligation to notify your client's existing insurance company in writing of the replacement within 5 days of receiving the application. The purpose behind all of these requirements is to make sure that the Applicant is given enough information to make a decision in his or her own best interest.

Replacement again

30 Day free look

Standards for Marketing

1   Companies marketing Long-Term Care and Medicare Supplement Policies must:

- Establish marketing procedures to assure that any comparison of policies by its Agents will be fair and accurate, and that excessive insurance is not sold or issued.

- Prominently display on the Policy face the following:

    Notice to Buyer: This Policy may not cover all of your medical expenses/costs associated with LTC.

- Find out whether an Applicant already has insurance coverage, and if so, the types and amounts.

- Establish auditable procedures for verifying compliance with the above requirements.

Prohibited Acts and Practices

2   **TWISTING** – This is knowingly making any misleading statement or incomplete or fraudulent comparison of any insurance policies or insurance companies for the purpose of inducing a client to allow to lapse, forfeit, surrender, terminate, assign, borrow on or convert any insurance Policy or to take out a Policy with another insurance company.

3   **HIGH PRESSURE TACTICS** – This is using any sales method which has the effect of inducing the client to purchase insurance by means of explicit or implied force, fright, threat, or undue pressure.

4   **COLD LEAD ADVERTISING** – This is directly or indirectly using any method of marketing which fails to disclose in a conspicuous manner that the purpose of the advertising is to solicit insurance and that an Agent will call.

no-no's

Permitted Compensation Arrangements

5   In the sale of LTCs and MSPs, the model regulation limits Agents' compensation in order to address the potential for marketing abuses resulting from the large difference between first year and renewal commissions. For the first year commission, the insurance company may not pay the Agent more than **200% of the second year (renewal) commission**. All renewal commissions from the second year onwards must remain the same, and they must continue for a reasonable number of years (for LTCs) and at least 5 years (for MSPs).

Note to Student:

6   *Compensation* includes not just commissions, but also bonuses, gifts, prizes, awards, finders fees, etc.

200% = 2X

1   What about the commission on a *replacement* MSP? Well, it's up to each state to decide whether the Agent should get a first year commission or just a renewal commission, but the NAIC has encouraged the states **to not allow a first year commission in a replacement sale** because it would not be prudent in light of the standardized MSP plans. In the sale of LTC insurance, the states may adopt similar restrictions on replacement commissions because LTC is primarily sold to the senior citizen market . . . a market that has been identified as being susceptible to abusive marketing practices.

Conclusion

2   In this chapter, we examined both private policies and government programs that can provide care for the elderly. **Long-Term Care (LTC)** insurance is designed to pay for the necessary services of at-home care or nursing home care for at least **12 consecutive months**. This type of coverage is appropriate for someone who will need help with getting in and out of bed, preparing and eating meals, dressing, bathing, and those types of daily activities. The care may be furnished in a nursing home, or in the Insured's own home.

3   Title 19 of the Social Security Act is **Medicaid – a medical expense welfare program for the needy**. To qualify for Medicaid, a person must be at the poverty level **and** over age 65, blind, permanently and totally disabled, or a member of a family with dependent children under age 21. Unlike Medicare, Medicaid does not have deductibles or coinsurance and the benefits, although of the medical expense variety (doctor bills, hospital bills, medical supplies, etc.), are much broader than those of Medicare. The benefits vary from state to state because Medicaid is a federal-state partnership and some states have expanded their benefits. Funding comes from not only federal taxes, but also state and sometimes local taxes. In most states, Medicaid is administered by the state Department of Welfare.

4   Title 18 of the Social Security Act is **Medicare – a medical expense insurance program primarily for people age 65 or older**. Anyone, regardless of age, who has received Social Security Disability Income benefits for two years or who has chronic kidney disease is also eligible for Medicare. The benefits under Medicare are divided into two parts: **Hospital Insurance (Part A)**, which is automatic (no additional premium required) for anyone eligible for Medicare and includes essentially inpatient hospital types of expenses, and **Supplementary Medical Insurance (Part B)**, which pays benefits for other medical expenses, such as physicians' and surgeons' bills. In order to get the Part B benefits, a person must pay a small "premium" which is deducted out of his or her Social Security retirement income. Medicare, like most medical expense insurance programs, has deductibles, coinsurance, limits, and exclusions. Medicare is administered by the Centers for Medicare and Medicaid Services and is funded by federal Social Security taxes.

5   A **Medicare Supplement Policy (MSP)** pays for many of the hospital, medical, and surgical costs which are not paid for by the federal Medicare program. These policies are designed to complement – not duplicate – Medicare. With MSP insurance, companies are prohibited from rejecting (or even rating) someone for an MSP who is 65 or older and who for the first time has enrolled in Medicare Part B within the last 6 months. The trend in MSP insurance is toward standardization and simplification of Policy forms and benefits.

1 LTC and MSP insurance have much in common in terms of Policy requirements and sales practices. For example, both require that:

- Policies issued be **guaranteed renewable** or **noncancellable**.

- A covered group member be given the opportunity to convert to an individual Policy without proof of insurability (**conversion right**) and without any new probationary periods or preexisting conditions.

- A **preexisting condition** not be defined more restrictively than a condition for which medical advice or treatment was recommended by, or received from a provider of health care services within **6 months** preceding the effective date of coverage. Losses due to a preexisting **condition may not be excluded after 6 months** of the effective date of coverage.

- The Policy contain a **30 Day Free Look**.

- The Applicant be given an **Outline of Coverage** (a summary of the principal benefits and coverages of the Policy).

- You, as the Agent, not sell or replace LTC or MSP insurance unless it is **appropriate** for the purchaser.

AD&D AND LIMITED HEALTH POLICIES

1 In terms of relative importance to the insurance industry, the insuring public or the average life and health Agent, some insurance contracts fall close to the bottom of the list. To dedicate an entire chapter to them is almost ridiculous. The reason we have chosen to do so is that they do not fit into the medical expense, nor the disability income categories that we established in Chapter 10. But, neither are they so insignificant that they can simply be ignored. Essentially, these policies do not fit anywhere, but they show up everywhere. Therefore, we will give them their own chapter, but it will be a short one.

2 We will discuss the following limited policies in this chapter: Accidental Death & Dismemberment, Hospital Indemnity, Critical Illness, Accident Only Policy, and the Travel Accident Policy.

Accidental Death and Dismemberment (AD&D)

The Odd Ducks

3 The first Policy issued in this country which resembles life and health insurance as we know it today was an accident Policy for railroad passengers written in 1864 by the Traveler's Insurance Company of Hartford, Connecticut. That Policy was the direct forerunner of a Policy known today as **Accidental Death and Dismemberment.**

Looks like Life, but it's Health

4 As the name implies, the Policy protects against **accidental** death and **accidental** dismemberment. **Death or dismemberment stemming from sickness is not covered.**

Accident only

5 As you would expect, both *accidental death* and *dismemberment* are rather carefully defined in the contract. Accidental death is often defined as death resulting directly and independently from:

- An accidental injury visible on the surface of the body or disclosed by an autopsy, or

- A disease or infection resulting from an accidental injury, or

- An accidental drowning.

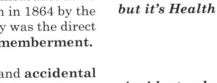

EYES

HANDS

6 Most policies further stipulate that death must **occur within 90 days of the accident**, although a few companies will allow up to 180 days.

FEET

© 2010 Pathfinder Corporation

Notes

1 The dismemberment coverage first lists the parts of the body for which coverage is provided – hands, feet, and eyes – the **primary parts**. The loss of hands or feet is generally very narrowly defined as, **"the complete severance at or above the wrist or ankle joints."** Loss of use of a hand or a foot would not qualify for benefits under this definition. Most policies are a bit less restrictive with the eyes and only require the "complete and irrevocable loss of eyesight."

Cut it off!

2 The benefit structure of an AD&D contract is based upon an amount called a **principal sum** – essentially a face amount. The principal sum is payable in the event of **accidental death** or the loss of any two of the **primary parts** – two eyes, two hands, two feet, an eye and a hand, an eye and a foot, or a hand and a foot. (Unfortunately for most of us, it pays nothing for "foot in mouth.")

principal - death or two "parts"

3 A secondary benefit (sometimes called the **capital sum**) is available if there is a loss of only one of the primary parts. Most commonly, the capital sum is an amount equal to **one-half** of the principal sum. Therefore, if Joe Insured owned an AD&D contract with a principal sum of $10,000 and severed one foot in an auto accident, he would receive $5,000. If both feet were severed (or if he died) in the accident, he (or his beneficiary) would receive $10,000.

capital - one "part"

4 The fact that the AD&D Policy **pays a death benefit** and has provisions for naming a beneficiary, but is still classified in most states as a health contract makes it a rather odd duck from the outset. And the more you learn about it, the odder it gets. For instance, since most companies writing AD&D do not exclude job-related accidents and because your occupation is a greater factor in predicting accidents than your age, the job classification of the Insured has a great deal more to do with price than age. With some companies, the most the Policy will pay under any circumstances is the principal sum, but others will pay double (or triple) the principal sum if your death was the result of being a passenger on a common carrier.

5 While few Agents sell AD&D as a stand-alone Policy, it is often sold on its own through direct mail. On the other hand, nearly every other product we sell can incorporate AD&D coverages (in whole or in part) as an inherent part of the product or attach those coverages as a rider.

- **Life Insurance**, individual as well as group, often utilizes the accidental death part of AD&D to build the **multiple indemnity rider** which can **double or triple the death benefit** of the basic Policy if death occurs as the result of an accident.

Double indemnity

- **Medical Expense** policies often have a full-blown AD&D rider attached.

- **Disability Income** contracts can attach a complete AD&D rider, or another approach uses only the dismemberment coverage and actually pays disability benefits for a specific number of weeks for a single dismemberment and twice as long for a double dismemberment.

- **Travel Accident** policies may make use of all of the AD&D benefits or simply the accidental death portion.

6 Suffice it to say that you will see the AD&D contract used in conjunction with just about every life and health product in the marketplace.

Hospital Indemnity

1   The Hospital Indemnity contract is another which is hard to classify as a square peg or a round peg. Most state regulatory authorities view it as a medical expense Policy, but in many respects it functions more like a disability income Policy.

Face Amount contract

2   The basic promise of a Hospital Indemnity contract is straightforward and simple. The company promises to pay you a **specific number of dollars each day that you are confined in a hospital.** It might be $50 per day, $100 per day, or $200 per day. It is implied that you will use these dollars to pay your costs of hospitalization. And, since its apparent purpose is to pay medical costs, thinking of it as a medical expense Policy is quite reasonable. However, as a medical expense Policy, it has several major limitations.

- It is almost never sold as a family coverage. Therefore, one of your major concerns, your children's health, is not addressed by this contract.

- Since most accidents and illnesses do not require hospitalization, coverage from this contract is seldom triggered.

Dollars per day while you are IN the hospial

- Even when hospitalization is required, it is likely that you will spend more time in recuperation outside the hospital than inside. Under this Policy, benefits stop when you are discharged.

- Because the Policy benefits are fixed, there is no relationship between the hospital charges and your benefits. For a five-day stay, you might receive $1,000 and owe $10,000.

3   Another way of viewing Hospital Indemnity is to think of it as a **disability income Policy where disability is defined as hospital confinement**. Like disability income policies, this contract does pay you and the benefits are a fixed amount. But, again, there are major limitations:

- The length of most disabilities is far longer than whatever period of hospitalization may have been required.

- The benefit has nothing to do with your income. Even if you earn $500 per day, you may only be able to buy a benefit of $200 per day.

- No insurance regulator in this country would approve a disability income Policy with a hospital confinement definition.

1

While it may be difficult to classify a Hospital Indemnity plan, it is not difficult to find one – they show up everywhere in health insurance.

- Despite its obvious limitations, some Hospital Indemnity plans are sold to people who have no other coverage. While the benefits do not amount to much, neither do the premiums.

- Hospital Indemnity contracts are often sold to people who are covered under a group medical expense Policy with a high deductible and heavy coinsurance. Here, the idea is for the Hospital Indemnity to cover a big share of the up front expenses if the Insured is hospitalized.

- Hospital Indemnity coverage is often included or added as a rider to a disability income Policy for the first 30 to 60 days. This is done because most Insureds cannot imagine any lengthy disability which would not start with at least some time in the hospital. Since the elimination period in the disability income contract likely precludes income from that source, the Hospital Indemnity coverage at least starts a stream of income to the Insured.

Critical Illness / Dread Disease Policy

*Example:
"Cancer Policy"*

2   A Dread Disease Policy provides Major Medical or Comprehensive Major Medical type benefits **but only for the named disease**. While this contract could be written on practically any disease, it seems to work best for high cost illnesses that anyone can get, and everyone is afraid of. Policies written exclusively to cover heart disease or cancer are the most common contracts today.

Accident Only Policies

3   As we pointed out in Chapter 10 of this text, 90% of health insurance claims stem from sickness and only 10% arise from accidents. While the policies we've examined to this point cover both perils, it is certainly possible to design a Policy that only covers accidents. Though it can be sold on an individual basis, it is more commonly marketed as group insurance on a blanket basis.

Travel Accident Policies

4   This is one use of the aforementioned Accident Only contracts. Generally, this Policy provides coverage for injuries resulting from accidents occurring while the Insured is a fare-paying passenger on a common carrier (bus, airplane, cruise ship, etc.). Other Travel Accident Policies are written to cover accidental losses (AD&D) while operating a motor vehicle.

Narrow coverages

UNIFORM INDIVIDUAL HEALTH POLICY PROVISIONS LAW

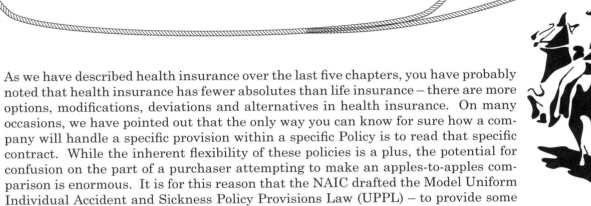

1   As we have described health insurance over the last five chapters, you have probably noted that health insurance has fewer absolutes than life insurance – there are more options, modifications, deviations and alternatives in health insurance. On many occasions, we have pointed out that the only way you can know for sure how a company will handle a specific provision within a specific Policy is to read that specific contract. While the inherent flexibility of these policies is a plus, the potential for confusion on the part of a purchaser attempting to make an apples-to-apples comparison is enormous. It is for this reason that the NAIC drafted the Model Uniform Individual Accident and Sickness Policy Provisions Law (UPPL) – to provide some degree of uniformity to contracts which are by nature very non-uniform.

The NAIC and the Model Law

2   The NAIC's first attempt to regulate the language of individual (as opposed to group) health contracts came back in 1912. By 1950, a total rewrite was in order due to the popularity of policies that had evolved after the passage of the original model. In 1979, a *readable version* was adopted by the NAIC to meet the simplified Policy language requirements of many of the states. This 1979 revision addressed language only – every attempt was made to preserve the meaning of the 1950 document.

3   Every state adopted the UPPL, and very few made any changes to the provisions of the model. In 1975, the state of Wisconsin repealed the law and replaced it with legislation requiring a few of the same provisions.

4   As we will see, the law contains 12 required and 11 optional provisions as well as a list of additional Policy structure requirements. While there is no requirement that companies incorporate these provisions into their policies *word for word*, most contracts simply use the wording found in the law. Obviously, any deviation from the Uniform Provisions would have to be approved by the state insurance regulatory agency and must be *at least as favorable* to the Policyowner as the language used in the law.

NAIC model law

5   Since there are 12 required and 11 optional provisions, you might at first glance assume that there must be at least 12 of these provisions in any Policy. But, as we will discover, some of these 23 provisions apply only to a specific type of coverage. For example, amongst the 12 required provisions, we will find one called the Change of Beneficiary Provision which tells us that the Policyowner has the right to name and change beneficiaries. Obviously, this provision is important if the contract has AD&D coverage because it is the only health Policy with a death benefit. On the other hand, this same provision is not applicable to a Major Medical Policy, and can therefore be omitted.

© 2010 Pathfinder Corporation

How to Proceed and What to Learn

1　To help you to familiarize yourself with the 12 required and 11 optional provisions, we will discuss each as it appears in the NAIC model. As you read each, notice the **name** given that particular provision, and try to tie it back to the objective of that provision. This is important as some of the names are quite similar and tend to run together. In our comments which follow each major provision, we will discuss its **purpose**, explain how it functions and point out any **key numbers** that you should know. If your purpose of reading this text is to pass a licensing exam, you should be aware that most entrance level exams concentrate heavily on the *required* uniform Policy provisions, thus making this an important area of study.

Name

Purpose

Key #'s

Required Versus Optional

2　As the names would imply, the required provisions **must** be included in an individual health Policy if appropriate, and the optional provisions **may** be included if the company wishes. As you might guess, the required provisions tend to protect the Policyowners and the Insureds, whereas the optional provisions tend to protect the company. The logic of the NAIC in separating these provisions into two piles is that the consumer **must** be protected (so the consumer protection-type provisions are required), but the insurance company should have enough sense to protect itself (therefore the provisions which protect the company are optional).

Must

May

Individual Versus Group

3　The required and optional provisions discussed in this chapter **only apply to individual policies.** However, since the purpose of all 23 provisions is to spell out the *rules of conduct* between the company and the Policyowner . . . the rights, duties, and responsibilities of each under any conceivable circumstances, there is a **similar set of provisions in group insurance** to establish the working relationship between the parties of the group contract. You will soon discover that the provisions governing the group health contracts are not markedly different from the provisions contained in this chapter. As a matter of fact, the provisions found in a life Policy, health Policy or group Policy differ very little conceptually from one to the other. Therefore, the things you know from life insurance will help you here, and the points you learn in this section will aid you as we move to group insurance.

The Required Provisions

ENTIRE CONTRACT; CHANGES

1 The **Entire Contract** provision states that:

- Only those **documents** which are **included or attached to the Policy** are legally part of the contract.

- Changes to the Policy must be in **writing**, attached to the Policy and signed by an executive officer of the company.

- No Agent has the authority to change or modify the agreement in any way.

2 This provision protects the Policyowner by **limiting the contract to the Policy and its attachments.** A statement in a Policy which says that "all promises are subject to the charter and by-laws of ABC Mutual" would have no legal bearing unless those documents were part of the Policy. Said another way, the Policyowner is not at the mercy of provisions he or she has not seen.

3 Further, this provision informs the Policyowner of the limits of the Agent's authority to modify the agreement in any way and outlines the procedure that must be undertaken if a change is desired.

TIME LIMIT ON CERTAIN DEFENSES (INCONTESTABLE)

4 This provision is made up of two paragraphs, and the company is given two options from which to choose. Typically, medical expense policies use the first choice and disability income policies use the second.

Option 1: TIME LIMIT ON CERTAIN DEFENSES

After three years (two years in most states) from the date of issue of this Policy, no misstatements, except fraudulent misstatements, made by the Applicant in the application for such Policy, shall be used to void the Policy or to deny a claim for loss incurred or disability (as defined in the Policy) commencing after the expiration of such three year period.

Option 2: INCONTESTABLE

After this Policy has been in force for a period of three years (two years in most states) during the lifetime of the Insured (excluding any period during which the Insured is disabled), it shall become incontestable as to the statements contained in the application.

5 With either option, the company is restricted to **a period of three years** (two in most states) in which to **rescind a Policy or contest a claim due to a misrepresentation or concealment in the application.** Simply put, if Joe lies on his application, the company has three years to do something about it. After three years, they are stuck with Joe . . . lies and all – they may no longer contest a claim or the Policy because Joe lied on the application; it is **incontestable**. As with the incontestable provision in life insurance, this does not mean that the company cannot contest a claim; it means only that they cannot contest on the basis of *statements made in the application* after the allotted time period. If Joe fakes a claim 10 years after purchasing a Policy, the company can contest. Their reason for contesting in this case though has nothing to do with statements Joe made on his application.

APPLICATION

1   How do these two options differ? They differ in two ways:

- Option 1 allows the company to contest after the three year period if they can establish **fraud** on the part of the Applicant. Option 2 does not allow the company to contest after three years even if they can prove fraud (which is close to impossible anyway).

- In Option 2, any period that an Insured is **disabled** does not count as part of the three year period. For example, if Joe Insured purchased the Policy three years ago but has been disabled six months in the meantime, the company would have three years and six months from the Policy date to contest the application. Option 1 does not have this disability time-cushion.

2   As you read the two options, you probably noticed that the NAIC model allows three years as a contestable period under either option, but in most states the law was enacted using two years instead of three. Obviously, this is better for the consumer.

3   Regardless of which option a company uses for its first paragraph, the second paragraph reads as follows:

No claim for loss incurred or disability (as defined in the Policy) commencing after three years (two in most states) from the date of issue of this Policy shall be reduced or denied on the grounds that a disease or physical condition, not excluded from coverage by name or specific description effective on the date of loss, had existed prior to the effective date of coverage of this Policy.

4   This paragraph limits to three years (again, two in most states) the company's right to deny a claim as being a preexisting condition **unless** that condition was specifically excluded by name with an Exclusion (Impairment) Rider when the contract was originally issued.

Grace Period

5   Obviously, the purpose of a Grace Period in any installment transaction is to allow for human error, human nature, and circumstances beyond anyone's control. To allow a health Policy to lapse because Joe is 45 hours late in paying his premium is not fair or reasonable. Suppose Joe bought a *Guaranteed Renewable to Age 65* medical expense Policy at age 45. Further assume that at age 55 he becomes uninsurable and that he retires at age 60. Without a Grace Period, Joe could be in serious trouble if he even takes a three day trip to celebrate his retirement unless he remembers to pay his premium before leaving.

Frequency of premium payment defines grace period

"7-10-31"

6   In health insurance, the length of the Grace Period varies according to the premium mode (the frequency of premium payments). For industrial weekly-premium policies, it is **7 days** (if the Agent misses collecting one weekly payment, the Insured is covered until the next weekly visit). For a monthly premium, it is **10 days** (the logic being that most monthly bills are payable by the 10th of the month). For all other premium modes (quarterly, semi-annually or annually), it is **31 days**. Remember that the coverage remains in force during the Grace Period and the Policy will only lapse at the expiration of the Grace Period.

REINSTATEMENT

1 We should first point out a major difference between health insurance and cash value life insurance. In health insurance, if the Policyowner does not pay the premium on time or within the Grace Period, **the company has no obligation to reinstate coverage**. If Joe has never filed a claim, the company probably wants him back. But, if Joe is the all-time company leader in claims dollars received, the company is not about to reinstate him, and there is no requirement to do so.

2 If the company wants to reinstate Joe (or at least consider doing so), there are two possible approaches:

Company is in control

- The company, or its duly authorized Agent, can accept Joe's past due premium. Could there be a time where you should simply refuse to accept Joe's money? Absolutely!

- Most of the time the company prefers to obtain up-to-date information on Joe and make a completely new decision. This can be done by taking a **reinstatement application** (most companies use the same application as they do for new Applicants), collecting his **overdue premium**, issuing a Conditional Receipt, and making a decision. Under this approach, if Joe has not been notified of his acceptance or rejection by the **45th day** following the date of the Conditional Receipt, he is automatically reinstated.

45days
look over app

3 With either approach, there are two further restrictions on this process.

- While the company is authorized to collect past due premium from Joe utilizing either of the reinstatement methods we've outlined, it can collect **no more than 60 days past due premium** regardless of how long Joe's payment has been delinquent.

60days
back premium

- If Joe is reinstated under either procedure, **accident coverage begins on the reinstatement date** but there is a **10 day waiting period before sickness losses are covered**. Once again, it's much easier to spot a preexisting accident than a preexisting sickness and the 10 day waiting period serves as a blanket probationary period. Of course, a sickness starting on the 11th day or after would be covered.

10days
waiting period

Preview:

4 The next four provisions, Notice Of Claim, Claim Forms, Proof of Loss, and Time of Payment of Claims, relate to the process of submitting claims and getting paid. The four step process is clearly stated in the Policy to avoid any confusion over the responsibilities of the Policyowner and the insurance company. The sequence begins when **Joe Insured notifies** the company that he has sustained a loss. The company then acts by **mailing claim forms** to Joe. Next, Joe, with the help of the doctor(s) involved, completes the claim forms and returns his **proof of loss** to the company. As the last step, the company **pays the claim**.

NOTICE OF CLAIM

1   The claims process begins with the Policyowner as soon as a loss is suffered. The purpose of the **Notice Of Claim** provision is to advise the Policyowner that in order to collect benefits under the Policy, timely notice of loss must be given to the insurance company. The Insured must give **written notice** of a claim to the company within **20 days** of the loss, or as soon thereafter as is reasonably possible. The *or as soon thereafter as is reasonably possible* phrase is included so that Joe is not denied a claim if timely notification is prevented due to circumstances beyond his control (such as being in a coma for six weeks). The Insured can send written notice to either the insurance company or to an authorized Agent of the company.

notice within

20 *days*

2   The second paragraph in this provision states that under a disability income Policy with a benefit period exceeding two years, the Insured must notify the company **at least once every six months** of a continued disability in order to continue to receive benefits. (Most companies ask for proof of continued disability on a monthly basis.)

CLAIM FORMS

3   Certainly, the insurance company is not going to pay a claim just because a Policyowner says there was a loss. The company needs *proof* that there was, in fact, a loss. This is accomplished by having the Policyowner complete claim forms. This provision establishes the company's responsibility to **provide the Insured with claim forms** within **15 days** of notification of the claim. It would be unfair to allow the company to sit on the claim forms, thereby delaying the claims process.

send out forms within

15 *days*

4   If the company fails to meet the 15 day deadline, then the Insured can write out a description of the loss in his or her own words which must then be accepted by the company as adequate proof of loss.

PROOF OF LOSS

5   The next step in the claims sequence is the Policyowner's responsibility. Under the Proof of Loss provision, the Policyowner is required to **provide written proof of loss to the company** within **90 days** from the date of loss. Late proof of loss is acceptable if furnished *as soon thereafter as reasonably possible*, but usually within one year. In cases of legal incapacity (for example, coma or extensive brain damage), proof will even be accepted after **one year** from the time it was contractually required.

send back forms within

90 *days*

6   If it is a medical expense type of loss, the medical provider (doctor's office, hospital) generally takes responsibility for completing the Proof of Loss statement and filing it with the company. Remember that in a significant number of cases, benefits have been assigned to the medical provider, and, therefore, the provider has a vested interest in completing this task in a timely manner.

7   On a disability income claim, it is primarily the responsibility of the Insured to complete the paperwork, although, in this case, a doctor's statement would in all likelihood be required along with the completed Proof of Loss forms.

TIME OF PAYMENT OF CLAIMS

1 The last event in the claims process is the payment of the claim by the company. The Time of Payment of Claims provision states **how long** the company can wait before it pays a claim. For medical expense or AD&D claims (lump-sum payments) the company must pay **immediately** upon receipt of due proof of loss. Even though the law says *immediately*, the company is not working against a three minute egg timer. Most insurance regulators translate *immediately* to mean within a **reasonable time** and are satisfied with payment in the realm of 30 days. Disability income benefits must be paid according to the contract, but **no less frequently than monthly**.

2 The key words in this provision are *time of payment* and the provision refers to how long the company has to pay claims. The question of to whom claims are paid is the subject of the next provision.

TIME

PAYMENT OF CLAIMS

3 The Payment of Claims provision states to **whom claims will be paid.** Under medical expense and disability income policies, there is rarely a question regarding who should get paid. The company simply **pays the Policyowner.** Even if Little Joe suffers a loss, the company still pays to Joe Insured.

Owe the **O**wner

4 However, if the Policy contains an AD&D benefit, there can definitely be a question of who gets paid if the Insured dies, and this question is answered by the Payment of Claims provision. Just as in life insurance, death benefits are payable to the Named Beneficiary. If no Beneficiary is named, then the company pays the benefits to the estate of the Insured. Any other benefits remaining unpaid at the Insured's death (for example, medical expense or disability income benefits) are also payable to a Beneficiary or the Insured's estate.

To whom

5 There are two additional paragraphs that the insurance company may include in the Payment of Claims provision if it so chooses.

6 The purpose of the first is to speed up payments to the family in situations where the proceeds are payable to the estate of the Insured. An estate may take years to settle, and some families do not have the resources to wait for settlement to bury the deceased Insured. This provision allows the company to pay up to $1000 to a relative that the company deems to be entitled to receive the money. The recipient is usually the individual who pays the funeral costs.

facility of payments provision

7 The second optional paragraph simply states that the company will, at the direction of the Policyowner, pay medical expense claims directly to the vendors of the medical services. This allows for the assignment of benefits.

PHYSICAL EXAM AND AUTOPSY

8 This provision is the most obvious exception to our rule of thumb that the required provisions protect the Policyowner. This one protects the company (and only indirectly the other Policyowners).

Xception

9 This provision gives the company the right to physically examine the claimant in the event of a medical expense, disability or dismemberment claim. Unless prohibited by state law, the company has the right to conduct an autopsy on the deceased Insured in the event of an accidental death claim.

LEGAL ACTION

1 Can the Insured sue the company if dissatisfied with the handling of a claim? —Yes, but in order to prevent premature litigation, the Legal Action provision states that the **Insured must wait at least 60 days** after submission of written proof of loss before initiating a lawsuit. This allows the company time to investigate the claim. Any such suit must be brought **within three years** after proof of loss in order to limit the company's liability to a known time frame. The intent of the Legal Action provision is to establish a **time period for resolving claim disputes** between the company and the Insured.

60 days - 3 years

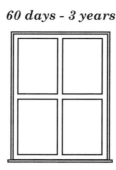

window of opportunity

CHANGE OF Beneficiary

2 This last required provision is an easy one . . . as it is in life insurance. It states that, unless an irrevocable Beneficiary has been named, the Policyowner may change the Beneficiary, surrender the Policy, assign it, or make any other changes desired. The intent of the Change of Beneficiary provision is to legally establish the Policyowner's **right of ownership** under the contract.

The Optional Provisions

3 As we have noted, the **optional provisions tend to protect the insurance company.** The attitude of the insurance regulatory authorities is that the companies have been around the block a time or two and should, therefore, know the circumstances in which they need to use these provisions to protect themselves.

4 While there are 11 optional provisions, many are seldom used. We will address the most important ones first, using the same approach as with the required provisions. We will then give you a thumbnail sketch of the others.

CHANGE OF OCCUPATION

5 With individual disability income and medical expense policies, it is typically a requirement that the Insured notify the company in the event of a change of occupation. If Joe goes from *librarian* to *construction worker*, his rates will go up. If he goes from *construction worker* to *librarian*, his rates will go down. The **Change of Occupation** provision tells us that Joe is supposed to notify the company when he changes occupations.

6 Since Insureds frequently fail to notify the company of an occupational change, this provision further outlines the process of settling a claim if Joe is in a more or less hazardous occupation when a claim is filed than he was in when he purchased the coverage.

7 If Joe simply moves to another job at the same risk level, nothing changes. But, there are two other possibilities that would trigger major changes.

Rule of two "R's"

Higher - reduce benefits

Lower - refund premium

- **Change to a higher risk occupation** – If Joe moves to a higher risk occupation, fails to notify the company and submits a claim, **the company will pay only the benefits his premium would have purchased** at the more hazardous occupation level.

- **Change to a lower risk occupation** – In this situation, the company will **pay the benefits of the Policy Joe purchased**, and return the overpayment of premium which has accrued since Joe changed to a less hazardous job.

1 Why is it that this provision handles Joe's occupational move so differently depending upon whether it's higher risk or lower risk? The move to a higher risk occupation is handled under the philosophy of "make it right" by adjusting benefits. Why do we not use the same philosophy if he goes to a lower risk occupation? Well, the reason is obvious once you analyze it. If Joe went from very high risk to very low risk, his benefits would have to be adjusted drastically. His disability income benefits might double, and under a medical expense Policy, the company might have to pay him 110% of his loss instead of 80%. Obviously, that solution would undermine the whole purpose of insurance, and therefore the approach we outlined is the system that is used.

MISSTATEMENT OF AGE

make it right

2 This provision contains the same solution we used in life insurance for this very common problem. If Joe Insured understates his age, thus increasing the company's risk, the company will **only pay an amount based on what Joe's premium payments would have purchased** in coverage if Joe had given his correct age. The reverse is also true. If Joe overstates his age, then the benefits would be increased accordingly.

ILLEGAL OCCUPATION

no cash for cons

3 This provision simply tells us that if Joe is **injured in the commission of a felony** or while engaged in an illegal occupation, the company does not have to pay his claim.

The Stacked Benefits Provisions

4 As we have pointed out all along in health insurance, benefits from health coverages cannot be stacked. If you have three medical expense policies, they will not all pay you 80% of the cost of your broken leg. If you earn $40,000 each year, you cannot buy three disability income policies to pay you $30,000 each if you are disabled. If overinsurance and its resultant duplication of benefits were allowed, the current health care crisis would look like a rather puny problem.

Double dipping our way to disaster

5 Three of the optional provisions address this **problem of overinsurance**. Basically they all say the same thing. **Each Policy will pay its pro rata share of the loss and refund the overpayments in premium** the Insured has made in purchasing duplicate coverage. It makes no difference if Joe has multiple policies with the same company or several companies. Nor does it matter if he buys duplicate medical expense coverage or duplicate disability income coverage.

OTHER INSURANCE IN THIS INSURER

pro rata

6 This provision provides for a pro rata benefit reduction and return of premium in the event of multiple policies with the same company.

INSURANCE
WITH OTHER INSURERS: EXPENSE INCURRED BASIS

7 This provision provides for a pro rata reduction of medical expense benefits and a return of premium in the event of duplicate coverage with more than one company.

INSURANCE WITH OTHER INSURERS: OTHER BENEFITS

Different rules for Group

8 This provision provides for a pro rata reduction of disability income benefits and a return of premium in the event of insurance with more than one company.

1 **Comment:** A concern that many students have when they look at the provisions concerning multiple policies is, "How does this apply to me? I'm covered under a Policy at my job, but I'm also covered under my spouse's Policy at his or her place of employment." Remember, these provisions regulate **individual policies – not group policies**.

2 As you will see, it is well understood that multiple coverage situations are often unavoidable in group insurance, and, therefore, we have a completely different mechanism for dealing with this problem in a group context.

The Remaining Optional Provisions

3 The final group of optional provisions are not as important as the first three nor do they address one basic problem like the three we just discussed. Some companies use them and some do not. Their purposes are all over the map.

RELATION OF EARNINGS TO INSURANCE: AVERAGE EARNINGS CLAUSE

4 Disability income policies can contain this clause which proportionately reduces the benefits paid if Joe is earning less at the time of his claim than he was at the time he bought the Policy. Under this provision, the company can base Joe's benefit upon the amount he made in the month prior to his disability, or **his average earnings over the 24 months immediately preceding his claim.**

Less is less

UNPAID PREMIUM PROVISION

5 As in life insurance, this provision allows the company to deduct any past due premiums from a claim payment owed the Policyowner and pay only the net amount.

pay us now or later

CANCELLATION

6 Since premiums are paid in advance, cancellation by either party triggers a refund of unearned premium. This provision requires that a **mid-term cancellation by the company** calls for a **pro rata refund**. If you pay annually in advance and are cancelled after 6 months, you receive a refund of 6 month's premium. If, on the other hand, **you cancel the contract** you are penalized and are paid a **short rate refund**. In some states this is a mandatory provision.

Pro Rata Refund

7 In the few states that allow companies to sell cancellable policies (see forms of renewal in Chapter 10), this provision requires at least **5 days written notice**. In the handful of states where this is still an issue, the 5 day requirement of the NAIC model has been increased to 30 days.

CONFORMITY WITH STATE STATUTES

8 This provision says that if a Policy does not conform with state statutes on the day it is issued, it is to be interpreted as if it did conform.

INTOXICANTS AND NARCOTICS

9 This provision eliminates the company's responsibility for losses sustained or contracted by the Insured as a consequence of his being intoxicated or under the influence of any narcotic not administered by a physician.

No bucks for drunks

State Mandated Policy Provisions or Benefits

1   The Uniform Policy Provisions Law is not the only law that addresses the contents of a health insurance Policy. Almost every state has laws which mandate other provisions or coverages. Obviously, companies doing business in those states must comply with the additional requirements.

2   For the most part, these state mandated requirements focus on medical expense policies rather than on disability income. Among the more common requirements you will find the following:

- maternity expenses
- newborn care
- well-baby care
- handicapped children
- mental health care
- allied practitioners (other health care professionals)
- alcohol and drug addiction
- ambulatory surgical car
- home health care
- transplant surgery

3   While these state mandated requirements are generally considered a plus for the Policyowner, they also tend to increase the costs of coverage. Whether or not individual states continue to legislate the benefits of medical expense policies in the face of sky-rocketing prices remains to be seen.

Conclusion

4   The purpose of this chapter has been to acquaint you with the Model Uniform Individual Accident and Sickness Policy Provisions Law. This law, adopted by all states (although repealed and replaced with a few of the same provisions in Wisconsin), sets out 12 required provisions and 11 optional provisions. A company may deviate from the wording of the model law as long as the language is at least as favorable to the Insured as the model law and is approved by the commissioner of insurance of that state.

5   The required provisions, in essence, state the following:

1. **ENTIRE CONTRACT** – The Policy, the application, and any attached riders constitute the entire agreement of insurance. Any changes to the Policy must be in writing, attached to the Policy, and signed by an executive officer of the company. No Agent has the authority to change or modify the agreement in any way.

2. **TIME LIMIT ON CERTAIN DEFENSES OR INCONTESTABLE** – After the health Policy has been in force for three years (two years in many states), the insurance company cannot (1) rescind the Policy or deny a claim for misrepresentation or concealment in the application, or (2) deny a claim as being a preexisting condition unless it was specifically excluded by name or with an Exclusion (Impairment) rider.

Notes

3. **Grace Period** – The Policyowner must be given a Grace Period, which in individual health policies is linked to the premium mode: **7 days** for a weekly premium mode, **10 days** for monthly premium mode, and **31 days** for any other premium mode. **Coverage remains in force** during the Grace Period. If the premium is not paid by the end of the Grace Period, the Policy will lapse.

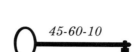
7-10-31

4. **REINSTATEMENT** – An insurance company is not obligated to reinstate a lapsed health insurance Policy. The company may, if it wishes, accept past due premium and immediately reinstate the Policy. Usually, however, the company will take a new reinstatement application, collect no more than 60 days worth of past due premium, issue a new Conditional Receipt, and require proof of insurability. The company may accept or reject the coverage. If no decision is made, the Policy is automatically reinstated on the 45th day. If the Policy is reinstated, coverage for accidents begins on the reinstatement date, but there is a 10 day waiting period before sickness losses are covered.

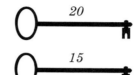
45-60-10

5. **NOTICE OF CLAIM** – The Insured must notify the health insurance company of a loss within **20 days** *or as soon thereafter as reasonably possible.*

20

6. **CLAIM FORMS** – The company must get claim forms to the Insured within **15 days** of being notified. If not, the Insured can write out a description of the loss and the company has to accept it as valid.

15

7. **PROOF OF LOSS** – The Policyowner must provide the company with written proof that there was a loss within **90 days** of the loss.

90

8. **TIME OF PAYMENT OF CLAIMS** – The insurance company must pay medical expense and AD&D claims **immediately** (which means within a *reasonable* time), and disability income benefits according to the contract but **at least once a month**.

9. **PAYMENT OF CLAIMS** – The insurance company pays the Policyowner. If it is an AD&D death benefit, the company pays the named Beneficiary. If no Beneficiary is named, then the company pays the estate.

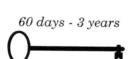
1000

10. **PHYSICAL EXAMINATION AND AUTOPSY** – The company has the right to physically examine the Insured during a claim and, where not prohibited by law, to perform an autopsy on a deceased Insured.

11. **LEGAL ACTION** – The Policyowner must wait at least **60 days** after submission of written proof of loss before initiating a lawsuit, and must bring the suit within **3 years** after proof of loss.

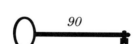
60 days - 3 years

12. **CHANGE OF Beneficiary**—Gives the Insured the right to change the Beneficiary, unless named on an irrevocable basis.

The optional Policy provisions are as follows:

1. **CHANGE OF OCCUPATION** – If Joe moves to a higher risk occupation, fails to notify the company and submits a claim, the company will pay only the benefits his premium would have purchased at the more hazardous occupation level. If he changes to a lower risk occupation, the company will pay the benefits of the Policy Joe purchased and return the overpayment of premium which has accrued since Joe changed to a less hazardous job.

2. **MISSTATEMENT OF AGE** – Benefits will be adjusted to match the Insured's actual age in the event it was misstated.

3. **ILLEGAL OCCUPATION** – The company does not have to pay the claim if the Insured is injured while committing a felony or while engaged in an illegal occupation.

4. **OTHER INSURANCE IN THIS INSURER** – This provision provides for a pro rata benefit reduction and return of premium in the event of other policies with the same company.

5. **INSURANCE WITH OTHER INSURERS: EXPENSE INCURRED BASIS** – This provision provides for a pro rata reduction of medical expense benefits and a return of premium in the event of duplicate coverage with more than one company.

6. **INSURANCE WITH OTHER INSURERS: OTHER BENEFITS** – This provision provides for a pro rata reduction of disability income benefits and a return of premium in the event of insurance with more than one company.

7. **RELATION OF EARNINGS TO INSURANCE: AVERAGE EARNINGS** – If Joe is earning less at the time of his disability claim than he was at the time he bought the Policy, the company can reduce his benefit.

8. **UNPAID PREMIUM** – This permits the company to deduct any past due premium from the claim at the time of claim payment .

9. **CANCELLATION** – This provision allows the insurance company to cancel a Policy at any time as long as it gives a 5 day written notice. (However, only a few states still allow cancellable policies, and all concerned require 30 days.)

10. **CONFORMITY WITH STATE STATUTES** – If, on its effective date, a Policy does not conform to state law, it will be interpreted as if it did.

11. **INTOXICANTS AND NARCOTICS** – The company does not have to pay benefits for losses resulting from the Insured's being intoxicated or under the influence of any narcotic not administered by a physician.

2 R's

make it right

Part IV
GROUP INSURANCE

GROUP CONCEPTS AND GROUP LIFE

one contract

many Insureds

1 Up to this point in the text, our principal focus has been on insurance contracts written for individuals. In the next two chapters, we will see how these same contracts can be written to insure a large number of individuals (Group insurance) rather than insuring a single individual. The products we have already studied . . . Term, Whole Life, Universal Life, Disability Income, and Medical Expense function almost identically to the way they functioned as individual Policies. Therefore, this chapter will concentrate on the ideas that distinguish Group Policies from individual Policies and on the legal requirements that are unique to the Group insurance business.

2 In a nutshell, Group insurance is an insurance plan that **provides coverage to a number of persons under one Policy.** You will discover that only certain Groups are eligible to purchase a Group Policy, such as an employer for its employees, or an association for its members. However, the **organizing entity cannot** (in almost all cases) **be the Beneficiary**. You will also learn that the underwriting of Group insurance varies somewhat from the individual arena. Insurance companies writing Group Policies must include certain standard Policy provisions, as you have seen in individual insurance, as well as comply with regulations which may restrict the types and amounts of coverage that can be written as Group insurance.

© 2010 Pathfinder Corporation

A Brief History

1   In many respects, the great success of Group insurance in this country was very predictable. In all three areas of insurance discussed in this text – life, disability income
and medical expense – the idea of providing coverage on a Group basis came from
the people who needed the coverage, the consumers, rather than from the insurance
industry itself. In terms that an economist might use, it was a *market driven* need
that resulted in the Group product. The insurance industry did not invent a hula
hoop and try to force market acceptance; instead, the consuming public demanded
a product which the insurers then produced. In 1910, Montgomery Ward & Co.,
Inc., was investigating the possibility of insuring a disability income-type employee
benefit that they had previously self-Insured. By 1911, they had placed the coverage with London Guarantee and Accident of New York. This contract is generally
regarded as the first Group Policy written in this country. During the same time
period, Montgomery Ward entered into negotiations with the Equitable Life Assurance Society to provide Group life insurance for its employees. An Equitable actuary, William J. Graham (the "father of Group insurance"), developed an acceptable
contract. While Montgomery Ward was studying the plan, five other big employers
actually purchased contracts. By the time Ward took action, they could claim only to
have purchased the sixth Group life plan sold in the United States . . . the very first
covered the employees of the Panasote Leather Company in 1911.

2   In a similar vein, in 1929 a Group of Dallas, Texas, schoolteachers approached Baylor
Hospital with the idea of prepaying hospital services on a Group basis. With the
collapse of the national economy in October of that same year, hospitals across the
country saw the Baylor Hospital Plan as a method by which they could get paid for
the services they would have to provide even in the face of a Great Depression. As
the hospitals formed the Blue Cross organization, the doctors and surgeons took note
(they, too, had problems getting paid), and they formed the Blue Shield.

New Federal laws may change the Group Health business

3   Though consumers triggered the beginnings of Group insurance, the insurance companies were quick to realize the potential profitability of the Group business. Since
1911, the Group life and health insurance business has become a major industry in our
country. Group insurance has become a major component of most employee benefit
plans and, as such, has considerable economic, social, and political significance. With
the high degree of flexibility possible in a Group program, the insurance company can
design benefit packages according to the exact needs of the customer, which is not
possible with individual Policies. Today, approximately 80% of all health insurance
and over 40% of all life insurance is written on a Group basis . . . a huge industry
with incredible potential for growth and innovative marketing strategies.

4   As we saw with individual Policies, the National Association of Insurance Commissioners (NAIC) has developed model legislation in the area of Group life and health.
The first statutory definition of Group insurance was recommended by the NAIC in
1917. Today, most states have adopted the NAIC models regulating Group insurance
almost verbatim. Our discussion will ignore any minor modifications made by the
states and utilize only the NAIC models.

Regulation

1 Since it is very likely that a Group Policy sold to an employer in Ohio could cover employees in Illinois, it is important to know who has jurisdiction in the event of a legal dispute. Generally speaking, **the state in which the coverage was delivered,** Illinois in our example, would have jurisdiction.

State regs in which Policy is delivered dictates benefits

2 Most state laws governing Group insurance say that such multi-state Policies are acceptable if the Policy is:

- Approved by the issuing state.

- Written in substantial compliance with the laws of the delivery state.

- And, if the laws governing Group insurance are substantially similar between the issuing state and the delivery state.

CHARACTERISTICS OF Group INSURANCE

3 Group insurance is characterized by:

- Legally acceptable Groups.
- A Group contract.
- Experience rating.
- Group underwriting.

4 We will address each of these in turn.

Legally Acceptable Groups

5 While most states limit by statute the types of Groups eligible to buy Group insurance, others have no restrictions whatsoever and rely solely on the underwriting practices of admitted companies to determine eligible Groups. Shortly, we will examine the most commonly acceptable types of Groups which, interestingly enough, are the ones listed in the model law. They are:

- Single Employer
- Labor Union
- Negotiated Trusteeship
- Association
- Credit Union
- Creditor
- Multiple Employer Trust (MET)

good Groups

6 Another major variation from state to state has to do with the minimum number of persons required to form an eligible Group. Even the model law was amended on this point. At one time, the model law contained a minimum number for each Group type . . . 10 for single employer Groups, 25 for labor union Groups, and so on. The 1984 and 1985 amendments eliminated all the minimum number requirements except for association Groups which remains at 100.

Single Employer Groups

1 This is a Group formed by one employer for the benefit of its employees. An example of a single employer Group would be the employees of Acme Ink, Inc. As you would guess, this is the type of Group for which most Group insurance is written. In this text, our discussion of Group insurance will frequently use the words *employee* and *employer*. This is *not* because other configurations are not possible, but because the most likely situation is an employer Group.

Single employer

2 Under a single employer Group, the definition of *employee* may include the individual proprietor running the business, or the partners of a partnership. It may also include retired employees, former employees, or directors of the corporation. A Policy insuring the employees of a public organization, such as a state government, may also cover elected or appointed officials.

Fairly Inclusive

Labor Union Groups

3 Labor unions may establish Group insurance plans to provide benefits for their members, with the labor union as the Policyowner. In reality, labor union Groups account for very little Group insurance due to the impact of two laws.

Labor Union

4 The first is a federal law known as the Taft-Hartley Act. It prohibits employers from paying money directly to a union for the purpose of providing Group insurance for its members. Secondly, most states have laws which prohibit Group plans in which union members pay for the coverage entirely from their own pockets. Consequently, the only payment option remaining is for the union to pay the premiums entirely from union funds or to share the cost with the membership.

New Federal Laws may change this

Negotiated Trusteeship (Taft-Hartley Trust)

5 As we have said, the Taft-Hartley Act does not allow the employer to pay money directly to the union for the purpose of purchasing Group insurance. However, this legislation *does allow* the employer to pay into a trust fund established for the same purpose. Negotiated trusteeships are formed as the result of collective bargaining over benefits between a union and the employer(s) of the union members. Generally, the union members are in the same or a related industry, like trucking or construction. Furthermore, these industries are characterized by frequent movement of union members among employers.

Association Groups

6 An association Group, like an alumni Group or professional Group (state Teachers' Association), can buy Group insurance for its members. This is the one Group type for which the model law still maintains a minimum numerical requirement. The association must have at the outset at least one hundred (100) members; it must have been organized for a purpose other than buying insurance; it must have been active for at least two years; it must have a constitution and by-laws; and it must hold regular meetings not less frequently than annually.

Associations

100
minimum

Credit Union Groups

7 A credit union, such as the General Motors Credit Union, can offer insurance to its members as a credit union Group.

Credit Unions

Creditor Groups

1   While it is certainly possible to buy individual Policies to offset a debt obligation (e.g. Decreasing Term against a mortgage), most of what we know as credit insurance is sold as Group insurance. This Group is formed by a creditor, such as a bank or a lending institution, to **insure the lives of its customers.** An example of a Creditor Group would be the First National Bank of Joeville insuring all of its borrowers (debtors).

2   In most respects, this **Group type breaks all the normal rules of Group insurance.** Normally in Group insurance, someone else pays all or most of the premium (like your employer), and you or your family are the beneficiaries of this arrangement. With Group Creditor, everything is backwards. **You and I as debtors of the bank pay for the insurance,** and **the bank is the Beneficiary** of the insurance. You and I (and our families) benefit only in the sense that our payments are made to the bank if we become disabled, and the **loan is paid in full if we should die with an outstanding obligation to the lender**. Many of us who have purchased Credit Life or Credit Disability insurance when taking out an installment loan did not even realize that we were buying Group insurance – a Group made up of all the debtors of that particular lending institution.

3   In addition to the normal requirements for Group insurance, Group Creditor has three special requirements as follows:

- The **amount** of insurance on the life or health of any debtor **may at no time exceed** the greater of the scheduled or actual **amount of indebtedness** to the creditor. For example, if you borrow $22,000 from the bank, the bank can only insure your life up to $22,000; or if the monthly payments on the loan are $800, then the maximum disability income amount is $800 per month.

- Unlike normal Group insurance, the **proceeds of the insurance are payable to the bank** as the creditor and the **Beneficiary** of the Policy. Each payment made by the insurance company to the bank must be used to reduce or pay off the unpaid balance due, and any excess insurance over the unpaid balance must be paid to the estate of the Insured. The insurance company must provide each Insured with a certificate describing the coverages and stating that the death benefit will first be applied to reduce the indebtedness with the lending institution.

- Agricultural credit needs are treated differently. A farmer will generally establish a line of credit with his bank of, say, $100,000. At times he may have borrowed up to his maximum credit line, and at other times he may have a balance of zero. Rather than selling Term life insurance whose face amount would have to increase, decrease and then increase again repetitively, the law allows credit life sold on agricultural credit transactions to be written as level (non-decreasing) Term insurance. Therefore, a farmer with a $100,000 line of credit could have $100,000 of Term life coverage even though he has not yet borrowed nearly that much from his lender. Under these circumstances, the Policy would pay the lender the amount of the loan and pay the difference to the farmer's beneficiaries.

4   To summarize, Creditor Group, also called **Credit Life and Health insurance,** or simply Group Credit, is a specialized use of Group life and Group health insurance. It protects **a lending institution (creditor) from losing money as the result of a borrower's (debtor's) death or disability.**

Multiple Employer Trust (MET)

1   The Employee Retirement Income Security Act of 1974 (ERISA) allowed small employers with too few employees to purchase Group insurance a way in which **two or more employers in similar businesses** could join together to form a Multiple Employer Trust.

*METs
A group of
ONE*

2   As you would guess, this blew the top off the Small Group market, and generally rendered useless the number requirements that had existed in the laws. If Joe Insured's restaurant is a corporation, he is technically an employee – let's suppose he is the *only* employee. Under ERISA, Joe could join a MET and provide Group insurance for himself and his family. While not quite true legally, in Joe's eyes, he is a *Group of one.*

3   After the passage of ERISA, two types of MET's evolved. One type was where a Group of employers would establish a trust. This trust would then contract with an insurance company to provide a fully Insured product for those employers who joined the trust. This arrangement was regulated by state departments of insurance.

Bunches of bosses

4   The second type of MET which developed was one which was **not covered** by a fully Insured Policy of insurance. Instead, the trust was self-funded by the premiums of the employers participating in the trust and claims were paid out of the accumulated premiums. In effect, these self-funded MET's operated as unlicensed insurance companies and were essentially unregulated. Unfortunately, many of these self-funded trusts met with financial troubles when claims exceeded premiums collected. Worse, some of these trusts were run by unscrupulous operators who took the assets of the trusts for themselves rather than to pay claims.

Some Insured

5   When a self-funded MET is unable to pay claims for any reason, the debt owed the health care provider does not go away. Instead, the debt falls back on the individual (the employee) or, under several legal decisions, to the employer who signed the employees up for coverage through the MET. Obviously, many individuals who have relied on "insurance" through a MET have found themselves deep in debt and without coverage.

Some not

6   To address this problem, Congress added the definition of a Multiple Employer Welfare Arrangement (MEWA) to ERISA in 1982. Under this definition, a MEWA is an employee welfare benefit plan which offers medical expense, AD&D, and other benefit programs to the employees of two or more employers.

MEWAs

7   If a plan was fully Insured by an insurance company, it continued to be known as a MET and was regulated by the various state departments of insurance. If a plan was unInsured (i.e., self-funded and, therefore, not *insurance*), it was referred to as a MEWA and regulated by the U.S. Department of Labor (DOL). Since the DOL regulates all other ERISA plans, this arrangement seemed to make sense. However, the DOL was singularly unqualified to regulate any aspect of the insurance business as that had always been the business of the states.

8   By the late 1980's, the unInsured MEWA's were beginning to fail regularly, often leaving Insureds with huge, unpaid medical bills. The DOL had neither the expertise nor the interest to regulate these plans and, therefore, gave that responsibility back to the states.

9   At the present time, **the terms MET and MEWA are beginning to be used interchangeably**. The real question is not one of terminology; it is a question of soundness. If a MET/MEWA is fully Insured, insurance departments have no real problem with it. The Insured MET/MEWA is regulated as it has always been.

1   However, insurance departments around the country do have a problem with the unInsured self-funded MET/MEWA plans, and they deal with the problem in generally one of three ways:

- All unInsured MET/MEWA's are evil as they run the risk of leaving people unInsured and deeply in debt if they fail. Therefore, they may not operate at all in the state.

- UnInsured MET/MEWA's are by definition "insurance companies" as they accept the risk of loss from unrelated employers. All insurance companies in the state are regulated by the department of insurance. Therefore, since a MET/MEWA is considered an insurance company, it must be licensed and regulated by the state department of insurance as an insurance company.

- UnInsured MET/MEWA's are hybrids which serve a useful purpose but they must be regulated in order to protect those that they cover. Therefore, they will be allowed to operate but must be certified by the state department of insurance as a qualified MET/MEWA. They must submit periodic coverage data and financial information so that the department of insurance can make sure that they are financially sound.

2   There are serious consequences which will befall the operator of an unInsured MET/MEWA – or the Agent who sells a client into one – if the rules of the local department of insurance are not followed. These include injunctions against the MEWA and large fines for those operating an illegal or unregistered insurance company or MEWA. Concerning Agents, **many states will hold the Agent personally responsible for all unpaid claims from a failed MEWA**.

3
Unless you have a few hundred thousand dollars stashed away, be careful how you deal with a MEWA.

A Group Contract

4   In contrast to individual contracts, Group Policies cover a number of people under one contract which is issued to someone other than the Insureds. This contract is known as the **master contract**, and it provides coverage to the Group of individuals who have a specified relationship to the *organizing entity* – the Policyowner. Normally, Group contracts cover individuals who are employees, and the **Policyowner of the master** contract is the employer. As we have seen, other possibilities exist – members of a labor union, members of an association, debtors of a creditor and the rest. While the Insureds are not parties to the contract, **it is generally true that the Policy must be written for the benefit of persons other than the master Policyowner** (creditor Groups being the single exception). Therefore, the Insured employees and their beneficiaries do have legally enforceable rights under the contract and are often referred to as **Third Party Beneficiaries.**

Contract to Policyowner

5   Individuals covered under the master contract are **given certificates of insurance** as evidence of their coverage. Today, this *certificate* normally consists of a laminated plastic card and a booklet summarizing the coverage of the master Policy. Normally, the certificate is not a legal contract and contains a disclaimer to that effect. However, in instances where the explanatory booklet and the master contract varied considerably, some courts have held the promises of the booklet to be legally enforceable.

Certificates to insurance

Experience Rating v. Community Rating

1 In individual insurance, companies use the mortality and morbidity tables to predict the risk they are assuming. Also, with medical expense Policies, insurance companies will take into account the costs of medical care within a particular geographic area (called *community rating*).

2 With Group insurance, the **claims history of the Group** seeking to purchase insurance can be utilized. This approach, called **experience rating**, has two positive results on the price of Group insurance.

How did the Group do

Federal law may dictate community rating

- Since it is more accurate, Groups with a clean claims record can save significant amounts of premium.

- Because the premium charged has a direct relationship to the loss experience, the employer has a vested interest in minimizing losses to maintain a favorable track record. This can lead to management initiated weight loss, exercise, and stop-smoking programs for employees.

3 Obviously, the downside to experience rating is that Groups that have had higher than average claims experience pay a higher premium. Under the original Blues program of community rating, everyone living in a specific community paid premiums on the same scale. Therefore, if you are in a Group with a poor claims history, community rating works to your advantage and experience rating works against you.

Group Underwriting Requirements

4 One of the most important distinguishing characteristics of Group insurance is the substitution of **Group risk selection** for individual risk selection. With individual selection, each applicant's health status, morals, habits, occupation, and credit status are all thoroughly and carefully reviewed. In Group selection, the insurance company normally does not require a physical examination, nor is it concerned with the morals or habits of any particular individual. Instead, Group selection is directed at determining the **average age of the Group, the ratio of men to women, the occupational and geographic environment, and the general physical and moral status of the Group as a whole**. The Group itself becomes the standard of measure, and the same insurance principles are applied to the Group as a whole that are normally applied to an individual.

The Group is the unit of classification

Averages

5 While most of the public does not understand Group underwriting, the one thing that the average Joe and Jolene do know about Group insurance is that it **costs less** than an individual insurance Policy. This cost advantage is due primarily to two concepts – **reduced adverse selection** and **reduced administrative costs**.

Reduced Adverse Selection

1 As you remember from Chapter 3 of this text, **adverse selection is the greater tendency of bad risks to purchase insurance than good risks,** and the tendency of bad risks to buy insurance in higher amounts than good risks.

2 To use an extreme example of the importance of **adverse selection**, assume you are an insurance company doing business in country X. Country X has an adult population of 100 million people. Ninety million of those people are healthy, and 10 million are sickly. If you priced your life and health insurance assuming a 90% healthy/10% sickly ratio, you would go bankrupt. What you need to know is that only 50 million people in country X buy life and health insurance, and that all 10 million who are sickly are part of that 50 million. Therefore, your odds of insuring a sickly person are 1 out of 5 instead of 1 out of 10. To further compound your problem, the sickly people tend to buy in amounts which are double the norm which only increases the odds against you . . . the adverse selection.

Taking the good with the bad

3 In Group insurance, particularly Employer Group, adverse selection is a considerably smaller factor. First of all, if the Insureds are all employees, they must be in reasonably good health or they would not be working. Furthermore, since the employer is likely paying most or all of the premium, many healthy employees who would not otherwise feel any urgency to purchase a Policy on their own will accept insurance as an employee benefit. Finally, there are a number of Group insurance *rules* (some law, some tradition, **some underwriting guidelines**) which further protect the insurance company against adverse selection.

more underwriting guidelines

- **Purpose of the Group** – This is fundamentally important in protecting against adverse selection. The National Association of Nearly Dead formed for the purpose of buying Group insurance will not fly. The members of the Group must be together for some purpose other than to purchase inexpensive Group insurance. The insurance must be incidental to the purpose of the Group. The rationale is that Groups organized solely for the purpose of purchasing low-cost insurance would probably include an excessive number of individuals in poor health, engaged in hazardous occupations, or having other undesirable characteristics.

only real Groups need apply

- **Eligible Members** – One way to reduce adverse selection within a Group is to guarantee that all insurable individuals are eligible for coverage. Therefore, under a Single Employer Group, all of the employees must be eligible. It is possible to sub-divide the employees into logical Groups, such as union versus non-union or salaried versus hourly. However, within any one Group, there can be no discrimination . . . all members would be entitled to the same set of benefits. Also, any individuals in a Group not wishing the coverages may reject them in writing if they wish.

New Federal laws may change this

the more the merrier

- **Set Benefit Schedule** – As a further safeguard against adverse selection, the plan benefits must be beyond the control of the employer or the employee. They must be automatic, not optional. If the employees themselves could select the level of benefits, then the poor risks would tend to select more insurance, and healthy risks would tend to select minimum coverages. To avoid this adverse selection, the benefit plan must be pre-established, maintaining the same coverage for the individual within the Group or class with no chance to "pick and choose."

- **Contributory vs. Non-contributory** – Group insurance premiums can be paid for entirely by the employer, entirely by the employees, or the costs can be shared. If the employees contribute some or all of the money, then the plan is referred to as **contributory (or participating)**. If the employer pays all of the premium, then the plan is called **non-contributory**.

  In a non-contributory plan, the employer must cover 100% of the eligible and insurable members. In a contributory plan, where the employee pays part of the cost, it would be unfair to require everyone to join . . . to pay for something that they may not need or want. To reduce adverse selection, a few states and most companies require that at least 75% of the eligible persons join the Group. The theory is that if there are no minimum percentage participation requirements, then only the poor risks will join.

  With non-employer Groups, like association Groups, each member pays 100% of his own insurance costs - there is no employer to pay a part. Such arrangements are sometimes referred to as **fully contributory**.

- **Changes in Status** – If an employee drops out of the plan (or chooses not to participate in the first place) and later decides to join, this could be adverse selection at its worst. Under the circumstances of re-entry or delayed entry into the plan, it is customary to require a medical examination.

- **Turnover** – Most Group insurance plans cover people who work full-time. The age range is typically from about 18 to retirement age. The older the employee gets, the greater the risk of health problems or death. The risk becomes very high after age 65. However, when an individual retires, he or she typically leaves the Group plan. This is **called turnover.** The older employees leave the plan at about the time they become higher insurance risks, thus substantially reducing the risk to the insurance company and, consequently, the premium that must be charged. As the older employees retire, they are replaced with younger, lower risk employees.

Reduced Administrative Costs

1 The second major reason that Group insurance costs less is that it is cheaper to issue and service a single master contract covering 10,000 employees than it is to issue and service 10,000 separate contracts. A big plus for the insurance company is that the Group typically has a **Plan Administrator** (in an Employer Group, someone from human resources, for instance) who has the **responsibility for running the Group insurance program**. The Plan Administrator is responsible for adding or dropping employees from the plan, explaining coverages, collecting premiums if it is a participating plan, and may even help with the initial steps in the claims process.

- **Reduced Lapse Rate** – A big plus for the insurance company with Group insurance is a reduced Policy lapse rate - **persistency**. As we pointed out in Chapter 3 of this text, a Policy which is cancelled early in the coverage period is very costly to the insurance company. With Employer Group, the employer is responsible for paying the premium (even if the employees share in the cost), and therefore Policy lapses are rather unlikely.

- **Lower Commission Rate** – Another big savings for the insurance company directly affects the Agency force. The commissions paid on Group insurance are a much smaller percentage of the premium than in an individual sale. Though everyone would like to be the Agent that sells IBM its Group plan, the commission paid on that sale is much lower than if that Agent sold the same coverages to every IBM employee individually. (Of course, by the time you made that many individual presentations, you would be too old to have any fun spending your money anyway.)

- **Almost No Medical Exams** – Though medical exams can still be required for Group Life and Group Disability Policies, most Group Policies are issued **without any medical exam whatsoever.** This is a tremendous savings in administrative costs for the insurance company.

- **New Employees Entering the Group** – A new employee frequently must wait a period of time before becoming eligible for Group insurance. This **waiting period** (or **probationary period**) minimizes the record-keeping and administrative expenses that would be involved in enrolling short-term employees. After the waiting period, eligible employees will be given a period of time, known as the **eligibility period**, to join the Group plan. Other plans use an **open enrollment period**, in which case all new employees must wait until the next enrollment period (for example, November of each year) before joining the Group plan. Those who do not enroll at the first opportunity can be required to take a medical exam if they choose to join later.

New Federal Laws may change this

New use of old word

STANDARD PROVISIONS

1   Now that you understand how Group insurance functions, you need to be familiar with the provisions which must be part of any Group Policy. As with health insurance, the NAIC has drafted model legislation dealing with both Group Life and Group Health which has been enacted into law in most states. Because Group insurance so often covers people living in several states, most states have adopted this legislation with almost no variation as there is an obvious need for uniformity.

2   While some of these model provisions are unique to Group Life or Group Health, the majority apply to both. Therefore, we will first outline those which apply to both life and health, and then discuss those which are unique to one Policy or the other. You will notice that most of these provisions parallel those which you have already learned in studying the individual life and health products. Therefore, our explanations will be exceedingly brief except to point out any differences which do exist between Group and individual contracts.

Group Life & Health Standard Provisions

3   **GRACE PERIOD** – The Policy must provide a Grace Period of at least **31 days** in case of nonpayment of premium. As in individual life and health, the Insured(s) are still covered during the Grace Period.

4   **INCONTESTABLE** – The Policy must contain an incontestable clause which states that, except for nonpayment of premium, the Policy is incontestable after the Policy has been in force for **two years**, even if there were misstatements on the application. In addition, no statement made by an Insured may be used by the insurance company in contesting the validity of the coverage unless: a) the Policy has been in force for less than two years during the lifetime of the Insured, and b) the statement is a written statement signed by the Insured person.

5   **COPY OF THE APPLICATION** – If an application is used in the purchase of the Group Policy, a copy of the application must be attached to the Policy when it is issued if it is to be considered part of the contract. All statements made by the Policyowner or persons Insured under the Policy are deemed **representations** – not warranties.

6   **EVIDENCE OF INSURABILITY** – The insurance company must state in the Policy what an Insured must furnish as evidence of individual insurability.

1 **MISSTATEMENT OF AGE** – The Policy must set forth a reasonable method of adjusting premiums and/or benefits if an Insured misstates his or her age.

2 **Beneficiary DESIGNATIONS** – The Policy must state that any payment of claims under the Policy will be paid to the Insured or a Beneficiary designated by the Insured person. However, if there is no Beneficiary designation or if the designated Beneficiary pre-deceases the Insured, the insurance company at its option may pay up to $2,000 (in health, up to $5,000) to any person appearing to the insurance company to be equitably entitled to the money (such as someone who paid the funeral expenses). The remainder of the benefits would be paid to the estate of the Insured.

3 **INDIVIDUAL CERTIFICATES** – The Policy must state that the insurance company will issue an individual certificate to each Insured person which states:

- The insurance protection provided by the Policy.

- To whom the benefits will be paid.

- Any coverages for dependents provided by the Policy.

4 **CREDIT LIFE AND HEALTH** – Group Credit Life and Health Policies must provide each debtor covered under the Policy with a **certificate of insurance** describing the coverages and specifying that the benefits will be paid to the creditor to reduce or eliminate the indebtedness. Any benefits left over would then be paid to the debtor.

Group Life Insurance

5 While it is theoretically possible to sell just about any life insurance product we have addressed in this text on a Group basis, three of the life products account for about 99.9% of the Group life sold. They are Guaranteed Renewable Term, Whole Life, and Universal Life.

Guaranteed Renewable Term

6 More than 95% of Group life is written as **Guaranteed (Annually) Renewable Term**. In the Group environment, the Policy remains in force for one year and may then be renewed without evidence of insurability at the option of the master contract owner. As with individual coverage, the price per $1000 of coverage increases at an increasing rate each year. Despite this, the employee's contribution (in a contributory plan) normally remains level. Therefore, the employer's contribution for a given employee must increase each year. However, the employer's contribution to the over-all plan may remain the same or even decline depending upon the contributions required of new employees, their age and sex, and the experience of the plan.

TERM insurance is KING

7 If Term insurance is used with a Group, it is not at all unusual to extend the plan to cover **dependents of the employees** as well. The expense of adding dependents may be shared or paid completely by the employee or by the employer. Obviously, if the employer pays the entire cost, the plan cannot discriminate; it must cover every employee's spouse and/or children. Since most states have adopted the 1984 amendments to the NAIC model bill, the company does have the right to exclude dependents who are deemed uninsurable.

New Federal Laws may change this

1   While some states have dollar maximums written into law for dependent coverage, most follow the model law and use a percentage maximum. The model law says that the amount of insurance for any covered spouse or dependent child under a Group Life Policy **may not exceed 50% of the amount of insurance for which the employee is Insured**. For example, if you are the Insured employee and you are covered for $40,000 under the Group Life plan, then the maximum amount of life insurance under the Group plan for your spouse and for each dependent would be $20,000.

$$\frac{1}{2}$$

for dependent

Cash Value Life Insurance (Group Permanent)

2   As in individual insurance, the use of permanent insurance in the context of a Group plan both provides protection and builds cash value. The cash value is used to provide for life insurance following retirement.

Group Annuities

3   Group Annuities are most frequently used in funding a corporate pension or profit sharing plan. In a Defined Contribution plan this approach is referred to as a *Money Purchase* plan. A specific amount (say, 5% of salary) is paid as premium for each employee. Employee benefits at retirement will depend upon contributions made, the earnings of the Annuity and the employee's length of service.

4   In a Defined Benefit plan, the employer estimates the pension desirable when an employee reaches normal retirement age. In this *Annuity Purchase* plan, the insurance company is asked to quote a level premium for each covered employee and guarantees that if the indicated premium is paid, the company will pay the guaranteed benefit as retirement. This is sometimes referred to as a Level Premium Group Annuity contract.

Other Important Elements

5   Whether a Group life plan is constructed with Term, Whole Life, or Universal Life, it is quite common for the employee to be given the right to buy additional insurance beyond that which is provided under the Group plan. This is known as **Supplemental Life Insurance** and is typically made available up to a maximum based upon the employee's earnings (for instance, three times the employee's earnings).

6   Another common benefit found along with Group Life is AD&D coverage with the principal sum equal to the death benefit of the employee's Group insurance. Therefore, if the cause of death is accidental, the Group plan and the AD&D contract both pay the same amount, thus providing a double indemnity benefit. The AD&D contract can be purchased by the employer or the employee. If the employee pays for it, it is often known as **Voluntary AD&D**. If the employer pays, the premium costs are deductible as a business expense.

1   While we have seen that it is possible for an employee to slightly modify the amount of his or her coverage, it is important to emphasize that this is only true within limits. If every employee could select the amount of coverage he or she wished, adverse selection would be a terrible problem. There must be a **predetermined benefit schedule** which assigns each employee to a specific category based upon salary, position, or seniority. All employees within that category must be offered the same amount of insurance coverage under the Group plan. The master Policy will specify one of the following four methods for determining Group life benefits:

- Employee earnings (each salary range receives a fixed amount of coverage). This is the most common form of benefit schedule.

- A flat amount (everyone gets the same amount of coverage regardless of the length of service or income).

- The type of position, or position schedule (officers have one amount, superintendents another, managers another, etc.).

- The length of service (so many dollars of coverage per year of service).

2   Whichever system is used, no individual can select his or her own coverage outside the parameters offered.

Life Conversion Privileges

3   Earlier in this chapter, we looked at some of the provisions that must be included in a Group Policy if it is to conform with the NAIC model bill. Those provisions applied not only to Group Life, but to Group Health as well. We now turn our attention to provisions from the model bill that **apply only to Group Life**, the Conversion Privileges.

4   Each of these provisions is written to address the same basic problem. Let's suppose that since age 20, Joe Insured has been an employee of Acme Ink, Inc. Under Acme's Group Life Plan, Joe has $100,000 of life insurance. Jolene and each of the children have $50,000 under Joe's Group plan, and this is all the life insurance that Joe's family has. What happens if Joe and his entire family are uninsurable, and he is fired at age 40? What happens to Jolene's coverage or the children's coverage if Joe dies? What happens if Acme Ink, Inc. loses so much business to ballpoint pens that it discontinues its Group Life program? What if Acme's program is only for *active* employees and Joe is disabled for five months? What happens to the children's coverages when they are no longer Joe's dependents? What happens to Jolene's Policy if she and Joe get divorced? The NAIC model addresses each of these concerns.

Convert from Group to individual Policy

5   **The Conversion Privilege gives Joe and his dependents the right to convert their Group coverages to individual Policies in the same (or lesser) amount without providing evidence of insurability** if Joe's employment terminates or if any of his dependents are no longer considered qualified family members due to age or divorce.

KNOW THIS!

CONVERSION PRIVILEGE

no proof needed

1 While the above is a good overview of Joe's and his family's rights, there are some important details.

- Application for the individual Policy must be made and the first premium paid **within 31 days** of the Group coverage termination date.

31 days

- If Joe or his dependents are not made aware of their rights to convert, they are given an additional **15 days** extension. For instance, assume that Joe is fired and not told of his rights. Thirty-one days later (the normal time his rights expire), he receives a letter from his former employer or the company which issued the Group Policy informing him of his right to convert. He then has 15 days to act.

- No matter when he learns of his right to convert, the conversion period will never exceed **60 days** from the date Group benefits expire.

2 Though Joe or his dependents can convert to an individual Policy of any type available from the Group insurer, **the company may exclude Term** insurance as an option. The rates for the converted Policy are standard individual Policy rates based upon the Insured's attained age.

might not have option of Term

3 If Joe leaves Acme to go to work for Printer's Ink, Inc., any Group Life provided by his new employer within 31 days of Joe's last day at Acme will reduce the amount that his company must convert to individual insurance. If Joe had $100,000 of Group life at Acme and Printer's provides $40,000, he may convert no more than $60,000 from his previous Group plan.

1   **DEATH DURING THE CONVERSION PERIOD** – A Group life Policy must provide that if an Insured dies during the conversion period, then the Group Policy must pay the death benefit, **whether or not application for the individual Policy was ever made**.

Like Joe was still part of the Group

2   **Group Policy TERMINATION** – If the master contract itself is terminated, then the contract must allow every person who has been Insured under the Policy for at least five years to convert his or her coverage to an individual Policy of insurance. The amount of insurance issued under this conversion privilege shall be the amount of coverage being terminated less the amount of any new coverage that will be obtained from another company within 31 days after the termination of the old Policy, or $10,000 – whichever is less.

3   **TOTAL DISABILITY** – If active employment is a condition for Group insurance, then the Policy must state that the Insured may continue his or her life insurance coverage for up to six months after total disability. The Insured has to pay the premium, but the rate must be at the normal rate.

Conclusion

4   The purpose of this chapter has been to acquaint you with the distinguishing characteristics of Group insurance from individual life and health and to familiarize you with the legal requirements unique to the Group insurance business.

5   Group insurance is life or health insurance that covers a Group of persons, such as employees of a corporation or members of an association, under just one Policy. The Policy is called a **master contract** and it covers the entire Group. Each covered member receives a **certificate of insurance** verifying that there is coverage in force and a booklet summarizing the coverages of the master Policy. The same types of Policies sold on an individual basis which we've seen in previous chapters can also be sold on a Group basis. Most Group Life is Guaranteed Renewable Term, although permanent forms of life insurance are also possible, such as Whole Life (Group Ordinary) or Universal Life (GULP). In the health insurance area, Disability Income, Medical Expense, Medicare Supplements, Long-Term Care, and AD&D are frequently sold on a Group basis.

6   Most states limit the types of Groups eligible to buy Group insurance. The most commonly acceptable Groups are:

- **Single Employer Group** – for the benefit of the employees.
- **Labor Union Group** – covers the members of the labor union.
- **Negotiated Trusteeship** – an employer pays into a trust fund to pay for coverage for labor union members.
- **Association Group** – covers members of a professional or trade association.
- **Credit Union Group** – for the credit union members.
- **Creditor Group** – insures debtors and makes their loan payments to the bank if they become disabled or die. Also called Credit Life & Health.
- **Multiple Employer Trust (MET/MEWA)** – two or more small employers join together and establish a trust which either (1) purchases insurance from an insurance company (fully Insured – GOOD), or (2) pays the health care providers out of the funds collected from the members (unInsured/self-funded – BAD). **Many states will hold the Agent personally responsible for all unpaid claims from a failed MEWA.**

1. In some states, there are minimum number requirements for the size of the Group, such as 10 for a single employer Group or **100 for an association**. Many states, however, have eliminated the number requirements. A Group cannot be formed, however, solely for the purpose of obtaining insurance at reduced rates.

2. In Group insurance, there is no individual underwriting. The insurance company utilizes **Group risk selection** . . . determining the average age, ratio of men to women, occupational and geographic environment, and so on. The company may also use **experience rating** . . . examining the claims history of the Group. With Group underwriting, the company does not scrutinize each individual so closely, and medical exams normally are not required.

3. Group insurance tends to cost less than purchasing an individual Policy. This is due to **reduced adverse selection** and lower administrative costs. The Groups which can be covered are formed for some purpose other than obtaining cheap insurance; there is a set benefit schedule beyond the control of any individual employee; almost no medical exams are required; there is a reduced Policy lapse rate in Group insurance; and the Agent's commission rate is lower in Group than in individual sales.

4. Group insurance premiums can be paid for either entirely by the employer (called a **non-contributory** plan), or the employees can pay for all or a part of the premium (called a **contributory** plan). In non-contributory plans, 100% of the eligible (insurable) employees must be covered. In most contributory plans, at least 75% of the eligible persons must join the Group . . . to reduce adverse selection.

5. For a new employee entering a Group insurance plan, there is normally a **waiting period** before he or she can be covered. In a contributory plan, the waiting period is followed by an **eligibility period** (or **open enrollment period**) during which time the new employee can join the Group if he or she is insurable.

6. As we saw with individual life and health Policies, there are standard provisions in Group Policies as well, such as a Grace Period provision, an Incontestable Clause, a Misstatement of Age provision, etc. Unique to Group life is the **Conversion Privilege**. An employee leaving a Group life plan has the right to purchase, *without evidence of insurability*, an individual life Policy in the same or lesser face amount as the Group coverage. The insurance company may, however, exclude Term from the offering. The employee's covered dependents also have this life insurance conversion privilege. Application for the individual Policy must be made and the first premium paid within **31 days** of the Group coverage termination date, and the coverage remains in force during that period whether or not application for the individual Policy was ever made. If not made aware of the right to convert, the departing Group member gets a **15 day** extension from the date of notification, but not to exceed **60 days** from the date the Group benefits expire.

New Federal Laws may result in changes to Group rules

Group Health

17

As we pointed out earlier in this text, Long Term Disability Income is about the only Health Policy more likely to be sold on an individual basis than a Group basis. The others – like short term Disability Income, medical expense, Medicare Supplements, and Long Term Care – are actually more likely to be found as a Group product than as an individual Policy. AD&D, which we said earlier is a common benefit found along with Group Life, is actually more commonly found with Group Disability Income and Group Medical Expense.

While the coverages of the Group Health contracts are almost identical to the coverages provided by the individual policies, there are some important differences.

- **No Medical Exam** – Typically, Group Health policies do not require the Group members to take a full-fledged medical exam.

Medical

- **Occupational Accidents and Sicknesses** – While individual Health policies normally cover you 24 hours a day, **Group Health policies usually exclude accidents or sicknesses suffered on the job**. This is because occupational accidents and sicknesses are covered by **Workers Compensation**. Some Long Term Disability Income policies pay for disability claims caused by the job, but they provide for the **coordination of benefits** with Workers Compensation disability benefits which accomplishes the same objective. If AD&D benefits are provided as part of the Group plan, they almost always cover job-related losses, even if Workers Comp also pays benefits.

WC is king

- **Renewability** – Though individual Health policies generally provide for Long Term renewability guarantees, Group Health is normally written to give the company the option to renew or not renew at each Policy anniversary. As you remember from Chapter 10, this form of renewability is known as *Optionally Renewable*.

- **Maternity Benefits** – Although it is common for individual Health policies to exclude pregnancy coverage or to make it available only at extra cost, the 1978 Civil Rights Act requires that employer Groups **insuring 15 or more employees treat pregnancy** the same as any other sickness. The maternity benefits required by this law can be included in the Group Policy or can be self-Insured by the employer.

Group Kids

Standard Provisions
Unique to Group Health

1 In addition to the NAIC model bill provisions which applied to both Life and Health, there are some which apply only to Health insurance. Most are identical to the *individual* Health provisions you have already studied. Therefore, we will emphasize the differences which exist.

2 **NOTICE OF CLAIM** – The Policy must state that the Insured must give written Notice of Claim to the insurance company within **20 days** after the occurrence of the loss. Failure to make this notification will not jeopardize the claim in any manner if it was not reasonably possible to give the notice within the 20 day period.

Same as individual

3 **CLAIM FORMS** – The insurance company must provide the Insured with claim forms within **15 days** after receiving the Insured's written notice of claim. If not, then the Insured can submit the claim in his or her own format, and it must be accepted as adequate proof of loss.

20

15

4 **PROOF OF LOSS** – The Insured must provide the insurance company with written proof of loss within **90 days** of the loss. Subsequent written proof of a disability must be furnished to the insurance company at reasonable intervals as specified by the company. If it was not possible to provide the Proof of Loss within 90 days, then the Insured must provide such proof as soon as reasonably possible, but not to exceed one year.

90

5 **TIME OF PAYMENT OF CLAIMS** – Please note that there is a difference here as compared to individual policies . . . medical expense and AD&D claims must be paid within **60 days** (as opposed to *immediately* in individual policies) of receipt of due Proof of Loss. Just like with individual policies, Group Disability Income claims must be paid **no less frequently than monthly**.

not the same

6 **PHYSICAL EXAM AND AUTOPSY** – The insurance company has the right to conduct a physical examination of any Insured for whom a claim is being made under the Policy. The insurance company also can conduct an autopsy in the case of the death of an Insured if it is not prohibited by state law.

same as individual

7 **LEGAL ACTION** – Group Health contracts must state that the Insured may not sue the insurance company within 60 days after having submitted a proof of loss for a claim. This provision also states that any lawsuits must be started by the Insured within three years after the date of the loss.

*New Federal
Laws will
change the
terminating
age to 26*

and

*eliminate
the
Preexisting
Conditions
Exclusions*

1 Although not part of the NAIC model, most states require and most companies include at least two other provisions in nearly every Group Health contract. One is fairly standard from state to state and company to company while the other is all over the map. The one which is fairly standard governs the way in which companies handle children who remain dependent upon the Insured after reaching the limiting age contained in the Policy. The other deals with our old nemesis – preexisting conditions.

2 **DEPENDENT CHILDREN** – This section provides the same coverages for dependent children under Group Health insurance as you have already studied in individual policies.

3 **PREEXISTING CONDITIONS** – Because most Group Health policies do not require a medical exam, most companies would like to erect a rather large barrier to screen out preexisting conditions. If the companies were allowed to screen as broadly as they might like, the Insureds might find that their Policy is virtually worthless because *everything is a preexisting condition*. This is where the legislators and the regulators come in. Most states have laws which specifically state how far back in a person's Health history a company can go to identify a preexisting condition and how long any preexisting conditions can be excluded. Most commonly, a preexisting condition is defined as **a disease or physical condition for which medical advice or treatment was received by the Insured during the 6 months prior to his or her effective date of coverage**.

4 If a condition is classified as preexisting, it may be excluded from coverage for:

- up to one year, or

- until the Insured has a period of 180 consecutive days during which no medical advice or treatment for that specific disease or illness was received . . .

    . . . whichever comes first.

5 Federal and state laws are **changing rapidly regarding the exclusion of preexisting conditions**. Many states have eliminated the use of preexisting conditions exclusions **of any kind** for Groups above a certain population (like 50 lives). The federal government has recently eliminated such exclusions for people moving from a job where they were covered to a small Group (50 lives and under) where they used to encounter new problems with preexisting conditions.

Change of Insurance Companies

6 Most jurisdictions now require that if Employer Group coverage changes from one insurance company to another, the impact on the Insured employees and their families must be negligible - **no loss - no gain**. There can be no new probationary periods or preexisting conditions exclusions. Under most laws, the dollars spent by the Insureds to meet deductibles or coinsurance requirements of the original insurer must be **carried over** to meet any such requirements of the new insurer.

Group Health Plan Termination

7 Some states require that if the Group Health Policy is terminated, any benefit which is already being paid, must continue until coverage is no longer necessary. This requirement is known as an **extension of benefits provision**.

© 2010 Pathfinder Corporation

Additional Laws Unique to Group Health

1   With the numerous provisions we have studied from the NAIC model on Group Health insurance as well as the laws concerning dependent children and preexisting conditions, you would think that every possible problem that you could encounter with Group Health insurance is behind us. But, you would be wrong. We have two more problems and two more pieces of legislation with which to concern ourselves.

- **Multiple Coverages** – What if Joe Insured is covered under two Group medical expense plans? Can he collect twice? –Well, that one is easy. No! Then what does happen? –That one is not so easy, but it is the subject of another NAIC model law adopted by most states concerning the **Coordination of Benefits (COB)** between two Group plans.

- **Continuation of Coverage** – We handled Joe's termination of employment problem in Group Life with the Conversion Privilege. However, we have yet to address the problem of continuing coverage under a Group Health Policy if Joe or his dependents lose coverage due to termination of employment, death, or divorce. The **Consolidated Omnibus Budget Reconciliation Act of 1985** (better known as **COBRA**) established new federal law to ease this dilemma. In 1996, the **Health Insurance Portability and Accountability Act (HIPAA)** offered a different solution to essentially the same problem.

Let's review them one at a time.

Coordination of Benefits

2   As we have said, it is certainly possible to be covered under two similar Health policies at the same time. While this is beginning to become a problem with Disability Income, the major difficulty today is with medical expense policies. Therefore, we will talk primarily in the context of medical expense policies.

3   First of all, how would someone get two, let's say, Comprehensive Major Medical policies? Seemingly, the answer is **on purpose** or **by accident**. If Joe has two individually-purchased Comprehensive Major Med policies, then he bought them on purpose. Why would he do this? Without wishing to sound harsh, he is either an idiot or a crook. A person with absolutely no understanding of medical expense policies might buy two thinking that it is okay to collect twice. If anything in the last six chapters has registered, you are well aware that medical expense policies are designed to *make you whole (or nearly) but not make you rich.* If you have a $2,000 loss, you will not receive any more than $2,000 no matter how many policies you own. Since few idiots have enough money to buy duplicate Comprehensive Major Medical policies, it is more likely that Joe is a crook. By purchasing multiple policies, Joe plans to enrich himself at claim time. With individual policies, this situation is easily handled. Suppose Joe has a Comprehensive Major Med Policy with Company A and an identical Policy with Company B. Both call for a $200 deductible and 80/20 coinsurance. If each company is aware of the other's coverage and both have utilized the optional provisions relating to overinsurance in their policies, each will pay its share of the cost. Using the Policy described above, let's assume that Joe suffers a loss and had $2,200 of covered expenses. After the deductible, the company's 80% of $2,000 is $1,600. Company A would pay $800 and so would Company B.

4   The second way that we said Joe could wind up with double coverage is *by accident*. If Joe works for ABC Corporation, and Jolene works for XYZ Corporation, both could have a non-contributory Comprehensive Major Medical Policy as part of their

1 compensation package. If both plans cover the family, then Joe's entire family has double coverage even though he did not seek out such an arrangement. Joe is not a crook; he simply took what was given to him. The **Coordination of Benefits** clause in the NAIC model takes the approach that while Joe should not profit from a loss, he should get some benefit from each plan. Let's see how it works.

2 Suppose Joe is doubly covered under two Group Health plans – once under his own at work and once as Jolene's spouse under her plan at work. Under the Coordination of Benefits clause, Joe would fare better. Essentially, **the second company pays what the first company will not pay** (the deductibles and coinsurance). In double coverage situations, the company covering the injured/sick employee is called the **primary insurance company**, and the employee's spouse's company is called the **secondary, or excess, insurance company**. The spouse with the birth date occurring the earliest in the calendar year has its company designated as primary for the children. For example, if your birthday is in January and your spouse's birthday is in March, then your insurance company will be the primary insurer for your children.

JOE'S GROUP

JOLENE'S GROUP

PRIMARY SECONDARY

3 In our example above, Joe's Policy would pay *as if no other company is involved.* Therefore, Joe has paid $600 ($200 deductible plus $400 coinsurance) and his company paid $1,600. **Jolene's company is secondary,** and **it would pay what Joe's did not pay** . . . $600. The covered expenses were $2,200, and the two companies paid $2,200. Joe did not profit from the loss, but he did gain some advantage from each of the two plans that are part of his family's compensation package.

Secondary pays what the primary won't

4 It should be noted that some states are beginning to toy with the idea of requiring the secondary company to pay only 80% of what the primary company did not. How far this cost savings attempt will go is yet to be determined.

THE PORTABILITY PROBLEM

5 Joe and/or one of his dependents loses coverage because:

- Joe retires, quits or gets fired from his job.
- Joe dies.
- Joe and Jolene get divorced or legally separated.
- One of the kids is no longer a dependent because of age or marriage.

Federal law. . .

6 Any of these events could leave Joe or his family without coverage at least temporarily. There are several possible solutions:

- Most Group Health policies offer a Conversion Privilege from a Group to individual coverage without any new preexisting conditions exclusion. The price is high, the coverage is often not as generous and there may be limited rights of renewal.

- If everyone is Healthy (without current treatment ongoing), then Joe (or Jolene after a divorce, or Joe College at age 26) gets a job and is covered under the new employer's plan.

HIPAA

7 The most likely negative scenario is that Joe leaves employer A to work for employer B. **But**, if Joe or a dependent has an ongoing Health problem it would be excluded as a preexisting condition under the new employer's plan. What is needed is a bridge to provide coverage until the new Group picks up coverage. **For employer Groups over 20, COBRA** can do the job. A slightly different solution can be found with Groups of 2 or more employees under a 1996 federal law know as HIPAA.

COBRA

1 The purpose of COBRA (**The Consolidated Omnibus Budget Reconciliation Act of 1985**) is to **provide for Health benefits during the time that you and your dependents leave one employer's Group Health coverage until you obtain coverage under another.** Under COBRA, Congress shifted the burden of providing Health care from the government (Medicaid, local county or city owned hospitals) to employers who in turn pass the responsibility to their Group benefit plans.

Federal law...

2 **COBRA mandates the continuation of Group Health coverages** for you as an Insured employee and/or your dependents who are protected by your coverage if you lose your Group Health coverage because you:

COBRA = CONTINUANCE

- Terminate your employment voluntarily.
- Get fired (unless it was for *gross misconduct*).
- Go from full to part-time employment.

3 If you lose your Group Health coverage because of one of these reasons, you and your dependents are called **qualified Beneficiaries**. Each one of you has an independent choice to continue to be covered for up to **18 months** from the date of the event which resulted in the loss of coverage.

18 Months

CANNED JOE

4 Covered dependents of an Insured may keep their Group Health coverage for up to **36 months** if they lose their coverage because:

36 Months

- The covered employee dies.
- Divorce or legal separation from the covered employee occurs.
- The covered employee was taking COBRA coverage and lost eligibility because he or she became eligible for Medicare coverage.
- He or she no longer meets the definition of *dependent* (usually due to marriage or being over the eligible age).

5 The **benefits under COBRA coverage must be the same** as those contained under the original Group Health plan. The premium charged to you for the coverage must not exceed 102% of the total cost to provide for the coverage. For example, if you normally contribute $250 a month towards your Group Health coverage from Widgets, Inc., and your employer contributes $750, the total monthly cost is $1000. For COBRA coverage, the monthly premium would be no more than $1020.

102%

6 The Omnibus Budget Reconciliation Act (OBRA) modified COBRA to extend coverage from 18 months to 29 months if you or a covered dependent are fully disabled under the Social Security definition on the date (or within 60 days of the date) you become eligible for COBRA. A person who has been disabled for 29 months under Social Security becomes eligible for Medicare regardless of age. Therefore, COBRA becomes a bridge to Medicare.

24 months + 5 month waiting period

29 months

7 A *qualified Beneficiary* must be given notice of his or her right to take COBRA coverage soon after the *qualifying event*. He or she then has 60 days in which to choose to take the coverage. This is called **the election period**. Once the election period ends, the right to COBRA continuation coverage ends as well.

1 Benefits under COBRA continuation coverage will end if:

- The 18, 29, or 36 month coverage period ends.
- The employer terminates all Group Health plans.
- The covered person does not make a timely premium payment (30 day grace period).
- The covered person becomes covered by another Group Health plan which does not have a preexisting condition limitation applicable to the covered person.
- The covered person becomes actually covered by Medicare.
- During the additional 11 months of disability coverage the disability ends.

New Federal laws may change this

2 As noted above, when a COBRA covered person becomes covered by another Group Health plan, he or she can still retain the COBRA coverage if the new coverage has a preexisting condition limitation clause which impacts the covered person. In that case, the new Group coverage becomes the person's *primary* coverage and claims are submitted to the new carrier first. If the new carrier denies the claim or limits payment, the claim is then sent off to the COBRA carrier. Once the preexisting condition limitation clause is no longer effective, the COBRA coverage ends.

3 In summary, you can see that **COBRA continuation coverage provides for the continuation of Group Health insurance coverages upon the termination, death or divorce of an employee.** This continuation privilege parallels the conversion privileges previously discussed under Group Life.

⸺ HIPAA ‡

4 The **Health Insurance Portability and Accountability Act of 1996 (HIPAA** or the Kennedy-Kassebaum Act) also addresses Health insurance portability, but from an entirely different perspective. Whereas **COBRA builds a coverage bridge** from the old Policy, **HIPAA requires the new Group Policy to accept most new entrants - warts and all.**

HIPPA = Portability

5 Here's how it works. Suppose Joe has worked at ABC Corporation for 5 years and has been covered under their Group Health plan during his employment. Further assume his employment is terminated. He goes to work for XYZ Corp and applies for coverage under the XYZ plan which currently covers all 37 XYZ employees. Even though he had heart surgery last month while still employed at ABC, he would be fully covered under the XYZ plan from day one. Yes, the XYZ plan has a preexisting conditions exclusion, but Joe's *time in service* at ABC satisfies it.

NO Preexisting Conditions Exclusions

6 The details are fairly straightforward. HIPAA applies to **Groups of 2 or more** employees (thus employee Groups of 21 or more could be subject to COBRA or HIPAA). Joe must have been Insured coming into the new Group under:

- an individual Health Policy
- a Group Health Policy
- Medicare
- his state high risk pool
- a public Health, Indian Health or Peace Corps plan

HIPAA plugs up "holes" in coverage

7 with no more than a 63 day gap in coverage. If he makes a *timely entry* into the new Group, the new plan's preexisting conditions exclusion can apply only to problems for which Joe has received treatment in the last 6 months. These problems can, then, only be excluded for up to 12 months into the future. **But** if Joe has been previously Insured immediately prior to joining the new Group, his old coverage must give him **a certificate of prior creditable coverage.** If Joe has more than 12 months of creditable service under his old plan, there would be no applicable preexisting conditions limitation under his new plan.

1 Others under Joe's Policy (e.g. Jolene or Joe College) would have the same rights as Joe if they were leaving Joe's Policy to seek coverage through a Group at their new job.

2 In addition to portability, the other major impact of HIPAA is that Employer Group Health plans can no longer medically underwrite an individual and deny coverage due to his medical condition, past claims, genetic makeup or potential need for services. This allows people with less than perfect Health to be covered under a new employer's Group Health plan - a situation where coverage was often denied in the past.

Automatic Coverage

STATE LAWS REGARDING PORTABILITY

3 Many states have passed laws which are intended to aid Insureds in moving from one Health plan to another. This is particularly true with Groups of 2-50 employees which, under the NAIC Model Law, are considered to be Small Groups. Obviously there are places where such laws overlap COBRA and HIPAA. In these situations, the plan (state, COBRA, HIPAA) which is the most generous to the Insured takes precedence.

OTHER Group PLANS

4 Up to this point, we have not introduced any new products in this chapter. We have viewed Group insurance solely as a distribution system for products that are also sold as individual contracts. At this point, we need to introduce about a half a dozen products that almost do not exist outside the Group environment. Some are becoming more important, others less important, and some are on the borderline of extinction already. Though none will test you intellectually, they are products with which you should be familiar.

Dental Insurance

5 Though seldom sold as an individual basis, Dental Care insurance is becoming an increasingly important benefit provided to many employees through Group Dental Plans. While there are many differences in types of plans, how they function and what they cover, they do share some common factors.

"The tooth and nothing but the tooth. . ."

Types of Plans

6 **Scheduled** - Scheduled Dental care policies work with schedules that specify a maximum dollar amount that the Policy will pay for each Dental procedure covered.

New federal laws may mandate dental coverages

7 **Comprehensive (Non-Scheduled)** - Comprehensive Dental care policies do not have schedules; instead they will normally pay a portion of usual and customary charges for covered procedures.

8 **Combination Plans** - Combination plans incorporate features from Scheduled and Comprehensive plans. For example, preventive care may be offered on a *usual and customary* basis, while more complex (and expensive) procedures may be scheduled.

9 **Pre-Paid Dental Plans** - Pre-paid plans work much like an HMO in that a monthly fee is paid for each Insured (**subscriber**) and, in exchange, Dental treatment is offered by a **licensed provider**. Pre-Paid Plans can contract with any licensed dentist in the geographical area.

How Dental Policies Work ‡

1 Typically all Dental Policies will provide for routine, preventive care such as cleaning. It would not be unusual to find a dollar limit on preventive care or certain other restrictions (no more than one or two cleanings per year). Other procedures can be covered either on a scheduled basis or a *usual and customary* basis. For example, most Dental Policies will provide coverage for:

- Diagnostic Care - X-Rays
- Restoration - Fillings, crowns, etc.
- Prosthodontics - Bridge work
- Periodontics - Treatment of gum disease
- Endodontics - Root Canals
- Orthodontics - Teeth straightening
- Oral Surgery

2 Although routine, preventive care may be covered without a deductible, Dental Policies usually feature both a **deductible and coinsurance** for most procedures. The deductible may be a per person maximum or a per family maximum. In some cases, where an Insured has both Group Medical Expense and Group Dental insurance, an **Integrated Deductible** may be used which applies to both medical expenses and Dental expenses. After the Insured has met the deductible, a cost sharing or coinsurance feature is normally found that involves the Insured and the insurance company sharing the cost of Dental care. For example, the Insured might pay for 20% of their Dental costs, while the company might pay 80%. Typically, there will be a total maximum dollar limit on coverage for the year on a per person or per family basis ($1000/person, $5000/family).

Deducts coinsurance

Limitations and Exclusions

3 Dental Policies have built-in mechanisms designed to protect against adverse selection. Normally, there is a **probationary period** for new employees who join the Group after the effective date of the Policy. Additionally, treatment limits can be imposed on employees who at first rejected coverage and now are trying to claim it.

New federal laws may change this

4 As you might guess, Dental Policies are not too keen on covering **pre-existing conditions** and they are normally excluded from coverage. Also, most plans will exclude cosmetic dentistry performed simply because the Insured is tired of being compared to David Letterman or wants to have really shiny white teeth. Dental Policies offer **no conversion privilege**. In other words, when you leave the Group plan, you cannot convert your Group Dental plan to an individual plan.

Prescription Drug Expense Insurance

5 Another very popular employee benefit is a plan which covers the cost of prescription drugs. Almost always, the employee pays a small, flat fee per prescription and the Policy pays the rest. Because of the large number of small claims inherent in a program such as this, only streamlined approaches to claims and administration allow the company to offer this kind of a program on a profitable basis.

Vision Care Expense Insurance

1 Like Dental Care and prescription medicines, Vision Care is an exclusion under medical expense programs but can still be very expensive for the average family. Thus, it too can be a very popular employee benefit. Though most vision care plans do not have a deductible, they minimize over-utilization by restricting their benefits. A common limitation is to allow no more than one exam and one pair of lenses in any 12 month period and no more than one pair of frames in any 24 month period.

Blanket Health Policies

2 A Blanket Health Policy is most often a Group Medical Expense Policy which is written on an accident only basis. It differs from traditional Group insurance in that **no individual Insureds are named and no certificates of insurance are issued**. Blanket insurance is usually only used for Groups whose membership periodically and frequently changes, or where there is a very high turnover of members. Groups eligible for blanket insurance vary from state to state depending on the local state law, but typical examples include school districts or colleges that wish to cover the students and teachers at school, common carriers (planes, trains, buses, etc.) wishing to cover their passengers, volunteer fire departments, and summer camps. These are situations where the Group membership changes frequently, and the blanket Policy automatically covers the changing membership. The key point to remember is that each individual is not specifically named in a blanket Policy.

No individual Insured named. . .

school teams camps

Franchise and Wholesale Insurance

3 Historically, the law in most states specified minimum Group membership numbers in order to qualify as a *Group*. In the beginning, it took 10 people in one Group to qualify as a true *Group*. Obviously, numerous Groups did not have 10 people. Franchise and Wholesale insurance was developed to serve as a sort of *imitation Group*. The term *Franchise* usually refers to Health insurance, while *Wholesale* refers to Life insurance, although this distinction is fading. As the NAIC model bill now totally ignores minimum Group sizes for all plans except association Groups (minimum of 100 members), and with Multiple Employer Trusts you can conceivably have a Group of one, the future existence of Franchise and Wholesale insurance will be relegated to the Museum of Insurance Trivia.

semi Group

4 Franchise and Wholesale insurance provides Health and Life coverages for small Groups which have inadequate numbers to qualify for true Group insurance. Franchise and Wholesale insurance is not, strictly speaking, Group insurance because **individual policies are issued for each participant** rather than one master contract. Individual underwriting is done and each individual can be charged a different premium rate. Each participant submits his or her own application, including a medical history. The insurance company will, for each applicant, then issue a standard Policy, a rated Policy or reject the coverage. The premiums charged are less than for an individual Policy, but more than for true Group coverage.

Many policies, not just one

Conclusion

1 Group Health policies have many of the same provisions that individual Health policies have, such as the provisions for Notice of Claims, Claim Forms, Proof of Loss, Legal Action, etc. Like individual Health, there is also generally a provision for coverage of dependent children until age 19, and a **continuation privilege** for handicapped dependents who are chiefly dependent on the Group member for support and maintenance. Also like in individual policies, the definition of a **preexisting condition** in a Group Health Policy is usually restricted by state law in terms of how far back in time a company can go in labeling a condition as *preexisting* and how long after coverage starts coverage can be excluded for that condition.

2 Group Health has some unique twists of its own though in terms of coverages. For example, in Group Health, employer Groups insuring 15 or more employees must include **maternity benefits**. Another difference from individual Health is that the provision for renewal in Group Health policies is usually only *Optionally Renewable*, giving the insurance company the option to not renew the Policy at each Policy anniversary. Also, Group Health policies usually exclude coverage for accidents or sicknesses *suffered on the job* (because of Workers Compensation coverage). Group Health policies may have a **Coordination of Benefits** clause to handle a situation of double coverage. In such a case, one insurance company is *primary* and it pays as if no other company were involved. The other company is *secondary* and it pays covered expenses that the primary company does not, such as the deductible and the Insured's coinsurance portion.

3 A federal law which impacts Group Health is **COBRA**. COBRA mandates the continuation of Group Health coverages for you as an Insured employee and/or your dependents who are protected by your coverage if you lose your Group Health coverage for just about any reason other than being fired for *gross misconduct*. The time period that the coverage must continue in force is generally 18 or 36 months, depending on the event that triggered COBRA. The **Health benefits under COBRA must be the same** as what they were under your original Group plan, and the premium cannot exceed 102% of the total cost that was paid to provide for the coverage. You, however, are responsible for paying the premium – not your employer.

4 Another federal law greatly impacting small Group (2-50) medical expense insurance is the Health Insurance Portability and Accountability Act of 1996 (HIPAA). It mandates that a previously Insured person who is entering a new Group plan due to a change in employment will not face an unInsured period due to preexisting conditions exclusions in the new Policy. If the new employee makes a *timely entry* into the new plan, his **prior creditable service** in his previous coverage will count against any preexisting conditions limitations of the new plan. Furthermore, HIPAA eliminates medical underwriting in small employer Group medical expense plans.

1   Other Health coverages found almost exclusively on the *Group* market include **Dental, Prescription Drug,** and **Vision Care Expense Insurance**. Structured like the medical expense policies examined earlier in this text, these plans often have a deductible, coinsurance, and dollar limits.

2   A Group Health Policy which differs from traditional Group insurance is **Blanket Health**. It is used to cover Groups which have a frequent change in membership, like the children in a school system, and is unique in that no individual Insureds are named in the Policy. Blanket insurance is normally written on an accident only basis. Another type of Group insurance which differs from traditional Group is Franchise/Wholesale insurance – historically sold to Groups too small to qualify as a *Group*. With **Franchise** and **Wholesale** insurance, **individual policies** were issued instead of one master contract, and individual underwriting was done.

Part V
APPENDICES

Glossary & Index

A

A&H POLICY
Accident and Health. A policy that pays benefits for losses resulting from generally either an accident or a sickness. The three major classifications of A&H benefits are medical expense benefits, disability income benefits, and dismemberment benefits. A&H policies are also referred to as Health policies. Page 10-2

ABSOLUTE ASSIGNMENT
The complete and absolute transfer of all of the legal rights and benefits contained in a policy from one policyowner to a new policyowner. Also see *Assignment*. Page 5-10

ACCELERATED DEATH BENEFIT
See *Living Benefit Option*.

ACCEPTANCE
A necessary element in the formation of a contract; the acceptance is the complete assent to an offer. Page 2-3

ACCEPTANCE (APPROVAL) FORM OF RECEIPT
A type of interim insuring agreement in which coverage starts on the date the application is approved at the company's home office. Page 2-13

ACCIDENT
In health insurance, an unintended and unforeseen (unpredictable, unexpected) event which results in bodily injury. Accident and sickness are perils which can be covered by health policies. Some policies cover only accidents, while others cover both accident and sickness. Page 10-8, 10-27

ACCIDENT & HEALTH INSURANCE
Another common name for health insurance. The abbreviation is A&H insurance. Page 10-2

ACCIDENTAL BODILY INJURY
An unforeseen and unintended bodily injury resulting from an accident which takes place in a known place and at a known ti me. Page 10-26

ACCIDENTAL DEATH
Death resulting from an accident. Some life and health policies only pay benefits if death occurs as the result of an accident, as opposed to death as the result of a sickness. Page 14-1

ACCIDENTAL DEATH AND DISMEMBERMENT BENEFIT
Pays a stated amount in case of accidental death or in case of the loss of limbs or sight as a result of an accident. Also see Accidental Death & Dismemberment Policy. Page 14-1

ACCIDENTAL DEATH AND DISMEMBERMENT (AD&D) POLICY
A health insurance policy that provides two types of benefits: a death benefit paid for accidental death, and a dismemberment benefit for the accidental loss of parts of the body, such as hands, feet and eyes. An AD&D policy is conceptually a combination of life insurance and health insurance. It is accident only coverage (does not pay benefits for losses due to sickness). Page 14-1

ACCIDENTAL DEATH BENEFIT
In life and health insurance, a payment for loss of life due to an accident. Also, a rider added to a life insurance policy for payment of an additional benefit, related to the face amount of the basic policy, when death occurs as the result of an accident as defined in the policy. Page 7-12, 14-1

ACCIDENTAL DISMEMBERMENT
See *Dismemberment Insurance*.

ACCUMULATE AT INTEREST
A dividend option in which the policyowner leaves the dividends with the insurance company to invest and earn interest. This dividend option works much like a savings account. See *Accumulated Dividends*. Page 6-5

ACCUMULATION PERIOD
The "pay in" period of an annuity unless it is the funding vehicle for a qualified retirement plan, contributions are in after-tax dollars. Interest grows on a tax-deferred basis and is then fully taxable at withdrawal Page 4-33

ACQUIRED IMMUNE DEFICIENCY SYNDROME (AIDS)
Special legal considerations dictate extreme sensitivity on the part of the insurance companies when examining, underwriting or refusing to underwrite people who have the AIDS antibodies in their systems. Page 3-9

ACTUARY
An insurance professional trained in mathematics, statistics, accounting, and the principles of insurance, annuities, and retirement plans. Insurance companies rely heavily on actuaries to determine, on the basis of past experience, the estimated claims costs for future losses. In life and health insurance, the mortality and morbidity tables are the basis for many of the calculations. *

AD&D
See *Accidental Death and Dismemberment Policy*.

ADL
Activities of daily living - eating, dressing, bathing etc. Long Term care policies are designed to provide nursing home type benefits when people can no longer perform the activities of daily living. Page 13-2

ADHESION
See *Contract of Adhesion*.

ADJUSTABLE LIFE
A relatively modern life insurance policy which allows flexibility in (1) face amount, (2) premium, and (3) the policy plan (which includes the period of protection and the payment period). Page 9-4

ADMINISTRATIVE SERVICES ONLY (ASO) CONTRACT
When a Self-funded group health plan contracts with an insurance company to serve as a Third Party Administrator Page 10-17

ADMITTED COMPANY
An insurance company licensed to do business in a particular state. The company's license is called a Certificate of Authority and is issued by the state's Department of Insurance. Also called an *Authorized Company* or a *Licensed Company*. Page 1-12

ADULT DAY CARE
Allows a family member to serve as the primary care giver and still go to work. Most policies provide coverage in both a true Adult Day Care facility or in the home. Page 13-6

* definition only, term not found in text

ADVERSE SELECTION

Selection against the company; the tendency of less favorable insurance risks to seek or continue insurance to a greater extent than better risks. Also, the tendency of a policyowner to take advantage of favorable options in insurance contracts.

Page 3-11

ADVERTISING

In insurance law advertising is any communication to the consuming public - broadcast, telecast, written or spoken.

Page 5-1

AGE

For life and health insurance, the age in years of an applicant, insured, or beneficiary. Some companies use the age as of the most recent birthday. Other companies use the age at the nearest birthday, either the last or the next. Page 3-7

AGENCY AGREEMENT OR AGENCY CONTRACT

A legal document containing the terms of the agreement between the agent and the insurance company, signed by both parties. The agency agreement clearly defines what an agent can and cannot do, and how he or she will be compensated.

Page 2-19

AGENT/PRODUCER

Anyone who sells or aids in the selling of insurance, the delivery of policies, or the collection of premiums on behalf of an insurance company; a legal representative of an insurance company.

Page 2-19

AGENT'S AUTHORITY

The power specifically granted to the agent in the agency contract and/or the power which the public may reasonably expect the agent to have. The agent's authority virtually never includes the power to change or waive the provisions of a policy, to alter an application, or to make an amendment or add a rider to the contract. Also see *Express Authority* and *Implied Authority*.

Page 2-19

AGENT'S REPORT

A written report submitted by the agent along with the application, telling the company what the agent knows about the applicant's habits, health, financial standing, morals, other insurance in force, etc. Page 3-4

AGREEMENT

An offer and an acceptance of that exact offer form an agreement. For the agreement to be considered a contract, it must be supported by consideration. Also see *Contract*. Page 2-3

ADJUSTABLE LIFE

Its primary advantage is that insureds can periodically adjust the amount of death benefit, the amount of premium or even the type of coverage as their needs change over their lifetimes

Page 9-4

ALEATORY CONTRACT

An aleatory contract is one in which one party is only obligated to pay if a fortuitous event occurs and in which one party may obtain far greater value under the agreement than the other. There is a possibility that the company will never be obligated to pay. An insurance contract is an aleatory contract as there may be an uneven exchange of values. Page 2-17

ALIEN COMPANY

A company incorporated or organized under the laws of a country or state outside of the United States or its territories or possessions. In the United States, Sun Life Of Canada would be considered an alien company. Page 1-12

ALL CAUSE DEDUCTIBLE

This deductible establishes a calendar year total (like $200 for an individual) for which the policyowner is responsible. After the stated amount has been paid, either as the result of one claim or several, the policyowner has fully satisfied the deductible for that calendar year. For the remainder of the calendar year, the policy will pay benefits in accordance with the coinsurance percentage stated in the policy. This approach is most commonly used with the Major Medical policy or the Comprehensive Major Medical policy and is by far the most popular deductible arrangement in today's marketplace. Also called a *Calendar Year Deductible*.

Page 12-15

AMOUNT CERTAIN ANNUITY

See *Annuity Certain*.

ANCILLARY BENEFITS

In a Basic Hospitalization medical expense policy, the extra expense payments provided for miscellaneous hospital expenses, such as drugs, X-rays, lab fees, and sometimes ambulance charges. Also called *Miscellaneous Expense Benefits*.

Page 12-5

ANNIVERSARY

See *Policy Anniversary*.

ANNUAL PREMIUM

The total dollar premium amount which must be paid on an annual basis to keep the policy in force. Page 3-13

ANNUALLY RENEWABLE TERM

A Term Life insurance contract which gives the policyowner the right to renew the policy each year up to a specified age (such as age 65) or for a specified period of time (such as 10 years) without proof of insurability. Premiums increase with each renewal because the rates are based on the insured's newly attained age. Also called *Yearly Renewable Term*. Page 4-9

ANNUITANT

One who receives the proceeds of an annuity (or upon whose life payments depend). Page 4-20

ANNUITY

A contract guaranteeing an income for a certain period of time or for life to the annuitant. Page 4-19

ANNUITY CERTAIN

Unlike a Life Annuity, the Annuity Certain is a contract which pays a specified income for a set period of time whether the annuitant lives or dies. The Fixed Period and Fixed Amount settlement options are examples of Annuities Certain. For contrast, see *Straight Life Annuity*. Page 4-25

ANNUITY UNITS

With a Variable Life Annuity, the promise made to the annuitant is to pay the value of a specified number of annuity units at each payment interval for life. The value of the annuity unit fluctuates according to the value of the underlying investments made by the company in common stocks and bonds. Also see *Variable Annuity*. Page 4-35

ANTI-REBATE LAWS

State laws which prohibit an agent or a company from giving part of the premium back to the insured as an inducement to purchase insurance. *

Glossary & Index

ANTI-SELECTION
See *Adverse Selection.*

ANY OCCUPATION (ANY OCC)
This is the most restrictive definition of total disability because you are considered to be disabled only if you cannot do your job or any other job for which you are reasonably suited by education, training, or experience. For contrast, see *Your Occ.* Also see *Presumptive Total Disability.*   Page 11-6

APPARENT AUTHORITY
Power that the public reasonably assumes you to have as an agent, whether you actually do have that power or not. As an agent, you can obligate your company by acting under apparent authority even though you do not have the actual (express or implied) authority to do so. For contrast, see *Express Authority* and *Implied Authority.*   Page 2-21

APPLICANT
Any individual applying for a policy of insurance either on his own life or health or for someone else; one who fills out and signs a written application for insurance.   Page 2-7, 2-8

APPLICATION
A printed form supplied by the insurance company and usually filled out by the agent and a medical examiner (if applicable) on the basis of information received from the applicant on the life or health of the proposed insured. The form is signed by the applicant and becomes part of the insurance contract if a policy is issued. If the proposed insured is someone other than the applicant, then the proposed insured must also sign the application, thereby giving consent to the issuance of the policy. The application provides information to the home office underwriting department so that it may classify the risk and determine whether to issue the policy.   Page 3-3

ASSIGNMENT
The legal transfer of policy ownership or policy benefits from the policyowner to another party. When the company is given written notice of the assignment, the policy benefits will then accrue to the person named as assignee.   Page 5-9

ASSIGNMENT OF BENEFITS
In health insurance, the authorization by the policyowner to have benefits payable under a claim paid to someone else, usually to a physician or hospital under a medical expense policy, or to an attorney as legal guardian under a disability income policy.   Page 12-16

ATTAINED AGE
The age an insured has reached or attained. For life insurance, the attained age is based on either the actual age or the insured's age prior to the last birthday, depending upon the limits set by state law.   Page 4-9

ATTENDING PHYSICIAN'S REPORT
A report or statement from the proposed insured's own physician detailing the specifics of an accident or disease, the treatment and the prognosis. The information in such statements is privileged in nature and is given in confidence to the insurance company.   Page 3-5

AUTHORIZED COMPANY
See *Admitted Company.*

AUTOMATIC PREMIUM LOAN PROVISION
A provision in a life insurance policy authorizing the insurance company to automatically use the loan value (if adequate) to pay any premium not paid by the end of the grace period. The amount so paid is charged against the policy as a policy loan.   Page 7-13

AVERAGE EARNINGS CLAUSE
In Disability Income policies, an optional provision which permits the company to limit an insured's disability income benefits to the amount of his or her average earnings for the 24 months prior to the disability. Typically, if, at the time the disability commences, the total benefits payable under all coverages owned by the insured exceed the average earnings of the insured over the preceding two years, the benefits will be reduced pro rata to the average income amount. Also called *Relation of Earnings to Insurance Clause.*   Page 15-10

AVIATION CLAUSE/EXCLUSION
Limits or excludes life or health coverages when the insured is killed or injured in specified types of air travel. Coverage may be confined to fare paying passengers on regularly scheduled flights of commercial airlines or it may be considerably less restrictive.   Page 5-15

AVOID RISK
A way to respond to risk by taking specific steps to eliminate a specific exposure.   Page 1-2

B

BASE (BASIC) PLANS
Developed originally in the 1930's, the Base Plans (or Basic Plans) were divided into three separate areas: Basic Hospital, Basic Medical, and Basic Surgical. They were characterized by low dollar limits of coverage, no deductible, and they required that the insured actually be hospitalized to receive any benefits. Nowadays, a Base Plan is most often seen as a segment of a Supplementary Major Medical plan.   Page 12-3

BASIC HOSPITAL POLICY
A basic medical expense health plan that provides benefits for daily room and board expenses (DBR) plus miscellaneous (ancillary) expenses for nursing services, lab fees, drugs and sometimes ambulances, usually on a first dollar basis but with low total amount of coverage. Also called a *Hospital Policy.*   Page 12-4

BASIC MEDICAL POLICY
A basic medical expense health plan covering doctor visits while hospitalized. The Basic Medical Policy is generally very restrictive in that it will only pay for a limited number of doctor visits per day at a limited number of dollars per visit and for a limited number of visits per hospital stay. Also called *Medical Expense.*   Page 12-5

BASIC SURGICAL POLICY
A basic medical expense health plan covering surgical expenses. It is characterized by a list of surgical operations with listed amounts payable for each operation. Also called *Surgical Expense.*   Page 12-5

BENEFICIARY
The person to whom the proceeds of a life or health insurance policy are payable when the insured dies. The *primary* beneficiaries are those who are first entitled to the proceeds. The *secondary* beneficiaries are entitled to the proceeds if no primary beneficiary is living when the insured dies. The *tertiary* beneficiaries are those entitled to the proceeds if no primary or secondary beneficiaries are alive when the insured dies. Secondary and tertiary beneficiaries are also referred to as *contingent* beneficiaries.   Page 5-17, 16-12

* definition only, term not found in text

BENEFICIARY PROVISION

A provision in a life or health policy which gives the policyowner the right to name the beneficiary and to change the designated beneficiary unless the beneficiary is named irrevocably.

Page 5-16

BENEFIT PERIOD

In health insurance, a maximum period of time for which the policy will pay benefits.

Page 11-7

BLACKOUT PERIOD

The period of time between the youngest child turning 18 and a widow(er) reaching retirement age during which no Social Security benefits are paid following the death of a fully insured spouse.

Page 4-33, 18-3

BLANKET INSURANCE

A group health insurance policy covering a number of individuals who are not individually named in the policy. Only certain groups, dictated by state law, are eligible to purchase Blanket policies such as high school athletic teams, children's summer camps, newspaper carriers, school districts, etc.

Page 17-10

BLUE CROSS/BLUE SHIELD

Service organizations which promise services to the *subscriber* (insured) rather than a reimbursement of dollars. The Blues contract with the provider hospitals and physicians as well as with the subscriber. Traditionally, Blue Cross was designed to pay hospitals, and Blue Shield was designed to pay doctors. Both are generally nonprofit organizations which usually operate on a state-wide basis.

Page 10-10

BREACH OF CONTRACT

The violation of, or failure to perform, the terms of a contract; the breaking of a legally binding agreement. An insurance policy is a legal contract, and failure to comply with the terms or conditions incorporated in the policy constitutes a breach of contract. As insurance policies are unilateral contracts (only the company makes any promises), only the company can be sued for breach of contract.

Page 2-17

BROKER

Brokers legally represent the customer, whereas agents are the legal representatives of the companies who have appointed them as agents.

Page 2-20

BURIAL INSURANCE

A slang term usually referring to a small policy of life insurance ($1,000 to $5,000) intended to pay the funeral expenses of the deceased insured.

Page 4-1

BUSINESS CONTINUATION PLANS

See *Buy And Sell Agreements* or *Cross Purchase Plans*.

BUSINESS OVERHEAD EXPENSE

A modified disability income policy designed to pay for the monthly expenses of a business, generally of a self-employed professional or a sole proprietor. The Business Overhead Expense policy is written on the businessowner, but it pays the business so that the office rent, the employees' salaries, and other business expenses can be paid. However, BOE never covers the salary of the businessowner, and benefits are paid on a reimbursement basis for the business expenses actually incurred.

Page 11-17

BUY AND SELL AGREEMENT

A contract that establishes what will be done with a business in the event an owner dies or becomes disabled. Life insurance normally provides the funds necessary to implement the Buy and Sell Agreement in case of an owner's death because it can provide the exact amount of money needed at exactly the time it is needed. Similarly, in health insurance, Disability Buy-Sell coverage is designed to provide benefits to a corporation to buy out a disabled stockholder/director's share of the business. If one of the primary stockholder/directors becomes disabled, the policy will generally pay an installment benefit to the corporation for up to a year and then finally pay out a lump sum benefit to the corporation so it can buy out the disabled partner.

Page 7-12, 8-14

BUYER'S GUIDE

Provides generic information designed to educate the applicant concerning the types of insurance available, to better enable him to make an informed and appropriate choice.

Page 2-16

C

CALENDAR YEAR DEDUCTIBLE

See *All Cause Deductible*.

CANCELLABLE CONTRACT

A health insurance policy that may be terminated by the insurance company at any time, even during the policy period, as long as the policyowner is given a five day written notice. This type of policy is illegal in most states.

Page 10-23

CANCELLATION PROVISION

A provision in a health policy that permits the company to terminate the contract during a period for which premium has been paid. This provision is now prohibited by most states.

Page 15-10

CAPITAL SUM

In an Accidental Death and Dismemberment (AD&D) health policy, the dollar amount provided for dismemberment of a *primary* body part (hand or foot) or loss of sight in one eye. The capital sum is usually fifty percent of the principal sum. For contrast, see *Principal Sum*.

Page 14-2

CAPTIVE AGENT

An insurance agent who has signed an agency agreement with a company which provides that he or she represent that company only. For contrast, see *Independent Agent*.

Page 3-13

CASH OR DEFERRED ARRANGEMENT PLANS

Includes Tax Sheltered Annuities (TSA's) (TDA) (403-B), 401(k) Plans and Section 457 Deferred Comp.

Page 8-5

CASH VALUE

In a life insurance policy, the cash value is the equity amount legally available to the policyowner when the policy is surrendered. The cash surrender option is one of a life insurance policy's nonforfeiture options.

Page 4-10

CATASTROPHE INSURANCE

See *Major Medical Expense Insurance* and *Comprehensive Medical Expense Insurance*.

CATASTROPHIC LOSSES

Losses which impact many insureds simultaneously. Such as war or nuclear hazards. These types of losses are excluded in most forms of insurance.

Page 3-2

CERTIFICATE OF AUTHORITY

A license issued by a state department of insurance to an insurance company granting it the right to conduct business in that state.

Page 1-12

CENTER FOR MEDICARE & MEDICAID SERVICES
Medicare is administered by the Center for Medicare & Medicaid Services.   Page 13-13

CERTIFICATE OF INSURANCE
In group insurance, since there is only one policy (called the *Master Contract*), each covered member is given a document called a Certificate of Insurance which states the benefits provided under the group contract. Also called an *Individual Certificate*.   Page 16-12

CHANGE OF BENEFICIARY PROVISION
A provision in life and health policies specifying the right of the policyowner to change the beneficiary at any time unless the beneficiary has been named on an irrevocable basis.
Page 5-19, 15-8

CHANGE OF INSURED RIDER
When a joint policy is used to fund a Buy-Sell Agreement, one of the insured's could leave that employment before any of the principals die. If a new partner joins the company this rider allows the other partners to continue their coverage without an age change or new proof of insurability.   Page 7-13

CHANGE OF OCCUPATION PROVISION
An optional provision contained in health policies stating that if the insured changes occupation, he or she must notify the company for the premium rate adjustment.   Page 15-8

CLAIM
In insurance, a request or demand by the policyowner of the insurance company for payment of benefits according to the provisions of the policy.   Page 15-6

CHURNING
The buying and selling of securities within a client account for the purpose of generating commission income.   Page 9-16

CLAIM FORMS PROVISION
In health policies, a mandatory provision which requires the insurance company to provide forms for the submission of proof of loss by the policyowner within 15 days after receipt of a notice of claim.   Page 15-6

CLASS
In insurance, a group of insureds with the same general characteristics who are exposed to the same perils and are grouped together for rating purposes.   Page 3-2, 6-2, 10-22

CLASSIFICATION
In insurance, the systematic arrangement of defined classes or groups of risks; the grouping of persons for the purpose of determining an underwriting or rating group into which a particular risk must be placed.   Page 3-7

CLAUSE
A provision of an insurance policy. *

CLOSE (CLOSELY HELD) CORPORATION
A corporation which has substantially identical ownership and management, i.e., the stockholders are also the managers. This is compared to a large corporation in which the managers own very little, if any, of the company. *

CLOSED PANEL
If an HMO contracts with a Group Practice to provide medical services for its members *exclusively*, it is a closed panel arrangement. See *Open Panel*.   Page 10-14

COBRA
(CONSOLIDATED OMNIBUS BUDGET RECONCILIATION ACT OF 1985)
The Federal statute which governs the continuation of Group health insurance benefits in specific circumstances.
Page 17-6

COINSURANCE
In health insurance, a provision whereby the insurance company and the policyowner share covered losses in agreed proportions. An 80/20 Coinsurance Clause is typical of Major Medical type policies. Excluding the amount of the deductible, the company agrees to pay 80 percent of the insured's covered expenses and the insured pays the remaining 20 percent. Also called *Percentage Participation* or *Cost Sharing*.   Page 12-10

COLLATERAL ASSIGNMENT
The limited assignment of an insurance policy to a creditor as security for a debt. Under a collateral assignment, the creditor is entitled to be reimbursed out of policy proceeds for the amount owed. The beneficiary is entitled to any excess of the policy proceeds over the amount due the creditor in the event of the insured's death. For contrast, see *Absolute Assignment*.
Page 5-9

COMMISSION
In insurance sales, the percentage of the premium paid by the insurance company to the agent or broker as compensation for making the sale. Commissions are sometimes regulated by law, as is often the case with Medicare Supplement and Long-Term Care policies.   Page 3-12

COMMISSIONER
A public official in charge of a government agency. An insurance commissioner is the head of a state insurance department and is charged with the supervision of the insurance business in the state and the administration of the state's insurance laws. Called Superintendent or Director in some jurisdictions.   Page 5-1

COMMISSIONERS' STANDARD MORTALITY TABLE
A mortality table approved by the National Association of Insurance Commissioners as a standard for valuation and for computing rates and nonforfeiture values for life insurance policies. When new tables are issued (approximately every twenty years), they typically reflect longer life expectancies and improved investment yields which result in reduced costs of life insurance for the insuring public.
Page 3-2

COMMON ACCIDENT PROVISION
A medical expense policy provision which states that if two or more insureds under the same policy are injured in the same accident, then the company will charge only one deductible. This provision only works with accidents – not sicknesses. *

COMMON DISASTER PROVISION
A life insurance policy provision which states that if the beneficiary dies within a stated period of time (such as 30 or 60 days) of the insured, then the insurance company will proceed as if the insured had outlived the beneficiary. Also called a *Death of Beneficiary Clause*. In health insurance, a provision which states that if two or more insureds are injured in the same accident, then only one deductible will be charged against the claim.   Page 5-23

* definition only, term not found in text

COMMUNITY RATING

A method for setting premium in Group insurance which is dependent not on the history of a specific group, but rather all of the groups in a designated geographic area. See *Experience Rating*. Page 10-14, 16-8

COMPARATIVE INTEREST RATE METHOD

A way of comparison shopping while purchasing life insurance. With this approach (sometimes called the internal rate of return) you simply compute an interest rate based upon premiums paid versus cash developed under the contract. Page 5-3

COMPOUND INTEREST

Interest earned on interest. First, interest is earned on the principal over a given period, and is then added to the original principal to become the new, higher principal upon which interest is earned during the new period, and so on from period to period. *

COMPREHENSIVE MAJOR MEDICAL POLICY

A medical expense policy with a Base Plan and Major Medical coverages fully integrated into one policy. It is structured exactly like Major Med – i.e., a deductible followed by coinsurance and a Stop Loss – but the big difference is that the deductible is low ($100 to $500 range). Page 12-13

COMPREHENSIVE MEDICAL EXPENSE POLICY

See *Comprehensive Major Medical Policy*.

CONCEALMENT

The intentional failure to disclose a material fact; the hiding of the truth or telling a partial truth. Concealment, like misrepresentation, may be grounds for cancellation of a policy or denial of coverage. Also see *Misrepresentation*. Page 2-6

CONCURRENT REVIEW

See *Utilization Review*.

CONDITIONAL

Insurance policies are conditional in nature because certain future conditions or acts must occur before any claims can be paid. Conditional statements are "If . . ., then . . ." in nature: "If there is a loss, then the company is obligated to pay". Page 2-16

CONDITIONAL RECEIPT

In life and health insurance, a type of interim insuring agreement under which the insurance company agrees to start coverage on the later of either the application date or the date of the medical exam IF the proposed insured is insurable as applied for on that later date. If the policy applied for is rejected or issued differently than applied for, then there is no coverage at all under the Conditional Receipt. Also see *Interim Insuring Agreement*. Page 2-12, 15-5

CONDITIONALLY RENEWABLE

A renewal provision in a health insurance policy which gives the policyowner the right to renew the contract until a stated age IF specified events (like the early retirement of the insured) do not occur. Page 10-20

CONFORMITY WITH STATE STATUTES PROVISION

A widely used optional provision found in health policies which states that if the policy does not conform to the minimum requirements of the state law of the insured, then the policy will be interpreted as if it did. Page 5-10, 15-15

CONSENT

Approval; permission. In order to purchase life or health insurance on another person, you must have an insurable interest in that person and, generally, his or her written consent. Consent is indicated by having the proposed insured sign the application. Page 2-8, 5-9, 7-11

CONSIDERATION

A necessary element of a contract; consideration is something of value, such as money, promises, property, etc. In life and health insurance, the insured's consideration is the payment of the first premium and the statements on the application; the company's consideration is the promises contained in the policy itself. Also see *Contract*. Page 1-6, 2-3

CONSIDERATION CLAUSE

A statement in a health insurance policy which specifies that the policy was issued based on (a) the application, and (b) the payment of premium. The Consideration Clause also often states when coverage begins and ends. Page 10-31

CONTEST

To deny payment of a claim due to fraud, material misrepresentation, or concealment on the application for insurance. Also see *Incontestable Clause*. Page 5-6, 15-3

CONTESTABLE PERIOD

The period of time during which an insurance company may contest a claim under a policy because of fraud, misrepresentation, or misleading or incomplete information furnished on the application. The contestable period is determined by state law and is usually one to three years from the policy's date of issue. Also see *Incontestable Clause*. Page 5-6, 15-3

CONTINGENT BENEFICIARY

A contingent beneficiary is an alternate beneficiary designated to receive payment in the event that the primary revocable beneficiary dies before the insured. Page 5-17

CONTINUOUS PREMIUM WHOLE LIFE

A Whole Life policy for which the policyowner makes premium payments for the whole of life (until death or reaching age 100, whichever comes first). Also called *Straight Life*. For contrast, see *Limited-Pay Whole Life Policy*. Page 4-14

CONTRACT

An agreement between two or more parties which is supported by consideration and which is legally enforceable. An insurance policy, for example, is a contract. The chief requirements for the formation of a valid contract are: (1) an offer made by one party; (2) an acceptance by another party; (3) an exchange of consideration between the parties. To be enforceable, the parties to the contract must be legally competent, the contract must have a legal purpose, and there must not be fraud or misrepresentation by either party. Page 2-1

CONTRACT OF ADHESION

In insurance, a contract in which the buyer must accept the established policy form offered by the company. Because the company is entirely responsible for drafting the policy, any ambiguities in the policy will be resolved in favor of the policyowner. Page 2-17

CONTRACT OF INSURANCE

A legal and binding contract whereby an insurance company agrees to pay a policyowner for losses, provide other benefits, or render service to, or on behalf of, an insured. In life and health insurance, the contract of insurance consists of the policy, the application, and any attached riders. Page 2-2

* definition only, term not found in text

Glossary & Index

CONTRIBUTORY PLAN
A group insurance plan under which the employees contribute to the payment of premium for the insurance coverage. Employee contributions are generally made through periodic payroll deductions. For contrast, see *Noncontributory Plan*.
Page 16-10

CONTROLLED BUSINESS
An insurance account that an agent or broker can control by virtue of personal influence with that buyer. The definition of "controlled business" varies according to state law, but a typical example is insurance that you write on your immediate family, your employees, or your own company. *

CONVENTIONAL ANNUITY
See *Fixed Dollar Annuity*.

CONVERSION
In life insurance, a contractual right allowing the policyowner to exchange his or her insurance policy of one kind for a policy of a different kind. For example, Convertible Term can be converted to Whole Life. Also see *Conversion Privilege*.
Page 4-9

CONVERSION PERIOD
In group life insurance, the period of time a departing group member has to convert his or her group life insurance coverage into an individual policy without proof of insurability. Also see *Conversion Privilege*.
Page 16-15

CONVERSION PRIVILEGE
In group insurance, the right of an insured individual who is leaving the group to convert to an individual policy of insurance without proof of insurability.
Page 16-14

CONVERTIBLE TERM POLICY
A Term life insurance policy which may be converted into a permanent type of coverage (such as Whole Life) without proof of insurability if converted within a specified period as stated in the contract. The new premium will be based upon the attained age of the insured at the time of conversion.
Page 4-9

COORDINATION OF BENEFITS CLAUSE
A provision in some group health insurance policies specifying that if the insured is covered under another group plan in addition to his or her own group health plan, then benefits will be coordinated by the two insurance companies so that double benefits are not paid. One policy will be primary and it will pay as if no other coverage existed; the other company will be secondary and will pay the covered expenses not paid by the primary policy (the deductible and the insured's portion of the coinsurance).
Page 17-4

CORPORATE-OWNED NONQUALIFIED ANNUITY
The premiums paid would be deductible to the employer as a business expense but taxable income to the employee as income in the year they are paid. The earnings of the Annuity (left undisturbed until 59 1/2) would grow tax deferred until withdrawn. At retirement, only the earnings would be taxable.
Page 4-31

CORPORATE PENSION PLAN
is defined by the IRS as one "established and maintained by the employer primarily to provide for the payment of definitely determinable benefits to employees over a period of years, usually for life, after retirement." The corporation must contribute to the plan, and there are normally provisions for the employees to contribute additional amounts.
Page 8-4

CORPORATE PROFIT SHARING PLAN
Rather than committing the employer to either a fixed benefit or to a fixed contribution plan, which must be paid regardless of the company's financial condition, the Profit Sharing Plan allows the employer to vary the contribution to the plan at the discretion of the board of directors. See *Profit Sharing Plan*.
Page 8-4

CORRIDOR DEDUCTIBLE
The deductible in a Supplementary Major Medical policy, so called because it is not applied until after the Base Plan benefits of the policy are exhausted. The Corridor Deductible of a Supplementary Major Medical plan is typically $100-$500.
Page 12-13, 12-15

COST OF LIVING OPTION
On a disability income policy, this option would automatically increase the disability benefit at a given rate after the insured starts receiving benefits. Depending upon the company, this can be done by stating a guaranteed percentage (typically between 5 - 10%) or tying the benefits to an inflation index like the Consumer Price Index (CPI).
Page 11-13

COST OF LIVING RIDER
The Cost of Living rider allows the policyowner to increase the face amount of the policy as the designated cost-of-living index increases.
Page 11-12

COST SHARING
See *Coinsurance*.

COUNTER-OFFER
In the process of forming a contract, if the first party makes an offer which is unacceptable to the second party, the second party can suggest another alternative, which would be called a counter-offer. There is no limit to the number of counter-offers that may occur. Counter-offers are not mandatory to the formation of a contract. Also see *Offer* and *Acceptance*.
Page 2-8

COVERED EXPENSES
In an insurance contract, covered expenses typically include costs such as reasonable and customary hospital room charges, doctors fees, and miscellaneous medical service charges incurred by the insured and for which the policyowner is entitled to receive benefits. Expenses which exceed the policy's limits are not covered and therefore must be paid by the insured.
Page 12-19

CREDIT A&H POLICY
A form of disability income insurance designed to protect a creditor (a lending institution) against the nonpayment of a loan as the result of the disability of the debtor (borrower). The creditor is the owner and beneficiary of the policy and the debtor is the insured. Also see *Credit Life Policy*.
Page 16-5

CREDIT LIFE POLICY
Life insurance issued on the life of a borrower (debtor) to cover the repayment of a loan in case of the borrower's death before the loan has been repaid. The creditor (generally a lending institution) is the owner and beneficiary of the policy and the borrower is the insured. Credit Life insurance is usually written using Decreasing Term on a relatively small, decreasing balance installment loan. In the event of the borrower's death, the death benefit is used to pay off the outstanding balance of the loan. Credit Life is normally written on a group basis.
Page 16-5

* definition only, term not found in text

CROSS-PURCHASE PLAN
A method of funding a Buy and Sell Agreement where each partner in the company buys a policy on each of the other partners. If there are three partners, six policies are purchased. Page 7-12

CURRENTLY INSURED
Under Social Security, a status of limited eligibility that provides only death benefits to widows or widowers and children; it does not provide old-age or disability benefits. For contrast, see *Fully Insured*. Page 18-11

CUSTODIAL OR RESIDENTIAL CARE
Help in performing the ADL's and can be performed by someone without medical skills or training but still based on doctor's orders. Page 3-6

CUSTOMARY AND REASONABLE CHARGES
In health insurance, medical expense policies generally cover reasonable, customary and necessary medical expenses, but not excessive fees, costs for unusual procedures or unnecessary expenses. The insurance company determines the most common charge for similar medical fees and services in the area where the insured receives the medical care and may refuse to cover excessive costs if the charges were not within the customary and reasonable limits. Page 12-8

D

DAILY HOSPITAL BENEFIT
In a medical expense policy, a benefit designed to pay for hospital room and board charges that are charged to the patient on a per diem (daily) basis. Also called *DBR* (daily board and room). Page 12-5

DBR
See *Daily Hospital Benefit*.

DEATH BENEFIT
The policy proceeds to be paid upon the death of the insured. In life or AD&D health policies, the face amount, as stated in the policy, to be paid to the beneficiary upon proof of death of the insured. Also see *Principal Sum*. Page 9-7, 9-12

DEBIT AGENT
An agent who sells Industrial Insurance. Generally, a Debit Agent sells small amounts of coverage house-to-house in a limited territory and collects premiums on a regular weekly or monthly basis at the policyowner's home. Also see *Industrial Insurance*. Page 4-3

DECLARE A DIVIDEND
Stock insurance companies periodically pay part of their profits to their stockholders as a return on investment. These payments are called dividends and are taxable because they are considered to be income. On the other hand, a mutual insurance company may pay a *policy dividend* to its policyowners if it finds that the actual experience in mortality, interest and expenses is more favorable than expected. Policy dividends paid to policyowners by a mutual company are not taxable as they are considered a return of unneeded premium. Page 6-4

DECREASING TERM
Term life insurance in which the face amount decreases over time in scheduled steps from the date the policy goes into force until the date the policy expires. The premium, however, usually remains level. The intervals between the decreases are usually either monthly or annually. Page 4-7

DEDUCTIBLE
In many health insurance policies, the amount of covered expenses which must be paid by the policyowner before the policy pays any benefits. The company pays benefits only for losses in excess of the amount specified in the deductible provision (subject to the coinsurance provision). There are various types of deductibles and ways they can be applied. Also see *Corridor Deductible* and *Elimination Period*. Page 10-6, 11-8, 12-15

DEFERRED ANNUITY
A Life Annuity contract under which the first payment is not made to the annuitant until the expiration of a fixed number of years or until the annuitant attains a specific age; often used to provide retirement income. Page 4-37

DEFERRED ARRANGEMENT PLANS
See *Cash Arrangement Plans*.

DEFERRED COMPENSATION
Describe arrangements whereby work done today is compensated in the future. The obvious purpose is to lower income (and taxes) today, and pay the deferred monies out tomorrow when the employee is hopefully in a lower tax bracket. A nonqualified plan. Page 8-6

DEFINED BENEFIT PLANS
This plan is just the opposite of a Defined Contribution Plan. Here, you know what will come out, but it requires a constant process of estimating to determine what must go in. These fixed benefit plans, sometimes called Annuity Purchase plans, establish a set benefit formula for employees. The defined benefit may be a percentage of pay for each year of service in the plan, or a flat sum, or some combination of the two. The dollar amount of the benefit may vary, as with a variable annuity plan, but the formula must be fixed in the plan. Page 8-4

DEFINED CONTRIBUTION PLANS
Sometimes called Money Purchase Plans, these pension plans require a set rate of contribution from the corporation. Employee benefits at retirement will depend directly upon the amount of contributions made, the plans earnings, and the employee's length of service in the plan. Estimated benefits are derived from actuarial projections which obviously use age and sex as considerations. Under a Defined Contribution Plan, you know exactly what will be put in, but you can only guess at what will come out. Page 8-4

DELIVERY RECEIPT
A receipt signed and dated by the policyowner stating that he or she has received the policy. Page 2-16

DENTAL EXPENSE INSURANCE
A form of medical expense health insurance covering the treatment and care of dental disease and injury to the insured's teeth. Dental insurance is most frequently sold on a group basis. Page 17-8

DEPARTMENT OF PUBLIC WELFARE
Administers each state's the Medicaid program within established federal guidelines. Page 13-9

DIRECT RESPONSE MARKETING SYSTEM
The insurance company advertises for clients to mail their applications directly to the company, which bypasses the agent altogether. Page 3-13

Glossary & Index

DISABILITY

A physical or mental impairment caused by accident or sickness which partially or totally limits your ability to work. There are several standard definitions of "disability": *Your Occupation (Own Occupation), Any Occupation, Presumptive Total Disability, Partial Disability, Residual Disability*. In order to be eligible for disability income benefits, the insured must fit the definition of disability stated in the policy or, in the case of Social Security Disability Income, the definition required by the Social Security Administration.   Page 11-6

DISABILITY BUY-SELL

A coverage designed to provide benefits to a corporation to buy out a disabled stockholder/director's share of the business. If one of the primary stockholders/directors becomes disabled, the policy will generally pay an installment benefit to the corporation for up to a year and then finally pay out a lump sum benefit to the corporation so it can buy out the disabled partner.
                                                     Page 11-18

DISABILITY INCOME

A cash benefit paid on a periodic basis (such as monthly) and designed to replace income during a period of the insured's disability. Also, under some life insurance policies, a limited disability income may be provided by means of a rider in the event of total and permanent disability of the insured.
                                              Page 10-4, 11-2

DISABILITY INCOME BENEFITS

The type of benefits payable under a Disability Income policy. They are periodic payments (usually monthly) that replace income while the insured is disabled.   Page 11-2

DISABILITY INCOME INSURANCE

A health insurance policy that provides periodic payments when the insured is disabled and unable to work. It is a stated amount (valued) contract. Disability Income policies are sometimes called Loss of Time or Income Protection policies. For contrast, see *Medical Expense Insurance*.   Page 11-2

DISCHARGE PLANNING

See *Utilization Review*.

DISCOUNTED OR PRESENT VALUE OF MONEY

The value today of a future payment discounted at some appropriate compound interest rate. For example, if I promise to give you $100 ten years from now, that is worth about $39 today. This principle is used by investors such as insurance companies to determine how much money they must invest today to produce a certain amount at a future date. Also called the *Time Value of Money*.   Page 5-2

DISMEMBERMENT INSURANCE

A form of health insurance which provides a fixed payment in the event of the accidental loss of one or more body parts (usually hands or feet) or the sight of one or both eyes. Dismemberment insurance frequently is combined with Accidental Death insurance in a form called Accidental Death And Dismemberment (AD&D) insurance. Dismemberment is usually defined as "severance of the limb(s) at or above the ankle or wrist joint," and for eyes, "the complete and irrevocable loss of sight." Also see *Accidental Death & Dismemberment Policy*.
                                                     Page 14-1

DIVIDEND

In participating life insurance policies, the return of that part of the premium paid at the beginning of the year which still remains after the company has set aside the necessary reserves and has made the deductions for claims and expenses. The dividend includes a share in the company's investment, mortality, and operating profits. Because the dividend paid to a policyowner under a participating policy is simply a return of premium overcharge, it is not taxable.   Page 6-1

DIVIDEND CLASS

Dividends are paid by participating companies to policyowners by dividend class. The company determines dividend classes by grouping policyowners according to type of coverage, age at policy issuance, year of issue, etc. The reason for paying dividends by class is for fairness.   Page 6-2

DIVIDEND OPTIONS

In life insurance, the choices a participating policyowner has to receive his or her dividends. Dividend options available vary from one company to another. Some of the dividend options include: *Cash, Reduction of Premium, Accumulate at Interest, Paid-up Additional Insurance, One-Year Term, Paid-up Life,* and *Accelerated Endowment*.   Page 6-4

DOCTRINE OF REASONABLE EXPECTATIONS

One of the basic legal principles guiding insurance law which says that an insurance policy should do for the insured what he would reasonably expect it to do.   Page 2-2

DOCTRINE OF UTMOST GOOD FAITH

A general principle concerning the relationship between the policyowner and the insurance company. The insurance company and the policyowner each have a duty of good faith and fair dealing. Neither party may do anything which would injure the right of the other party to receive the benefits of the agreement. The company relies on the insured to tell the truth and the insured relies on the company to honor the promises it makes in the policy. Also see *Representation, Misrepresentation,* and *Concealment*.   Page 2-2

DOMESTIC COMPANY

A company is a domestic company in the state under whose laws it was organized.   Page 1-12

DOUBLE INDEMNITY RIDER

A life insurance policy rider which obligates the insurance company to pay double the face amount of the policy if the insured dies as the result of an accident. This rider generally stipulates that the death must occur prior to a specified age and result from an accidental bodily injury and not be contributed to by any other cause. Also, the death must occur within 90 days of the accident in order for the double benefit to be paid. Also known as a *Double Benefit Provision* or a *Multiple Indemnity Rider*.   Page 7-15

DREAD DISEASE POLICY

Provides Major Medical or Comprehensive Major Medical type benefits but only for the named disease. While this contract could be written on practically any disease, it seems to work best for high cost illnesses that anyone can get, and everyone fears.   Page 14-4

DUAL CHOICE PROVISION

Federal law which required employers with 25 or more employees to offer a federally-qualified HMO as a health insurance alternative to their employees.   Page 10-12

* definition only, term not found in text

E

EARNED INCOME
Gross salary, wages and commissions resulting from employment. Earned income does not include income from investments, rents, annuities, or insurance policies (unearned income).
Page 11-4

EFFECTIVE DATE
See *Policy Date*.

ELIGIBILITY PERIOD
In group life and health insurance, a limited period of time during which members may enroll in the group plan.
Page 16-11

ELIMINATION PERIOD
In a Disability Income policy, a stated period of time beginning at the onset of the insured's disability during which no income benefits will be paid. It is a deductible expressed in time rather than in dollars. For example, if Joe has a 30 day Elimination Period and he is disabled for a total of three months, then he would be eligible for a total of two months of disability income benefits. Also called a *Waiting Period*.
Page 10-7, 11-8

ENDORSEMENT
See *Rider*.

ENDOW
A life insurance policy is said to endow when its cash value equals the face amount, and the policyowner receives, in cash, the face amount. Whole Life policies are normally designed to endow when the insured reaches age 100.
Page 4-16

ENDOWMENT POLICY
A form of life insurance which offers death protection for a stated period of time (the endowment period), and which also accumulates cash value. Endowment policies are designed so that the cash value will equal the face amount at the end of the endowment period. If the insured dies during the endowment period, the policy matures and the death benefit is paid. If the insured does not die, but lives to the end of the endowment period, then the policy matures and endows the face amount.
Page 4-17

ENHANCED ORDINARY LIFE
Also known as Economatic or Extra Ordinary Whole Life. Combines Whole Life and Term for a constant death benefit. Over time, dividends are used to purchase Single Premium Paid Up Adds to replace the Term portion.
Page 7-7

ENTIRE CONTRACT CLAUSE
An insurance policy provision stating that the policy and the application, if attached, constitute the entire agreement between the insurance company and the policyowner. No promises or special agreements of the agent can be part of the insurance company's obligation unless they are set out in writing as a part of the contract and signed by an executive officer of the company.
Page 5-5, 10-19

EQUITY INDEXED LIFE INSURANCE
Permanent insurance with cash value guaranteed to grow at a conservative rate but could show higher returns as it is linked with a public equity index like the S&P 500.
Page 7-19

ERISA (EMPLOYEE RETIREMENT INCOME SECURITY ACT)
A federal law governing the operation of most private pension and benefit plans. This law establishes guidelines for the management of pension funds. In insurance, this law allows employers to provide employee benefits like medical expense insurance with a self-funded plan or by banding together with other employers to do so. These plans can be either insured or uninsured.
Page 8-3, 16-6

ESTATE TAXES
See *Federal Estate Tax*.

ESTOPPEL
A legal principle based on fairness which prevents someone from enforcing a legal right he or she would otherwise have.
Page 2-18

EVIDENCE OF INSURABILITY
Any statement or proof of a person's physical or mental health, personal character, occupation, living habits, etc. affecting the insurance company's acceptance of an applicant /proposed insured. Also called *Proof of Insurability*.
Page 5-9

EXCLUSION RIDER
See *Impairment Rider*.

EXCLUSIONS
Losses that are not covered. Life insurance policies usually only exclude suicide, and then it is usually only temporarily excluded. Health insurance policies on the other hand typically contain many exclusions, such as losses due to pre-existing conditions, suicide, war, hernia, self-inflicted intentional injuries, pregnancy, etc.
Page 5-14, 10-24

EXECUTIVE BONUS PLAN
an arrangement by which an employer can provide life insurance for selected employees. The employee, usually a key executive, purchases a policy on his or her own life and names someone other than the employer as the beneficiary. The employer then pays a cash bonus to the executive each year in an amount equal to the premium.
Page 8-14

EXECUTIVE DEFERRED COMPENSATION
See *Deferred Compensation*.

EXECUTORY
A characteristic of certain types of contracts, such as insurance contracts, in which the execution or completion of the agreement takes place in the future. *

EXPENSE FACTOR
In calculating the gross premium, the insurance company must charge enough to cover costs such as agent commissions, company overhead costs, administration, and other costs of maintaining the business.
Page 3-12

EXPERIENCE RATING
In group health insurance, a review of the previous year's group claims experience (loss ratio) in order to establish premiums for the next period. The lower the claims experience, the lower next year's premium will be.
Page 10-14, 16-8

EXPIRATION DATE
The date when insurance coverage ends. Also called *Termination Date*.
Page 5-7, 5-8, 16-5

* definition only, term not found in text

EXPRESSED AUTHORITY

The power expressly or specifically granted in writing to the agent in the Agency Agreement. For contrast, see *Implied Authority* and *Apparent Authority*.   Page 2-21

EXTENDED TERM OPTION

In life insurance policies that have cash value, Extended Term is a non-forfeiture option which allows the policyowner to receive the equity of the policy in the form of Term insurance in the same face amount as the policy being surrendered. The length of the Extended Term is stated in the non-forfeiture table and is directly related to the amount of equity accumulated in the policy.   Page 6-10

EXTENSION OF BENEFITS

A provision in some states regarding a terminated group health policy which requires that any benefits being paid at termination continue until no longer necessary.   Page 17-3

F

FACE AMOUNT

In a life insurance policy, the amount payable in the event of death as stated on the policy face. The face amount will be decreased by any outstanding loan against the policy, and increased by any additional benefits payable such as accumulated dividends, paid-up additions, or multiple indemnity benefits.
                   Page 2-17, 4-5

FACILITY OF PAYMENT CLAUSE

A clause which allows the insurance company to pay the death benefit to someone who seems reasonably entitled in case there is no beneficiary named in the policy or all beneficiaries have predeceased the insured or the beneficiary cannot be located. The person reasonably entitled to receive the proceeds is typically the person who paid the funeral expenses.   Page 15-7

FACULTATIVE REINSURANCE

Reinsurance is negotiated on a policy by policy basis.   Page 1-8

FAIR CREDIT REPORTING ACT

A federal law whose purpose is to protect consumers in regards to their credit history. The Act requires written notification to an individual whose credit is to be investigated; sets out specific guidelines to the credit reporting agency concerning the collection and distribution of credit information; sets a limit on how long adverse information can be kept; and grants the consumer access to his or her information. Additionally, the consumer has the right to have incorrect information corrected.
                   Page 3-6

FAMILY INCOME POLICY

A policy which combines Decreasing Term and Whole Life to offer income protection and a death benefit in the event of the premature death of the breadwinner. The policy provides that if the insured dies within a specified period (say 20 years), the family will receive a stated amount of income from the date of death until the end of the specified period. At the end of that period, the Whole Life death benefit is paid to the beneficiary. For contrast, see *Family Maintenance Policy*.   Page 7-17

FAMILY INCOME RIDER

Same concept as the Family Income policy except that the Decreasing Term part of the coverage is written as a rider on a Whole Life policy rather than combining both coverages into the policy itself. Also see *Family Income Policy*.   Page 7-14

FAMILY MAINTENANCE POLICY

This policy combines Level Term and Whole Life to offer income protection and a death benefit in the event of the premature death of the family breadwinner. The policy stipulates that if the insured dies within a stated period (say 20 years), the family will receive a monthly benefit from the date of death for the stated period of time. At the end of the monthly income benefit period, the face amount of the policy is paid to the beneficiary. For contrast, see *Family Income Policy*.

FAMILY MAINTENANCE RIDER

A Level Term rider added onto a Whole Life policy in order to achieve the characteristics of a Family Maintenance policy. Also see *Family Maintenance Policy*.

FAMILY (PROTECTION) POLICY

A policy which combines Convertible Term and Whole Life to provide a moderate amount of insurance on each member of the family. These coverages are packaged into units. Typically, a unit consists of $5,000 of Whole Life protection on the breadwinner, $1,250 Convertible Term coverage on the spouse and $1,000 of Convertible Term on each child. Of course, the family can buy as many units of coverage as desired.   Page 7-2

FEDERAL ESTATE TAX

A federal tax levied upon the property of an individual at death. The ownership of a life insurance policy, like the ownership of a house, constitutes property and is, therefore, subject to this tax. If a deceased insured owned the policy on his own life, then the value of that policy becomes part of his gross estate for federal estate tax purposes. The cash value of life insurance policies owned by the deceased on the lives of others is also taxable.
                   Page 5-11

FINANCIAL NEEDS APPROACH

A method of determining how much insurance a person should have. The focus of this approach is not on the proposed insured but on the needs of his surviving family.   Page 4-3

FIXED AMOUNT SETTLEMENT OPTION

A life insurance policy settlement option under which the beneficiary receives the death benefit proceeds in regular installments (usually monthly) in a specified dollar amount.
                   Page 6-16

FIXED DOLLAR OR FIXED AMOUNT ANNUITY

A Life Annuity that guarantees a fixed dollar payment at regular intervals during the lifetime of the annuitant. For contrast, see *Variable Annuity*.   Page 4-28

FIXED PERIOD SETTLEMENT OPTION

A life insurance policy settlement option in which the beneficiary receives an income for a stated period of time (fixed period), such as for 10 years, from the death benefit proceeds.
                   Page 6-16

FLAT DEDUCTIBLE

A set dollar amount deductible whereby every time there is a claim, the deductible must be satisfied.   Page 12-15

FLEXIBLE PREMIUM ANNUITY

A Deferred Annuity under which premiums may vary from year to year within stipulated limits; often used to fund an IRA.
                   Page 8-7

FOREIGN COMPANY

A company is considered to be a foreign company in any state other than the one in which it is incorporated or chartered, but within the United States or its possessions. For contrast, see *Alien Company* and *Domestic Company*.   Page 1-12

* definition only, term not found in text

FORTUITOUS
Unexpected or unforeseen; accidental; something which happens by chance. Insurance companies will take on fortuitous risks but reject risks of foreseeable or intentional losses.
Page 3-2

401(k) PLAN
A qualified retirement plan in which the employer generally matches the employee's contribution, and the amount contributed works like a salary cut for income tax purposes.
Page 8-14

401(k) ROTH PLAN
Works like a 401(k) with after-tax contributions.
Page 8-14

403B PLAN
See *Tax Sheltered Annuity.*

FRANCHISE INSURANCE
A group life or health insurance plan for very small groups (usually 3 to 10 members). With Franchise insurance, an individual policy is issued to each member of the group and individual underwriting is done. This type of insurance is generally written for groups that are too small to qualify for traditional group coverage. Formerly called *Wholesale Insurance* in the life insurance area.
Page 17-10

FRATERNAL BENEFIT SOCIETY
An organization which provides life and health insurance benefits to members of a fraternity or lodge. Fraternals usually receive favored treatment under regulatory and tax laws, but are operated much like a mutual insurance company.
Page 1-10

FRAUD
In general terms, any misrepresentation of a material fact, made knowingly and intentionally, with the intent that another person will rely on it and suffer financial injury as the result; an act of deceit or cheating.
Page 2-19

FREE LOOK PROVISION
A life or health insurance policy provision, usually required by law, which gives the policyowner a stated number of days to review a newly issued policy. If the policyowner is dissatisfied with the policy for any reason, he or she can return it to the insurance company within the stated period of time for a 100% refund. If the policy is returned, the coverage is cancelled from the date of issue and the company is not liable for any claims which occurred during that period of time. Also called *Right to Examine the Policy.*
Page 5-13, 10-23

FULLY INSURED
Under Social Security, an individual acquires the status of fully insured after working 40 quarters (10 years). In order to qualify for most Social Security programs (retirement benefits, disability benefits, and most survivor benefits), an individual must be fully insured. For contrast, see *Currently Insured.*
Page 8-13

FUNDED
In pension plans, one in which the funds necessary to meet the future financial obligations under the plan are accumulated in a reserve while the plan is in operation.
Page 8-7

FUTURE INCOME OPTION
A rider which may be available on a disability income policy which allows the insured to purchase additional amounts of disability income coverage in the future regardless of health (no proof of insurability). The specific benefit available and frequency of option dates varies greatly from one company to another.
Page 11-12

G

GATEKEEPER
The primary care physician in an HMO who decides if a member needs to see a specialist and, if so, which one.
Page 10-15

GENERAL ACCOUNT
An account which contains the regulated, or guaranteed, funds of a life insurance company. See *Separate Account.*
Page 4-32

GOVERNMENT INSURANCE
A general term referring to just about any insurance available through the government. Examples include *Social Security*, SGLI, CHAMPUS, Medicare and Flood insurance.
Page 1-11

GRACE PERIOD PROVISION
A period of time after the premium due date during which the policy remains in force. Losses occurring during the grace period are covered. The length of the grace period is determined by state law, and may vary depending on whether it is a life or health policy, and whether it is an individual or a group policy. Also see *Unpaid Premium Provision.*
Page 5-8, 15-12

GRADED PREMIUM WHOLE LIFE
A form of Whole Life with a redistribution of premium. Premium payments are lower than traditional Whole Life in the early years of the policy, and higher in the later years. The objective is to make the initial premiums more affordable during the early years of the policy and still offer permanent protection. Also called *Modified Life.*
Page 7-8

GROSS PREMIUM
In the calculation of premium rates, the gross premium is the estimated cost of claims (risk) plus the expenses (agent commissions, overhead, etc.) less interest (a credit because the premiums are paid in advance). Gross Premium = Risk + Expenses − Interest. For contrast, see *Net Premium.*
Page 3-12

GROUP
A number of people classified together by common risk factors such as age, sex, occupation, smoking habits, etc. In group insurance, the persons covered by the Master Policy.
Page 16-3

GROUP ANNUITY
See *Group Insurance.*

GROUP HEALTH INSURANCE
See *Group Insurance.*

GROUP INSURANCE
Life or health insurance which covers a group of persons under just one policy (called a *Master Contract*). The group must have been formed for a purpose other than to obtain insurance. State law determines what types of groups are eligible. Typical eligible groups include: employee groups, association groups, debtor groups, and labor union groups. Group insurance utilizes the same types of coverage as individual insurance: Term Life, Major Medical, Disability Income, AD&D, etc.
Page 16-3

GROUP LIFE INSURANCE
See *Group Insurance.*

* definition only, term not found in text

Glossary & Index

GROUP PERMANENT INSURANCE
A group plan in which the policy purchased is a Whole Life policy. During the employment years, the policy provides death benefits to the employee's survivors in the event of premature death. Upon retirement, the cash value of the policy can be used to provide retirement income to the employee.
Page 16-13

GROUP PRACTICE MODEL HMO
Under this arrangement the HMO practice contracts with an independent group practice (or clinic/hospital) to provide health care benefits for its subscribers.
Page 10-13

GROUP TERM POLICY
A group life policy written using Term life insurance. Also see *Group Insurance*.
Page 16-12

GUARANTEED CASH VALUE
In a Whole Life policy, the guaranteed amount payable to the policyowner upon surrender of the policy according to the policy's table of guaranteed values. The cash value table is scaled according to the number of years the policy is in force. Also see *Cash Value*.
Page 4-10

GUARANTEED INSURABILITY PROVISION
A provision which allows the policyowner to purchase additional insurance in specified amounts at various future dates without proof of insurability. Rates for the insurance purchased under this option are based on the insured's attained age at the time of purchase. This benefit may also be accomplished by means of a rider. In a disability income policy, this provision may also be called a *Future Income Option*.
Page 7-15, 7-20

GUARANTEED RENEWABLE
A form of renewability in health insurance which gives the policyowner the right to continue coverage until a stated date or age. During the policy period, the insurance company may not make any changes in the policy except for the premium charged. Premiums may be adjusted over time by class. This is usually the highest form of renewal available for medical expense policies. Also see *Noncancellable*.
Page 10-20

GUARANTY ASSOCIATION
A state-mandated association of all companies writing life and health insurance in a given state. Collectively, the Association endeavors to aid policyowners of insolvent companies up to specific dollar limits.
Page 5-3

GUERTIN LAWS
The nonforfeiture laws which have been standard in all states since 1947. (Named for Alfred Guertin, who was an actuary for the New Jersey Insurance Department and head of the NAIC committee developing the model bill.)
Page 6-6

H

HAZARD
Increases the likelihood that a peril will occur. If the peril is death, then a dangerous job would be a hazard.
Page 1-3

HEALTH INSURANCE
The generic name which has been accepted by the insurance industry as the broad term for the branch of insurance that includes all types of disability income, medical expense and the accidental death and dismemberment coverages due to accident or sickness. It is also known as accident and health insurance, sickness and accident insurance, etc.
Page 10-2

HEALTH INSURANCE PORTABILITY AND ACCOUNTABILITY ACT OF 1996 (HIPAA)
Federal law directed at small groups (2-50 insureds) which makes it easier for an individual to change from one group to another without losing benefits temporarily due to preexisting conditions exclusions in the new policy.
Page 17-7

HEALTH INSURING CORPORATIONS (HIC)
Another name for HMO's (in some states).
See *HMO*.

HEALTH MAINTENANCE ORGANIZATION (HMO)
A type of health care service provider. The classic HMO is a program that operates by hiring its own doctors to staff its own local clinics. The HMO approach emphasizes preventive health care, so routine physicals, immunizations, and office visits are covered and there are usually no deductibles or coinsurance.
Page 10-13

HEALTH POLICY
An insurance policy which indemnifies for loss (income and/or expenses) resulting from accidental bodily injury or sickness.
Page 10-2

HEALTH SAVINGS ACCOUNT
A cross between a Self-Funded Plan and a traditional Medical Expense Contract with a very high deductible. It can be sold on an individual (or family) basis or to groups.
Page 10-7

HOME HEALTH CARE
In most policies, intermediate or custodial care performed at the patient's own home.
Page 13-6, 18-7

HOSPICE CARE
A public agency or private organization that is primarily engaged in providing pain relief, symptom management, and supportive services to the terminally ill and their families.
Page 13-11

HOSPITAL EXPENSE POLICY
See *Basic Hospital Policy*.

HOSPITAL/SURGICAL EXPENSE POLICY
A basic medical expense health policy combining Basic Hospital coverage with Basic Surgical coverage into one policy. Also see *Basic Hospital* and *Basic Surgical*.
Page 12-3 to 12-5

HOSPITAL INDEMNITY
A medical expense plan that pays a stated amount for every day that the insured is in the hospital.
Page 14-3

HOSPITAL ROOM BENEFITS
In health insurance, the benefits payable up to a specified daily maximum for the purpose of paying hospital room and board charges.
Page 12-4, 12-5

HOSPITALIZATION POLICY
See *Basic Hospital Policy*.

HR-10 PLAN
See *Keogh Plan*.

HUMAN IMMUNODEFICIENCY VIRUS (HIV)
Special underwriting considerations. See *Acquired Immune Deficiency Syndrome (AIDS)*.

* definition only, term not found in text

HUMAN LIFE VALUE APPROACH
A method of determining how much insurance a person should have. The human life value approach totally focuses on what the proposed insured reasonably anticipates earning and contributing to his family.   Page 4-3

I

ILLEGAL OCCUPATION PROVISION
A health insurance optional provision which states that if the insured is injured as the result of engaging in an illegal occupation, then the insurance company does not have to pay the claim.   Page 15-9

IMMEDIATE ANNUITY
A Life Annuity contract under which the first income payment will be received by the annuitant immediately (usually one month, three months, six months, or 12 months) after the payment of the purchase price.   Page 4-26

IMPAIRMENT RIDER
A health insurance rider which excludes coverage for one part or system of the body on one specific insured. It can be written so that if the insured can reasonably go without treatment for a specified period of time, the company will drop the rider and the ailment will be covered. Also called an *Exclusion Rider*.
Page 10-25

IMPLIED AUTHORITY
Power that is not specifically granted to an agent in the agency agreement, but that an agent can imply or assume that he or she has. Implied authority is necessary to do the day-to-day activities of an agent. An example might be the power to take a personal check rather than cash in collecting the first premium. For contrast, see *Apparent Authority* and *Express Authority*.
Page 2-21

INCOME REPLACEMENT CONTRACT
A relatively new alternative to traditional disability income policies, Income Replacement is a policy under which the insurance company agrees to replace an insured's income up to a stated percentage, like 70% or 80%, if he or she suffers a loss of income due to a covered accident or sickness. Even if you are working full time doing all the same duties you did before, if you suffer a loss of income because of a covered accident or sickness, you get paid.   Page 11-14

INCONTESTABLE CLAUSE
A mandatory provision for life and health policies which limits the amount of time (usually one to three years) that an insurance company can rescind a policy or contest a claim due to misrepresentation or concealment on the application – except for nonpayment of premium (or fraud, in many medical expense policies). Also called *Time Limit On Certain Defenses* in health insurance.   Page 5-6, 15-3, 16-11

INCREASING TERM
Term life insurance coverage in which the face value increases periodically (each year or month) during the policy period. The premium for Increasing Term may be level, or it may increase over time along with the face amount. For contrast, see *Level Term* and *Decreasing Term*.   Page 4-8

INDEMNIFY
To make an insured financially whole again; to restore an insured who has suffered a loss to his or her original financial condition, but not to profit from the loss.   Page 2-17, 10-4

INDEMNITY
A fundamental insurance concept based on the premise that an insured is not supposed to profit from a loss. Otherwise, the insured would be inclined to incur losses rather than try to prevent them. This means that in general, in cases of double coverage or overinsurance, the company(s) involved will reduce the claim payment or exclude coverage.
Page 2-17

INDEPENDENT AGENT
An insurance agent who represents multiple companies. His agency agreement with each company does not restrict his ability to contract with other companies.   Page 3-13

INDEPENDENT PRACTICE ASSOCIATION MODEL HMO
The HMO contracts with independent providers throughout the coverage territory to provide health care benefits for its subscribers.   Page 10-13

INDIVIDUAL CERTIFICATE
See *Certificate of Insurance*.

INDIVIDUAL RETIREMENT ACCOUNT (IRA)
A qualified retirement plan for any individual with earned income; contributions to an IRA may be deductible for tax purposes (depending on income and whether the individual is in another qualified plan), and interest earned on an IRA is tax deferred until withdrawn. Along with the tax advantages, there are also restrictions, such as the amount of the deductible annual contribution, and when and for what purpose money can be withdrawn.   Page 8-10

INDUSTRIAL INSURANCE
Sometimes called Debit insurance. Insurance issued on individuals, usually without a medical examination, in small amounts with premiums payable weekly or monthly to an agent who calls at the home to collect the premium. Also see *Debit Agent*.   Page 4-3

INPATIENT HOSPITAL CARE
The reasonable charges that result from hospitalization in a semi-private room for medically necessary care. This includes room and board, regular nursing services, drugs taken in the hospital, medical tests (X-rays, lab, etc.), and the use of oxygen tents, wheelchairs, crutches, operating rooms and other supplies and services.   Page 13-10

INSIDE LIMITS
In health insurance policies, the maximum amount the policy will pay for specified types of medical expenses, such as $75 per day for a semi-private hospital room, $300 per claim for x-rays, $2,500 per policy for psychiatric care, etc.   Page 12-9

INSPECTION REPORT
A written report concerning an applicant's or an insured's habits, lifestyle, avocations, character, etc. Insurance companies may conduct their own inspection reports, or purchase them from outside companies (such as Equifax). The collection and retention of this type of information is governed by the Fair Credit Reporting Act.   Page 3-7

INSURABILITY
In life and health insurance, insurability is anything pertaining to an individual's acceptance for insurance . . . items which affect his or her health, susceptibility to injury, life expectancy, etc. These factors are considered in determining the risk. If an individual is uninsurable according to the company's underwriting standards, the company will reject the coverage.
Page 3-3, 3-7

* definition only, term not found in text

Glossary & Index

INSURABLE INTEREST

In life insurance, an insurable interest is generally a financial interest in the life of another person, but may also be an interest existing between family members. For example, a creditor has an insurable interest up to the amount of the debt in the debtor; business partners have an insurable interest in each other; an employer has an insurable interest in a key employee; also, there is an insurable interest in family relationships such as between spouses, and between parents and their children. An individual is considered to have an unlimited insurable interest in his or her own life. In order to purchase insurance on someone else, you must have an insurable interest in that person's life at the time of application. Page 2-7

INSURANCE

Insurance is the transfer of risk of financial loss from an individual to a company which, for consideration, assumes that risk for a stated period of time against a stated peril(s) up to a stated amount. Page 1-3

INSURANCE COMPANY

As commonly used, any corporation, association or fraternal benefit society which is primarily engaged in the business of furnishing insurance protection to the public. Also see *Insurance*. Page 1-7

INSURANCE POLICY

The printed form prepared by an insurance company to serve as the contract between the policyowner and the insurance company. The policy contains all the terms and conditions of the agreement between the parties to the contract. Page 2-1

INSURANCE PREMIUM

The designated amount of money payable by the policyowner to the insurance company which is required to keep the policy in force. Page 3-12

INSURANCE WITH OTHER INSURERS PROVISION

An optional provision found in individual medical expense health policies designed to limit double or multiple payment of benefits where the insured has several policies covering the same loss. Under the principle of indemnity, the insured is to receive only one payment for each claim, not multiple payments, which would let the insured profit from the loss.

Page 15-9

INSURED

The individual(s) covered by the policy of insurance. Page 2-7

INSURER

The company underwriting the insurance and assuming the risk. Page 1-7

INSURING CLAUSE

The Insuring Clause is the heart of an insurance policy because it contains the general promise to the policyowner and states, in general terms, the type of coverage provided and the policy limits. Page 5-10, 10-20

INTEGRATED DEDUCTIBLE

In a Supplementary Major Medical plan, a deductible positioned (integrated) between the Base Plan and Major Medical benefits. Under this arrangement, the deductible applied is the higher of (1) a substantial stated amount, like $1,000, or (2) whatever the Base Plan pays. Also called a *Variable Deductible*. Page 12-15

INTEREST FACTOR

One of the factors taken into account by an insurance company when calculating premiums rates. This is an estimate of the amount of money which will be earned by the company on the insured's invested premium payments. The other factors in calculating the gross premium are risk and expenses. Also see *Gross Premium* and *Net Premium*. Page 3-11

INTEREST OPTION

A settlement option under which the insurance company holds the insurance proceeds and invests them on behalf of the beneficiary, and the beneficiary receives the interest from the investment. The proceeds remain the property of the beneficiary and are ultimately paid in accordance with the settlement agreement. Page 6-15

INTEREST SENSITIVE WHOLE LIFE

Under this contract the company sets the initial premium based upon current assumptions about risk, interest and expense. If the actual experience differs from what is expected, then premiums can be raised or lowered. Additionally, cash value growth is projected using a rather conservative guarantee. If the company earns more it can pay higher than the guarantee - but never lower. Page 7-10

INTERIM INSURING AGREEMENT

An agreement separate from the policy which may be used to speed up coverage for the insured before actually receiving the policy. Interim Insuring Agreements require payment of the first premium, but *do not* guarantee that a policy will be issued. Examples of Interim Insuring Agreements include: *Conditional Receipt*, Acceptance Form of Receipt, and *30 Day Interim Term Receipt*. Page 2-11

INTERIM TERM RECEIPT

Term Life insurance issued to an applicant for a period of 30 or 60 days during which time the insurance company will either issue a permanent insurance policy or reject the application. It is one form of *Interim Insuring Agreement*. Page 2-11

INTERMEDIATE CARE

Nursing and rehabilitative care which is required occasionally and can only be performed by a skilled practitioner under doctor's orders. Page 13-5

INTESTATE

One who dies leaving no will; the condition of dying without a will. In general, life insurance policy death benefits are payable to the named beneficiary (or beneficiaries) regardless of whether the insured dies with or without a will. Page 5-17

INTOXICANTS AND NARCOTICS PROVISION

An optional provision found in individual health policies which states that the insurance company is not liable for any losses which occur while the insured is intoxicated or under the influence of drugs not prescribed by a physician. Page 15-10

INVITATION TO MAKE AN OFFER

An optional element of contract formation. An invitation to make an offer is not a true offer because some of the essential elements are missing. To have a true offer, all of the details must be complete, both parties must have full knowledge, and there must be consideration present. An invitation to make an offer is nothing but a signal that one party is open to offers. Page 2-9

IRA

See *Individual Retirement Account*.

* definition only, term not found in text

IRREVOCABLE BENEFICIARY
A beneficiary designation whereby the policyowner cannot change the designated beneficiary, surrender the policy, take out a policy loan, or exercise any other policy feature without the consent of the irrevocable beneficiary. Upon the death of the insured, the death benefit goes to the irrevocable beneficiary (or the irrevocable beneficiary's estate if he or she predeceased the insured, unless named on a reversionary basis). For contrast, see *Revocable Beneficiary*.   Page 5-23

J

JOINT AND SURVIVOR LIFE ANNUITY
An Annuity that makes payments to two (or more) annuitants throughout their lifetimes. When the first annuitant dies, the insurance company continues to make payments (in whole or in part) until the last annuitant has died.   Page 4-28, 6-18

JOINT LIFE
Two or more persons covered by one policy. Death benefits are paid upon the death of the first insured.   Page 7-9

JUMPING JUVENILE POLICY
Juvenile insurance on which the face amount automatically increases by a multiple (usually five), of the original face amount when the insured child reaches a predetermined age (like 18, 21, or 25). No proof of insurability or additional premium is required when the face amount is increased. Sometimes called an Estate Builder policy. Also see *Juvenile Life*.
                    Page 7-10

JUVENILE LIFE
Life insurance policies written on the lives of children within specified age limits (usually under age 15), generally with the parents or grandparents as the policyowners.   Page 7-10

K

KEOGH PLAN (HR-10)
A qualified retirement plan for self-employed professionals and their eligible employees. Contributions to a Keogh Plan are deductible from income (up to certain limits) and interest earned on a Keogh account is not subject to taxation until the money is withdrawn. Like IRA's, there is a penalty for early withdrawal of the money and other restrictions on the plan.
                        Page 8-15

KEY EMPLOYEE INSURANCE
Life or disability income insurance designed to indemnify a business against financial loss caused by the death or disability of a vital member of the firm; the business (employer) is the owner and beneficiary of the policy, and the key employee is the insured.   Page 8-2, 11-17

L

LAPSED POLICY
A policy whose coverage has terminated because of nonpayment of premiums.   Page 5-8, 15-5

LAW OF LARGE NUMBERS
A principle which states that the larger the size of a group, the more accurately the experience of that group can be predicted; a fundamental statistical principle for establishing the actuarial tables used by insurance companies to predict losses.
                        Page 1-6

LEGAL ACTION PROVISION
A mandatory health insurance policy provision which states that the policyowner must wait 60 days after submitting the Proof of Loss before suing the insurance company, and if the policyowner intends to sue, such action must be taken within three years.   Page 15-8

LEGAL CAPACITY
The capacity to bind oneself contractually, i.e., being of legal age, sane, and sober. An individual with legal capacity is considered a legally competent party.   Page 2-6

LEGAL GUARDIAN
An adult who has been charged with looking after the legal affairs of a minor or an incompetent.   Page 2-7

LEGAL PURPOSE
An essential element of any contract. The purpose of the contract itself must be legal. To eliminate the possibility that the insurance contract be misused, two reasonably simple safeguards have been built into the laws governing the formation of an insurance contract. These are *Insurable Interest* and *Consent*.
                        Page 2-7

LEGAL RESERVE
In life insurance, the amount of money that must be set aside by the company each year to fund future claims and to offset the increased risk as the insured's age advances. Minimum reserve levels are established by state law.   Page 1-9

LEGALLY COMPETENT PARTY
See *Legal Capacity*.

LEVEL PREMIUM
An insurance premium which remains fixed throughout the life of a policy.   Page 4-5

LEVEL TERM POLICY
Term Life coverage in which the face value remains unchanged from the date of issue to the date the policy expires. For contrast, see *Increasing Term Policy* and *Decreasing Term Policy*.
                        Page 4-6

LICENSE
With respect to an insurance agent, certification issued by the appropriate state department of insurance that an individual is qualified to solicit insurance applications. License requirements vary according to state law. *

LICENSED COMPANY
A company duly authorized by a state insurance department to operate in that state. Also known as an *Admitted Company* or an *Authorized Company*.   Page 1-12

LIFE ANNUITY
An annuity that promises to pay a guaranteed income for life.
                        Page 4-26

LIFE ANNUITY WITH PERIOD CERTAIN
A Life Annuity contract providing income to the annuitant for at least a definite and specified period of time, such as 10 years, with payment going to a designated beneficiary if the annuitant dies before the end of the specified period. If the original annuitant is still alive at the end of the designated period, annuity payments continue until the annuitant's death. In life insurance, as a settlement option, this annuity is called *Life Income with Period Certain*.   Page 4-28, 6-16

* definition only, term not found in text

LIFE INCOME OPTION
In life insurance, one of the optional modes of settlement under which the proceeds of the policy may be taken in the form of an annuity payable to the beneficiary for life. Also see *Straight Life Annuity*.   Page 6-17

LIFE INCOME WITH PERIOD CERTAIN OPTION
See *Life Annuity With Period Certain*.

LIFE INSURANCE
A contract (policy) under which an insurance company agrees to pay a stated amount to a beneficiary upon the death of the insured.   Page 1-4, 4-1

LIFE INSURANCE COMPANY
An organization chartered by a state for the purpose of furnishing life insurance protection and annuities. Many life insurance companies are also chartered to issue health insurance.
                    Page 1-7

LIFE PAID-UP AT AGE _____ POLICY
A Whole Life policy in which premiums are paid for a designated period of time rather than for the whole of life; a limited-pay Whole Life policy. The coverage is for life, but the premiums are paid for a designated period. If a 40-year-old man bought a Life Paid-Up at Age 65 policy, he would pay premium for 25 years and enjoy coverage for life. Another way of expressing this same policy is "25-Pay Life."   Page 4-14

LIFETIME EXTENSION
A disability income policy rider which extends the income benefits for total disability until death as long as the insured becomes disabled before some limiting age.   Page 11-13

LIFETIME MAXIMUM BENEFIT
Under Major Medical policies, the maximum dollar benefit that each insured is entitled to receive under the policy for expenses incurred for all diseases or injuries suffered during his or her lifetime.   Page 12-10

LIMITED ASSIGNMENT
See *Temporary Assignment*.

LIMITED HEALTH INSURANCE POLICY
A health insurance policy which provides protection against specifically designated accidents or a specific illness. For example, a Cancer policy is similar to a Major Medical policy, but it limits coverage to one specific illness – cancer. Also see *Limited Policies*.   Page 13-15, 14-1

LIMITED-PAY WHOLE LIFE POLICY
A permanent life insurance policy for which premiums are paid for a specified number of years or to a specified age of the insured. Limited-Pay policies can be expressed as ___-Pay Life or Life Paid at Age ___.   Page 4-14

LIMITED POLICIES
Health insurance policies which restrict benefits to specified accidents or diseases. Examples of limited policies are travel accident policies, dread disease policies, and ticket insurance. Also see *Limited Health Insurance Policies*.   Page 13-15, 14-1

LIVING BENEFIT OPTION
A life insurance benefit which pays a portion (up to 50%) of the face amount to the insured/owner prior to death.   Page 6-17

LIVING DEATH (DISABILITY)
This sounds worse than death and it probably is. If you become disabled, you have not one problem, but several. Your income stops, your normal expenses continue, and on top of it all, you have a new layer of expenses in the form of medical bills. Disability Income policies can replace lost income and Medical Expense policies can pay for medical bills.   Page 1-5

LLOYD'S OF LONDON
An English institution within which individual underwriters or groups of individuals accept insurance risks. Lloyd's provides the support facilities for such activities and is not, in itself, an insurance company.   Page 1-7

LOAN VALUE
In life insurance, the cash value which has built up in the policy and which can be borrowed from the policy by the policyowner. If the policy matures or is surrendered when there is an outstanding loan against the policy, this amount (plus interest) is deducted from the amount payable.   Page 5-11

LONG-TERM CARE INSURANCE
Long-term care policies provide coverage for medically necessary services which a person receives in a setting other than a hospital, such as a nursing home or, perhaps, even one's own home. Long-term care policies are generally considered to be health insurance, but a life insurance policy can also provide long-term care benefits through its policy provisions or by means of a rider. The NAIC defines long-term care as any insurance policy (group or individual) or rider designed to provide coverage for not less than 12 consecutive months for each covered person for necessary diagnostic, preventive, therapeutic, rehabilitative, maintenance or personal care services provided in a setting other than an acute care unit of a hospital. Also see *Nursing Home Insurance*.   Page 13-2

LONG TERM DISABILITY INCOME (LTD)
Usually, a disability income policy with a benefit period of two years or more (in group policies) or five years or more (for individual policies). For contrast, see *Short Term Disability Income*.   Page 11-7

LOSS
A financial hurt; the basis for a claim under an insurance policy.   Page 3-2

LOSS OF INCOME POLICY or LOSS OF TIME POLICY
See *Disability Income Insurance*.

LOSS RATIO
The cost of claims paid as compared to the premiums collected for the coverage.   Page 13-7, 13-13

M

MAJOR MEDICAL EXPENSE INSURANCE
A health policy designed to reimburse the policyowner for medical expenses incurred by the insured. Generally, Major Medical insurance provides benefit payments for 80 percent of all reasonable and customary medical expenses which exceed the deductible (generally in the $500 to $5,000 range), up to the maximum limit of liability and within the time period provided by the policy.   Page 12-7

MAJOR MEDICAL POLICY
See *Major Medical Expense Insurance*.

MANAGED CARE
Approaches to health care that attempt to minimize expense. Can include *HMO's*, *PPO's* and *Self-Funded Plans*.
                    Page 10-15

* definition only, term not found in text

MASTER CONTRACT

In group insurance, only one policy is issued and it is called the Master Contract. It contains all the provisions, benefits, and conditions of the agreement. Individuals covered by the group plan do not receive a policy; they receive Individual Certificates (Certificates of Insurance).   Page 16-7

MATERIAL FACT

A significant statement of fact given to an insurance company by an applicant. A fact is material if the company would have rejected the risk or charged the applicant a different premium if it had known the truth about the statement.   Page 2-6

MATERNITY BENEFITS

Medical expense health insurance benefits which cover all or a portion of the costs arising from pregnancy and childbirth. In individual health policies, maternity benefits are frequently excluded from coverage.   Page 17-1, 15-11

MATURE

In life insurance, the time when the policy's face amount becomes payable. Term Life insurance matures only upon the death of the insured during the term. A Whole Life policy matures in one of two ways: (1) upon the death of the insured; or (2) when the cash value equals the face value of the policy (normally at age 100).   Page 4-9, 4-16

MEDICAID

A joint federal-state welfare (assistance) program, administered by states and subsidized by federal government grants, under which various medical expenses will be paid for low income needy people who qualify. Generally, those who qualify are persons whose income and resources are below the poverty limits set by state law.   Page 13-8

MEDICAL EXAMINATION

The physical examination of a proposed insured, usually conducted by a licensed physician or other medical examiner; the results of the medical examination become part of the application, which is attached to the policy and made part of the contract.   Page 3-6

MEDICAL EXAMINER

In life and health insurance, a doctor who examines proposed insureds and claimants for the insurance company.
                                                        Page 2-20

MEDICAL EXPENSE INSURANCE

One of the two major categories of health insurance (the other is disability income insurance). Medical expense policies reimburse the policyowner for medical expenses such as hospital and doctor bills. There are various types of medical expense plans, including *Basic Hospital, Basic Medical, Basic Surgical, Major Medical, Comprehensive Major Medical* and *Dental*. For contrast, see *Disability Income Insurance*.
                                                        Page 12-1

MEDICAL INFORMATION BUREAU (MIB)

The MIB is an organization that stores and makes available to insurance companies key underwriting information on applicants for life or health insurance. The major purpose is to help guard against concealment or fraud by new applicants. Member companies check with the MIB to uncover pertinent health facts discovered by another company on an applicant.
                                                    Page 3-4, 5-20

MEDICARE

A federal medical expense health insurance program primarily for persons age 65 and older. Medicare consists of Hospital Insurance protection (Part A) and Medical Insurance protection (Part B). Medicare is administered by the Center for Medicare & Medicaid Services. Social Security Administration offices take applications for Medicare and provide general information about the program.   Page 13-9

MEDICARE PART C (ADVANTAGE)

Expands health care options for Medicare beneficiaries. Instead of receiving benefits through the traditional Medicare program, recipients can choose to obtain their benefits through an HMO, PPO, an HSA and several other managed care plan types.   Page 13-12

MEDICARE SUPPLEMENT POLICY

A Medicare Supplement Policy (MSP) is an individual or group medical expense health policy which is designed primarily as a supplement to the hospital, medical or surgical expense reimbursements available under the federal Medicare program. For example, an MSP could pay for deductibles, coinsurance, and exclusions under Medicare. MSP's, however, must not duplicate the benefits provided by Medicare. MSP's are heavily regulated by state law.   Page 13-13

MEDIGAP COVERAGE
See *Medicare Supplement Policies*.

MET/MEWA
See *Multiple Employer Trust*.

MILITARY SERVICE CLAUSE

A clause contained in some life and health policies that excludes losses resulting from war (declared or undeclared) or which occur while the insured is on active duty in the Armed Services. Most life policies issued today contain no military service clause.   Page 3-9, 5-14

MINOR BENEFICIARY

A beneficiary who is under legal age; when there is a minor who is to receive proceeds under a policy, it is generally best that a trust, parent, or a legal guardian be named to accept the benefits on behalf of the minor.   Page 5-20

MISCELLANEOUS BENEFITS
See *Ancillary Benefits*.

MISREPRESENTATION

A false statement intentionally made; a lie. If an applicant for insurance misrepresents a material fact, the insurance company may cancel the policy or deny payment of a claim under the policy for up to a specified period of time such as two or three years (dictated by state law). An agent who misrepresents a policy, a company, a competitor, etc. may be guilty of violating the law and found guilty of a misdemeanor and subject to penalties such as fines, jail, loss of license, etc. as prescribed by state law. Also see *Concealment*.   Page 2-6

MISSTATEMENT OF AGE PROVISION

A provision in most life and health policies setting forth the action to be taken by the insurance company if a misstatement of age is discovered after the policy is issued. The usual procedure is to adjust the benefit payable of the policy to what the premiums paid would have purchased had the correct age originally been stated.   Page 5-7, 15-9, 16-12

* definition only, term not found in text

MISSTATEMENT OF SEX PROVISION
A life insurance policy provision which states that, in cases of misstatement of gender on the application, the insurance company can adjust the benefits payable under the policy to reflect the premiums paid using the correct information concerning the insured's gender. Page 5-7

MODE
See *Premium Mode.*

MODIFIED ENDOWMENT
The 1988 tax revenue act proscribes that any cash value policy which builds cash value faster than a Seven-Pay Whole Life contract is deemed to be a Modified Endowment. All withdrawals must be first made with untaxed dollars and al withdrawals prior to age 59 1/2 are subject to a 10% tax penalty. Page 4-18

MODIFIED LIFE
A form of Whole Life insurance with reduced premiums during the early years but higher than regular rates during the later years. Modified Life can be constructed by combining Term and Whole Life, or by simply redistributing the premium of a Whole Life policy. Page 7-7

MOODY'S INVESTORS SERVICE
One of the best known bond rating agencies in the United States; Moody's publishes manuals, reports, and statistics on the financial ratings of various bonds, securities, and corporations. Page 1-13

MORAL HAZARDS
Intentional losses, such as fraudulent claims, which companies try to screen out with careful underwriting, probationary periods, exclusions and other underwriting devices. Page 1-3

MORALE HAZARDS
When an insured ignores the financial impact of a loss because the company pays for it. Companies control this hazard with deductibles, coinsurance and other policy limitations. Page 1-3

MORBIDITY
The rate of disease or probability of accident or illness. Morbidity is part of the risk which insurance companies take into account in calculating health insurance premium rates. Page 3-2

MORBIDITY TABLE
A statistical table which is used to estimate the amount of loss due to accidents and sickness of persons at different ages. Morbidity tables are used in the computation of health insurance rates, similarly to how the mortality tables are used in life insurance underwriting. Page 3-2

MORTALITY
The rate of death. Mortality is part of the risk which insurance companies take into account in calculating life insurance premium rates. Page 3-2

MORTALITY SAVINGS
The savings which occur when the actual losses are less than the amount estimated from the mortality table used. When the actual losses (claims) are less than estimated, then it is said that the company had a savings in mortality. Page 6-2

MORTALITY TABLE
A statistical table which, based on age and sex, states the life expectancy of persons and the percentage of persons in any given group who are expected to die. Mortality tables are used in the computation of life insurance rates. Page 3-2

MORTGAGE PROTECTION INSURANCE
A type of Decreasing Term insurance designed to correspond directly to the amount of outstanding loan and length of time remaining on a mortgage. If the insured dies during the mortgage period, the outstanding balance is paid by the insurance company to the beneficiary or directly to the mortgage company. Also called *Mortgage Redemption.* Page 4-7

MORTGAGE REDEMPTION INSURANCE
See *Mortgage Protection Insurance.*

MULTIPLE EMPLOYER TRUST
Many small groups, particularly small business owners and their employees, need life and health insurance, but have too few people in the business to qualify for true group insurance. To meet this need, some states allow the formation of Multiple Employer Trusts (MET's), which is a group formed by banding together several small business owners and their employees for the purpose of purchasing life and health insurance at more favorable rates. Also called *MEWA's.* Page 16-6

MULTIPLE INDEMNITY RIDER
A life insurance provision which states that some or all of the benefits under a policy will be increased by a stated multiple (such as double or triple indemnity) in the event the insured dies an accidental death. Also see *Double Indemnity Rider.* Page 7-15

MULTIPLE-OPTION PLAN
See *Point of Service (POS) Plan.*

MUTUAL COMPANY
An insurance company which has no capital stock or stockholders, and is essentially owned by its policyowners. It is managed by a board of directors chosen by the policyowners. Any earnings in addition to those necessary for the operation of the company are returned to the policyowners in the form of policy dividends (return of unneeded premium). For contrast, see *Stock Company.* Page 1-9

N

NAIC
See *National Association of Insurance Commissioners.*

NASD
See *National Association of Securities Dealers.*

NATIONAL ASSOCIATION OF INSURANCE COMMISSIONERS (NAIC)
An association made up of the state insurance commissioners; the NAIC is active in resolving insurance regulatory problems and in the formation and recommendation of model legislation and regulations (much of which is designed to gain uniformity from state to state to simplify marketing of insurance on a regional and national basis). Page 15-1

NATIONAL ASSOCIATION OF SECURITIES DEALERS (NASD)
A national organization, operated under the supervision of the Securities and Exchange Commission (SEC), which was established to represent the securities industry with the SEC; the NASD sets high moral and ethical standards in securities trading, serves as a liaison between government and investors, and establishes and enforces rules in securities trading. Page 4-38, 9-9

* definition only, term not found in text

NATIONAL HEALTH INSURANCE

Any system of socialized health insurance benefits covering all or nearly all citizens, established by federal law, administered by the federal government, and subsidized by taxation. Examples are *Medicare* and *Medicaid.* *

NATURAL GROUP

For purposes of group insurance coverage, a natural group is defined as a group organized for some purpose other than obtaining group insurance, and which has been in existence for a specified period of time (usually two years). Page 16-3, 16-9

NET PREMIUM

In the calculation of premium rates, the net premium is the estimated cost of claims (risk) less interest to be earned (a credit because the premiums are paid in advance). Expenses are not calculated into a net premium. Net Premium = Risk – Interest. For contrast, see *Gross Premium*. A second meaning of net premium, sometimes used by policyowners, is the gross premium less any policy dividends. Page 3-11

NO LOSS ~ NO GAIN

State laws regarding individual and group health policies which require that new policies provide the same benefits from the onset that would have been available from the original policy. Page 12-18 17-3

NON-ADMITTED COMPANY

A company not licensed to do business in a particular state. Also called an Unauthorized Insurer. For comparison, see *Admitted Company*. Page 1-12

NONCANCELLABLE

A form of renewal in a health insurance policy which not only allows the policyowner to keep the coverage in force until a stated date or age, but which also guarantees the premium. During the policy period, the insurance company has no unilateral right to make any changes, or to cancel the policy as long as the premiums are paid. Also called *Noncancellable* and *Guaranteed Renewable*. Also see *Guaranteed Renewable*. Page 10-21

NONCONTRIBUTORY PLAN

A group insurance plan in which the employer pays the entire premium for insurance coverage and the employee/insured pays nothing. For contrast, see *Contributory Plan*. Page 16-10

NONFORFEITURE OPTIONS, PROVISIONS OR VALUES

In life insurance, nonforfeiture values are benefits available by law to the policyowner should he/she choose to stop paying for the policy and surrender it to the company. The nonforfeiture options usually available are: *Cash, Reduced Paid-Up Insurance*, and *Extended Term Insurance*. Page 6-7

NONPARTICIPATING INSURANCE POLICY

An insurance policy, usually issued by a stock company, which does not pay policy dividends, and under which the policyowner is not entitled to share in any surplus of the company. For contrast, see *Participating Insurance Policy*. Page 1-8

NON-QUALIFIED RETIREMENT PLANS

A retirement plan that does not qualify for special tax treatment by the Federal government. Page 8-6

NONRENEWABLE TERM RENEWAL PROVISION

See *Term Renewal Provision*.

NOT-FOR-PROFIT ORGANIZATION

An organization established solely for charitable, educational, humanitarian, religious, or other such limited purposes, and not as a profit-making business. Examples include schools, colleges, churches, and hospitals. Also known as a nonprofit organization (501C-3 organization). Page 8-5

NOTICE OF CLAIM PROVISION

A mandatory health insurance policy provision which states that the policyowner must give written notice to the insurance company that a loss has occurred within 20 days of the loss, or as soon thereafter as is reasonably possible. Page 15-6

NURSING HOME INSURANCE

Generally, a health insurance coverage designed to pay a stated amount for time spent in a nursing home, or to pay for medically necessary services received in a setting other than a hospital, such as a nursing home or, perhaps, even one's own home. Nursing home insurance is usually classified as either Long-Term (Custodial or Residential) Care, or Short Term (Convalescent) Care. Also see *Long-Term Care Insurance*. Page 13-2

O

OCCUPATION PROVISION

See *Change of Occupation Provision*.

OFFER

A necessary element in the formation of a contract. As applied to life and health insurance, the legal offer may be made by (1) the applicant, by submitting an application and paying the first premium, or (2) the company, where no premium payment has been submitted with the application, by delivery of the policy as applied for and request for premium payment. Page 2-3

OLD AGE SURVIVORS DISABILITY INSURANCE (OASDI)

Social Security retirement, survivors and disability insurance (OASDI) is part of the Social Security Act and is administered by the Social Security Administration. It provides what are commonly called "social security benefits" to workers who are retired, disabled workers, and survivors of deceased workers. Also see *Social Security Act*. Page 8-10

OPEN PANEL

If an HMO contracts with a Group Practice to provide medical services for its members or subscribers, the group practice may retain the right to treat patients who are *not* members of the HMO. See *Closed Panel*. Page 10-12

OPTIONAL PROVISIONS

See *Uniform Policy Provisions Law*.

OPTIONALLY RENEWABLE

A health insurance form of renewability in which the insurance company reserves the right to terminate the coverage at any anniversary date, or in some cases, at any premium due date, but does not have the right to terminate coverage between such dates, i.e., the policy is renewable at the company's option, not the policyowner's. Page 10-31

ORDINARY LIFE

Ordinary Life is one method of marketing life insurance. It is essentially individual life insurance whereby an agent collects the first premium with the application and then premiums after the first are mailed directly to the home office of the company that issued the policy. Ordinary Life has traditionally included *Term, Whole Life,* and *Endowment* insurance. Sometimes, *Continuous*

* definition only, term not found in text

Premium Whole Life (Straight Life) is inaccurately referred to as Ordinary Life.   Page 4-4

OTHER INSURANCE PROVISIONS
Optional individual health insurance policy provisions that address the problem of duplicate coverages . . . the policyowner having more than one policy covering the loss, either from the same company or with two or more companies. These provisions state that in such a situation, the insurance company will reduce the benefit payable on a pro rata basis and return the appropriate amount of premium. This is consistent with the principle of indemnity . . . to make the insured whole again, but not to let the insured profit from having a loss. This situation is handled differently with group medical expense coverage. See *Coordination of Benefits Clause.*   Page 15-9

OUTPATIENT
A person who receives diagnosis or treatment at a hospital or medical facility but is not admitted to the hospital as an overnight patient.   Page 10-13

OVERHEAD
Financial charges of a fairly fixed nature which do not vary substantially with the volume of sales activity. Rent, utility bills, insurance, employees' salaries, and some taxes are examples of overhead items.   Page 11-17

OVERINSURANCE
An excessive amount of insurance carried by an insured, which might create a temptation to deliberately cause a loss or prolong a disability. While insurance companies cannot control the amount of insurance a policyowner purchases, health insurance companies may reduce the payment of a claim in situations of overinsurance. This is handled with certain optional policy provisions such as the *Average Earnings Clause* and *Other Insurance* provisions.   Page 15-9

OWN OCCUPATION (OWN OCC)
See *Your Occ.*

OWNER
In life and health insurance, the owner is the person who has all the rights contained in the policy, such as the right to name and change beneficiaries, the right to borrow against the policy, the right to cash in the policy, the right to assign the ownership to another person, etc. The owner is designated on the application by the applicant and may or may not be the insured. Also called the *Policyowner.*   Page 5-9, 15-7

OWNERSHIP PROVISION
A life insurance policy provision stating that during the insured's lifetime, the rights and privileges of the policy belong exclusively to the owner. The owner may or may not be the insured.   Page 5-18

P

PAID-UP ADDITIONS
A dividend option in which fully-paid additional insurance of the same type as the original policy is added to the policy. It is as if the dividend were used as a single premium to purchase as much insurance as possible of the same type as the original at the insured's attained age.   Page 6-5

PAID-UP AT AGE _____ LIFE POLICY
See *Limited-Pay Whole Life Policy.*

PARTIAL DISABILITY
In health insurance, a transitional benefit for an insured who has been totally disabled and can return to work, but cannot resume all of his or her duties or cannot yet work full-time. Typically, the partial disability benefit is 50% of the total disability benefit for a period not to exceed six months. The use of this benefit is generally on the decline. For contrast, see *Total Disability* and *Residual Disability.*   Page 11-9

PARTIAL SURRENDER
Under a UL policy, loans can work just as they do with other cash value policies, it is also possible to make a cash withdrawal from a UL policy that neither has to be repaid nor requires the payment of interest. Principle comes out first therefore the tax ramifications are minimal.   Page 9-15

PARTICIPATING INSURANCE POLICY
A plan of insurance normally issued by a mutual company or a fraternal benefit society under which the policyowner is paid policy dividends, which are a return of unneeded premium (overcharge). A company which issues this type of policy is a *Participating Company.* For contrast, see *Nonparticipating Insurance Policy.*   Page 1-9

PAYMENT OF CLAIMS PROVISION
A required individual health insurance policy provision which states to whom the insurance company will pay any claims.   Page 15-7

PAYOR BENEFIT RIDER
A rider usually attached to a life insurance policy written on the life of a child. This rider waives the right to premium should the person paying for the policy, e.g., the parent, die or become disabled.   Page 7-13

PAYROLL DEDUCTION
In insurance, an arrangement whereby the premium an employee pays for insurance is deducted directly from his or her paycheck and forwarded to the insurance company by the employer. Also used to indicate similar handling of an employee's contributions to an employee benefit plan. *

PENSION PLAN
A plan under which an employer (or other organization such as a labor union) provides retirement benefits for employees and both employer and employee benefit by way of favorable tax treatment.   Page 8-7

PER CAUSE DEDUCTIBLE
With a per cause deductible, a separate deductible is charged for each cause that necessitates medical treatment. If all the claims stem from the same cause, however, only one deductible applies (subject to other policy limitations, such as the Accumulation Period, Benefit Period, and Per Cause Maximum).   Page 12-8

PER CAUSE MAXIMUM
A limitation on a medical expense policy in that once a specified dollar limit has been reached for expenses stemming from one cause, the policy pays no more benefits for losses from that particular cause. *

PER DIEM
Per day, or a daily charge. *

PERCENTAGE PARTICIPATION
See *Coinsurance.*

* definition only, term not found in text

PERIL
A cause of loss. In life insurance, the peril is death; in health, there are two perils: accident and sickness. Page 1-2

PERIOD CERTAIN
A specified period of time. Also see *Life Annuity with Period Certain*. Page 4-28

PERMANENT AND TOTAL DISABILITY
A continuous disability which meets the definition of total disability as stated in the policy (e.g., Your Occ, Any Occ, Presumptive Total Disability). Page 11-6

PERMANENT INSURANCE
Generally refers to Whole Life insurance. The insured is guaranteed the right to keep the policy in force for his or her entire life as long as the premiums are paid, and the policy builds cash value. Page 4-10

PERMANENT PARTIAL DISABILITY
The insured is only partially disabled, but will be that way forever. Page 11-9

PERSISTENCY
The tendency of a policy to stay in force, i.e. group policies typically have greater persistency than individual policies. Page 16-10

PERSONAL CONTRACT
Insurance is generally considered to be a personal contract. I cannot insure your life because I have no financial interest in you life. Page 2-17

PHYSICAL DEATH
A breadwinner dies during the earning period of life. All life policies are designed to provide for the contingency of premature physical death. Page 1-4

PHYSICAL EXAMINATION AND AUTOPSY PROVISION
A required health insurance policy provision which states that the company has the right to physically examine the claimant in the event of a medical expense, disability or dismemberment claim, and unless prohibited by state law, the right to conduct an autopsy on the deceased insured in the event of an accidental death claim. Page 15-7

PHYSICAL HAZARDS
Tangible circumstances such as a heart condition or a high-risk hobby which might cause a company to decline or charge more to insure a risk. Page 1-3

POINT OF SERVICE (POS) PLAN
Plan where the insured joins the HMO. If for some reason they wish to use a doctor who is not part of the HMO, they may do so but will pay a higher coinsurance percentage for the privilege. Page 10-19

POLICY
In insurance, a written contract between the insurance company and the policyowner. The policy, the riders, and a copy of the application, if attached, constitute the entire contract of insurance. Page 2-1, 2-3

POLICY ANNIVERSARY
In insurance, the anniversary date of issuance of a policy, as shown on the policy. This date is important in exercising policy benefits, such as purchasing additional coverage. *

POLICY CHANGE PROVISION (CONVERSION OPTION)
A life insurance policy provision which states that the policyowner has the right to change from a lower premium form of insurance, such as Term, to a higher premium form, such as Whole Life, without evidence of insurability. This provision also states that to change from a higher premium form to a lower premium form does require proof of insurability. Page 5-10

POLICY DATE
The date on which insurance coverage becomes effective, as shown in the policy. Also see *Termination Date*. Page 2-13, 4-4

POLICY DIVIDEND
See *Dividend*.

POLICY FEE
A small annual charge (or sometimes a one-time charge) to the policyowner, in addition to the premium, which covers the cost of issuing the policy and/or the cost of policy administration, such as collecting the premium and paying policy taxes. *

POLICY LOAN PROVISION
A provision in cash value life policies which states that the policyowner has the right to borrow up to the amount of the cash value in the policy without cancelling or surrendering the policy. The insurance company, however, may charge interest on the loan in advance. Page 5-11

POLICY PERIOD
In insurance, the period of time during which the policy remains in force. Page 4-5. 10-17

POLICY SUMMARY
Provides specific information that highlights the critical parts of the policy issued by your company and provides an easy way for you to review the coverages, riders, exclusions and costs of your product. Page 2-16

POLICY YEAR
In insurance, a 12-month period which begins on the effective date of coverage. Page 6-4

POLICYOWNER
See *Owner*.

POST MORTEM EXPENSES
Final expenses, funeral, ambulance, hospital and cemetery expenses. Page 4-3

PREADMISSION REVIEW
See *Utilization Review*.

PREDETERMINED LIMIT
The maximum the insurance company will pay for the loss; in Life Insurance this is the death benefit or face amount. Page 1-6

PREEXISTING CONDITION
A medical condition which exists on the policy's effective date and during the past (period of time dictated by state law) either caused you to receive medical advice or treatment, or caused symptoms for which an ordinarily prudent person would seek medical advice or treatment. The policy generally excludes coverage for a preexisting condition for some specified period of time. The time periods and the exact definition of a preexisting condition vary depending on state law and the type of policy. Page 10-25

* definition only, term not found in text

PREFERRED PROVIDER ORGANIZATION (PPO)

A health care plan under which the covered individual can choose the health care provider he or she wants. The PPO contracts with a large number of medical providers (hospitals, doctors, etc.) across a community and lists them. If the claimant utilizes a physician or hospital on the PPO's preferred list, benefits are structured somewhat as they would be with an HMO – small (if any) deductible, low cost sharing and some coverage for preventive care. However, the insured may choose medical providers not found on the preferred list and still have coverage. With this alternative, benefits are paid similarly to what the insurance companies or the Blues would pay on a Major Medical type contract – the claimant would be responsible for a deductible and about 20% of the costs after the deductible – plus some penalty for choosing an outside provider. PPO's can be *comprehensive* in nature or offer a *limited range of services*. Page 10-14

PREFERRED RISK

In life insurance, a person whose physical condition, occupation, mode of living and other characteristics indicate an above average chance for a long life. For contrast see *Standard Risk*. Page 3-10

PREMIUM

The payment required to keep an insurance policy in force. Premiums are paid in advance, and may be paid in a lump-sum payment or periodically. Also see *Premium Mode*. Page 3-12

PREMIUM DETERMINATION

Risk + Expenses - Interest = Gross Premium and Risk - Interest = Net Premium. Page 3-12

PREMIUM MODE

The frequency with which the policyowner elects to pay the premium, such as annually, semiannually, quarterly, or monthly (or weekly in Industrial insurance). Page 3-13

PREMIUM PAYMENT CLAUSE

A provision which states that premiums are payable in advance at the home office of the company. Generally, the agent should not accept premium payments except for the first, which is taken at the time of application. Page 5-6, 5-21

PREMIUM PAYMENT PERIOD

Under a Limited-Pay Whole Life policy, the number of years during which premiums are payable. For example, a 20-Pay Whole Life policy would have a premium payment period of 20 years. Page 4-13

PRESUMPTIVE TOTAL DISABILITY

A benefit included with most disability income policies in which you are automatically considered to be totally disabled (even if you can and are doing your job or any job) if sickness or injury results in the loss of (1) sight in both eyes, (2) hearing in both ears, (3) power of speech, or (4) use of any two limbs. Page 11-7

PRIMARY BENEFICIARY

The beneficiary who is first entitled to the proceeds of a policy upon the death of the insured. For contrast, see *Contingent Beneficiary*. Page 5-17

PRIMARY INSURANCE AMOUNT (PIA)

Under the federal Social Security Act, the PIA is the basic unit used to determine the amount of each monthly benefit payable for Social Security benefits. Page 8-11

PRINCIPAL SUM

In an Accidental Death and Dismemberment (AD&D) health policy, the amount payable for the accidental loss of life or of two primary body parts (hands, feet, eyes). Also see *Capital Sum*. Page 14-2

PRO RATA

In proportion; proportionately. Page 15-9

PROBATIONARY PERIOD

In health insurance policies, a specified period of time beginning on the policy's effective date (start date) during which there is no coverage. The main purpose of the Probationary Period is to screen out preexisting illness. In group insurance, the term Probationary Period is sometimes used to refer to the period of time a new employee must wait before he or she is eligible to join the group plan. Page 10-27

PROFIT SHARING PLAN

Similar in nature to a pension plan, but the employer is not required to make constant contributions every year - just regular and substantial contributions during years of profitability. Page 8-3

PROOF OF LOSS PROVISION

A required individual health insurance policy provision which states that the insured must submit the proof of loss (completed and signed claim form) to the insurance company within 90 days of the date of the loss. Page 15-6

PROSPECTIVE REVIEW

See *Utilization Review*.

PURE RISK

Inherent risk, insurable risk; only a chance for loss. Page 1-2

Q

QUALIFICATION PERIOD

In a disability income policy with a residual disability income benefit, the qualification period is a specified period of time which (1) modifies the elimination period by stating that the elimination period can be satisfied with just *partial disability*, and (2) states that the insured must be totally disabled for the length of the qualification period. In order to get residual disability benefits, the insured must go through both the elimination period and the qualification period, but the time periods can run concurrently. *

QUALIFIED RETIREMENT PLAN

A retirement plan which meets certain federal requirements and which qualifies for special tax treatment. The major requirements are that the plan (1) be for the benefit of employees or their beneficiaries, (2) not discriminate (such as in favor of highly compensated employees), (3) be in writing, (4) define the contributions or the benefits, and (5) be permanent. Contributions are deductible for income tax purposes (within certain limits) and the funds accumulate interest on a tax deferred basis. *Keogh Plans, IRA's, and 401(k) Plans* are examples of qualified retirement plans. Page 8-2

R

RATE

The cost of a given unit of insurance. In life insurance for example, it is generally expressed as the price per $1000 of coverage. In disability income insurance, it is usually the price of $100 per month benefit. The premium is the rate multiplied by the number of units of insurance purchased, plus a policy fee (if any), which is sometimes added to the initial premium payment. Also see *Premium* and *Policy Fee*. Page 3-12

* definition only, term not found in text

RATED POLICY

An insurance policy issued to a person who is a substandard risk and is billed at a premium rate which is higher than that charged for a standard risk.   Page 3-10

REBATE

In insurance, a portion of the agent's commission, or anything of value, given to a client as an inducement to buy insurance from that agent; sharing a commission with an unlicensed person. Rebates are illegal in most states, usually both for the agent to give and for the applicant to receive. *

RECIPROCAL

An unincorporated insurance company managed by an attorney-in-fact. The insureds are known as subscribers. From the insured's viewpoint, a Reciprocal Insurance Exchange functions much like a Mutual.   Page 1-10

RECURRENT DISABILITY PROVISION

In a disability income policy, a provision which states that a later, separate period of disability will be considered a continuation of a prior period of disability if it starts within six months after the end of the prior period of disability and is the result in whole or in part of the same or related injury or sickness. With the recurrent disability provision, the insured is not penalized for trying to go back to work.

Page 11-11

REDUCE RISK

By living a healthier lifestyle or by living and working under safer conditions.   Page 1-2

REDUCED PAID-UP INSURANCE

In life insurance, a nonforfeiture option under which the insured's cash value is used as a net single premium to purchase as much paid-up insurance of the same type as the original policy as is possible, given his or her attained age. The face amount of the policy is thereby reduced, but it is completely paid-up.   Page 6-10

RE-ENTRY TERM

A specialized form of Renewable Term which allows the insured to re-establish insurability at regular intervals in order to gain more favorable rates.   Page 7-8

REFUND LIFE ANNUITY

A Life Annuity contract which provides that upon the death of the annuitant, the company will pay to a designated beneficiary the difference between the annuity value and the income payments made. This may be done as a continuation of the income payments or in a lump sum. As a life insurance settlement option, the Refund Life Annuity guarantees that the beneficiary gets an income for life plus a guarantee that at least the settlement amount will be paid out.

Page 4-27, 6-18

REHABILITATION BENEFIT

In a disability income policy, a provision which states that the company will cover costs not covered by other insurance or public funding for the disabled insured to participate in a rehabilitation program designed to help him or her return to work. Some policies have a stated limit (like 12 times the monthly indemnity) for this benefit, and others are open-ended.

Page 11-11

REIMBURSEMENT CONTRACT

An agreement whereby one party (the insurance company) agrees to pay the other party (the policyowner) for expenses incurred on a lump-sum basis. Medical expense policies, for example, are reimbursement contracts.   Page 2-17, 10-5

REINSTATEMENT PROVISION

A required provision in both life and health insurance policies which states whether and how the policyowner can reinstate a lapsed policy. In life insurance, unless the policy has been surrendered for its cash value, the policyowner can reinstate within a specified period (determined by state law) by providing proof of insurability and payment of all past due premium plus interest. In health insurance, the company is not obligated to reinstate a lapsed health insurance policy. The company may, if it wishes, accept past due premium and immediately reinstate the policy. Usually, however, the company will take a new reinstatement application, collect no more than 60 days worth of past due premium, issue a new conditional receipt, and require proof of insurability. The company may accept or reject the coverage. If no decision is made, the policy is automatically reinstated on the 45th day. If the policy is reinstated, coverage for accidents begins on the reinstatement date, but there is a 10 day waiting period before sickness losses are covered.

Page 5-8, 15-5

REINSURANCE

The sharing or spreading of a risk which is too large for one insurance company to accept. This is done by transferring part of the risk to another insurance company, called a reinsurer. For example, most life insurance companies place a limit on the amount of insurance they will accept on any single life. Consequently, when issuing policies for larger amounts than their own limit, they reinsure the excess with another company, which accepts the excess risk for a portion of the premium.

Page 1-8

RELATION OF EARNINGS TO INSURANCE

See *Average Earnings Clause*.

RENEWABLE TERM

A Term life insurance policy under which the policyowner has the right at the end of the specified term to renew the policy for another term of the same length without proof of insurability. The premium will increase upon renewal, however, because it is based on the attained age of the insured at the time of renewal.   Page 4-9

RENEWAL

In life or health insurance, the continuance of a policy beyond its original policy term. Also, the agent's commissions on second and subsequent years' premiums.   Page 4-9, 10-20

RENEWAL PROVISION

A provision in a health insurance contract stating the policyowner's right to renew the policy, such as *Noncancellable, Guaranteed Renewable, Conditionally Renewable, Optionally Renewable, Cancellable* or *Term*.   Page 10-20

REPLACEMENT

The substitution of a new policy for an existing policy. Strictly regulated in most jurisdictions.   Page 12-18

REPRESENTATIONS

Statements made by an applicant or an insured which are true to the best of his or her knowledge and belief. For contrast, see *Warranties, Misrepresentation,* and *Concealment.*   Page 2-4

RESERVE

A sum, required by law, that must be set aside by an insurance company to assure the payment of future claims.

Page 1-13

* definition only, term not found in text

RESIDUAL DISABILITY

A residual disability benefit pays a portion of the difference between what the insured can earn while partially disabled as compared to what he or she earned before the disability, and the residual benefit continues for the same period as total disability benefits would have been paid under the same policy. The precise definition of residual disability depends on whether the definition of total disability in the policy is Own Occ or Any Occ.

Page 11-10

RESPITE CARE

Many LTC policies provide the cost of temporarily replacing a family member as primary care giver for a day or a weekend.

Page 13-6

RETAIN RISK

Self-insuring or accepting deductibles. Your willingness to retain some of the risk reduces the company's exposure and allows the subsequent rate reduction.

Page 1-2

RETENTION OF CAPITAL

Life Insurance can be written in quantities large enough that the beneficiary can live off the interest earned on the death benefit, thus retaining the capital for the next generation.

Page 4-3

RETIREMENT ANNUITY

See *Deferred Annuity*.

RETIREMENT DEATH

A breadwinner (or two of them) reaches retirement without accumulating adequate cash to provide for a reasonable retirement income.

Page 1-4

RETURN OF CASH VALUE RIDER

A life insurance rider in which the insurance company agrees to pay, upon the death of the insured, an amount equal to the cash value of the policy at the time of the insured's death in addition to the regular face amount.

Page 7-15

RETURN OF PREMIUM RIDER

A life insurance policy rider which promises that, in the event of the death of the insured within a specified period of time, the policy will pay, in addition to the face amount, an amount equal to the sum of all premiums paid to date.

Page 7-17

REVERSIONARY BASIS

An irrevocable beneficiary can be named on a reversionary basis, which means that if the irrevocable beneficiary predeceases the insured, then all of the owner's rights will revert to the policyowner.

Page 5-18

REVOCABLE BENEFICIARY

A beneficiary designation that may be changed at the policyowner's request without the consent of the beneficiary. For contrast, see *Irrevocable Beneficiary*.

Page 5-19

RIDER

A written modification to a policy which may add or delete benefits, usually printed on a separate page, signed by an executive officer of the company, and attached to the policy. The terms *rider* and *endorsement* are interchangeable, although the life and health business tends to use the term *rider*, and the property and casualty business tends to use the term *endorsement*. The purpose of each is to modify the original agreement to fit the needs of a specific policyowner.

Page 7-15

RIGHT TO EXAMINE THE POLICY

See *Free Look Provision*.

RISK

Chance of loss; uncertainty of loss; also, an individual or group of individuals being considered for or covered by a life or health policy. Regarding premium determination, risk is the estimated cost of future claims, based on the mortality tables for life and morbidity tables for health insurance. The factors for determining risk include age, sex, build, physical condition, medical history, occupation, family history, habits, and hobbies. Risk is one factor considered in calculating the gross premium. Also see *Gross Premium*.

Page 1-2, 3-12

RISK RETENTION GROUP

An insurance organization typically not regulated as a company by the state authorities. Most often addressing commercial casualty concerns. If all the liquor stores in a state pool their resources to pay liquor liability claims against any of the participants, that would be a Risk Retention Group.

Page 1-11

ROTH IRA

A non-tax deductible individual retirement account introduced in 1997.

Page 8-8

S

SAVINGS INCENTIVE MATCH PLAN FOR EMPLOYEES (SIMPLE PLAN)

An alternative for businesses with less than 100 employees. Participating employees can defer income up to a specific dollar ceiling and the employer matches dollar for dollar any contribution up to a percentage of the employee's annual compensation.

Page 8-10

SEC

See *Securities and Exchange Commission*.

SECONDARY BENEFICIARY

See *Contingent Beneficiary*.

SECTION 457 DEFERRED COMP

Section 457 of the IRS code makes non-qualified Deferred Compensation arrangements possible for employees of state and local government and for employees of not-for-profit organizations. In most cases, this plan can be viewed as a salary reduction retirement plan for state and local government employees

Page 8-6

SECURITIES AND EXCHANGE COMMISSION

A federal regulatory agency composed of five commissioners appointed by the President and confirmed by the Senate. The SEC administers the securities laws, which were designed to promote full disclosure and to protect the investing public. All national securities exchanges and associations are under the supervision of the SEC.

Page 9-7

SELF-FUNDED PLANS

An approach to employer-sponsored health care which allows the employer to put money aside and pay claims themselves. Above a certain stop-loss, reinsurance is purchased, and often the claims work is subcontracted to a Third Party Administrator.

Page 10-17

SELF-INSURANCE

Any time an individual chooses to pay for all or any part of a loss himself, he is self-insuring. Chooses to pay a deductible in health insurance. See also *Self-Funded Plan*.

Page 1-2

* definition only, term not found in text

SEPARATE ACCOUNT
The account in which a life insurance company places non-qualified, i.e. **variable**, funds. See *General Account*.

Page 4-33, 9-7

SERVICE CONTRACT
This type of contract is never intended to pay money to the insured or a beneficiary. Under this arrangement, the insured is simply provided with whatever services are needed at the time of loss. Service contracts are generally found in health insurance. The traditional Blue Cross plans and Health Maintenance Organizations (HMOs) are excellent examples.

Page 2-17

SERVICE ORGANIZATION
Blue Cross, Blue Shield, Health Maintenance Organizations, and Preferred Provider Organizations are all service organizations (or *service providers*). Rather than obtaining health coverages on a reimbursement basis, you pay a fee in exchange for medical services. A service organization arrangement generally requires that you only utilize the services of providers participating in the plan. Also see *Blue Cross/Blue Shield, Health Maintenance Organization,* and *Preferred Provider Organization*.

Page 10-10 to 10-12

SERVICE PROVIDER
See *Service Organization*.

SETTLEMENT OPTIONS
In life insurance, the various methods by which the beneficiary or the policyowner may have policy proceeds paid upon maturity of the policy. The settlement options usually available are (1) Cash, (2) Interest, (3) Fixed Period, (4) Fixed Amount, and (5) Life Income.

Page 6-13

SHORT TERM DISABILITY INCOME (STD)
A disability income policy with a benefit period of less than two years (for group policies), or less than five years (for individual policies). For contrast, see *Long Term Disability Income*.

Page 11-7

SICKNESS
The exact definition of sickness varies with each health insurance policy, but a typical definition is an illness or disease which first manifests itself or which is first diagnosed and treated while the policy is in force. Contrast with *Preexisting Condition*.

Page 10-8

SIMPLIFIED EMPLOYEE PENSION (SEP)
A hybrid of a Profit Sharing plan and an IRA. The employer simply contributes money to each eligible employee's IRA.

Page 8-10

SINGLE PREMIUM POLICY OR ANNUITY
A life insurance or annuity contract paid for in full by one premium payment when the policy is issued, with no further premiums due during the term of the contract.

Page 4-13, 4-20

SKILLED NURSING CARE
Nursing and rehabilitative care which is required daily and can only be performed by a skilled practitioner under doctor's orders.

Page 13-5

SOCIAL INSURANCE
Insurance programs which are set up and administered by the government. Examples are *Medicare*, Social Security Disability Income, and Social Security Retirement Income.

Page 11-5

SOCIAL INSURANCE RIDER
See *Social Security Rider*.

SOCIAL SECURITY
Government programs created under the federal Social Security Act including OASDI (retirement, disability, and survivor's benefits), Medicare, Medicaid, and a variety of other social insurance and public assistance and welfare services. The programs are intended to provide economic security to the public. Also see *Social Security Act*.

Page 8-10

SOCIAL SECURITY BENEFITS
Retirement, disability, and survivor's benefits available to retired or disabled workers and their families. Also see *Old Age Survivors and Disability Insurance (OASDI)*.

Page 8-10

SOCIAL SECURITY DISABILITY INCOME
Pays qualified individuals a monthly disability income if the worker is totally disabled.

Page 8-11

SOCIAL SECURITY RETIREMENT INCOME
Pays covered individuals and their eligible dependents lifetime monthly retirement benefits.

Page 8-11

SOCIAL SECURITY RIDER/SOCIAL INSURANCE SUPPLEMENT (SIS)
A rider which can be added to a disability income policy which will pay the amount of monthly benefit the insured would be entitled to under the Social Security Disability Income program, but is denied. Also called a *Social Insurance Rider*.

Page 11-5

SOLICITOR
In some states, mostly in Property and Casualty insurance, a licensed individual appointed by an agent to market that agent's product line. A solicitor has no power to speak for the company; his authority comes from the appointing agent.

Page 2-20

SPECULATIVE RISK
Gambling, a chance of gain or loss.

Page 1-2

SPENDTHRIFT CLAUSE
Legislation in all states allows the inclusion of a spendthrift clause in a policy which protects the cash value and the death benefits from the creditors of the owner/insured.

Page 5-21

SPLIT DOLLAR PLAN
A non-qualified retirement plan using life insurance as a vehicle. The employer and the employee split both the premium and the proceeds.

Page 8-4

STAFF MODEL HMO
Under this arrangement the HMO employs doctors and owns the clinic or hospital in which its subscribers or members receive treatment.

Page 10-13

STANDARD RISK
A person who qualifies for insurance protection without being charged more premium than standard rates; a risk that meets the same conditions of health, physical condition, etc. as the average risk. For contrast, see *Substandard Risk*.

Page 3-10

STATE LIFE AND HEALTH GUARANTY ASSOCIATIONS
Aid policyowners of companies that cannot be financially rescued. Operating somewhat like the FDIC, which guarantees bank deposits, these organizations aid policyowners of insolvent companies, within certain limitations.

Page 5-3

* definition only, term not found in text

STATED AMOUNT CONTRACT
A policy that pays a specified amount to the insured or beneficiary regardless of the amount of the actual loss sustained by the insured. These policies have a face value which is the amount that will be paid in the event of a loss. Life insurance and disability income policies are stated amount contracts. Also called a *Valued Contract*. Contrast with a *Reimbursement Contract*.
Page 2-17, 11-2

STATED PERIOD OF TIME RENEWAL PROVISION
See *Term Renewal Provision*.

STATEMENT OF CONTINUED GOOD HEALTH
Statement the insurance company wants the insured to sign to verify that the insured is in essentially the same physical condition as he was when he completed the application.
Page 2-11

STOCK COMPANY
A company that is owned and controlled by its stockholders who have invested money in the corporation in exchange for shares (stock). The stockholders share in the profits (and losses) of the company. A stock company is managed by a board of directors elected by the stockholders. Stock insurance companies issue non-participating policies. For contrast, see *Mutual Company*.
Page 1-8

STOCK REDEMPTION PLAN
A buy-sell agreement under which the corporation agrees to purchase a deceased owner's share of his estate.   Page 7-12

STOCKHOLDER
A person who owns a part of an incorporated stock company. The shares of stock represent the proof of ownership. The stockholders elect the company's board of directors and share in the company's profits or losses.   Page 1-8

STOP LOSS FEATURE
A provision found in some Major Medical type health policies which states that once the total costs have exceeded a specific amount (like $5,000 or $10,000), the company pays 100% of the eligible expenses above that amount.   Page 12-10

STRAIGHT LIFE
A Whole Life policy for which the policyowner makes premium payments for the whole of life (until death or reaching age 100, whichever comes first). Also called *Continuous Premium Whole Life*. For contrast, see *Limited-Pay Whole Life Policy*.
Page 4-14

STRAIGHT LIFE ANNUITY
An Annuity contract that promises to pay a guaranteed income for life, but makes no provision for the return of unused premium after death. With a Straight Life Annuity, you cannot outlive the benefits because they are guaranteed for life. Also called a *Life Annuity*.   Page 4-27, 6-17

SUBSCRIBER
The insured under a Blue Cross - Blue Shield plan.
Page 10-10

SUBSTANDARD RISK
In life and health insurance, a risk which is below the standard or average; high risk. A person who is a substandard risk, if covered at all, is issued a rated policy.   Page 3-10

SUICIDE CLAUSE
A life insurance policy provision which states that if the insured commits suicide within a specified period after policy issuance (usually one or two years), the company's obligation will be limited to a return of premiums paid. After the time period has passed, suicide is covered.   Page 5-14

SUPPLEMENTARY MAJOR MEDICAL POLICY
Structured exactly like Major Medical (i.e., a deductible followed by coinsurance and a Stop Loss) but it is intended to be a supplement to a Base Plan, and its deductible is low (in the $100 to $500 range). The Base Plan, which could be from the same or another company, provides most of the initial dollars. After the Base Plan benefits are exhausted, then the Major Med takes over, beginning with the deductible. Because the deductible is placed between the Base and the Major Medical benefits, it's called a corridor deductible.   Page 12-12

SURGICAL EXPENSE POLICY
See *Basic Surgical Policy*.

SURPLUS LINES TRANSACTION
A transaction that makes it possible to buy insurance from an unauthorized insurer through a Surplus Lines Agent.
Page 1-12

SURRENDER
In life insurance, to return a policy to the insurance company in exchange for the policy's cash value or other equivalent nonforfeiture value. Also see *Nonforfeiture Options*.
Page 6-6

SURVIVOR BENEFITS
Pays survivors of covered workers lifetime or temporary monthly payments and/or a lump-sum death benefit.
Page 8-13

SURVIVOR LIFE ANNUITY
See *Joint and Survivor Life Annuity*.

SURVIVORSHIP LIFE
Two or more persons are covered by one policy. Death benefits are paid upon the death of the last insured.
Page 4-29, 7-9

T

TAFT-HARTLEY ACT
The Act prohibits employers from paying money directly to a union for the purpose of providing group insurance for its members.
Page 16-4

TAX SHELTERED ANNUITY
A retirement program for employees of not-for-profit organizations like schools and churches. Qualified employees can have their employer set aside up to 20% of their annual salary after the reduction. They pay income taxes as if they had taken a salary cut, so it's even more advantageous than a deduction. Tax Sheltered Annuities are not really tax "sheltered" – they're tax deferred.   Page 8-5

TEMPORARY ANNUITY
Opposite of a *Life Annuity with Period Certain*. Pays for a specific period of time or life, whichever is less.   Page 4-6

TEMPORARY ASSIGNMENT
The transfer of the policy benefits from one policyowner to another party temporarily.   Page 5-10

TEN-DAY FREE LOOK PROVISION
See *Free Look Provision*.

* definition only, term not found in text

TERM LIFE INSURANCE
A life insurance contract which provides coverage for a specified period of time and expires without value if the insured
survives the stated period. The face amount can be structured
to remain constant throughout the term (Level Term), increase
over time (Increasing Term), or decrease over time (Decreasing
Term). Many Term policies are also renewable and convertible
up to some stated age. As a general rule, Term life insurance
does not accumulate cash value. For contrast, see *Whole Life
Insurance*. Page 4-4

TERM RENEWAL PROVISION
A Term health policy (unlike a Term life policy) gives the insured/
policyowner no rights of renewal whatsoever. Policy is for a
specific period of time only (like a plane trip), if the insured
wants more coverage they have to buy another policy.
Page 10-31

TERMINATION DATE
The date on which insurance coverage under a policy stops.
Page 4-4, 10-21

TERTIARY BENEFICIARY
See *Contingent Beneficiary*.

THIRD PARTY ADMINISTRATOR (TPA)
Under a self funded plan employers are better off to subcontract
the claims work to an insurance company under an Administrative Services Only (ASO) contract. Page 10-17

THIRD PARTY OWNERSHIP
When someone other than the insured owns the policy - a wife
on her husband, a business on an employee, or partners on each
other. Page 5-9

TIME LIMIT ON CERTAIN DEFENSES
See *Incontestable Clause*.

TIME OF PAYMENT OF CLAIMS PROVISION
A required health insurance policy provision that specifies
how long the insurance company has to pay claims. Medical
expense and AD&D claims must be paid immediately for individual policies (group – 60 days); for disability income claims,
according to the policy but no less frequently than monthly.
Page 15-7

TOTAL DISABILITY
While there are several definitions of total disability, all require
that the disability result from a sickness or accident not excluded
under the policy, and that during a period of disability, the insured
be under the care of a physician. The most generous definition
of total disability is the *Your Occ (Own Occ)* definition. Other
definitions include *Any Occ* and *Presumptive Total Disability*.
Page 11-6, 18-4

TRANSFER RISK
Give your risk to a professional risk-bearer and pay for the
privilege accordingly. Page 1-2

TRANSPLANT BENEFIT
In a disability income policy, this provision states that if the
insured becomes disabled as the result of donating an organ for
transplant, the company will treat the disability as if it were
the result of a sickness. Page 11-11

TRAVEL ACCIDENT POLICY
A limited medical expense health insurance policy that provides
coverage for injuries resulting from accidents which occur while
the insured is traveling as a fare-paying passenger on a common carrier (bus, airplane, cruise ship, etc.). Accidental Death
& Dismemberment coverages are also often included in Travel
Accident policies. Page 4-1

TREATY REINSURANCE
A blanket agreement in which company B automatically reinsures 25% of all policies written by company A. Page 1-8

TRUST
A legal arrangement in which property (such as money) is held
by a person or corporation (trustee) for the benefit of others
(beneficiaries). The grantor (person who transfers the property
to the trustee) gives legal title to the trustee, subject to the
terms set forth in a trust agreement. A trust can be named as
beneficiary of a life insurance policy. Page 5-17

TURNOVER
In group health insurance, the process of the older, higher risk
employees retiring and leaving the group, and being replaced
by younger, lower risk employees. The result is that the average age and risk of the group stays constant. Page 16-10

TWISTING
Knowingly making any misleading statement or incomplete or
fraudulent comparison of any insurance policies or insurance
companies for the purpose of inducing a client to allow to lapse,
forfeit, surrender, terminate, assign, borrow on or convert any
insurance policy or to take out a policy with another insurance
company. Twisting is a violation of the insurance law in many
states. *

U

UNAUTHORIZED INSURER
See *Non-admitted Company*.

UNDERWRITE
In insurance, to assume risk in exchange for premium; to as-
sume liability in the event of specified loss or damage; to insure.
Page 3-1

UNDERWRITER
A person, such as an insurance company employee, who evalu-
ates a risk, decides on its eligibility for coverage (accepts or
rejects the risk), and determines the appropriate rate. The
term is also sometimes loosely used to refer to an insurance ag
ent. Page 3-1, 3-2

UNIFORM POLICY PROVISIONS LAW (UPPL)
A set of 12 required and 11 optional model health insurance
policy provisions drafted by the NAIC. The UPPL has been
passed in all states (although repealed and replaced in Wisconsin with legislation requiring a few of the same provisions)
and must be included in virtually every individual (not group)
health policy. The provisions set out the working relationship
between the policyowner and the insurance company and spell
out the rights and obligations of the parties, such as grace periods, reporting claims, paying claims, handling misstatement of
age, etc. Page 15-1

UNIFORM SIMULTANEOUS DEATH ACT
A statute which directs that, in a life insurance policy, if the
insured and the sole revocable beneficiary die at the same time,
or when it cannot be determined who died last, the benefits are
payable as if the insured survived the beneficiary. Therefore,
the death benefit would be paid to the estate of the insured.
Page 5-19

* definition only, term not found in text

Glossary & Index

UNILATERAL CONTRACT
A contract, such as an insurance policy, in which only one party makes a promise. The insurance company makes a promise contained in the policy. The policyowner can continue the coverage in force by paying premium (no promise is required on the policyowner's part to forever pay premium). Page 2-17

UNIVERSAL LIFE
Considered to be an interest sensitive form of permanent protection, Universal Life combines Term life insurance with a tax deferred savings plan (cash value). The death benefit, premium amount, payment period, cash value growth, and protection period are all flexible. Page 9-10

UNPAID PREMIUM PROVISION
An optional health policy provision which states that the insurance company has the right to deduct a policyowner's past due premium from a claim payment and pay only the net amount. Also see *Grace Period*. Page 15-10

UTILIZATION REVIEW
A managed care concept which requires continuous reviews of a case to assure that treatment is appropriate and cost effective. Before a hospitalization a preadmission (or prospective review) is used; during the hospitalization a concurrent review and prior to leaving the hospital - discharge planning. Page 10-15

V

VALUED CONTRACT
See *Stated Amount Contract*.

VARIABLE ANNUITY
A Life Annuity contract similar to a traditional Fixed Life Annuity in that payments will be made periodically to the annuitant over the remaining years of that person's life, but differing in that payments vary in dollar amount. The Variable Annuity promises to pay a fixed number of annuity units to the annuitant at each payment period. The value of an annuity unit fluctuates with the underlying value of the investment in common stocks and bonds. The purpose is to keep the purchasing power of the annuity payments current with the rate of inflation. There is no guaranteed minimum annuity payment. Also see *Annuity Units*. Page 4-33

VARIABLE DEDUCTIBLE
See *Integrated Deductible*.

VARIABLE UNIVERSAL LIFE
An advanced and sophisticated life insurance product which gives the policyowner the ability to increase, decrease or even skip premiums altogether (within limits), dump large amounts of money into the plan (as permitted by law), increase (with evidence of insurability) or decrease the amount of insurance, take money out of the plan as a partial withdrawal or a policy loan, and the right to select the investment vehicle for the policy's cash value from a number of different options. However, there is no guaranteed return on cash value. Variable Universal Life is considered a security product and the agent selling it must be dually licensed in life insurance and securities. Page 9-15

VARIABLE WHOLE LIFE
A permanent form of life insurance in which the death benefit and cash value vary based upon the investment performance of the cash value. Unlike traditional Whole Life, the cash value of a Variable Life policy is invested in common stocks which provides the potential for a higher return on the investment – but

greater risk. A minimum death benefit is guaranteed. To sell Variable Life, you must hold both a life insurance and a securities license, and, in some states, a separate Variable Contracts license. Page 9-6

VESTED
To be the property of some particular person(s); a vested interest cannot be denied to a vested individual without his or her consent. For example, in a vested pension plan, the rights to benefits cannot be denied to employees, even if they leave the plan. Page 8-8

VIATICAL SETTLEMENTS
Selling your policy to an investor at a discounted price to provide cash before death which pays for a terminal illness. Page 6-18

W

WAITING PERIOD
In group insurance, the Waiting Period is a period of time before a person is eligible to join the group plan. In disability income insurance, the Waiting Period is another name for the *Elimination Period*. Page 16-11

WAIVE
To give up a right or privilege. Page 2-18

WAIVER
The relinquishment of a right or privilege. In insurance, a waiver can take the form of a provision or rider (such as a Waiver of Premium), or it may occur if a party simply does not enforce his or her right. Page 2-18

WAIVER OF PREMIUM
A provision included in many life insurance and disability income policies which exempts the policyowner from further payment of premiums after he or she has been totally (and, in some cases, permanently) disabled for a specified period of time. Page 7-16

WAIVER OF PREMIUM WITH DISABILITY INCOME RIDER
A life insurance rider that not only waives the policyowner's obligation to pay any further premiums in case of a permanent and total disability, but also pays a monthly income to the disabled policyowner. Page 7-16

WAR CLAUSE
See *Military Service Clause*.

WARRANTIES
Statements which are the absolute literal truth, regardless of the speaker's knowledge. A warranty is an extremely strict definition of "truth" and except in cases of fraud, statements made by an applicant for life or health insurance are not considered to be warranties. For contrast, see *Representations*. Page 2-4

WHOLE LIFE INSURANCE
A form of life insurance which has a guaranteed level death benefit until death or age 100, whichever comes first, and which builds a guaranteed cash value which will equal the face amount of the policy at age 100. Premiums for a Whole Life policy are also level and may be paid for as long as the insured lives or age 100 (called *Straight Life* or *Continuous Premium Whole Life*), for a limited period (called *Limited-Pay*), or in one lump sum (called *Single Premium Whole Life*). Page 4-10

WHOLESALE INSURANCE
See *Franchise Insurance*.

* definition only, term not found in text

WILL
A written document, executed in a form required by state law, by which a person makes a disposition of his or her property to take effect upon death.   Page 5-18

WORKERS COMPENSATION
Insurance coverage purchased by an employer which pays benefits (medical expense, dismemberment, disability income, death benefits, etc.) for employees who are injured or killed on the job. Although Workers Compensation benefits are life-and-health-insurance-type benefits, it is treated for insurance licensing purposes as a casualty subject (because of its relationship to employer liability). Health insurance policies often exclude coverage for losses covered by Workers Comp.
                                                        Page 10-29

Y

YOUR OCCUPATION (YOUR OCC)
This is the most generous definition of total disability. Under this definition, you are considered disabled if you are unable to perform the important duties of your own occupation – the work in which you were engaged when the disability began – regardless of whether you can or want to do some other job. For contrast, see *Any Occ*. Also see *Presumptive Total Disability*.
                                                        Page 11-6

* definition only, term not found in text